Verdi

Verdi

A Life in the Theatre

CHARLES OSBORNE

Alfred A. Knopf
NEW YORK
1987

THIS IS A BORZOI BOOK
PUBLISHED BY ALFRED A. KNOPF, INC.

Copyright © 1987 by Charles Osborne

All rights reserved under International and Pan-American Copyright
Conventions. Published in the United States by Alfred A. Knopf,
Inc., New York. Distributed by Random House, Inc., New York.
Originally published in Great Britain by George Weidenfeld &
Nicolson, Ltd., London.

Library of Congress Cataloging-in-Publication Data

Osborne, Charles, [date]   Verdi: a life in the theatre.

Bibliography: p.
Includes index.
1. Verdi, Giuseppe, 1813-1901.   2. Composers—
Italy—Biography.   I. Title.
ML410.V4066   1988   782.1'092'4 [B]   87-45205
ISBN 0-394-54110-3

Manufactured in the United States of America

FIRST AMERICAN EDITION

For Ken

Torniamo all' antico: sarà un progresso.
(Let us turn to the past: that will be progress.)

Verdi, to Francesco Florimo
4 January 1871

Contents

Illustrations

Following page 172

Verdi acknowledging applause for *Falstaff* in Paris, April 1894 (*author's collection*)

Verdi's note to Boito, on 1 November 1886, the day he completed work on *Otello* (*author's collection*)

An 1866 cartoon (© *Biblioteca Nazionale Braidense, Milan*)

Teresa Stolz as Aida (*Museo Teatrale alla Scala*)

Caricature of the conductor Franco Faccio (© *Instituto de Studi Verdiani, Parma*)

Emanuele Muzio (*Museo Teatrale alla Scala*)

Teresa Stolz (*Museo Teatrale alla Scala*)

The conductor Angelo Mariani (*Archivo Storico Ricordi*)

Caricature of the first performance of the *Requiem* (*Museo Teatrale alla Scala*)

Verdi in the garden of his villa, Sant' Agata, *c.* 1899 (*Archivo Storico Ricordi*)

Giuseppina Strepponi in middle age (*Museo Teatrale alla Scala*)

First page of the *Requiem* manuscript, 1874 (*Museo Teatrale alla Scala*)

Verdi with the conductor and cast of *Otello* (*Museo Teatrale alla Scala*)

Verdi's study at Sant' Agata (*Archivo Storico Ricordi*)

Verdi, aged seventy-nine, with Arrigo Boito (*Archivo Storico Ricordi*)

Verdi with friends at the spa of Montecatini, 1898 (*Archivo Storico Ricordi*)

Victor Maurel, the first Falstaff (*Museo Teatrale alla Scala*)

Casa di Riposo, Milan (© *Aldo Garzanti Editore*)

Verdi on his death-bed, 27 January 1901 (*author's collection*)

The funeral procession, 26 February 1901 (*author's collection*)

Verdi

Chapter One

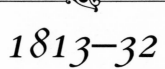

1813–32

It used to be assumed that the description of his childhood which Italy's greatest composer gave on his seventy-eighth birthday was the plain truth. 'Alas!' he wrote to a correspondent on that day, 'born poor, in a poor village, I had no means of educating myself. They put a wretched spinet under my hands, and some time after that I began to write musical notes . . . notes upon notes . . . that's all.'[1] It now appears, however, that Verdi was exaggerating somewhat, though his parents, innkeepers in a small village called Le Roncole, were by no means prosperous. The Verdis were not peasants but small land-owners, and the composer's father was not, as used to be claimed by Verdi commentators, illiterate, but merely uncultured, as one might expect of a village innkeeper in early nineteenth-century Italy.

Le Roncole (the name of the village means 'bill-hooks', thick knives used for pruning) is three miles outside the small market town of Busseto in the province of Parma. The inn, which also served as the family dwelling, is now a Verdi museum. From the outside, the two-storeyed stone building looks much as it must have done in October 1813 when Giuseppe Verdi was born, but the interior was badly damaged by a fire in 1814 caused by marauding Russian Cossacks, and the disposition of its rooms was changed in the rebuilding. In 1813 the upper storey contained three bedrooms, each with a small fire-place, while the ground floor housed the tavern and its kitchen, and a large living-room.

The Verdi family had been established in the nearby village of Sant' Agata since the middle of the seventeenth century, when Giovanni Verdi was the leaseholder of farms there. In the mid-1780s, Giuseppe Antonio Verdi moved to Le Roncole to open the inn where, in 1785, his son Carlo was born. In 1805 Carlo married Luigia Uttini, an innkeeper's daughter from Saliceto in the neighbouring province of Piacenza, and on 9 October 1813 their first child, Giuseppe Verdi, was born.

The date of the composer's birth is given in most reference books as 10 October, but the more likely date is 9 October, the day Verdi himself always celebrated. The confusion arose probably because the entry in the baptismal register in the village church, the Chiesa di San Michele Arcangelo, was dated 11 October and refers to the child having been born on the previous day. However, at that time days were counted from sunset to sunset: Verdi was born at eight o'clock in the evening, and most probably on 9 October. He was given the names Giuseppe Fortunino Francesco (or Joseph Fortunin François, since the birth certificate is in French, Parma then being part of Napoleon's empire).

Carlo Verdi's inn also functioned as the village grocery store selling flour, bacon, coffee, sugar, spices, salt and tobacco, according to the memoirs of a Roncole priest, Giovanni Fulcini.[2] By the time he was six or seven, Giuseppe helped his parents in the store. He was a quiet, reserved child who rarely played with the other village children, but he was already fascinated by music. According to Fulcini, when some barrel-organ player or fiddler passed through the village Giuseppe would immediately run to the door of the inn to listen. Noticing the boy's absorption in his music one day, an old strolling fiddler advised Carlo and Luigia to allow their child to study music. In due course his advice was followed. Giuseppe was already being taught the rudiments of reading and writing at the local school by Don Pietro Baistrocchi, who was also the church organist, and Baistrocchi was now engaged to instruct him in music. Carlo Verdi purchased an old, run-down spinet, which was repaired for Giuseppe's use by one Stefano Cavalletti. The instrument is now in the museum of La Scala, Milan, and a note affixed to the inside of the lid can still be seen:

> By me, Stefano Cavalletti, these hammers were renewed and lined with leather, and I adjusted the pedals, which I gave as a present, as I also renewed the hammers without charge, seeing the excellent aptitude of the young Giuseppe Verdi for learning to play this instrument, for this is sufficient to repay me completely. Anno Domini 1821.

When Verdi was born, Austria and France were at war, and the battleground included much of northern Italy. In 1814 during the flight of Napoleon's troops from the advancing Austrians and

Russians, the Cossacks pursued the French through the village of Le Roncole, pillaging and killing; the story goes that Luigia Verdi, with her year-old child clasped to her breast, climbed to the church belfry and hid there, for it was widely believed that Cossacks ate babies alive. The story is presumably true, for Verdi, showing a German visitor around Le Roncole in his seventieth year, pointed to the old bell-tower of the church, and said, 'Up there my mother, holding me in her arms, sought refuge in 1814 from the Russians, whose rioting caused the inhabitants of Roncole twenty-four hours of anxiety and terror. During all that time she hid up there in the bell-cage, accessible only by ladder, terrified that I might betray our hiding place by crying. Fortunately I slept almost continuously, and laughed with great satisfaction when I awoke.'

In 1815, the Congress of Vienna brought an end to the war, and gave the Duchy of Parma to Napoleon's estranged wife, the Austrian Duchess Marie Louise. From having been French, the country in which the child Verdi grew up now became Austrian.

In 1816, a second child was born to Carlo and Luigia Verdi, and was christened Giuseppa. Said to have been a gentle and attractive creature, perhaps mentally retarded as a result of meningitis, she died when she was seventeen. By the time he was nine, her brother Giuseppe had succeeded Baistrocchi, who had died, as organist in the village church. Earlier, Giuseppe used to serve as an altar boy at Mass. Years later, the composer told his friend the poet and caricaturist Melchiorre Delfico[3] that on one occasion, while serving at Mass, he was so absorbed in the sound of the organ that he failed to hear the priest ask for the water and wine. Three times the priest hissed at his assistant, watched by an amused congregation. Finally the priest gave the boy a shove which caused him to lose his balance and fall over. Picking himself up, Giuseppe shouted at the priest, 'May God strike you down!' and ran out of the church. The mature Verdi, an agnostic, enjoyed pointing out when he told the story that several years after the incident the priest was struck by lightning in another church and killed.

Giuseppe continued to be the organist at Le Roncole for nine years, long after he had ceased to live in the village, for when he was ten his father arranged for him to continue his education in the nearest market town, Busseto. Carlo Verdi may well have been advised to do so by Antonio Barezzi, a wealthy merchant in Busseto from whom he bought his provisions, and a leading figure in the musical life of the town. At any rate, Barezzi agreed to keep an eye on young Giuseppe, who went to school at the Busseto *ginnasio*, or grammar school, run by Don Pietro Seletti, and boarded with a cobbler, a native of Le Roncole, whose nickname was Pugnatta. It was in November 1823 that Giuseppe was enrolled at the grammar school and shortly afterwards began formal musical study at the music school under Ferdinando Provesi who, in addition to being its director, was also choirmaster and organist at the church of San Bartolomeo in Busseto and director of the Philharmonic Society.

The two principal sources of information about Verdi's childhood and youth are Melchiorre Delfico, already mentioned, and Giuseppe Demaldè, a distant relative and older contemporary of Verdi, whose *Cenni biografici* (Biographical Notes·), written during the 1840s, have never been published in full.[4] From Delfico comes the story that Verdi, who walked from Busseto to Roncole and back every Sunday to play the organ in the village church, set out one winter morning from Busseto before dawn. It was so dark and foggy that he could hardly see the road in front of him and had to trust to his familiarity with the route. Near the end of his journey,

> either because he had not discerned the turning in time or because he was not aware he was walking near the edge of the road, he suddenly missed his footing and fell into a quite deep ditch which ran from Roncole towards Busseto. The bottom was marshy, and the lad was trapped. The more he struggled to extricate himself, the deeper he sank into the treacherous mud. He would not have been able to save himself had not his cries been heard by a peasant woman on her way to church who rushed to his help.[5]

It is from Demaldè that one learns of a certain rivalry between Verdi's teachers Seletti (of the grammar school) and Provesi (of the music school), exacerbated no doubt by the fact that their pupil was clearly more interested in his musical studies than his non-musical education. When Giuseppe had to explain to Provesi that a musical task assigned to him had not been done because he was falling behind with his work at the grammar school and feared that he might be expelled, Provesi replied: 'Listen, my boy. If you continue to apply yourself to your work as in the past, you will become a first-rate musician. I could not predict the same for you in general scholarship, not because you lack ability, but because of your inordinate love of music.'

The young Verdi thereafter did his best to keep up with both his musical and non-musical studies, but it was in music that he excelled.

In his fifteenth year he was already assisting Provesi by giving lessons when his master was ill, playing the piano for the Busseto Philharmonic Society, and teaching the children of the merchant Barezzi. He had also begun to arrange and even to compose music for the Busseto town band. When Rossini's *Il barbiere di Siviglia* was performed at the Busseto theatre, Verdi composed an overture for the orchestra to perform. (Demaldè very oddly suggests that this was because, 'as everyone knows', Rossini's opera does not have an overture! Perhaps what he meant was that the piece known as the overture to the 1816 *Il barbiere* was, in fact, an overture which Rossini had already used twice: first for *Aureliano in Palmira* in 1813, and then for *Elisabetta, regina d'Inghilterra* in 1816. Having probably heard the overture at least twice already, when he encountered it for the third time in connection with *Il barbiere di Siviglia* Demaldè may well have taken the view that the new opera did not have an overture of its own.)

The fifteen-year-old composer's overture to Rossini's *Barber of Seville* was given a tumultuous ovation by the Busseto audience. This proved so stimulating to Verdi's talent, says Demaldè, that within a short time he had composed several other overtures, arias, duets, concertos, and variations on themes of other composers. One of the most ambitious of these works was *I deliri di Saul* (The Madness of Saul), a cantata in eight movements for baritone and orchestra which Antonio Barezzi described as showing 'a vivid imagination, a philosophical outlook and sound judgment in the arrangement of the instrumental parts'. It was given several performances in Busseto and the surrounding district, but was never published. In later years the composer took care to suppress all of his juvenilia.

Verdi was sixteen when the church organist in the nearby small town of Soragna announced his retirement, and he decided to apply for the post. Although his application was supported by Provesi, it was not successful, and for a time he continued his studies in Busseto. From the autumn of 1829 until 1832, when he was in his nineteenth year, he acted as Provesi's assistant. But it was becoming clear that he would have either to develop as a musician by continuing with more advanced study elsewhere, or settle down to earning a living of some kind in or near Busseto. His father, Carlo, would have liked him to return to Roncole or at least live not too far away. Antonio Barezzi, however, considered that Verdi's talent deserved every opportunity to develop. In his view, not only was there no more young Verdi could learn in Busseto but there was also no one in the provincial capital, Parma, who could teach him. It was important that he should study in Milan, where the best conservatorium in Italy, and the most prestigious opera house, La Scala, were both to be found.

Barezzi encouraged Carlo Verdi to apply to a charitable institution in Busseto, the Monte di Pietà e d'Abbondanza, for a scholarship to enable Giuseppe, who was now seventeen and a half years of age, to 'perfect himself in the art of music, in which he has given evidence of extraordinary ability both as to execution and composition'. On the day that Carlo filed an application, Antonio Barezzi invited young Giuseppe to come and live at his house as a member of his family. Giuseppe had been in the habit of spending much time there, teaching the children on Barezzi's excellent Viennese piano, and occasionally helping with the merchant's accounts. The eldest of the Barezzis' five children, Margherita, was only a few months younger than Verdi, and an affectionate friendship had already grown between the young teacher and his pupil. During the months in which Giuseppe lived with the family, this friendship ripened into love.

When nothing had been heard from the Monte di Pietà after several months, at the instigation of Barezzi and Provesi Verdi's father petitioned his sovereign, the Duchess Marie Louise, through whose intervention the affair was expedited. In February 1832 the Mayor of Busseto, who was also President of the Monte di Pietà, wrote to inform Carlo Verdi that a grant of 300 lire per annum would be made to Giuseppe for a period of four years in recognition of his extraordinary talent. However, the first payment could not be made until November.

Fortunately, Antonio Barezzi was willing to advance the money necessary to pay for Giuseppe's expenses in the intervening months, and so on 22 May a passport was issued allowing Verdi to travel to Milan. It contains a physical description of the young composer: Age, 18. Height, tall. Hair, brown. Forehead, high. Eyebrows, black. Nose, aquiline. Mouth, small. Beard, dark. Chin, oval. Face, slender. Complexion, pale. Distinguishing marks, pock-marked.

His teacher Don Pietro Seletti had arranged for Verdi to lodge in Milan with his nephew, Giuseppe, who was also a school-teacher. In June 1832, accompanied by his father and his music teacher Provesi, who stayed only long enough to see him settled in, the young Verdi took up residence with Giuseppe Seletti, and on 22 June submitted his formal application for admission to the Milan Conservatorium. He was aware that, at eighteen, he was four years over the age limit, but expressed the hope that in any examinations to which he might be put, he would be found to possess talent unusual enough to cause the age limit to be waived. He sought no scholarship from the Conservatorium, as his grant from the Monte di Pietà in Busseto was sufficient to allow him to pay the institution's regular fees as a boarding student.

Chapter Two

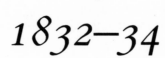

1832–34

Before he left Milan to return to Busseto, Provesi was able to introduce Verdi to Alessandro Rolla, a professor at the Conservatorium and a member of its board of examiners. Rolla, a successful composer and a conductor of opera at La Scala, was a man in his middle seventies who, when he was much younger, had led the Parma orchestra for twenty years, and still retained a friendly interest in the town and its musicians. However, despite Rolla's sponsorship, Verdi's application was rejected.

That a school of music should reject someone who in due course was to become a great composer might be, and for many years was considered to be, a typical example of academic short-sightedness and bureaucratic obtuseness. When one bears in mind, however, that the Milan Conservatorium was already overcrowded, that Verdi was four years past the age limit, and that as a citizen of the Duchy of Parma he was considered a foreigner in the state of Lombardy–Venetia, the decision of the examiners does not appear so outrageous. Unfortunately, the Conservatorium gave no reasons for its rejection. Nearly half a century later, in his reply to a biographer who had asked him about his student days, Verdi made it clear that he felt he had been treated badly:

> . . . I went through a sort of examination at the Conservatorium, producing some of my compositions, and playing a piece ['Capriccio' by Henri Herz] on the pianoforte before Basily, Piantanida, Angeleri and others, including the veteran Rolla, to whom I had been recommended by my master at Busseto, Ferdinando Provesi. About a week afterwards I called on Rolla, who said to me, 'Think no more about the Conservatorium, but choose a teacher in the town. I recommend either Lavigna or Negri.'

I knew nothing more about the Conservatorium. No one replied to my application. No one, either before or after the examination, spoke to me about the rule. . . .[1]

Verdi's account is not completely accurate, for there was a formal reply to his application, and it was forwarded by Rolla to Provesi. Basily's report to the Director of the Conservatorium gives reasons for the Board's rejection, though these were apparently not passed on to Verdi or Provesi:

Signor Angeleri, teacher of the pianoforte, found that the said Verdi would have need to change the position of his hands which, he said, would be difficult at the age of eighteen. As for his own compositions which he presented, I am in complete agreement with Signor Piantanida, teacher of counterpoint and vice-registrar, that if Verdi applies himself attentively and patiently to a study of the rules of counterpoint he will be able to control the genuine imagination he shows himself to possess, and thus turn out creditably as a composer.[2]

He had been examined by Francesco Basily (registrar of the Conservatorium), Gaetano Piantanida (teacher of composition), Antonio Angeleri (teacher of pianoforte) and Alessandro Rolla (teacher of violin). Basily pointed out to the Director that he was continually receiving complaints about overcrowding due to the large number of students who had to work in a restricted space, and also about the fact that all the pianoforte pupils had to share the use of only one instrument. The Director, in passing on Basily's report to the governing body, added, 'As I have many times reported, restrictions of space in the dormitory make it impossible to accept him unless some other paying pupil leaves in the new school year.'

Verdi's application was in due course returned to him. *'Fui respinto'* (I was rejected), he scrawled on the envelope before filing it away. Meanwhile, in Milan, he decided to study with Vincenzo Lavigna, one of the two teachers recommended by Rolla. For the next three years he worked assiduously with Lavigna, a minor composer of opera and a conductor at La Scala who appears to have been an excellent, if somewhat conservative, teacher. Forty years later, Verdi described him and his teaching methods:

Lavigna was very strong on counterpoint, was somewhat pedantic, and could see virtue in no other music but that of Paisiello [Lavigna's teacher]. I remember that in a sinfonia I wrote for him he corrected all the orchestration in the manner of Paisiello! 'I'm for it,' I said to myself, and from then on I never showed him any of my creative compositions. In the three years I spent with him I did nothing but canons and fugues, fugues and canons, in every possible way. Nobody taught me orchestration or how to handle dramatic music.[3]

Nevertheless, Verdi concluded, 'He was learned, and I wish all teachers were like him.' His studies progressed well under Lavigna, and Seletti was able to send good reports of Verdi back to the young musician's benefactor, Antonio Barezzi, in Busseto. Verdi made very few other acquaintances during these early years in Milan. He went to La Scala regularly, having been bought a season ticket by Barezzi, and also attended performances at the other two opera houses in Milan, the Teatro Carcano and the Canobbiana. Being deprived of the companionship and stimulation of fellow-students from which he would have benefited in an educational institution, Verdi was thrown back on his own resources, and must soon have acquired that discipline and self-sufficiency which were to be such prominent features of his mature character. Though his student compositions were mainly orchestral pieces, to be a composer in nineteenth-century Italy was to be a composer of opera, and Verdi's goal, from the very beginning, was to become a successful one. Nevertheless, the composers whose works he studied with Lavigna included Haydn, Mozart and Beethoven, as well as such earlier Italian composers as Palestrina, Corelli and Marcello.

In July 1833 Verdi's old music teacher Provesi died in Busseto, and in the following month the young composer's sister, Giuseppa, died in Le Roncole. Verdi could afford neither the money nor the time to attend their funerals. He dealt with his distress by working even harder at his studies. Some months later, the question of a successor to Provesi arose. He had held several posts in Busseto, among them the directorship of the Philharmonic Society and the music school, as well as being organist and choirmaster of the local cathedral. The Philharmonic Society decided not to make an appointment until Verdi had completed his studies in Milan. The Society also suggested to the Provost of the cathedral that no permanent appointment of an organist and choirmaster should be made until Verdi was able to apply.

The Provost, however, was opposed to Verdi's nomination. Instead, he appointed a musician named Sormani who proved so mediocre that, on many Sundays, there was no choir music at all. Other candidates for the combined posts came forward, and before long the town was divided into whose who thought Verdi should be appointed and those who favoured one of the others. Verdi forwarded to the Monte di Pietà certificates from Lavigna attesting to the progress he was making, one of which stated that, within a year, he would be fully equipped to assume the position of a musical director.

One evening in April 1834, Verdi attended a rehearsal of an oratorio. It is an account of this occasion that begins an autobiographical narrative which Verdi dictated forty-five years later to his publisher Giulio Ricordi. Though it is factually inaccurate in several details, Verdi's narrative is important, for it expresses vividly his sense of himself and reveals how the successful composer in his mid-sixties viewed the twenty-one-year-old student:

> In 1833 or 1834 there existed in Milan a Philharmonic Society which was made up of good voices. It was directed by Maestro Massini who, if he was no distinguished musician, was at least patient and persevering, which was exactly what was needed for an amateur society. They were preparing for a performance of an oratorio by Haydn, *The Creation*, at the Teatro Filodrammatico. My teacher, Lavigna, asked me if I would like to attend the rehearsals for the sake of what I might learn from them, and with great pleasure I accepted.
>
> Nobody noticed the young man who sat quietly in a corner. The rehearsals were conducted by three maestri: Perelli, Bonoldi and Almasio. One fine day, by some strange coincidence, all three of them were absent from the rehearsal. The performers were becoming impatient when Massini, who did not feel capable of sitting at the piano and playing from the score, turned to me and asked me to serve as accompanist. Perhaps lacking confidence in the ability of a young and unknown artist, he added, 'It will be enough if you simply accompany with the bass.' I was then still fresh from my studies and did not feel at all intimidated by an orchestral score. I accepted, and sat at the piano to begin. I remember very well the ironic smiles that passed among those amateurs. It seems that my youthful face, my thin figure and my not very elegant clothes commanded but little respect.
>
> However, we began the rehearsal, and little by little I began to warm to the task. As my excitement grew, I began not only to accompany but also to conduct with my right hand, while I played with my left. I had a real success, all the greater for being unexpected. When the rehearsal was over, I was complimented and congratulated by all, especially by Count Pompeo Belgiojoso and Count Renato Borromeo.
>
> Following this incident, either because the three maestri mentioned were too busy elsewhere to continue, or because of other reasons, the direction of the concert was finally entrusted to me. The public performance took place, and was so successful that it was repeated in the great hall

of the Casino de' Nobili in the presence of the Archduke and Archduchess Rainer and all the grand society of the day.

A little later, Count Renato Borromeo commissioned me to compose a cantata for voices and orchestra, the occasion, if I remember rightly, being the wedding of a member of his family. I ought to say, however, that I earned nothing from all this, as these were all unpaid assignments.

Massini who, it seems, had faith in the young musician, then proposed that I should write an opera for the Teatro Filodrammatico, which was under his direction. He gave me a libretto which, after being partly revised by Solera, became *Oberto di San Bonifacio*.

I accepted the offer with delight, and returned to Busseto where I had meanwhile been appointed as organist. I remained in Busseto for about three years. When I had completed the opera, I again undertook the journey to Milan, taking with me my score, finished and in perfect order. I had gone to the trouble of making separate copies of all the singers' parts myself.

But now the difficulties began. Massini was no longer director of the Teatro Filodrammatico, so he was in no position to stage my opera. However, either because he had real confidence in me or because he wanted to show his gratitude to me, for after Haydn's *Creation* I had assisted him several other times, rehearsing and conducting various other works (including *La Cenerentola*), without asking for any remuneration, he refused to be put off by any obstacle but said to me that he would do everything in his power to have my opera produced at La Scala on the occasion of the annual benefit performance for the Pio Istituto. Count Borromeo and the lawyer Pasetti promised Massini their support, but to tell the truth their support, as far as I know, consisted of a few conventional words of recommendation. Maestro Massini, on the other hand, went to a great deal of trouble, greatly assisted by the 'cellist Merighi whom I had known when he was in the orchestra at the Teatro Filodrammatico, and who also had faith in my talent.

Finally, everything was arranged for the spring of 1839, and it turned out that I had the double good fortune of having my opera staged at La Scala and of having four really extraordinary performers: Strepponi, the tenor Moriani, the baritone Ronconi, and the bass Marini.

The parts had been distributed and vocal rehearsals hardly begun when Moriani fell seriously ill! So everything came to a halt, and there could be no question of giving my opera! Left completely stranded I was thinking of returning to Busseto when, one morning, an employee from La Scala visited me and said, brusquely, 'Are you the maestro from Parma whose opera was going to be put on for the Pio Istituto? Come to the theatre, the impresario wants to see you.'

'Can that be possible?' I exclaimed, and the man replied, 'Yes, sir. I was instructed to bring the maestro from Parma who was supposed to have an opera produced. If that's you, then come.' I went.

The impresario at that time was Bartolomeo Merelli. One evening in the wings he had overheard a conversation between Signora Strepponi and Giorgio Ronconi, in the course of which Strepponi spoke very favourably of *Oberto* and Ronconi agreed with her.

I presented myself to Merelli who promptly informed me that, in view of these favourable judgments on my music, he would like to produce my opera during the coming season. However, if I accepted, I would have to make some adjustments to the score, since the cast would not be exactly the same as originally proposed. It was a handsome offer: young and quite unknown, I had encountered an impresario who had the courage to stage a new work without asking me for any kind of financial guarantee – a guarantee which, incidentally, I would have been unable to give. Taking upon himself all the expenses of the production, Merelli simply proposed to divide with me whatever sum I might receive from the sale of my score if the opera were to be a success. Nor should one believe that he was making an unfair proposal, for the opera was that of a beginner. As it happened the opera was successful enough for the publisher Giovanni Ricordi to purchase the rights for 2000 Austrian lire.

Oberto di San Bonifacio did not have a huge success, but it was sufficiently popular to be given a fair number of performances which Merelli decided to augment with a few non-subscription performances. It was performed by [Antonietta] Marini, mezzo-soprano; [Lorenzo] Salvi, tenor; and the bass [Ignazio] Marini. As I mentioned I had to make some adjustments to my music to suit the vocal ranges of the new singers. I also had to write a new number, the quartet, whose dramatic placing was suggested by Merelli himself, and I had the verses written by Solera; this quartet proved one of the best numbers in the score.

Merelli then made me an offer which was an extraordinary one for those times. He offered me a contract to compose, at eight-month intervals, three operas, to be performed either at La Scala or the opera house in Vienna of which he was also the impresario. In return he undertook to pay me 4000 Austrian lire for each opera, any profit from the sale of the scores to be divided equally between us. I immediately accepted the contract, and shortly afterwards Merelli, as he was leaving for Vienna, commissioned the poet Rossi to write a libretto. This was *Il proscritto*. I was not really satisfied with it and had not begun to set it to music when Merelli, returning to Milan in the early months of 1840, told me that for the autumn he needed to have a comic opera, for reasons of balance, in his repertory. He would seek out a libretto for me at once, he said, and I could work on *Il proscritto* later. I did not say no, and Merelli gave me several libretti by Romani to read, libretti which, either because they had been unsuccessful, or for some other reason, were lying forgotten. I read and reread them. Though none of them appealed to me, the situation became more and more pressing, so finally I chose the one which seemed to me the least bad of the lot. This was *Il finto Stanislao*, whose title was changed to *Un giorno di regno*.

At that time I was living in a modest apartment near the Porta Ticinese with my little family: my young wife, Margherita Barezzi, and our two little children. Hardly had I started work when I came down with a bad case of angina which kept me in bed for many days. I had just begun to convalesce when I remembered that in three days the rent was due, for which I needed 50 scudi. Though that was no small sum for me in those days, still it could not be called all that serious. But my painful illness had prevented me from providing in advance, nor did the communications then with Busseto (the mail went only twice a week) make it possible for me to write to my excellent father-in-law Barezzi in time for him to send me the said amount. I wanted at all costs to pay the rent on the day it was due, and so, although I was reluctant to resort to third parties, I decided to ask a friend, Pasetti, to approach Merelli for the required 50 scudi. There is no point in my relating here how it came about that Merelli did not lend me the 50 scudi. It was not his fault. But I was distressed at having to allow the rent day to pass without paying it. My wife, seeing my agitation, took her few jewels and left the house. She managed, I don't know how, to collect the required sum, and gave it to me. I was moved by this affectionate act, and promised to return it all to my wife, which I was in due course able to do, thanks to my contract.

But now the most terrible misfortunes began for me. At the beginning of April my little boy fell ill. The doctors were unable to discover what was wrong with him, and the poor child wasted slowly away and died in the arms of his mother who went nearly mad with grief. But that was not enough: a few days later my little daughter fell ill, and she too was taken from us! That was still not enough: at the beginning of June my young wife herself was stricken with acute encephalitis, and on 19 June 1840 a third coffin was carried out of my house! I was alone! Alone! Within about two months my three loved ones had gone. My family was destroyed! And in the midst of this terrible anguish, to honour the commitment I had undertaken, I had to write an entire comic opera!

Un giorno di regno failed to please. Certainly the music was partly to blame, but so, too, was the performance. With a mind tormented by my domestic tragedy, embittered by the failure of my work, I was convinced that I could find no consolation in music, and decided never to compose again! I even wrote to Signor Pasetti (who since the failure of *Un giorno di regno* had not been in touch with me) asking him to persuade Merelli to release me from my contract.

Merelli sent for me and treated me like a capricious child! He would not allow me to be discouraged by the failure of one opera, and so on. But I insisted, until finally he gave me the contract back, and said: 'Listen, Verdi! I can't force you to compose . . . . But my faith in you is undiminished. Who knows whether, one day, you may not decide to write again? In which case, if you give me two months' notice before the beginning of a season, I promise your opera shall be performed.'

I thanked him, but these words did not suffice to alter my decision, and I left. I took rooms in Milan, in the Corsia de' Servi. I had lost heart, and no longer thought about music, but one winter evening as I was leaving the Galleria de Cristoforis, I ran into Merelli who was on his way to the theatre. It was snowing heavily. Taking me by the arm, he asked me to accompany him to his office at La Scala. On the way we talked, and he told me he was having difficulty over a new opera. He had commissioned Nicolai who was, however, dissatisfied with the libretto.

'Just imagine!' said Merelli, 'a libretto by Solera. Superb!! Magnificent!! Extraordinary! Effective, grandiose, dramatic situations, beautiful verses! But that stubborn composer will not see reason, and declares it's an impossible libretto. I'm in a quandary, and can't think where to find him another quickly.'

'I can save you the trouble,' I assured him. 'Did you not have *Il proscritto* written for me? I haven't composed a single note of it. I put the libretto at your disposal.'

'Bravo! That's really good luck.'

In the course of our conversation we had arrived at the theatre. Merelli called Bassi, the stage-director, poet, librarian etc. etc. and told him to look at once in the archives to see if he could find a copy of *Il proscritto*. But at the same time Merelli picked up another manuscript and showed it to me, exclaiming:

'Look, here is Solera's libretto! Fancy refusing such a beautiful subject! Take it. Read it.'

'What on earth should I do with it? No, no, I'm not in the mood to read libretti.'

'Oh, come on, it won't bite you! Read it and then bring it back to me.' And he thrust the manuscript at me: a thick pile of paper written in big letters as was the custom then. I rolled it up, took my leave of Merelli and went back to my lodgings.

On my way back, I felt a kind of vague uneasiness, a profound sadness, an anguish that gripped my heart! I went home and, with an almost violent gesture, I threw the manuscript on the table and remained standing in front of it. In falling, it had opened; without meaning to, my eyes stared at the open page and at one line in particular:

'*Va, pensiero, sull ali' dorate . . .*'
[Go, thought, on golden wings . . .]

I glanced over the verses that followed, and was deeply moved by them, especially since they were almost a paraphrase of the Bible, which I have always loved reading.

I read one passage, then another. Then, firm in my intention never to compose again, I forced myself to close the manuscript, and went to bed! No use, *Nabucco* was whirling around in my head! Sleep would not come. I got up and read the libretto, not once, but twice, three times, so often that by morning I can say I knew the whole of Solera's libretto by heart.

Nevertheless I did not feel disposed to go back on my decision, so during the day I went back to the theatre to return the manuscript to Merelli.

'Beautiful, eh?' he said to me.

'Very beautiful.'

'Well then, set it to music!'

'Definitely not. I don't want anything to do with it.'

'Set it to music, set it to music!'

With these words he took the libretto and stuffed it into the pocket of my overcoat, seized me by the shoulders, and not only shoved me out of his office, but slammed the door in my face and turned the key.

Now what?

I returned home with *Nabucco* in my pocket. One day a verse, the next day another, here a note, there a phrase. Little by little the opera was composed.

It was the autumn of 1841 when, remembering Merelli's promise, I went to him and announced that *Nabucco* was completed and could be staged during the coming Carnival-Lent season.

Merelli declared he was ready to keep his promise, but at the same time he pointed out to me that it would be impossible to stage my opera the coming season, because he had already accepted three new operas by renowned composers: to give a fourth opera by someone who was virtually a beginner would be dangerous for all concerned, but especially for me: it would therefore be wiser to wait until the spring, when he had no other commitments, and he promised to engage good singers for me. But I refused: either during Carnival or not at all! And I had good reasons: for it would have been impossible to find two artists better suited to my opera than Strepponi and Ronconi, both of whom I knew had been engaged for the Carnival season, and on whom I had firmly set my hopes.

Merelli, though he wanted to oblige me, was in a difficult position as an impresario: four new operas in one season was a real risk. But I had good artistic arguments in my favour. In short, what with 'yes' and 'no', embarrassments, objections, time went by and the posters with the Scala repertoire for the season appeared, but *Nabucco* was not announced.

I was young and hot-blooded! I wrote a furious letter to Merelli in which I gave free rein to my bitterness. I must confess that no sooner had I sent it than I felt remorse, and I feared that I had ruined everything.

Merelli sent for me. When he saw me, he exclaimed gruffly: 'Is this the way to write to a friend? But, very well, you're right: we will stage this *Nabucco*: but you must realize that I will have very heavy expenses with the other new operas, so I cannot afford to have sets and costumes specially made for *Nabucco*! I shall have to arrange, as best I can, the most suitable material I find in the storeroom.'

I agreed to everything, so anxious was I to see the opera staged. A new poster came out on which, at last, I could read: NABUCCO!

I remember a comical scene I had with Solera a little earlier. For the third act he had written a love duet between Fenena and Ismaele. I didn't like it. It seemed to me to cool the heat of the action and to detract somewhat from the Biblical grandeur which characterized the drama. One morning when Solera was at my lodgings, I mentioned this to him: but he wouldn't consider my comment, not because he didn't find it reasonable but because it would have annoyed him to re-do something he had already done. We argued back and forth, he giving his reasons and I mine. At last, he asked me what I wanted in place of the duet, and I suggested a prophecy for Zaccaria, the prophet. He thought the idea not bad, and after a few 'ifs' and 'buts' he finally said he would think about the scene and write it later. That was not what I wanted, for I knew that day after day would pass before Solera made up his mind to write a single verse. I locked the door, put the key in my pocket, and said, half seriously, half jokingly, to Solera: 'You are not leaving here until you have written the prophecy. Here, take this Bible. The words are there already, you only have to put them into verse.' Solera, who was quick to anger, didn't take my joke well at first: there was an angry gleam in his eye; I had a nasty moment, for the poet was a huge man who could easily have overpowered the stubborn maestro. But suddenly he sat down at the table, and in a quarter of an hour the prophecy was written!

Finally, towards the end of February 1842, rehearsals began; and on March 9, twelve days after the first piano rehearsal, the premiere took place, my performers being Signora Strepponi and Signora Bellinzaghi, and the Signori Ronconi, Miraglia and Derivis.

With this opera it is fair to say my artistic career began. And in spite of the difficulties I had to contend with, it is certain that *Nabucco* was born under a lucky star. For even the things that might have harmed the work turned to its advantage. I had written a furious letter to Merelli who could easily have sent the young maestro packing. But the opposite occurred.

The costumes, refashioned in haste, looked splendid! The old scenery, touched up by the painter Perroni, made an extraordinary impression. The first scene in the temple, for instance, produced such an effect that the audience applauded for ten minutes.

At the dress rehearsal no one knew when or where the stage band was to come in. The conductor Tutsch was embarrassed. I pointed out a bar to him, and at the performance the band entered on the crescendo with such precision that the audience burst into applause!

But it does not always do to trust one's lucky stars! Experience later taught me the truth of the proverb: '*Fidarsi è bene, ma non fidarsi è meglio*' [To trust is good, but not to trust is better].[4]

Chapter Three

1834–42

Verdi's narrative of his early years, dictated to his publisher at the age of sixty-six, contains a large number of inaccuracies, though it essentially reflects the composer's feelings about his early days in Milan and though the actual anecdotes in it are no doubt true. Verdi has simplified the sequence of events which led to the composition of his first opera *Oberto*, and more surprisingly has telescoped the dates of the deaths of his wife and their two young children, making it appear that they died in Milan within the space of two and a half months between April and June 1840 while he was at work on his comic opera, *Un giorno di regno*. In fact, the three deaths occurred over a period of almost two years, between August 1838 and June 1840. The girl, Virginia, died first, in 1838, not the boy, Icilio, and her death occurred not in Milan but in Busseto. Icilio died in October 1839, in Milan, some weeks before the premiere of *Oberto*. Verdi did not begin to compose his second opera, *Un giorno di regno*, until March 1840, and it was while he was at work on it that his wife Margherita died, in June. It was not, therefore, 'within about two months' that Verdi's three loved ones were taken from him, but within two years. Nor did the composer's mood of despair in which he wanted nothing to do with music or opera last as long as he seems to suggest. A month after the failure of *Un giorno di regno* at La Scala, he was back at that theatre conducting a revival of *Oberto*. Some weeks later he was in Genoa, directing the same opera and even composing new music for it.

It is necessary, therefore, having accepted Verdi's narrative for its emotional truth, to set it aside and look again at the years 1834 to 1842 in order to discover factual detail which he had either forgotten or suppressed by the time he dictated his narrative in 1879.

It was as a result of Verdi's success as a conductor of Haydn's *Creation* that Pietro Massini, Director of the Teatro Filodrammatico in Milan, commissioned him to write an opera for that theatre. Verdi speaks of Massini giving him a 'libretto which, after being partly revised by Solera, became *Oberto di San Bonifacio'*. This phrase, however, cloaks a mystery which continues to intrigue Verdi scholars, for the libretto which Merelli gave Verdi, and which the young composer began to set to music early in 1836, was entitled *Rocester*. Either *Rocester* at some stage became *Oberto*, or they are two separate operas and *Rocester*, never having been performed, is lost.

The amateur performance of *The Creation* which Verdi conducted in Milan took place in April 1834. Two months later he was back in Busseto, competing for the local musical post which was a cause of such contention in the town. He remained in Busseto for most of the year, occasionally directing concerts of the town band. In December he returned to Milan for six months to complete his studies with Lavigna, and it was during this period that he conducted Rossini's *La Cenerentola* for Massini's Philharmonic Society. 'Praise to Massini,' wrote the critic of the theatrical paper *Il Figaro* on 8 April 1835, 'and to Maestro Verdi who conducted it; praise to the singers who performed it; to the orchestra, to the chorus, to everybody.'

In July Verdi returned to Busseto. Towards the end of the month he wrote to Massini:

> I am writing the opera (as you know) and by the time you return to Milan I hope to have sketched out all the pieces. Advise me about all the singers you have heard in the concert that by now you will have given, so that I can take into consideration the range of the voices.[1]

However, six months later, he wrote again:

> I am sorry not to have kept my word to you. I promised you before leaving Milan to return soon to write the opera, but then I was not free, and so I have not been able to keep my promise. If I am appointed Maestro, the municipality grants me two months' holiday, September and October, and then (if you consent) I am ready to keep my word.[2]

Eight months later, Verdi was able to tell Massini: 'I have finished the opera, except for those short passages that will have to be patched up by the poet.'[3] An opera, therefore, whether it was *Rocester* or *Oberto*, was composed by Verdi between January and September 1836, in Busseto. During these months, two other important events occurred.

After an inordinate amount of intrigue, scandal-mongering and lobbying, and the announcement of a competition for the post, the President of the Interior of the Duchy of Parma appointed Verdi as *Maestro di musica*. Within weeks the young composer had married his benefactor Barezzi's daughter, Margherita. The young couple went to Milan in May for their honeymoon, but by the end of the month they were back in Busseto, living in rooms at the Palazzo Tedaldi. Verdi began to teach members of the local Philharmonic Society, conduct concerts, write music for performance in the town and for the church, and also give private music lessons.

His compositions at this time included a setting of '*Domine ad iuvandum*' for tenor, with flute obbligato; '*Le lamentazioni di Geremia*' (The Lamentations of Jeremiah) for baritone; and '*Il cinque Maggio*', a setting of Manzoni's poem of that title on the death of Napoleon. In later life, Verdi refused to allow any of these pieces to be published. (Many of them remained in the possession of Antonio Barezzi until his death in 1867. After the death of Barezzi's second wife in 1895, Verdi retrieved his manuscripts and burned them.) A setting of '*Tantum ergo*' for voice and orchestra, with alternative organ accompaniment, which was composed in November 1836 and performed at the church of San Bartolomeo on 1 January 1837, has survived and is in the Museum of La Scala, while a number of other pieces of juvenilia are in the Library of Congress in Washington. (One of the surviving unpublished pieces written for the Busseto band was used in 1963 in Visconti's film of Lampedusa's novel *The Leopard*.)

On 22 January 1837 the twenty-three-year-old Maestro conducted a concert of the Busseto Philharmonic Society at which several of his own compositions were performed, among them a Sinfonia, an aria from *I deliri di Saul* arranged for solo bassoon, and a chorus. This is merely one of several such concerts conducted by Verdi during his period as *Maestro di musica*. Now that he was gainfully employed in Busseto, the Monte di Pietà suspended his grant, having paid him a total of 650 lire. In due course Antonio Barezzi, who had paid in all probably three-quarters of the expenses of Verdi's musical education, recovered from the Monte di Pietà the balance of the full four years' pension.

As early as the autumn of 1836, Verdi had learned from Massini that there was little hope of his opera being performed during the coming season in Milan. Writing to Massini on 21 September 1837, the composer for the first time mentions the opera's title:

It is not unlikely that I shall be able to put the opera *Rocester* on the stage at Parma this Carnival, so please go with the bearer of this letter (who is a confidential friend of mine) to the author of the libretto, Piazza, and put the matter before him. If Piazza wishes to alter the verses here and there we are still in time, and I do indeed beg him to prolong the duet for the two women, to make it a more grandiose piece.[4]

In October Verdi went to Parma to see the impresario of the Teatro Ducale, but nothing came of his hope that *Rocester* might be staged in Parma, and in November the composer wrote again to Massini asking him to approach Marelli, the impresario at La Scala, to see if it could be performed there. 'Tell him first of all', he added, 'that I would like the score to be submitted for examination by musicians of standing, and if their judgment were unfavourable I should not wish the opera to be performed.'[5]

In February 1838 Verdi directed at least three concerts of the Philharmonic Society, for which he wrote new compositions, overtures, arias and solo pieces for various wind instruments, none of which have survived.

Margherita Verdi had given birth to a daughter, Virginia, on 26 March 1837. A son, Icilio Romano, was born on 11 July 1838. On 12 August, only weeks after Icilio was born, Virginia died. Verdi and Margherita went to Milan for their autumn holidays, and Verdi tried to promote there the cause of his opera. Though it is not mentioned by name in any of the extant correspondence, it seems that the opera he hoped to have staged in Milan was then *Oberto*. A set of *Sei romanze* (six songs) which Verdi had composed in Busseto in January and February was published in Milan during the autumn. At the end of October Verdi submitted his resignation from the post of *Maestro di musica* in Busseto, and in February 1839 he moved to Milan with Margherita and their surviving child, Icilio. In April two more songs and a Notturno for soprano, tenor and bass, with flute obbligato, were published in Milan, and on 17 November the premiere of *Oberto*, postponed from the spring, took place.

Whether *Oberto* is a revised *Rocester*, or a totally new opera, cannot be known for certain. Verdi further confused the issue in 1871 in a letter to Emilio Seletti, the son of the man with whom he stayed when he first came to Milan:

> *Oberto di San Bonifacio* was altered and added to by Solera, on the basis of a libretto entitled *Lord Hamilton* by Antonio Piazza, a government employee, then writer of *feuilletons* for the *Gazzetta di Milano*. Neither in *Lord Hamilton* nor in *Oberto* is there a line by Luigi Balestra.[6]

Was *Lord Hamilton* an alternative title for *Rocester*? They are, after all, both English names. Were they both, somehow, transmogrified into *Oberto*, a story of love and betrayal among the Italian nobility of the thirteenth century? Until or unless a copy of *Rocester* (or *Lord Hamilton*) is discovered, one cannot know. It is tempting, however, to imagine a lost Verdi opera (or two!) waiting to be found, and such speculation might be encouraged by the condition of the manuscript score of *Oberto* now in the Ricordi archives. Although, like other Verdi manuscripts, it is untidy and much worked-over, there are no changes in the names of the characters or the details of the plot. It seems to be a piece which began its life as *Oberto*. It is, of course, possible that, having revised *Rocester*, Verdi drafted a fresh manuscript of the work which had become *Oberto*, but in that case one would have expected a neater, cleaner manuscript.[7]

In October 1839, while *Oberto* was in rehearsal, the boy Icilio died. The premiere of the opera on 17 November was recalled by Verdi in his 1878 narrative as having been a moderate success, but in fact it was something more than that. Ricordi, the leading Italian music publisher, would hardly have purchased the vocal score for a considerable sum, nor would La Scala have given the young composer a contract for three more operas, to be produced at eight-monthly intervals, had *Oberto* not been enthusiastically received by the public.

The press comments support this. The critic of *La Fama* wrote of Verdi's generously lavish melody, his beautiful orchestration, the sweetness of his song and the purity and novelty of his ideas. He singled out several arias and the quartet in Act II as 'masterly numbers, which reveal great musical knowledge and which bear the stamp of inspiration'. With the exception of Antonietta Marini, who sang the leading female role of Leonora, he did not care for the singers, who 'seemed to be competing at singing off pitch', and he considered the English contralto Maria Shaw, who sang Cuniza, a novice in both singing and acting who was 'not made for a principal theatre such as ours'. The critic ended his review with the comment that, if the sets and costumes had been better and more suitable, his entertainment would have been complete.

The Leipzig *Allgemeine Musikalische Zeitung*, in the course of a long and detailed review, described *Oberto* as having pleased 'in an extraordinary fashion' and being 'in a small way, epoch-making'. 'A journey for it across the Alps in the near future cannot be lacking,' the critic considered. Listing Donizetti, Mercadante, Ricci and Verdi as the leading active composers of opera in Italy, he wondered if Verdi could rise higher: 'It is much to be wished, for he could surpass all his colleagues.'

The plot of *Oberto* is simple, if one remembers that the earlier part of it was not set to music, and that about a third of the action has taken place before the curtain rises. In two acts, the opera is really a three-act piece with Act I missing. Set in the year 1228, it tells the story of Riccardo, Count of Salinguerra, who has seduced and subsequently abandoned Leonora, daughter of Oberto, Count of San Bonifacio. At the beginning of the opera, Riccardo has fled to a neighbouring state and is about to marry Cuniza, sister of the local potentate. Leonora arrives on the day of the wedding to seek revenge upon the man who has treated her so cruelly, and she is followed by her father, Oberto, who, though at first he disowns his daughter, forgives her when she tells him she now hates Riccardo. They inform Cuniza of the real nature of the man she is about to marry, and she in turn confronts Riccardo. Riccardo confesses his shame, Leonora discovers that she still loves him, Oberto challenges him to a duel in which he, Oberto, is killed. A distraught Riccardo flees the country, and the opera ends with Leonora in despair. Verdi clothed this unexceptional, if not silly, operatic plot in music which combines a Bellinian delicacy with an energy in which the young composer's own voice can be clearly discerned. His opera is no masterpiece, but it contains a wealth of enjoyable melody, much of which would not disgrace the pages of the composer's middle-period masterpiece *Il trovatore*.

Oberto, like all of Verdi's operas, has been recorded for the gramophone, but it is only rarely heard in the opera house. In the two seasons following its premiere it was performed in Turin, Genoa and Naples. It was staged abroad in Barcelona in 1842, and in Malta in 1860. Performances after that were usually on commemorative occasions: at La Scala, Milan, in 1889 to mark the fiftieth anniversary of Verdi's operatic debut; at Busseto in 1939 on the hundredth anniversary; and in several Italian towns in 1951 on the fiftieth anniversary of his death. In recent years, the revival of interest in early Verdi has resulted in *Oberto* being occasionally performed. The opera's first stage production in Great Britain was in 1982 in London (where it had been heard in concert form in 1965). It was first seen in the United States in a small-scale production in New York in 1978; in 1985 an excellent production was mounted by the San Diego Opera.

Verdi began work in March 1840 on *Un giorno di regno*, the comic opera which Merelli needed for his forthcoming season, but broke off when he became ill and had to be nursed by Margherita. After some weeks he recovered, but Margherita herself then became seriously ill with encephalitis. Verdi summoned her father, Antonio Barezzi, from Busseto, and at midday on 18 June Margherita died in her father's arms. She was twenty-seven years old, the same age as her husband, who, distraught and unable to contemplate working on his comic opera, returned to Busseto, having asked Merelli to release him from his obligation.

As Verdi recalled years later, Merelli insisted on the contract being honoured. It appears to have been a kindly insistence, its object being to help the young composer live through his despair. So Verdi came back to the house in Milan which he had shared with Margherita, and completed *Un giorno di regno*.

The first performance on 5 September 1840 was a disaster, with hissing and booing from the audience, and the other performances were cancelled. The press notices were unfavourable, but not (as Verdi later claimed) brutally so. The *Figaro* drew attention to the singers' lack of aptitude for comedy and to the 'special circumstances that Verdi was forced to clothe his latest work with light-hearted music just at that time when a cruel and unexpected catastrophe had struck him'.[8] *La Moda* was also sympathetic to the young composer, and apportioned some of the blame for the opera's failure to its performance:

> . . . there is little hope that in the following evenings this harsh verdict can be modified, unless the singers decide, with a more strict performance, to underline some of the beautiful passages recognized by the intelligent listeners in the ensembles.
>
> To be sure, this is a misfortune for Verdi, but it must not make him dejected; let him bid farewell to this new path on which he has set out, and let him return to the impassioned inspirations of serious opera; let the author of *Oberto* not deliberately cut himself off from that atmosphere of emotion, of love, of sweet and moving song, that won him his first encounter, in order to be engulfed in this new labyrinth of outmoded forms, trite phrases, of motifs too close to a cold and servile imitation. The future is open to him, a future which will not deceive the man who spurns self-deception.[9]

The plot of the opera was based by the librettist Romani on an incident which occurred during the wars of the Polish Succession in the eighteenth century when it became necessary for Stanislaus

Leszczynski to travel incognito from France to Poland in order to be crowned king of Poland. Romani's libretto supposes a subterfuge, resorted to in order to distract attention from the exact whereabouts of Stanislaus until he was safely in Warsaw. The opera is set in the castle of Baron Kelbar, near the town of Brest on the Polish border. A double wedding is about to take place, the Baron's daughter marrying, against her will, a suitor of her father's choosing, and the Baron's niece, the Marchesa del Poggio, marrying the Commandant of Brest in the belief that the Cavalier Belfiore, whom she loves, has deserted her. The imminent arrival of Stanislaus, King of Poland, is announced, but when he enters, the Marchesa del Poggio recognizes him as Belfiore, though he plays his part so well that she later begins to think she may be mistaken. After a number of complications, all ends happily with the Baron's daughter allowed to marry the man she loves, the Marchesa and Belfiore reunited, and the real king safely arrived in Warsaw and acclaimed. Verdi's music is for the most part composed in the style of Donizetti, and occasionally Bellini. Although his opera is not the equal of the best of Donizetti's comedies, it is nevertheless an entertaining piece in the bel canto style, and one which certainly merits occasional revival.

Un giorno di regno surfaced again in Venice in 1845, in Rome the following year, and in Naples in 1859, after which it languished until the Verdi celebrations in Italy in 1951. For its British premiere it had to wait until 1961, and North America did not make its acquaintance until 1981.

Verdi took the advice of the critic of *La Moda* and did not attempt to write another comic opera until, at the end of his life, he embarked upon *Falstaff*. Nevertheless, *Un giorno di regno* is a not unentertaining example of opera buffa in the Donizettian vein. It passes an evening in the theatre pleasantly enough, though it gives no hint of the great heights which its composer was to scale within a few years.

After the failure of *Un giorno di regno* at La Scala, Merelli hastily revived *Oberto*, with Verdi directing the performances, the first of which was on 17 October, six weeks after the débâcle of the comic opera. This gives the lie to Verdi's claim, years later, that he abandoned the theatre for some time after the premiere of *Un giorno di regno*. Indeed, shortly after the autumn revival of *Oberto*, he went to Genoa to direct a production there of the same opera, for which he actually composed some new music: two duets and a chorus. The first performance of *Oberto* in Genoa at the Teatro Carlo Felice was on 9 January 1841, and Verdi wrote to Pietro Massini two days later:

Oberto opened on Saturday and was received coldly. There was applause for the Overture, the Introduction (enthusiastically, with a call for Catone, and for me), and La Marini's cavatina was applauded. The duet for Ferlotti and La Marini, cold (it's a new piece). The chorus that follows, also new, was also cold (I must point out that in this opera I have added the stage band). Scant applause for the duet that follows. Trio, cold. Also the finale. In the second act, all numbers applauded, but very coldly. . . .[10]

It was later that month, shortly after he returned to Milan, that Merelli handed Verdi the libretto of *Nabucco*. It cannot have taken the impresario very long to convince Verdi to set it to music, for in February the composer was busy meeting and discussing the opera with its librettist, Temistocle Solera. By October he had completed it, and in December he was already enlisting the aid of Giuseppina Strepponi, the soprano who was to create the role of Abigaille.

Strepponi, who was originally to have sung in Verdi's first opera, *Oberto*, at La Scala, had had to withdraw when its premiere was postponed. However, she had been largely instrumental in persuading Merelli to stage the opera. The mistress of the tenor Napoleone Moriani, who was the father of at least one of her three children, she was only twenty-four when she first met Verdi, though she had already been singing professionally for five years. She had been successful in a number of Bellini and Donizetti roles, but by the time of *Nabucco* her voice had seriously declined. At the early age of thirty-one she retired to Paris where she taught singing. She and Verdi were to become lovers, to live together and eventually to marry and share the rest of their lives, but in these early years in Milan their relationship was merely friendly and professional.

That Strepponi was an enthusiast for Verdi's work was already widely known. Donizetti, writing to a friend shortly before the first performance of *Nabucco*, claimed that 'her Verdi' had not wanted her in his opera, and that 'the management imposed her on him'.[11]

Strepponi's agreement to sing in *Nabucco* must certainly have influenced Merelli's decision to stage the opera as soon as possible. Under its original title of *Nabucodonosor* (the shorter title, *Nabucco*, was first used two years later for a production in Corfu) Verdi's third opera was given its premiere at La Scala on 9 March 1842 and was a resounding success. Verdi had now, without a doubt, established himself. *Nabucco* was given fifty-seven performances at La Scala in its first year: no other opera had ever had so huge a success at that theatre. The critic of the *Gazzetta di Milano* considered that, with *Nabucco*,

Verdi had placed himself 'in the small but select band of composers who, ignoring the bad taste that still clouds the spirit of many, use everything in their power to overcome, even partially, the well-worn but still long-used operatic conventions'.[12]

Although on the first night Giuseppina Strepponi was apparently not in good voice as Abigaille, the audience was wildly enthusiastic throughout the performance. It had been clear, days earlier, that the opera would be a success, for the back-stage staff, the dancers and the scene painters who crowded into the wings to listen to rehearsals were heard to exclaim at the novelty of the music.

The opera is based on Old Testament references to the Babylonian emperor Nebuchadnezzar and his subjugation of Jerusalem. The chorus '*Va, pensiero*', which had so moved Verdi when he first glanced at Solera's libretto, is sung by the captive Jews, toiling by the banks of the Euphrates. Verdi's heartfelt setting of it caused the Milanese audience to identify themselves, Italians suffering under the Austrian yoke, with the Jews of the Bible, and from that moment on Verdi became the unofficial composer of the Risorgimento, the movement for a united and free Italy. That the composer himself had any conscious intention to stir his audience politically is highly unlikely. But his sympathies were with the liberal cause of the Risorgimento, and there is no reason to think that he was at all displeased at the association made by his audiences.

The opera is in four acts, each of which is headed by a sub-title and a brief quotation from or paraphrase of the Book of Jeremiah, by way of preface. The action takes place in the year 586 BC, in the Temple of Solomon in Jerusalem and in Babylon. The Hebrews have been defeated by the Babylonian emperor Nebuchadnezzar (Nabucco), but the Hebrew prophet and leader Zaccaria has captured Nabucco's daughter Fenena, who is in love with a young Hebrew officer, Ismaele. Nabucco's other daughter, Abigaille, helps her father to invade and desecrate the holy temple of the Jews in Jerusalem, but later turns against Nabucco when she discovers that she is only his adopted daughter, and was originally a slave. When Nabucco blasphemes, he is struck down by Jehovah, and his reason deserts him. He is imprisoned by Abigaille who seizes the crown from him, and it is only when he prays to Jehovah that he recovers his senses, in time to save Fenena from execution. A dying and repentant Abigaille implores forgiveness of Jehovah, the God of the Jews, and with her last breath blesses the union of Fenena and Ismaele.

The German composer Otto Nicolai, for whom Solera's libretto was originally intended, never changed his opinion of it. He wrote in his diary, 'Verdi is the Italian opera composer of today. He has set the libretto which I rejected, and made his fortune with it. But his operas are absolutely dreadful, and utterly degrading for Italy.'[13]

Far from being dreadful, *Nabucco*, the opera with which, as its composer said, his artistic career really began, is a remarkably fine work, adding Verdi's own freshness, vigour and emotional intensity to the gracefulness of Bellini and the melodic fecundity of Donizetti. In musical characterization, too, it marks a distinct advance upon *Oberto* and the farcical *Un giorno di regno*: the neurotic Nabucco is, in many ways, an adumbration of the Macbeth Verdi was to create five years later, and the cruel Abigaille is clearly an ancestor of Lady Macbeth.

Donizetti attended the premiere of *Nabucco*, and it is said that the next day, travelling by coach to Bologna, he was heard to exclaim more than once, 'Oh, that *Nabucco*. Beautiful, beautiful, beautiful!' As one of Verdi's earliest biographers wrote:

> The great success of *Nabucco* roused such great enthusiasm as had never before been seen. That night Milan did not sleep, and the next day the new masterpiece was the topic of all conversations. The name of Verdi was in every mouth; even fashion, even cookery borrowed his name, making hats *alla Verdi*, shawls *alla Verdi*, and sauces *alla Verdi*.[14]

Chapter Four

1842–44

The success of *Nabucco* precipitated Verdi into Milanese literary, musical and social life. Still in his twenties, the young man from the country had few social graces, was shy to the point of brusqueness, and was not at ease in the coffee houses and salons which he now found himself frequently visiting. But he was intelligent, a good listener and keen to learn, and in time he made a few close friendships in Milan. Amongst the earliest were the Maffeis, the Countess Giuseppina Appiani, and the Countess Emilia Morosini.

The Cavaliere Andrea Maffei, a forty-four-year-old poet and man of letters, was one of the most influential men in the intellectual circles of Milan. His wife, Clarina, a countess in her own right, was only twenty-eight but had already made her salon an important part of social life in the city. They were not a well-matched couple, for Maffei was conservative by temperament while Clarina was more liberal in her ideas. She was an ardent supporter of the movement for Italian independence and unity: her husband had no strong feelings on the subject. Four years after Verdi met them, the Maffeis separated, and Clarina subsequently maintained for many years a relationship with Carlo Tenca, the statesman and editor of the literary and political magazine *Rivista Europea*. Verdi remained a friend of both Andrea and Clarina.

At the Countess Maffei's salon, Verdi met people interested in politics and literature. The salon of Giuseppina Appiani had a more musical bias, for Signora Appiani (born the Countess Strigelli), a forty-five-year-old widow, had been a friend of Bellini (who had composed *La sonnambula* while staying in her house), and Donizetti was a regular guest. With the departure of Donizetti to Vienna, where he was appointed composer to the Austrian court, Verdi became the centre of musical interest at Giuseppina Appiani's salon. He was also a welcome guest at the intellectual salon of Emilia Morosini, an Italian noblewoman of Swiss origin.

After the huge success of *Nabucco*, Merelli immediately commissioned another opera from Verdi, generously adding that the composer could name his own price. Verdi sought the advice of the singer Giuseppina Strepponi, who had already been so helpful to him, and she suggested that he ask for whatever sum Bellini had received for *Norma* more than ten years earlier. Merelli agreed, and Verdi and Temistocle Solera began to consider subjects for the new opera. Before long, they had decided upon the narrative poem *I lombardi alla prima crociata* (The Lombards at the First Crusade) by the Milanese poet Tomasso Grossi. When it was published in 1826, Grossi's poem about the eleventh-century defenders of the Christian faith helping to free Jerusalem from the Saracens had caused a great stir in northern Italy, for already there was a clear tendency amongst Italian patriots to place a modern political interpretation upon plots drawn from ancient history. Sixteen years later, when Verdi and Solera began work on the opera, *I lombardi*, the contemporary political implications were even more strongly noted.

Before beginning to compose *I lombardi*, Verdi spent some days in Bologna, where he paid a visit to Rossini, the living composer he most admired. To the Countess Emilia Morosini, he wrote that Rossini's polite welcome had seemed sincere.

In May he wrote a song, '*Chi i bei dì m'adduce ancora*' (its text a translation of Goethe's poem 'Erster Verlust'), to be copied into the album of another Milanese friend, Sofia de' Medici.

I lombardi was composed in the autumn and winter of 1842, partly in Milan and partly in Busseto, Solera having produced his libretto by the end of the summer. Whether Verdi accepted the libretto without question or whether he required it to be revised is not certain. His usual practice, as one knows from later correspondence, was to treat his librettists almost as secretaries, making frequent suggestions and even drafting parts of the finished libretto himself. But Solera, though a year or two younger than the composer, was already well known in Milanese theatrical and journalistic circles, and was a forceful and ebullient character. Although Verdi had stood up to him during the composition of

Nabucco, he may not have felt able to be too demanding with regard to *I lombardi*. In the event, Solera's libretto was muddled and perfunctory, doing considerably less than justice to Grossi's poem and apparently also plagiarizing a play on the same subject, whose author, Giulio Pullè, brought charges against the librettist a few weeks after the premiere.

Before the premiere, however, there were censorship problems to be overcome, not with the Austrian civil authorities, but with the church. The Archbishop of Milan, having heard about the forthcoming opera, wrote to the chief of police, Torresani, to complain that the work contained much that it would be sacrilegious to portray on the stage, in particular the sacrament of baptism. He threatened to appeal directly to the Emperor of Austria if Torresani did not agree to forbid performance of the opera.

The chief of police did not wish to incur the displeasure of the Archbishop, even less that of the Austrian Emperor. On the other hand, he did not want to have to deal with the riots which he was sure would follow any attempt on his part to suppress a new opera by the most popular young composer of the day. He summoned Merelli, Verdi and Solera to his office to discuss possible changes. Verdi, however, refused to appear. 'You two go,' he said to Merelli and Solera. 'As far as I am concerned, rehearsals are well under way, the opera is going well, and I shall not change a note of it. It will be given as it is, or not at all.'

The impresario and the librettist appeared before Torresani, and made the composer's attitude clear to him. The harassed chief of police is said to have replied, 'I shall not be the one to clip the wings of this young man who promises so much for the art of music. Go ahead, I assume the responsibility.' He asked only that the opening words of Giselda's aria be changed from '*Ave Maria*' to '*Salve Maria*', and he informed the Archbishop that, in order to prevent any rioting, he had agreed to allow the baptism to remain but had insisted on other important changes!

I lombardi was given its first performance at La Scala on 11 February 1843. The audience had begun to assemble outside the theatre early in the afternoon, bringing food with them, with the result that, as a contemporary observer noted, 'the curtain went up to a strong smell of garlic sausage'. The performance went triumphantly, the police rule that there should be no encores was broken time and time again, and it was clear that the Milanese audience identified themselves with the Lombards of old, and the Saracens with their nineteenth-century Austrian overlords. In the last act, when Arvino incites the Lombards to battle with the words '*La santa terra oggi nostra sarà*' ('Today the Holy Land shall be ours'), it was not only the chorus of warriors which responded '*Sì! guerra, guerra!*' ('Yes! war, war!') but also large numbers of the audience. Again Verdi had uncannily, and unconsciously, connected with the collective feelings of his fellow citizens. Without intending it, he was fast becoming the composer of the liberal cause, the musical voice of the Risorgimento.

I lombardi was a huge popular success, and was performed twenty-seven times before the end of the season. Critically, however, it was less successful, the correspondent of *France Musicale* going so far as to declare it was not worth a *sou*! Its story of the murderer Pagano who expiates his crime by becoming a hermit in the Holy Land and helping the Lombard forces, led by his brother Arvino, to capture Jerusalem is sheer operatic kitsch; but, as surely as Pagano is redeemed by his repentance, Solera's libretto is redeemed by the energy and dramatic intensity of Verdi's music. *I lombardi* is not the cohesive whole that *Nabucco* is, and some of its effects are crude. But its best pages are vigorously exciting, and occasionally of a delicate beauty. And it is nowhere dull, for Verdi is never boring. Known as 'the master of the quick tempos'[1] in later life, he was always concerned to hold the attention of his audience. ('The boring', he wrote in 1854 to the playwright Antonio Somma, 'is the worst of all styles.')[2]

Some weeks after the premiere of *I lombardi*, Verdi paid his first visit to Vienna, the capital of the Austrian Empire, where he stayed for three weeks, rehearsing and staging *Nabucco* which was given its first Viennese performance on 4 April 1843. Later that month, he was back in Italy, staging *Nabucco* in Parma with Giuseppina Strepponi as Abigaille, the role she had created the previous year in Milan. With the exception of a few days in Bologna, to hear two Donizetti operas, *Linda di Chamounix* and *Marin Faliero*, and in Busseto to visit his mother at Le Roncole, Verdi seems to have stayed in Parma from the middle of April to the end of May. *Nabucco*'s first performance there was on 17 April and its last on 1 June, so it is likely that the composer stayed in order to spend time with his prima donna. Perhaps the intimate relationship between them began at this time, as some biographers have speculated, though it is more likely that they were still only friends and professional colleagues. Verdi's reason for staying in Parma may have been in order to await the return from Piacenza of the Duchess Marie Louise, who granted him an interview at the end of May.

Returning to Milan in June, he began to think about his next opera. Four of his works had now been produced at La Scala, and Merelli was keen for the relationship between the composer and La Scala to continue. But other Italian theatres were interested in the most exciting new composer to have emerged since Donizetti, and when Count Nani Mocenigo, director of the prestigious Teatro La Fenice in Venice, asked Verdi to compose an opera for the Fenice, he immediately began to consider subjects. Mocenigo's proposal was that the Fenice should open its autumn season with *I lombardi*, and that Verdi should write a new opera for performance later in the season, the choice of subject and librettist to be made by the composer.

Verdi was willing to engage Temistocle Solera to provide a libretto, for they had now successfully collaborated on two occasions, though he was also not averse to a change. Most of the subjects he considered were plots derived from English drama or literature, among them Byron's *The Corsair* and *The Two Foscari* (both of which were, in due course, to become Verdi operas). Another possibility, drawn from English history, was an opera about Catherine Howard, the unfortunate fifth wife of Henry VIII.

The most fascinating of the subjects Verdi considered was Shakespeare's *King Lear*. He had read and re-read the plays of Shakespeare, the author he loved and revered above all others, and he was eventually to write three great operas based on *Macbeth*, *Othello* and *The Merry Wives of Windsor*. On several occasions throughout his career, even in extreme old age, Verdi kept returning to the possibility of making an opera out of *King Lear*, but always some valid reason prevented him, although he was obsessed with the idea. In 1843, there was the practical consideration that he would need a really first-class dramatic baritone for the role of Lear, and, in his opinion, the Fenice did not have a suitable one in their company. He needed for Lear, he said, someone of the calibre of Giorgio Ronconi, who had created the role of Nabucco.

Even before the subject of the new opera was decided upon, a contract was being drawn up and discussed with Verdi, who was very definite in his requirements. Three of the nine clauses in a draft contract were unacceptable to him: he was not prepared to submit a libretto for approval; he would not undertake to deliver a completed score by December, for his system of composition involved him in orchestrating an opera only during its piano rehearsals; and he would not wait until after the third performance before receiving the last instalment of his fee, his reason being that there might not be a third performance. (He had clearly not forgotten the *Giorno di regno* fiasco.)

On 6 June, however, he signed a contract, though the subject of the opera had still to be decided. At this point Francesco Maria Piave, a Venetian friend of Guglielmo Brenna, the secretary of the Fenice, wrote to Verdi offering to provide him with a libretto called *Cromvello* (Cromwell), based on *Allan Cameron*, a French novel which claimed to be a translation of Sir Walter Scott. Assured by Brenna that, although Piave had no experience as a librettist, he was an excellent lyric poet, Verdi encouraged Piave to complete *Cromvello*, as 'it might well be suitable for me, even if not for Venice'.

Thus began Verdi's relationship with the man with whom he was to collaborate on more operas than with any other librettist. Piave, three years Verdi's senior, had intended to be a priest, but found himself forced to leave the seminary to earn a living, which he did by writing light verse and short stories, reading proofs for a publisher and translating. The two men were to become good friends, and Piave remained Verdi's regular librettist for nearly twenty years until incapacitated by ill health. His value to Verdi lay in the fact that he was pliable, that he could be bullied without taking offence, and that he had an immense admiration for the composer.

Before becoming too involved with the Venice opera, Verdi spent three weeks in July 1843 rehearsing and, on 29 July, conducting a performance of *I lombardi* in Senigallia, a resort on the Adriatic.

Verdi's correspondence with Piave tells one a great deal about his intentions and methods. 'I do insist on brevity', he wrote to Piave in August 1843, 'because that's what the public wants.'[3] And a few days later,

> I have received this first act, which I find excellent both from the point of view of poetry and musical form. If anything should need to be altered, it will be only small things that can be done immediately on the spot. If you

decide to improve this line or that phrase, please do, for it won't bother me at all.

I am putting this first act on one side because I don't want to start work on it until I receive the complete libretto. This is my usual practice, and I find it works better because, once I have a general picture of the entire poem, the music then comes of its own accord. But don't hurry with the remaining two acts. As long as I have them by the end of next month I shall have time to compose them. Again I would urge you to give the last act finale all the pathetic colouring that you can.[4]

Piave's completed libretto proved unsatisfactory, and Count Mocenigo, during a meeting with Verdi in Milan, casually remarked that it was a pity another subject had not been chosen: Victor Hugo's *Hernani*, for example. Verdi's imagination was immediately fired. 'Oh, if only we could do *Hernani*!' he wrote to Mocenigo a few days later,

how wonderful that would be! It's true it would mean a lot of work for the poet, but I would make it my first duty to try to compensate him, and we would certainly create a much finer effect for the public.

After all, Signor Piave has great facility in versifying, and in *Hernani* he would only have to condense and tighten up; the action is all there, ready made, and it's immensely theatrical.[5]

Piave was paid one hundred florins for *Cromvello*, and instructed to begin work on adapting *Hernani* into an Italian opera, *Ernani*. This he did with an ill grace, accompanying his synopsis, which he sent to Mocenigo and Verdi for approval, with the statement that, in his view, the beautiful situations in the play were bound to lose much of their interest in the unavoidable compression they would undergo, 'especially when it all has to be done in such haste'.[6] However, after his synopsis had been passed by the censorship authorities, whose main concern was that the Emperor Charles v of Spain should be made to appear liberal and impressive and the conspirators as unthreatening as possible, Piave proceeded to write the libretto, which he submitted, scene by scene, to Verdi, who criticized and advised in great detail.

On 8 October Verdi attended a performance of *Nabucco* in Bologna, after which he spent a few days holidaying with the della Somaglia family at Cassano d'Adda. By the middle of the month, he was busily composing *Ernani*, the greater part of which he had completed by mid-November.

Mocenigo had requested Verdi to write the role of the youthful hero, Ernani, for the contralto Carolina Vietti, but Verdi was not keen on the old-fashioned practice of having women to play male heroes. He successfully resisted, and composed the role of Ernani for the tenor voice. It was expected that the company's leading tenor, Domenico Conti, would sing the role, but Conti sang so badly in *I lombardi* at the Fenice in December that Verdi flatly refused to consider him for *Ernani*.

Several other problems of casting had to be solved, and Verdi also had to fight a battle with the management of the Fenice who were opposed to a hunting horn being brought onstage and played by one of the characters, the vengeful Silva, in the last act. In their view, this would lower the tone of their distinguished theatre. However, Verdi stood firm and got his way. He arrived in Venice early in December to rehearse *I lombardi*. To Piave he had written:

> I shall find myself a room at the Luna or the Europa or the devil knows where else, near the post office. I don't know my way around Venice, whereas you do, and so, taking advantage of that sacred confidence which you keep telling me should exist between us, I beg you to come and find me. Come about ten, and if I'm still asleep wake me up. If you can't manage that time, I'll potter about myself until I find you.[7]

Verdi's first impression of Venice was that it was a beautiful and poetic city, but not the kind of place he would want to live in. After the premiere of *I lombardi* on 26 December, he wrote to Giuseppina Appiani:

> You are impatient to hear the news of *I lombardi*, so I hasten to speed it to you. It's not a quarter of an hour since the curtain fell.
> *I lombardi* was a great fiasco: one of the really classic fiascos. Everything was disapproved of, or just tolerated, with the exception of the cabaletta of the vision. That is the simple truth which I relate to you with neither pleasure nor sorrow.[8]

The failure of *I lombardi* in Venice was probably in large part due to the inadequacy of Domenico Conti. A few days after the performance, the Fenice management decided to take legal action against Conti's agent for having sold them a tenor 'who is absolutely incapable of assuming the responsibilities assigned to him',[9] and Conti left Venice to return home, 'hoping to derive some benefit from the quiet and from his native air'.[10] The next opera to be performed at the Fenice, Pacini's *La fidanzata corsa*, met with an even worse reception than *I lombardi*. Verdi, who was present, described the occasion and his present situation to a friend in Milan:

If I haven't written before now, it's because I have nothing very comforting to tell you. Quite apart from the outcome of *I lombardi*, I can see that the future will not be rosy in this theatre. The performance of *Fidanzata* is an example: they couldn't even finish the opera. The singers were whistled at, insults were shouted at the officials and especially Mocenigo, who has resigned his post as president. They even threw chrysanthemums onto the stage, though what that means I don't know. The tenor Conti has been released from his contract, but so far no substitute has been found. Meanwhile *I lombardi* continues to be performed with an absolute novice, Bettini, whom I have never heard.[11]

Apart from taking some days off to attend rehearsals in Verona of *Nabucco* in which Giuseppina Strepponi was appearing, Verdi remained in Venice to complete the composition of *Ernani*. As frequently and increasingly occurred when he was in the throes of composition, he fell ill and prey to melancholia, becoming somewhat more cheerful only after he had finished the orchestration towards the end of February.

During the rehearsal period the leading soprano Sophie Loewe, who was singing the role of Elvira, made it known that she disapproved of the opera ending with a trio. She had already suffered such an ending in *I lombardi* in Venice, and much preferred appearing in operas which ended with a brilliant cabaletta for the prima donna. She actually ordered Piave to provide the words for a final cabaletta, and that compliant librettist did so. Verdi, however, was adamant, and insisted that Piave throw it away. Madame Loewe gave in most unwillingly, and for some time her relations with Verdi were more than a trifle strained.

Ernani was given its first performance at the Fenice on 9 March 1844, and the following day Verdi wrote to Giuseppina Appiani:

Ernani, performed last night, was a pleasant enough success. If I had been given singers who were, I won't say sublime, but at least able to sing in tune, it would have gone as well as *Nabucco* and *I lombardi* did in Milan. Guasco [the tenor who sang Ernani] had no voice at all, and was so hoarse it was frightening. It is impossible to sing more out of tune than la Loewe did last night. Every number, big or small, was applauded, with the exception of Guasco's cavatina; but the most effective pieces of all were Loewe's cabaletta in Act I ['*Tutto sprezzo che d'Ernani*'], the cabaletta of the duet that ends as a trio ['*Tu se 'Ernani*'], the whole of the first act finale, the whole of the conspiracy act [Act III], and the trio of the fourth act. They took three curtain calls after the first act, one after the second, three after the third, and three or four at the end of the opera. That's the true story.[12]

Verdi's brother-in-law Giovanni Barezzi, writing home to his father, confirmed the composer's description of Guasco and Loewe, but said that the reception was very favourable and that the second performance, the following evening, was better sung and greeted at the end with twenty curtain calls. The *Gazzetta Privilegiata di Venezia* called the new opera 'a triumph, in which everyone was happy and contented',[13] while the critic of *Il Gondoliere* wrote:

> On the walls of our leading theatre there waves a banner on which there is written in letters of gold, '*Ernani*'. With a hundred voices the populace and the Senators applaud this Spanish bandit who has vanquished the *Lucrezias*, the *Gemmas*, the *Fidanzatas* and the *Giudittas*.[14] The original drama is by Hugo, the Italian adaptation by F. Piave, and the harmonies by Verdi, the delightful creator of *I lombardi* and *Nabucco*. His latest strains intoxicate, four times over, even the souls of grave pedants and severe matrons. /
>
> In the foyers, in the streets, in drawing-rooms, in cultivated gatherings, the new songs are on all lips. Accompanying the composer in his well-deserved triumphal carriage are the librettist and the singers. There were crowns, flowers, cheers, palms for all.
>
> The music is full of sweet melodies, choice harmonies, splendid instrumentation. The gem of this bracelet, the most intoxicating perfume in this brimming basket, is the trio in the last act of the drama.
>
> Sofia Loewe, Guasco, Superchi, and Selva were the principal interpreters of the new opera. The first-named because of her supreme art, the second through his rare gracefulness, the third through mastery, and the last – a youth not yet twenty – through the merit of his singing, were all worthy of our audience.[15]

On its own terms, *Ernani* is a thoroughly successful work. Piave's compression of Victor Hugo's play is expertly done. Even if Verdi must be given the credit for selecting the scenes and reshaping Hugo's plot, Piave deserves praise for his verses, which are simple, direct and singable. What has been lost in the process of adaptation is the incidental humour of Hugo's text, but for the most part Piave has followed the play closely.

The opera is set in Spain in the year 1519. Donna Elvira, though about to marry her elderly guardian, Don Ruy Gomez de Silva, is in love with the bandit Ernani. When she is abducted from Silva's castle by Don Carlo, King of Spain, Ernani and Silva join forces to rescue her and to plot against the king. Spanish concepts of honour lead Ernani to consider his life forfeit to Silva: he gives Silva a hunting horn and tells him that whenever Silva chooses to sound the horn, he, Ernani, will take his own life.

The plot against the king is discovered, but Carlo, at the moment of his election to the throne of the Holy Roman Empire, pardons the conspirators. It is then discovered that Ernani is of noble rank. In the last of the opera's four acts, the wedding festivities of Elvira and Ernani are interrupted by a sombre figure in a black mask who sounds a hunting horn. Ernani fulfils his pledge, stabs himself, and dies in Elvira's arms.

Musically, the weak pages in *Ernani* are comparatively few. What is most impressive is the opera's wealth of glorious melody. The characters may not be particularly interesting, and they are certainly not very subtly drawn, but they are painted by Verdi in strong colours. Forty years later, the Viennese music critic Eduard Hanslick, writing of *Tristan und Isolde*, used Verdi's comparatively primitive *Ernani* as a stick with which to beat Wagner. Why should Tristan take a whole hour to die, he asked, when Ernani managed it in a few modest bars?

Even before the premiere of *Ernani*, Verdi was accepting commissions from other opera houses. For Merelli and La Scala he had agreed to write an opera on the subject of Joan of Arc; for the Teatro Argentina, Rome, he undertook to compose *I due Foscari*, based on the Byron play which he had earlier considered for Venice; with Vincenzo Flauto, impresario of the Teatro San Carlo, Naples, he signed a contract to write *Alzira*; and in April 1844 he was already discussing *Attila* with Piave (though when the time came it was Solera who provided the *Attila* libretto). These four operas, and the half-dozen which followed them, were all written very quickly and under great pressure. This was the period which Verdi referred to later as his '*anni di galeria*', his years in the galleys, when he seemed for ever to be racing against time, always busy composing one opera while planning the subjects and libretti of the next one or two, and negotiating for those to follow.

The first of these operas to be composed was *I due Foscari*, but it was *Attila*, to be based on a play by the minor German playwright Zacharias Werner, that Verdi wrote about to Piave from Milan, in April, before they began work on *I due Foscari*.

Here is the synopsis of Werner's tragedy. There are some magnificent things in it. Read Madame de Staël's *De l'Allemagne*.

It seems to me there should be a prologue and three acts. We must raise the curtain on the burning of the town of Aquileia, with a chorus of townsfolk and of Huns. The people pray, the Huns threaten them, etc. etc. Then Ildegonda appears, then Attila etc., and the prologue ends.

I should like to begin the first act in Rome and, instead of having a scene of festivity, show an interior scene with Azzio meditating on the future etc. We could end the first act with Ildegonda giving Attila the poisoned goblet, which Attila thinks she does for love of him, but which she really does in order to avenge the deaths of her father and brothers etc.

It would be marvellous, in the third act, to have the whole of the scene with Leo on the Aventine, with the battle raging. But this may not be allowed, so we must try to conceal the point as best we can. This is how the scene should go, however.

I don't like the finale of the fourth act, but I shall think about it and see if I can come up with something better. You think about it, as well as me.

The three main characters are wonderful: Attila, who must not be altered in any way; Ildegonda, a beautiful character who wants to avenge her parents, brothers and lover; Azzio is handsome, and I like his duet with Attila when they propose to divide up the world. We need to invent a fourth character, and I think this would be Gualtiero, who thinks Ildegonda is dead, who flees, and who can be used among the Huns or among the Romans. He can have one or two fine scenes with Ildegonda. He could perhaps be in the scene of the poisoning, but above all in the fourth act, when he learns that Ildegonda wants to kill Attila. I don't want Azzio to die first, as I need him in the fourth act with Ildegonda etc.

It seems to me that this could be a really fine work and, if you give it serious study, you will do a really beautiful libretto. But you must take care with it. I shall send you the original Werner play in a few days, and you must have it translated, for there are passages of tremendous power in it. In short, make use of everything you can, but do a good job. Above all, read de Staël's *De l'Allemagne*, which will throw a great light on it for you. If you can find the original Werner play in Venice, that will save me some trouble. Let me know.

I advise you to study this subject thoroughly, and to keep everything well in mind: the period, the characters etc. etc. Then make your sketch, but in detail, scene by scene, with all the characters, so that all you have to do then is turn it into verse. That way you will encounter less difficulty. Read Werner, especially the choruses which are magnificent.[16]

That letter is a typical example of the tone which Verdi adopted with his librettists, especially Piave, and of the extent to which he involved himself with the writing of a libretto, from its earliest shaping through to its final draft. The opera which he and Piave began to write in the spring of 1844, however, was not *Attila* but *I due Foscari* which was needed for the winter season in Rome. *I due Foscari* was Verdi's second choice for Rome: his first suggestion, an opera about Lorenzino de' Medici, had not found favour with the Roman police.

At this time Verdi acquired a pupil who was to become a lifelong friend. This was Emanuele Muzio, an eighteen-year-old student of composition from Busseto. Like Verdi before him, young Muzio had benefited from the generosity of Antonio Barezzi who paid for him to study in Milan. He was an innocent young provincial, overawed by city life, who became devoted to Verdi. Muzio's letters to Barezzi provide much valuable information about Verdi's activities, and his methods of composition. On 22 April he wrote:

> Maestro Verdi has been giving me lessons in counterpoint for several days, since no foreigner nor anyone from the provinces can attend the Conservatorium. If eventually I am able to attend it will only be as a special favour to Signor Verdi on the part of the Viceroy and the Governor of Milan. What is more, he will be so kind as to make out a recommendation for me, which I shall send you as soon as I receive it. Many music students would pay as much as two or three *thalers* a lesson if Signor Verdi was willing to give them. But he does not give them to anyone except a poor devil like me to whom he has already done a thousand favours, and is now giving me lessons not two or three times a week but every morning. It amazes me. And, what's more, if he asks me to do some task for him he even offers me dinner. My maestro has such greatness of spirit, generosity, wisdom and heart that to match it I would have to set yours beside his, and then I could say that these are the two most generous hearts in all the world.[17]

In May, *Ernani* was staged in Vienna. Donizetti, now resident in that city, offered to attend rehearsals on Verdi's behalf, and the younger composer accepted his offer gratefully. 'It can only be of great advantage to my music for a Donizetti to interest himself in it,'[18] he wrote, adding that Donizetti should keep an eye on the stage direction in general and on any musical changes that might be necessary, especially in the tenor's part.

Verdi was now preparing to compose *I due Foscari*. To Piave, who had begun to send him drafts of the libretto, he wrote on 22 May:

> I have already sent the outline to Rome, and hope they will approve of it. Nevertheless, you can stop work for the time being, because I have plenty of other things to do. So think carefully, and try to continue as you have begun. So far everything is going beautifully, except for one small thing. I notice that, up to here, nothing has been said about the crime for which

Foscari is sentenced. It seems to me that should be emphasized.

In the tenor's cavatina, there are two things which don't work well: the first is that, having finished his cavatina, Jacopo remains on the stage, and this always weakens the effect. Second, there is no contrasting idea to set against the adagio. So write a little bit of dialogue between the soldier and Jacopo, and then have an officer say 'Bring in the prisoner'. Follow this with a cabaletta; but make it a strong one, for we are writing for Rome. And then, as I say, the character of Foscari must be made more energetic. The woman's cavatina is excellent. I think that here you should insert a very short recitative, then a solo passage for the Doge and a big duet. This duet, coming at the end, should be quite short. Work yourself into a proper state of feeling and write some beautiful verses. In the second act, write a romanza for Jacopo, and don't forget the duet for Maria, then the great trio, followed by the chorus and finale. In the third act, do just as we agreed, and try to make the gondolier's song blend with a chorus of citizens. Could it not be arranged for this to happen towards evening, so that we could have a sunset too, which would be beautiful?[19]

The work occupied Verdi throughout the summer of 1844. He was 'rising early now to write *I due Foscari*', his pupil and amanuensis wrote to Antonio Barezzi on 29 May, going on to describe the music in hyperbolic terms:

The introductory chorus, a meeting of the Council of Ten, is magnificent and awesome. In the music you can sense that mysterious atmosphere of those terrible gatherings that had power over life or death; you can imagine that the 'father of the chorus', as the Milanese call him, has set it well!![20]

By the end of June, the first act was almost finished, and early in August Verdi took time off to conduct *Ernani* in Bergamo, with Giuseppina Strepponi as Elvira. In mid-August, when he went to Busseto to stay with Barezzi and continue work on the opera, he was beset by the psychosomatic illnesses which for the remainder of his life were to attend his creative processes. He complained of headaches, stomach pains and a sore throat. From Busseto on 28 August he wrote to Giuseppina Appiani in Milan:

Just a word or two to let you know that very soon I shall be in Milan. As soon as my health improves a little, I shall set out for the Lombardian capital. The air of my native district isn't doing me any good. What a deserted place this has become. It's hardly even on the map. What more can I say? Be patient for a while and believe that no one will stand in my way, and that I am not making myself anyone's slave.

Are all your sons working furiously? I am dissatisfied with myself beause I am doing nothing, and there's still so much for me to do on *I due Foscari*! Poor me![21]

By the end of September, the opera was at last finished, and Verdi travelled by sea to Rome, congratulating himself that, although the sea was rough between Livorno and Civitavecchia, he was not seasick. This was his first visit to Rome, and he spent several days strolling about and marvelling at the classical sites before having to begin rehearsals. He orchestrated the opera during the rehearsal period in October, and *I due Foscari* was given its first performance at the Teatro Argentina on 3 November. As was customary, the composer conducted the first three performances. On the first night, although the opera was enthusiastically received, Verdi regarded it as a 'mezzo-fiasco'. Piave wrote to a Milanese friend, however, that Verdi was 'called at least twelve times to the stage, but that which would be for others a triumph is nothing to him'.[22]

If the reception was not all that Verdi had expected on the first night, this may have been due to an increase in admission prices. Subsequent performances, at regular prices, were greeted with cheers: on the second night Verdi took more than thirty curtain calls, and virtually every piece in the opera was applauded thunderously. The critic of the *Rivista di Roma* wrote: 'It seems to me that Verdi, even more than in *Ernani*, has endeavoured to shake off his former manner, and return to the springs of affection and passion. . . . Every personage speaks his own language; every character expresses his own passions in a manner eminently dramatic.'[23]

In the opera, Jacopo Foscari, son of the fifteenth-century Doge of Venice, Francesco Foscari, has been unjustly condemned to exile in Crete. Despite the pleading of Jacopo's wife, Lucrezia, the Doge is forced to uphold the verdict of the all-powerful Council of Ten. At the moment of his departure from his wife and the city that he loves, Jacopo suddenly falls dead. When the Doge is forced to abdicate, he too collapses and dies, as the bells of St Mark's are heard tolling to acclaim his successor.

Byron's *The Two Foscari*, though written as a play, was, according to the poet himself, 'not composed with the most remote view to the stage'. In the circumstances, Piave produced a masterly libretto which is entirely stageworthy, and Verdi in his music captured not only the 'Adrian sea-breeze' of Byron's poetry but also its vision of gloom and *accidia*. *I due Foscari* is one of the most original and affecting of the operas of Verdi's first period.

Chapter Five

1844–46

After the third performance of *I due Foscari* in Rome, Verdi returned to Milan to begin the composition of *Giovanna d'Arco*, the opera he had promised Merelli he would write for La Scala's carnival season of 1844–45, which was due to open on 26 December with a revival of *I lombardi*. Throughout December, the composer was busy rehearsing *I lombardi* and attempting to compose *Giovanna d'Arco*, and the rehearsals were not going well. Merelli had apparently cast *I lombardi* badly, and the orchestra was inadequate. 'I go to the rehearsals with the signor Maestro,' wrote young Muzio, 'and it makes me sorry to see him tiring himself out. He shouts as if he were desperate, he stamps his feet so much that you would think he was playing a pedal organ, and he sweats so much that it drops onto the score.'[1]

The leading singers in *I lombardi*, the soprano Erminia Frezzolini, the tenor Antonio Poggi, and the baritone Filippo Colini, were also those who were to play the three principal roles some weeks later in the new opera, *Giovanna d'Arco*. According to Muzio, they did not cover themselves with glory in *I lombardi*:

> Frezzolini is not singing with her old force and energy. She is mortified at getting less applause than she had hoped for, and then she cries because her voice is not what it used to be. Poggi is not liked. Yesterday in his cavatina he fluffed his high notes, and the audience began to hiss and grow restless. Colini's singing is too sweet, and in the ensembles he can't be heard because he is a baritone and the part is written for a deep bass.[2]

Gloomily, and in a state of exasperation with Merelli, Verdi continued working on *Giovanna d'Arco*. The admiring and completely uncritical Muzio, charting progress in his letters to Barezzi, wrote that the opera's 'terrifying introduction' was inspired by the mountainous precipices of the Apennines through which Verdi had travelled on his way back from Rome; and Joan of Arc, if she had not made herself immortal by her own deeds, would become so through Verdi's music. 'Every poor mortal' would be astounded by another piece in the opera, while

> the demons' choruses are original, popular, truly Italian. The first ('*Tu sei bella*') is a most graceful waltz, full of seductive motifs that, after two hearings, can be sung straight away. The second ('*Vittoria, vittoria, s'applauda a Satana*') is music of diabolical exaltation, that makes one shudder and tremble.[3]

On 22 December, Muzio reported that 'this morning, the signor Maestro wrote the march for *Giovanna*: how beautiful it is'; and a few days later boasted of having heard the love duet the previous day and found it 'the grandest and most magnificent piece in the opera'. The third act finale 'has one of the most beautiful melodies that has ever been heard'.[4]

Having rehearsed *I lombardi*, Verdi did not conduct it in public, and even refused to attend the first performance on 26 December. He spent the next few weeks composing and orchestrating *Giovanna d'Arco*, 'the mighty opera', according to Muzio, 'that will dumbfound all the Milanese'.[5] On 15 February the Milanese public, if not the critics, were duly dumbfounded. *Giovanna d'Arco* was applauded enthusiastically and was given on four nights every week until the end of the season, by which time its most popular tunes were being ground out on the streets of Milan by the city's barrel-organs: a monster barrel-organ, the largest ever seen in Milan, played (according to Muzio) almost the entire opera. The Scala season ended in March with an evening devoted to Verdi, the programme consisting of the last two acts of *Ernani* and the last two acts of *Giovanna d'Arco*. According to Muzio, there were flowers and applause for all, except the poor tenor:

> Poggi was received with hisses, and after his *romanza* various pieces of paper were seen flying through the air; everyone believed they were sonnets in his praise, and he even thanked the audience for its courtesy, with a smile on his lips and a number of bows; but there was surprise and a burst of laughter on seeing that instead of sonnets they were what the Milanese call *guzzinate*, songs the populace sings about a husband who beats his wife, a miser, a drunkard, a guzzler and so on. I can tell you that all the Milanese are still laughing about it.[6]

Verdi had by now become an internationally known composer. In 1845, *Nabucco* and the operas which followed it were being staged in France, Germany, Austria, Denmark, Hungary, Turkey, Algeria, Russia, England, Holland, Belgium and Spain. *Giovanna d'Arco* was heard in Rome three months after its Italian premiere, though the papal censorship insisted on a change of title to *Orietta di Lesbo*, with Joan turned into Orietta, a Genoese heroine leading the Lesbians against the Turks!

Though we do not know whether it was Verdi, or Merelli, or Solera who first proposed an opera about Joan of Arc, the probability is that the suggestion came from Verdi, for Solera's libretto clearly owes something (though not much) to Schiller's play *Die Jungfrau von Orleans* (The Maid of Orleans) and Verdi was a great admirer of Schiller. (Three of his later operas derive from plays by the German playwright.) Oddly, Solera denied that his libretto had any connection with Schiller. When the publisher Ricordi, knowing the lazy Solera's predilection for plagiarism, wrote anxiously to him, asking if there might be any problems of copyright with a contemporary French play, Solera replied:

> I have no knowledge at all of the play you mention. I assure you categorically that my *Giovanna d'Arco* is an entirely original Italian drama. I merely wanted, like Schiller, to introduce Joan's own father as her accuser; in everything else I have not allowed myself to be imposed upon by the authority either of Schiller or of Shakespeare, both of whom make Joan fall basely in love with the foreigner Lionel.
>
> My drama is original, and indeed I beg you to have it announced in your journal that, knowing that people would say I had naturally taken my plot from Schiller, I have been very careful to make it original.[7]

Despite Solera's protestations, there is no doubt that he based the outline of his libretto on Schiller's play, though he deleted several scenes and made a number of alterations. In doing so he reduced the action of the play to a purely personal level, the protagonists being Joan, her father and the Dauphin. It was not surprising that the romantic Schiller, like Byron and Victor Hugo, should have appealed both to Verdi's temperament and to his political liberalism. The pity is that the composer's librettist had not the intellect to understand the intentions of Schiller's plot. Fortunately, Verdi was soon to sever his relations with the unreliable Solera.

The plot of the opera has no basis in historical fact, but is a simplification of Schiller's fictionalized acount of the life of Joan of

Arc. Giovanna (Joan) is loved by Carlo (Charles), the Dauphin of France. Denounced by her father, Giacomo, at the coronation of the Dauphin, and accused of witchcraft, Giovanna is arrested and imprisoned. However, Giacomo later repents and helps her escape in order to lead the French forces. Giovanna dies not at the stake but from wounds received in battle. Her funeral procession is interrupted as she momentarily revives to see the heavens opening and the Virgin herself calling her. Ecstatically, Giovanna bids farewell to earth and dies.

Solera's characters may be two-dimensional on the page, but Verdi's music brings them fully to life. *Giovanna d'Arco* has a curiously primitive but pervasive charm of its own that sets it apart from bigger works such as *Nabucco* or *Ernani*. It is a perfectly viable and enjoyable work of art in a style which modern audiences have in recent years been learning to appreciate.

Verdi's business arrangements now become extremely complex. Not only is there usually more than one opera at some stage of gestation, but contracts are signed with one impresario who subsequently disposes of his interest to another. Verdi soon found himself not only committed simultaneously to several projects but having to offend one impresario or publisher in order to satisfy another. A contract he had entered into with the impresario Alessandro Lanari to write another opera for Venice was sold to Francesco Lucca, the publisher who was a rival of Verdi's regular publisher, Ricordi. Verdi thus found himself required to write an opera for Lucca, and it was perhaps to fend off the publisher for the time being that Verdi gave him a group of six songs, all of them settings of contemporary Italian poets, which he composed in the spring of 1845, shortly after the premiere of *Giovanna d'Arco*. These songs were published in the autumn by Lucca as *Sei romanze*. (In Julian Budden's *The Operas of Verdi* [Vol.1, p.269] these are described as 'Six Romances to words by Maffei', and '*Lo spazzacamino*' is mentioned as 'the best-known'. In fact, the poem of '*Lo spazzacamino*' is by Manfredo Maggioni. Only three of the six songs have words by Maffei.)

Verdi should have been working on his next opera for Naples, but on 28 April Muzio wrote to Barezzi that 'My Maestro . . . is not doing anything yet about the opera for Naples. At present he is busy only with me, giving me lessons from ten in the morning until two in the afternoon. He has me reading all the classical music of Beethoven, Mozart, Leidesdorf, Schubert, Haydn and so on.'[8] (Marcus Leidesdorf, the son of a Jewish merchant in Vienna, was better known as a publisher. His own compositions have been described as superficial, fashionable pieces, but he published Beethoven, Weber and Schubert.)

It was in May that Verdi received a visit from one of the Escudier brothers. Marie and Léon Escudier were publishers in Paris who, in due course, were to become Verdi's representatives in France. It was probably Marie who visited him in Milan, and who published in the brothers' review, *La France Musicale*, an acccount of the meeting which conveys a vivid impression of the composer:

> I saw Verdi for the first time last Monday, at his house. I had been given an utterly false idea of his character, imagining him to be cold, un-communicative and always engrossed in his art. Verdi welcomed me with great affability, and with a charm that was completely French [!] received several friends who visited him while I was there. We spoke a great deal about French music and those composers who are now writing for the Parisian theatres. He knows all the compositions that deserve to be known, and displays a keen liking for everything that comes from France. He expressed a desire to see the great score of Félicien David's *Le désert* which is soon to be performed in Milan. Having read the score avidly from beginning to end, he exclaimed, 'Ah, what excellent judges the French are! I had expected to see heavy music, overladen with notes; but instead I see a clear and straightforward instrumentation of the French school, combined with the simple and poetic melodies of the Italian school. Please inform M. David that I would be delighted to express personally to him one day my admiration of his genius.'
>
> Verdi is a handsome young man of twenty-eight or twenty-nine. [He was in his thirty-second year.] He has brown hair and blue eyes with an expression that is at once gentle and bright. His face lights up when he speaks; the constant mobility of his gaze reflects the diversity of his feelings; everything about him reveals a sincere heart and a sensitive soul.
>
> I requested Verdi to play me an extract from *I lombardi*, the '*Ave Maria*', which I have always considered the best piece in the work. He immediately sat down at the piano and sang with touching expression this page of music that he himself regards as one of his finest inspirations. . . .[9]

Verdi's agreement with the Teatro San Carlo in Naples regarding his next opera, *Alzira*, stipulated that the piece should be performed in June 1845. But this was only four months after the premiere of *Giovanna d'Arco* in Milan, and the composer seems to have found it difficult to concentrate so soon on his next major assignment. The *Alzira* libretto was being provided by the Neapolitan Salvatore

Cammarano with whom Verdi was collaborating for the first time; it was probably Cammarano or the Neapolitan impresario Flauto who had suggested Voltaire's play *Alzire* as the subject of the opera, for Verdi's letter to Cammarano of 22 March does not read as though it had been the composer's idea:

> I have received the synopsis of *Alzira*, and I am completely satisfied with it. I have read Voltaire's tragedy which, in the hands of a Cammarano, will make an excellent libretto. I am accused of liking a great deal of noise and handling the singing badly. Pay no attention to this. Just put passion into it, and you will see that I write reasonably well. I am surprised that Tadolini is not singing. I ought to let you know that, in my contract, article 3 reads as follows: 'The company to be engaged for the opera to be written by Signor Verdi will be chosen by him from those singers under contract to the management.' So, if Tadolini is under contract, Tadolini will have to sing, for I shall certainly not cede my rights for anything in the world.
>
> I should like this to be kept secret for the moment, and I should also be grateful if you could elucidate this matter for me, and also let me know what kind of singer Bishop is.
>
> To return to *Alzira*, may I ask you to send me some more verses quickly? There's no need for me to say keep it short, for you understand the theatre better than I do. We shall meet soon in Naples, meanwhile all my esteem.[10]

The tone of Verdi's letter is distinctly more respectful than that of his correspondence with Piave, not only because he did not yet personally know Cammarano, but also because the Neapolitan was an experienced man of the theatre. Eugenia Tadolini, the soprano Verdi was determined should sing in *Alzira*, had been the Elvira in the Vienna production of *Ernani* the previous year. The doubt about her availability was due to the fact that the lady was pregnant, but the birth of her child in April and the postponement of the premiere of the opera until August made it possible for her to sing the title role. (The soprano mentioned as a substitute, about whom Verdi requested information from Cammarano, was the English soprano Anna Bishop, wife of Sir Henry Bishop, the composer of 'Home, Sweet Home'. Donizetti had once rejected her with the words, 'No, for Christ's sake, not la Bishop! Are you pulling my leg?')[11]

The postponement of *Alzira* was due, however, not to Tadolini's pregnancy but to the illnesses which beset Verdi while he was composing. On 25 April Muzio wrote to Barezzi that he was rushing about Milan getting Verdi's medical certificates signed, and they were sent off to the impresario Flauto in Naples the following day. It was the middle of May before a reply was received, and when it arrived it not surprisingly infuriated Verdi, for Flauto clearly did not take the composer's indisposition at all seriously. He had written:

> We are immensely sorry to learn from your letters of the 23rd and 26th of last month that you are indisposed. The illness from which you are suffering is, however, a trifling affair, and needs no other remedies than those of tincture of absinthe and an immediate journey to Naples. I can assure you that the air here and the excitability of our Vesuvius will set all your functions working again, especially your appetite. Resolve then to come at once, and abandon that troop of doctors who can only aggravate the indisposition from which you are suffering. For your cure you can count on the air of Naples and on the advice that I shall give you when you are here, for I was once a doctor myself, though I have now abandoned such impostures. . . .[12]

This was not the way to deal with Giuseppe Verdi, whose reply was immediate and forthright:

> I am terribly sorry to have to inform you that my illness is not as minor as you think it is, and the absinthe tincture will be of no use to me.
>
> You say that the stimulating air of Vesuvius will improve my health, but I can assure you that what I need to get well again is calm and rest.
>
> I am not able to leave immediately for Naples as you invite me to, because, if I could, I would not have sent you the medical certificate. I inform you of this so that you can take whatever steps you think necessary during this period while I am trying to recover my health.[13]

On the same day, Verdi also wrote to Cammarano:

> I have today received a rather curious letter from Sig. Flauto. Without replying to my question, which was supported by a medical certificate, about delaying the performance of the opera by a month, he invites me to go directly to Naples. Furthermore, this letter is written in a style which I do not like. I have answered him in the same manner, and have told him that, for the time being, I cannot go to Naples.
>
> I wish this impresario would accept the situation in good part, and appreciate that I usually fulfil my obligations scrupulously, and that if it were not for a very bad stomach ache, which has prevented and which still prevents me from working, I would by now have had the good fortune to have finished my opera and be in Naples. If it were not for the pleasure of setting your libretto to music and writing for that theatre, I should have followed the advice of the doctor who advised me to rest all summer.

If you can contact the impresario and explain the matter, I should be very grateful since, to put it briefly, I cannot come now, and the opera cannot be produced in June.[14]

By the end of May, Verdi had not actually begun to compose the opera, being perhaps unwilling to do so until he had been assured by Flauto that he could have an extension of time. However, the impresario remained sceptical about the composer's illness, and reluctant to agree to a postponement. On 29 May Verdi continued this somewhat absurd and unseemly correspondence:

The medical certificate was issued in good faith, and no illness has been imagined or fabricated. What reason would I have? For two months now I have been unable to work, and even now I can work only at intervals, and short ones at that. Therefore it is impossible for the opera to be finished before the end of July.

I have never had a dispute with anyone, and I do not wish to have one with you. Let us, therefore, try to come to an agreement: I request of you the slight favour of postponing the opera for a month, or more if you wish.

You tell me I am under an obligation to the administration. But if even sick prisoners are shown consideration, why shouldn't I be?

Believe me, if I were really to take care of my health, I should rest for the whole of this year. But I am trying very hard to work. I shall write the opera, but I must ask you to allow me time.[15]

'We artists are never allowed to be ill,' Verdi complained to Cammarano. 'We should not always bother to behave like gentlemen, for the impresarios please themselves as to whether they believe us or not.'[16] He took the, for him, unusual step of enlisting the support of a nobleman, the Duke of San Teodoro, who was a friend of a member of the Neapolitan nobility, Marquess Imperiale di Francavilla, superintendent of the theatres of Naples. At the Duke's suggestion, Verdi wrote directly to the Marquess Imperiale, and in due course Flauto was forced to admit defeat. Verdi then composed *Alzira*, with the exception of the last act finale, within three weeks, and left for Naples on 20 June to begin to rehearse and orchestrate the opera.

The Naples correspondent of the *Rivista di Roma* described the reception Verdi received on this, his first visit to the city:

When the news spread through the city, not only that he had arrived, but that on the same evening he would certainly be present at the San Carlo theatre for a performance of *I due Foscari*, the public, moved by legitimate curiosity, gathered in crowds at the theatre to see the famous composer in person. The galleries and the vast auditorium of San Carlo, packed with spectators, presented a brilliant scene. The performers, inspired by Verdi's presence as if by a charge of electricity, surpassed themselves, so that the opera, although heard an infinite number of times in the past two seasons, seemed, judging by the effect produced in the theatre on that evening, quite new. All the singers were warmly applauded, but the enthusiastic audience wished to demonstrate its admiration for the composer of *I due Foscari*. Being called for repeatedly and vociferously, he appeared twice on the stage amid the most cordial, loud and unanimous applause.[17]

The soprano in *I due Foscari* was Anna Bishop, who, furious at not being wanted by Verdi for *Alzira*, became the composer's bitter foe. Verdi believed that she paid a number of Neapolitan journalists to write scurrilous stories about him; the animosity of the journalists in Naples towards Verdi is certainly difficult to explain otherwise, given his huge popularity with the Neapolitan public. 'With the exception of the journalists,' Verdi wrote to his Roman friend Jacopo Ferretti, 'I enjoy wholehearted public favour, and there seems no need to fear fatal cabals or intrigues on the night.'[18] His only serious living rival, the composer Mercadante, resided in Naples, and was certainly hostile to Verdi, though not to the extent of indulging in intrigues.

On 30 July Verdi was able to write to his friend Andrea Maffei in Milan:

I have finished the opera, except for the orchestration, so it will be ready for performance around August 9th. I am unable to give you an opinion of this opera of mine, because I have written it without any great care or much exertion, so if it fails I shan't mind very much. But don't worry, it won't be a fiasco. The singers enjoy singing it, so it must be quite tolerable, after all. I shall write to you immediately after the first performance. I shall be in Milan about August 17th, but I shall say nothing here about my departure. The Neapolitans are strange: one part of them is rough, almost uncivilized, whom you almost have to beat to get them to respect you; the other part almost chokes you to death with its kindness. To tell the truth, I cannot complain, as the management here have been very good to me.[19]

Alzira reached the stage on 12 August (the scenery not having been ready on the 9th) with Eugenia Tadolini in the title role, the tenor Gaetano Fraschini as Zamoro, and the baritone Filippo Coletti as Gusmano. Fraschini and Coletti were to serve Verdi well in other operas in years to come, but *Alzira* was no more than a moderate success. At the dress rehearsal, according to Muzio, enthusiasm ran so high that the members of the orchestra accompanied the composer home with applause and cheers. But, writing to Giovanna Lucca (the wife and business partner of the publisher Francesco Lucca) some days later, Verdi described the opera as 'a modest success on the first night and less on the second'.[20]

The haste with which Verdi composed *Alzira* is discernible in the finished work, some of whose pages are curiously perfunctory. The philosophical aspects of Voltaire's somewhat confused drama seem not to have interested the composer, and in any case Voltaire's moral concerns are lost in Cammarano's rather brutal adventure story in which Alzira, an Inca princess, is forced into marriage with the Spanish governor, Gusmano, who is stabbed at the wedding ceremony by the Peruvian chief Zamoro, to whom Alzira had been betrothed. Before he dies, Gusmano demonstrates the superiority of Christian forbearance over pagan savagery by forgiving his assassin. Verdi responded to this plot with one of his least innovative scores, and, though the opera displays the usual Verdian energy, it has not held the stage. When Jacopo Ferretti wrote to give him news of *Alzira*'s production in Rome some months after its Naples premiere, Verdi replied:

> I am very grateful for the news you have given me about that unfortunate *Alzira*, and even more for the suggestions you are kind enough to make. In Naples I too saw those weaknesses before the opera was produced, and you can't imagine how long I thought about them. But the flaw is too deeply rooted, and retouching would only make it worse. Then, how could I? I hoped that the overture and the finale to the last act would to a great extent outweigh the defects of the rest of the opera, but I see that in Rome this was not so. So that's the way it was.[21]

Verdi had lost whatever interest he ever had in *Alzira*. Years later he said of it, '*Quella è proprio brutta*' (That one is really ugly).[22] His judgment was far too harsh, but it may have been compounded partly of guilt at not having committed himself to the opera wholeheartedly during its composition.

Returning to Milan before the end of August, Verdi began to turn his thoughts towards the work he had agreed to write for the Fenice theatre in Venice. In March, some weeks after the Milan premiere of *Giovanna d'Arco*, he had gone to Venice to supervise a production there of *I due Foscari*, and had taken the opportunity to discuss with Piave the new opera for Venice which they had already agreed would be *Attila*, and about which Verdi had written to Piave the previous

April (see p. 40). On 24 June 1845, however, an announcement appeared in the magazine *Il Pirata* to the effect that Piave would write the libretti for the two operas Verdi was to compose for the 1846 season, and in exchange had ceded to Temistocle Solera the libretto for the forthcoming carnival season in Venice. Verdi had probably decided that Attila the Hun was too bloodthirsty a subject for Piave's gentle muse, but was ideally suited to the more robust témperament of Solera. By the time Verdi returned to Milan from staging *Alzira* in Naples, Solera had almost completed his *Attila* libretto. 'In a few days I shall begin *Attila* for Venice,' Verdi wrote to Léon Escudier:

> It is a stupendous subject! The poem is by Solera, and I am pleased with it. . . . How beautiful *Attila* would be for the Grand Opéra in Paris! One would only have to add a few things, and all the rest would go well. At other times you have written to me about having either *I lombardi* or *Ernani* translated this year; tell me now if *Attila* could not be done in two years' time. By then I shall be free, and if there were a chance of arranging something at that theatre I would not accept any engagements in Italy.[23]

Despite Verdi's extravagant enthusiasm for the opera before he had written a note of it, composition proceeded at a very leisurely pace throughout the autumn. Verdi's mood during these months was volatile: bursts of creative energy would be followed by days in which neurotic sloth overcame him, and he seemed to be overwhelmed by the weight of his commitments. In April he had written to his Busseto friend Giuseppe Demaldè: 'I look forward to the passing of these next three years. I have six operas to write, and then farewell to everything.'[24] He was, it appears, contemplating a very early retirement at the age of thirty-five.

He began *Attila* in September in Busseto but found life in his home town boring, and in the middle of the month moved back to Milan. In November, at work on *Attila*, his mood was sufficiently unstable to be reflected quite dissimilarly in two letters written on the same day to friends in Rome. To Ferretti he wrote: '*Attila* keeps me busy. What a wonderful, wonderful subject. The critics can say whatever they like, but I say "What a wonderful libretto for music".'[25] To a friend named Masi who had sent him news of the Rome production of *Alzira*, he wrote:

> Thanks for the news of *Alzira*, but more for remembering your poor friend, condemned continually to scribble musical notes. God save the ears of every good Christian from having to listen to them! Accursed notes!

How am I, physically and spiritually? Physically I am well, but my mind is black, always black, and will be so until I have finished with this career which I abhor. And afterwards? It's useless to delude oneself. It will always be black. Happiness does not exist for me.[26]

Some comfort was to be derived from the fact that his least popular opera, *Un giorno di regno*, was now being successfully revived in Venice under the title of *Il finto Stanislao*, not at the Fenice but at the second theatre. 'Do you want a good laugh?' Verdi asked the sculptor Vicenzo Luccardi. 'That opera of mine that was hissed off the stage at La Scala is now a sensation at the Teatro San Benedetto.'[27] (The San Benedetto theatre was later to perform a similar act of rehabilitation with *La traviata*.)

That Verdi was only fitfully occupied with *Attila* during the autumn is suggested by his purchase of a town house, the Palazzo Dordoni (now the Palazzo Orlandi) in Busseto, and by his taking a week off towards the end of October to visit the Countess Maffei, who was staying at Clusone, near Bergamo. He then returned to Milan where he had meetings with Léon Escudier from Paris and Benjamin Lumley from London, both of whom offered him contracts to compose for the following season.

Even if Verdi had been progressing more satisfactorily with *Attila*, he would have been held up by the fact that Solera had gone off to Spain with his wife, an opera singer, leaving the final act of the libretto unfinished. When the baritone Antonio Superchi, who was singing in the same company as Solera's wife in Barcelona, wrote to Verdi, the composer replied irritably:

> I hear with pleasure that Solera has written a hymn. What do you say? Has he sent me a copy of it? Just think! He doesn't even send me what he ought to send me for *Attila*, so you can imagine whether he would wish to send me one of his hymns. Indeed, as I know you see him often, I would beg you to goad him on a little to finish once and for all this little matter of *Attila*.[28] [Verdi seems not to have realized that the hymn had been intended for *Attila*.]

Solera's only response was to suggest that the composer find another librettist, and so Verdi turned to Piave. One of Piave's suggestions must have been that they make use of a popular Venetian band for a march in the last act, for this reply came from the composer:

> I know that the Kinschi band is an excellent band, as I heard them last year, but I am tired of these stage bands. Besides, the subject does not call for it.

There is no place for it unless we had a march for the arrival of Attila which would slow down the action for no good reason.

What's more, these bands no longer have the appeal of novelty. They are always nonsensical, and they make such a din. Anyway, I've written marches before – a warlike one in *Nabucco* and a slow, solemn one in *Giovanna*, and I shan't be able to improve on those. And what do you mean, there can't be a grand opera without the din of a band? Aren't *Guillaume Tell* and *Robert le diable* grand operas? Yet they don't have any bands. Nowadays the band is a piece of provincialism and quite unsuitable for use in the big cities.[29]

Verdi arrived in Venice early in December to orchestrate and rehearse the opera, which was meant to have its premiere on New Year's Eve. Piave, it appears, had produced an ending for the libretto, but Verdi delayed completing the composition as he was still in correspondence with Solera and wanted his comments. The premiere was postponed. Then early in January Verdi collapsed with a high temperature and was confined to bed for three weeks. He was seriously ill with gastric fever, and Piave devotedly nursed him. 'I shall never forget the care you lavished on me with more than merely fraternal love,' Verdi wrote to him some months later.[30] The illness was grave enough for the *Allgemeine Musikalische Zeitung* to have actually announced the composer's death!

Solera's comments on Piave's completion of the libretto arrived late in January, and were distinctly unfavourable:

My dear Verdi, your letter was a thunderbolt for me. I cannot conceal from you my indescribable sorrow at seeing a work with which I dared to feel satisfied now ending in parody. How was it that the solemnity of a hymn could not succeed in inspiring you, since it offered the possibility of providing your imagination with something new? In the ending that you send me I find only a parody. Attila pursues Odabella, Odabella flees from a nuptial bed in which she had placed all her hopes of vengeance, etc., all these seem to me things which ruin everything I thought I had instilled into my characters.

Fiat voluntas tua. The cup you make me drink is too painful. Only you could have convinced me that being a librettist is no longer a profession for me.

I very much hope that you will soon give me news of yourself, and of the opera when it is staged. Meanwhile, I beg you to change some of the verses that are not mine, so that the pill will taste less bitter to me. I return your own copy to you, so that you can more easily see the corrections.[31]

Recovering slowly from his illness at the end of January, Verdi still did not have the strength to work very hard on *Attila*. He proceeded slowly. On 11 February he wrote to his friend Luccardi, the sculptor, in Rome, asking him to provide a sketch and a description of the meeting of Attila with Pope Leo, as depicted in the tapestries or the Raphael frescos in the Vatican. He was always concerned to achieve historical accuracy in costume and decor. 'I particularly need the headdress,' he told Luccardi. 'If you do me this favour I will give you my holy blessing.'[32]

Finally, on 17 March 1846, *Attila* was given its premiere at the Fenice, and was reasonably successful. Some parts of the opera were greeted with immense enthusiasm: not surprisingly, the Venetian audience responded happily to the scene in which refugees from Aquileia arrive at the lagoon to found the city which was to become Venice, and tumultuously to the battles between Italians and Huns, whose contemporary political implications they were quick to seize upon. When, in his duet with Attila, the Roman general Ezio sang the line, '*Avrai tu l'universo, resti l'Italia a me*' (You take the universe but leave me Italy), there were cries from the audience of '*A noi! L'Italia a noi!*' After the performance Verdi was feted as a hero by the Venetians and escorted to his hotel with flowers, bands and torchlight. Writing to a friend afterwards he gave his usual cool report:

> *Attila* enjoyed a very good success. There were calls after every piece, but it was the whole of the first act that was applauded with the greatest enthusiasm. I had high hopes of the second- and third-act finales, but either I was mistaken or the public did not understand, because they were less warmly applauded.
>
> Perhaps this evening it will be better performed by the singers too, because, although they performed it with the greatest care, the effect did not match their good intentions. My friends try to tell me that this is the best of my operas, but the public disputes it. I believe it is not inferior to any of my other operas. Time will tell.[33]

The principal singers had been Ignazio Marini (bass) as Attila, Sophie Loewe (soprano) as Odabella, Carlo Guasco (tenor) as Foresto, and Natale Constantini (baritone) as Ezio. The *Gazzetta Privilegiata di Venezia* had this to say of the work and its performance:

> Maestro Verdi's opera began last night with the most splendid auguries. The Prologue was not only moving, it also roused the spirits, kindling them with the liveliest enthusiasm. It contains a lovely cavatina, sung with great mastery and expressiveness by La Loewe; a grand duet for two

basses, Marini and Constantini; a chorus of hermits; and a magnificent instrumental number in which with admirable skill the music imitates the awakening of nature at dawn. . . .

In the rest of the opera, the omens were less splendid. A sweet and melodious romanza sung by La Loewe was rightly applauded in the first part of a duet between her and Guasco. A beautiful and excellently crafted largo in the first act was pleasing, as was the rich and varied finale of Act II, but the effect of the music was less lively. Very lively, though perhaps not universal, were the applause and calls for the Maestro.

Justice demands, however, that we state that not all the arias were enjoyed as they had a right to be. In the grand finale, for example, some singers entered too soon, and the beauty of the ensemble was marred. Constantini had a fever, and Guasco did not seem in good voice, so one must hope for more from future performances. . . .

And now we address a request to Attila himself. He may dress himself and his men however he likes, taking no account of the pomp and magnificence of his house. That may or may not distress, but it does no harm. But will he please take pity on us and have the hundred flames of his banquet, which takes place in the dark anyway, consume some less odorous material, so people are not made ill when, at an evil moment, the flames are extinguished. Let the scourge of God not be the scourge of nostrils. . . .[34]

Shorn of the various pieces of local colour with which Verdi and Solera enlivened it, the plot of *Attila* is simple. Attila the Hun invades Italy, but is turned back before he can enter Rome. He is stabbed to death by Odabella, whose father he had defeated and killed in the battle for Aquileia. *Attila* is not one of the most successful of Verdi's early operas. In it, his imaginative use of the orchestra is confirmed and extended, but his skill in musical characterization is temporarily at a standstill. Odabella is an unconvincing figure, while Attila himself is as much a confusing as a confused character.

Five days after the premiere, Verdi returned to Milan still in poor health. There his doctors examined him and ordered a rest cure for six months, with no work, no composing, and no thought of future commitments. His constitution, strong though it was, could no longer stand up to the conditions of employment in the Italian opera industry.

Chapter Six

1846–48

Verdi's period of enforced inactivity was necessary not only for his health but quite possibly also for his future as a composer, for he was now in a state of nervous exhaustion, a condition to which his temperament rendered him peculiarly vulnerable and which had been hastened and exacerbated by the weight of the commitments he had entered into and by the consequent necessity of composing at great speed. For six months after the *Attila* premiere, Verdi concerned himself with business matters as little as possible, attempting to live the life of a complete invalid, looked after by the faithful Emanuele Muzio. His friends visited him, and occasionally he ventured out into the countryside, but he always dined at home and retired early to bed.

In April he felt obliged to send medical certificates to the English impresario Benjamin Lumley to support his claim that he was too ill to come to London, 'let alone write an opera'. Lumley, not disposed to take Verdi's illness too seriously, wrote back expressing sympathy, but added:

> I dare to hope that in a few days you will be back to normal and that, very soon, you will arrive here by short stages in the best of health – at the time of year when we enjoy our best weather, with a sky less blue than Italy's but also an air less exciting. . . . I am sure that a change of scenery and a visit to London in such a beautiful and prosperous season (I've never known such a brilliant time in our theatre) will be better for you than all the remedies imaginable.[1]

The impresarios with whom Verdi had to deal, among them Flauto in Naples and Lumley in London, tended to express themselves sceptically on the subject of Verdi's 'gastric fever' or, as it was more likely to have been, nervous collapse. In this they exhibited a distinct lack not only of sympathy but also of imagination. In the case of a busy professional such as Verdi, a sudden and prolonged unwillingness or inability to work is symptomatic of something other than mere malingering. To argue that Verdi simply wanted to extricate himself from unwelcome commitments is to fail completely to understand his creative temperament. Verdi was no simple young man from the country, healthy of mind and body. He had his fair share of the artist's schizophrenia: he was not only the healthy, shrewd, commonsensical farmer but also the melancholic, listless and pessimistic musician. The psychosomatic sore throats, headaches and stomach upsets were suffered by the musician: the musician's tantrums were tolerated by the peasant farmer.

Early in July, accompanied by his friend Andrea Maffei, who had just separated from his wife, Clarina, Verdi took the waters at Recoaro, a spa near the slopes of the Venetian alps, about thirty kilometres north-west of Vicenza. The two men took long walks and donkey rides in the mountains, but two weeks of this was enough for Verdi. On 14 July he wrote to Emilia Morosini, complaining:

> I am dying of boredom here. So many people about that those who arrive now are being turned away from the hotels. But they all keep to themselves. There is no society in the evenings, so after supper one goes to bed. I find this valley very pretty, but what is it compared with Como, Varese and so on? We take long walks, using the map which Peppina gave me as a present. I do not understand what benefit I shall derive from the waters: I think they are like that malvino ointment which does no good and no harm. I find them very easy to take, and we must hope they will be of future benefit. . . . What is good about this place is that no one plays music or talks about it. It was a real inspiration not to bring a harpsichord here. I don't feel like myself any more: I cannot believe I am able to write music or compose good and bad pieces, and I don't know whether I shall ever be able to return to work. How empty by contrast are the words 'fame', 'glory', 'talent' etc. I shall probably leave Recoaro on Thursday.[2]

He did leave Recoaro, returning to Milan by way of Venice, where he talked to Piave about *Il corsaro*, the opera based on Byron's play *The Corsair*, which Verdi thought would be a suitable subject for Lumley and London. He even began to sketch one or two scenes of the opera. (He had at first thought of writing his *King Lear* for London, on the understanding that Luigi Lablache, the great French-Irish bass, would be a member of the company and would undertake the role of

Lear. But with the breakdown in his health he had decided to postpone yet again the composition of so demanding a subject.)

By the beginning of August Verdi was back in Milan. Replying to a letter from the Naples impresario Flauto, he refused to commit himself to a definite date for his next opera to be composed for that city, and suggested that they pursue the matter some months later. 'I thank you for the friendship you show me,' he added. 'As for the good humour you wish me to display to the Neapolitans, I'm not certain what you mean, but I assure you I am in the most hilarious mood. Why should I feel bad-humoured towards the Neapolitans, or the Neapolitans to me? Do they lack colours in their prism that they have need of Verdi [i.e. '*verde*', Italian for 'green']?'[3]

By mid-August Verdi was beginning to feel that it might soon be possible for him to begin work again. His definite commitments included an opera to be written for London and published by Lucca; an opera to be written for Alessandro Lanari, the Florence impresario; and one for Naples. The London and Florence engagements were the more pressing, and he now gave simultaneous consideration to possible subjects for the two cities. In Recoaro, he and Maffei had no doubt talked of Schiller's play *Die Räuber*, which Maffei intended to translate and adapt: this was in due course to become *I masnadieri*, and it might, Verdi thought, be suitable for the company in Florence. But another subject had begun to appeal to him. This was Shakespeare's *Macbeth*, and on 19 August he wrote to Lanari in Florence. At this stage, the choice of subject depended to a large extent on the singers available. If Gaetano Fraschini (the tenor who had created the role of Zamoro in *Alzira*) was to be a member of the company, it is likely that Verdi would have composed *I masnadieri* for Florence, for he envisaged Schiller's Karl as a tenor hero. 'I do not wish to take a chance on other tenors, in the event of your not having settled anything with Fraschini,' he told Lanari, 'and in that case I would want to write a subject which did not require a tenor.'

Without at this stage letting Lanari know that *Macbeth* was the other subject he had in mind, Verdi said that the only singer in Italy who could portray the role he was thinking of was the baritone Felice Varesi, 'not only because of his singing, but also by virtue of his temperament and his appearance'. Other singers, even those better than Varesi, would be less suitable for the leading role in an opera which, he told Lanari, would be neither political nor religious, but 'a fantasy'.[4]

Verdi had already begun to compose *I masnadieri*, using Maffei's libretto, when it became clear that the tenor Fraschini would not be free to sing in Florence. He went to Bergamo to hear another tenor, Napoleone Moriani (who had been prevented by illness from being in *Oberto* seven years earlier), but found that Moriani's voice had deteriorated. He decided to compose *Macbeth* for Florence, and put *I masnadieri* aside for the time being. At the beginning of September he sent to Piave a summary of *Macbeth*, accompanied by a letter containing detailed instructions to his malleable librettist:

> Here is a scenario of *Macbeth*. This tragedy is one of the greatest creations of mankind! If we can't make something great with it, let's try at least to make something out of the ordinary. The scenario is clear: unconventional, simple and brief. I beg you to make your verses brief, too: the shorter they are, the more effect you will achieve. Only the first act is somewhat long, but it will be up to us to keep the numbers short. In your verses, remember there should be no superfluous words; everything must say something, and you must use an exalted language, except in the choruses for the witches, which must be common, but bizarre and original.
>
> When you've done the whole of the introduction, please send it to me. It is made up of four short scenes, which will need only a few verses. Once this introduction is done, I'll let you have all the time you want, because I know the general character and the colours as if the libretto were already finished. Oh, I beg you, don't treat this *Macbeth* of mine carelessly. I beg you on my knees, if for no other reason treat it well for my sake and for that of my health, which at the moment is excellent but will get worse at once if you upset me. Brevity and sublimity.[5]

Verdi worked on the composition of *Macbeth* slowly and carefully, refusing to discuss any future engagements: he clearly gave it a far deeper commitment than he had given to its immediate predecessors. Indeed, in dedicating the vocal score some months later to his old benefactor Barezzi, he wrote: 'Here now is this *Macbeth*, which is dearer to me than all my other operas, and which I therefore deem more worthy of being presented to you.'[6]

On 16 September, a terrible fire in Milan destroyed almost all of the suburb of Porta Orientale and continued to burn for a week. Verdi and Muzio went to watch the fire brigade coping with it, but unfortunately arrived just as the police were drawing a cordon around the onlookers, intending to press them into service at the pumps. In a letter to Barezzi, Muzio described their adventures as he and Verdi sought to evade the police cordon:

The Signor Maestro acted in time, and jumped down from the wall into the public gardens. But I was caught while covering the Signor Maestro's retreat, and had to work at the pumps until six in the morning when I managed to escape. I returned home covered in dirt and completely wet, looking like an assassin. On seeing me, the Signor Maestro began to laugh, which infuriated me. He is still laughing. But then, when he told me that he had had to stay concealed in the public gardens for an hour and a half, I began to laugh a bit, too. Now listen to this, which is even better. When the Signor Maestro jumped down from the wall into the public gardens, the gates were all shut and he couldn't get out. As I said, he stayed hidden for an hour and a half. When he saw that the people on the walls had dispersed, he tried to climb over, but he wasn't able to do so, as the wall was taller than he, and he had to wander about for more than an hour, gathering stones and building them up into a pile to use as a kind of ladder. He told me that he scrambled up and then fell back down again, and his hands, which look as though they had been scratched by a cat, vouch for the truth of his story.[7]

Before beginning work on *Macbeth*, Verdi had established that the baritone Felice Varesi would indeed be available to portray the title role. His first choice for Lady Macbeth (or 'Lady', as Verdi called her) was Sophie Loewe, who had created the soprano roles in *Ernani* and *Attila*, but in the autumn Loewe announced her immediate retirement from the stage, following (according to one of Muzio's letters to Barezzi) a fiasco in Florence in *Ernani* in which her virtual voicelessness was ascribed to her having had an abortion. Verdi accepted, in her place, Marianna Barbieri-Nini, who had been his first Lucrezia in *I due Foscari* in 1844. In 1887 her obituary was to describe her thus: 'Small and fat, poorly proportioned with a vast head twice the normal size, she had a face hardly likely to arouse sympathy at first sight.'[8]

Verdi wrote much of the *Macbeth* libretto himself, often using Piave merely to turn his prose into verse. Indeed, the composer supervised most aspects of the opera's production, sending off instructions to Lanari regarding the decor and costumes, which he insisted must be historically accurate, and the staging of various difficult scenes, especially those involving the witches. He was concerned, first and foremost, with the dramatic effect. When the singer engaged to portray Banquo made known his reluctance to reappear in the banquet scene as Banquo's ghost with nothing to sing, Verdi reacted angrily. 'Singers must be engaged to sing and to act,' he informed Lanari; 'What's more, it's high time we stopped being so easy-going about this kind of thing. It would be monstrous to have someone else play the ghost, for Banquo must continue to look like the same person when he appears as a ghost.'⁹

To discover how the appearance of Banquo's ghost was usually staged, Verdi wrote to London. He gave his publisher, Tito Ricordi, a lesson in British history: 'Macbeth assassinated Duncan in 1040, and was himself killed in 1057. In England in 1039 the king was Harold, called Harefoot. He was Danish, and was succeeded in the same year by Hardicanute, half-brother of Edward the Confessor. . . .'¹⁰ The composer advised on all aspects of the creation of this *Macbeth*, which he obviously considered to be the most important project he had embarked upon. Not surprisingly, he was visited by his usual birth pangs. On 14 December Muzio wrote to Barezzi:

> The Maestro has been somewhat unwell in the past few days. He has had intestinal pains, which led to a diarrhoea which did not give him a moment's peace. You can't imagine how it upset me to see him looking like this. Then he gave way to his melancholy, and said that his illness was worse than last year's, and so much else that it almost made me weep.¹¹

After a few days, Verdi recovered and resumed a routine which, according to Muzio, usually involved him in composing from nine in the morning until twelve at night. Muzio worked on his studies at the same large table as Verdi, and the composer, it seems, was always willing to interrupt himself to advise his pupil.

The first act of *Macbeth* had been completed by the end of October. In November the impresario Benjamin Lumley visited Verdi in Milan to discuss the opera he was to compose for London. Since Verdi was now writing *Macbeth* for Florence, he decided that the already partially composed *I masnadieri* would be suitable for London. Lumley was perfectly happy with this, but Lucca, the publisher who also had an interest in the London opera, had expected that it would be *Il corsaro*, had warmed to that particular subject, and now tried to hold Verdi to it. Despite this, Verdi concluded an agreement with Lumley to complete *I masnadieri* for production in London in 1847, and returned to *Macbeth*.

Early in January 1847, while he was still at work on the opera, Verdi wrote to the singers who were to portray Macbeth and Lady Macbeth, enclosing some of their music, explaining the characters as he conceived them, and even giving some precise instructions as to how the music was to be performed. 'First of all,' he told Marianna Barbieri-Nini, the character of your role is resolute, bold and extremely dramatic. The plot is taken from one of the greatest tragedies the theatre can boast of, and I have tried to draw faithfully from it all the dramatic situations, to have it put into good verse, to produce a new texture, and to write music tied, as far as is possible, to the actual words and the situation; and I wish this idea of mine to be understood well by the singers. In short, I wish the singers to serve the poet better than they do the composer.

Your first number is the cavatina. You appear, reading a letter, and then a recitative in a slow tempo. Then there comes an adagio of a grandiose kind, cantabile, but not too sweet a cantabile. I beg you to reflect well on the phrasing at the words:

> *Che tardi? accetta il dono,*
> *Ascendivi a regnar*
> [Why do you hold back? Accept the gift,
> Ascend the throne and reign]

and to sing it in such a way that the voice does not expand immediately but gradually, and to give significant emphasis each time to the words '*qui . . . qui . . . la notte?*' [here, here, overnight?]. These words are most significant and important in arousing applause. The first part of the cabaletta should go with a grandiose air, with haughtiness, but within this haughtiness there should also be joy. In the second part, perhaps the phrase at the words '*Tu notte ne avvolgi*' [You, night, enshroud us] etc. will be low for you, but it is exactly my intention to make it dark and mysterious (if necessary this phrase can be quickly changed) in order to have all the brilliance at the end . . . '*Qual petto percota*' [That the breast which is struck] etc. etc.

Note well that the little finale of Act I is completely unaccompanied, and so you will need to be very secure, especially you two principals.

You will also find enclosed the finale of Act II in which you have a drinking song. There is no need to tell you that this should go lightly, brilliantly, with all the appoggiaturas, gruppetti, mordents etc. I cannot remember well if you can trill easily: I have included a trill, but it can easily be taken out. The tempo of this *brindisi* is broad but not too much so. What follows is a vision scene for Macbeth in which you have splendid passages of reaction. The act ends with a concerted piece in which you almost always speak to Macbeth *sotto voce*.

Soon, I shall be sending you a duet. Then another aria, consisting however of a recitative and a single brilliant cabaletta. And then the great scene in which you sleepwalk, and reveal in your dreams all the crimes you have committed. It is a great scene in the play: if the music is at all good, it will make an effect.

In the numbers I am sending you now, pay attention to the tessitura (not to the music, which is difficult to make out from your simplified score), and let me know what you think of it. If there is any passage that does not lie well for you, let me know before I orchestrate it.[12]

Equally precise instructions were given to the Macbeth, Felice Varesi; and poor Piave, the librettist, was continually harangued. 'Oh no, indeed,' Verdi wrote sarcastically to him on 21 January,

> you're not the slightest bit at fault, except for having neglected these last two acts of mine in the most incredible manner. But don't worry. Saint Andrea [Andrea Maffei] has rescued both you and me, especially me because, if I may speak frankly to you, I couldn't have set your verses to music as they were, and you can see what a mess I'd have found myself in. Now everything is all right, but only because everything had to be changed. . . .[13]

Maffei had revised parts of Piave's libretto at Verdi's request, notably the witches' chorus in Act III and the sleep-walking scene. By the end of January, the opera was complete except for the orchestration, which took Verdi another two weeks. Rather exceptionally at this stage of his career, he finished the orchestration before the beginning of the rehearsal period. On 15 February he and Muzio travelled to Florence where *Attila* was being staged at the end of February. Verdi declined to attend any of the rehearsals and delegated responsibility to Muzio. He was concerned only with *Macbeth*, piano rehearsals for which began on 27 February, the day before the opening of *Attila*. Muzio described in one of his letters to Barezzi how he tricked Verdi into appearing at a performance of *Attila*:

> I am writing to you about the brilliant success *Attila* had at its third performance at the Teatro della Pergola. On Sunday the theatre was packed with people, and everyone had come to pay homage to the Maestro. They began, after Barbieri's cavatina, to shout, 'Come out, Verdi,' and this went on for a quarter of an hour. At last a spokesman appeared, and everyone was silent. He said, 'Maestro Verdi is not present in the theatre.' Then from all sides they replied, 'Send to fetch him, send to fetch him,' shouting even louder than before. The curtain was lowered and the performance couldn't continue. Finally they became quiet and the performance went on to the end. The finale of the third act had to be repeated, and here again they called for the Maestro, but they were persuaded to quieten down. But then there was a great murmuring, a general discontent, and they took it badly that the Maestro had not come to the theatre.
>
> Yesterday, Monday, I nagged at him from morning till evening to persuade him to go to the theatre, but he didn't want to go. Finally, I thought of a stratagem, and I told him that the leader of the stage band was in need of his instructions, and I also told him that a lens of the

fantasmagoria had been broken, and that he had to go to see about a replacement, and that I wasn't able to deal with these things, and that Barbieri needed a passage of her music changed, and that if he did not attend to all these things that very evening both the rehearsal and the evening performance would be ruined. Then he promised me he would go, but he delayed until the performance had begun. We went to the theatre after the Prologue, and we decided to enter by a small secret door by which you can get directly to the stage without being seen by a living soul. When he was in the theatre, I went into the stalls and told a few friends that Verdi was present. The word was passed around, and in a few moments, after the duet, everyone began to shout, 'Come out, Maestro!' Then he wanted to depart, but someone from the management came and persuaded him to show himself. He had to appear eight times altogether, amidst the most frenzied applause. I was happier than a prince. After the finale, they called for him again, and threw an immense number of bouquets to him. Finally he asked me where was this leader of the stage band, this alteration for Barbieri, this machine that needed attention, but I told him that while he was presenting himself to the public I had dealt with everything. He didn't believe me, and said, 'I'm angry with you,' but it wasn't true. I've never seen him angry with me. This morning, as soon as he was awake, I asked him if he was angry with me. And he said, 'You're a pain in the neck!'[14]

Finally, on 14 March 1847 (postponed from the 12th, because Verdi was indisposed) *Macbeth* was given its premiere at the Teatro della Pergola. Its success was immediate and enormous. Verdi had continued to rehearse his principal singers assiduously up until the final moment and, many years later, Marianna Barbieri-Nini recalled the experience:

The evening of the final rehearsal, with the theatre full of guests, Verdi made the artists put on their costumes; and, when he insisted on something, woe betide those who contradicted him. When we were dressed and ready, with the orchestra in the pit and the chorus already on stage, Verdi beckoned to me and to Varesi to follow him into the wings. We did so, and he explained that he wanted us to come out into the foyer for another piano rehearsal of that wretched duet.

'Maestro,' I protested, 'we are already in our Scottish costumes. How can we?'

'Put cloaks over them.'

Varesi, annoyed at this strange request, dared to raise his voice: 'But, for God's sake, we've already rehearsed it a hundred and fifty times.'

'I wouldn't say that, if I were you, for within half an hour it will be a hundred and fifty-one.'

He was a tyrant whom one had to obey. I can still remember the black look Varesi threw at Verdi as he followed the Maestro into the foyer. With his hand clutching the hilt of his sword, he looked as though he could murder Verdi just as later he would murder Duncan. But even Varesi gave in, and the one hundred and fifty-first rehearsal took place, while inside the theatre the audience clamoured impatiently.[15]

The singers were well aware that they had participated in an event of considerably greater importance than the usual operatic premiere. Writing to an official at the Fenice theatre in Venice three days later, Varesi referred to the success he had obtained with the role of Macbeth as the finest and most important of his career, and said that the second performance seemed to consist of one single, prolonged ovation.

Verdi had to acknowledge thirty-eight curtain calls on the first night, and after the performance he and Muzio were surrounded by an immense crowd, mainly of young people, who accompanied them with applause and cheers from the theatre to their hotel, almost a mile away. Over the next few days, the press notices appeared. The consensus was that Verdi had surpassed himself, though there were a few dissenting voices. The public, however, continued to applaud the opera with the greatest enthusiasm.

Eighteen years later, Verdi was to revise *Macbeth*, and it is this revised version which is usually performed today. But the opera as we know it is still basically the work of the thirty-four-year-old composer; with one or two exceptions, most of its great moments already exist in the 1847 score. Verdi's *Macbeth* is not unworthy to stand beside Shakespeare's; it is an opera in which, no doubt inspired by the great Elizabethan playwright whom he revered, Verdi has suddenly taken an immense leap forward, a leap away from the conventional demands of mid-nineteenth-century Italian opera, towards dramatic truth and a musical style which combines psychological depth with a continuing abundance of that prolific and individual melodic gift which was never to desert him. His intuitive feeling for Shakespeare was obviously to a large extent responsible for this.

Macbeth, however, caused something of a rift in Verdi's relations with Piave for, having entrusted Andrea Maffei with the revisions he thought necessary, the composer's last words to his librettist on the subject were, 'I assure you that I wouldn't take your drama for all the gold in the world.'[16] To Piave's dismay, Verdi had the librettist's

name omitted from the opera's title page. This was more than a trifle
unfair, for the greater part of the libretto, as set by Verdi, was written
by Piave. But the composer was capable of riding roughshod over
colleagues' feelings when he was convinced he was in the right.

Two weeks after the premiere of *Macbeth*, Verdi was back in Milan.
Bartolomeo Merelli, who had mounted the composer's first four
operas at La Scala, hoped to persuade him to write again for that
theatre, whose most recent Verdi premiere had been *Giovanna d'Arco*
two years previously. But Verdi, who considered that standards there
had become slipshod, would have nothing further to do with La Scala.
After *Giovanna d'Arco* he had refused Merelli's invitation to supervise
a revival of *Ernani*, and when some months later the impresario
mounted *I due Foscari* with the second and third acts in reverse order,
Verdi's decision to turn his back on La Scala was strengthened.

The 1847 carnival season at La Scala had opened on 26 December
1846 with *Attila*. Muzio, who was present at the first performance, no
doubt informed Verdi, as he did Barezzi, that the staging of the opera
was a mess. On 29 December, in a letter to his publisher Giovanni
Ricordi concerning arrangements for *Macbeth*, Verdi gave explicit
instructions with regard to La Scala:

> I approve the contract for my opera *Macbeth*, which will be staged during
> the next Lent season in Florence, and I agree to your making use of it, on
> condition, however, that you do not permit this *Macbeth* to be performed
> at the Imperial and Royal Theatre of La Scala.
>
> I have too many examples to persuade me that here they either do not
> know how, or do not want, to stage operas decently, especially mine. I
> cannot forget the awful staging of *I lombardi*, *Ernani*, *I due Foscari* etc. I
> have another proof of this before my eyes with *Attila*. I ask you, yourself, if
> this opera, in spite of a good cast, could overall be performed and staged
> any worse.
>
> I repeat, therefore, that I cannot and must not permit the performance of
> this *Macbeth* at La Scala, at least until things have changed for the better,
> and I myself give approval. I also feel obliged to advise you, for your
> guidance, that this condition which I now place on *Macbeth*, from now on I
> shall place on all my operas.[17]

Verdi was as good as his word, and a quarter of a century was to pass
before he relented. During that time Verdi's operas would be given
their first performances in Naples, Venice, Florence, Trieste, Rome,
London, Paris and St Petersburg, but not in Milan. The leading Italian
opera house was boycotted by the leading Italian composer.

Verdi's first concern in Milan in the spring of 1847 was to complete *I masnadieri* for Benjamin Lumley and Her Majesty's Theatre, London. When Lumley had first approached Verdi in 1845, his wildly unrealistic hope had been to persuade the composer to agree to compose one opera a year for a period of ten years! Verdi cautiously agreed to provide one opera only, and at some stage in the negotiations the publisher Lucca became involved in the agreement. The outcome of this was that, when Verdi finally decided that the opera he would compose for London was to be *I masnadieri* and not *Il corsaro*, he remained contractually obliged to write *Il corsaro* for Lucca. Since he found Lucca an irritating and insensitive person to do business with, Verdi was not disposed to lose any sleep over *Il corsaro*. Putting it out of his mind for the time being, he proceeded to complete the composition of *I masnadieri* to a libretto by Andrea Maffei, based on Schiller's play *Die Räuber*. He had already composed much of the opera before beginning work on *Macbeth*: he now completed his vocal score in May 1847, and on 26 May he left Milan with Muzio, bound for London by way of Paris.

Verdi decided to stay in Paris for a few days, and sent Muzio on ahead to London. His friend and colleague Giuseppina Strepponi had retired from the stage and was teaching singing in Paris. Perhaps Verdi wanted to spend some time with her: it may even have been now that their intimate relationship began. 'What I saw of Paris I liked very much,' he wrote to Clarina Maffei some days later from London, 'and above all I like the free and easy life that can be led in that country.'[18]

While Verdi was living or observing the free life in Paris, Muzio was coping with London:

> I have been in London since yesterday. I am here alone, without the Maestro who is still in Paris and will be arriving tomorrow evening. He sent me on ahead because in Paris they had told him that Signora Lind didn't want to sing any new operas. If this had been true, since it is in his contract that Signora Lind must sing in his opera, he would have made a protest to the management and not come to London, and I should have gone back to Paris, in ten hours, the way I came.
>
> As soon as I got to London I went to Lumley with a letter from Verdi, and he assured me the rumour was untrue and that Signora Lind could hardly wait to get her part and learn it, and he was very distressed not to see Verdi yet in London. So I wrote immediately to the Maestro, who is in Boulogne-sur-Mer, to let him know, and he will continue his journey tomorrow and be in London at six o'clock in the evening. . . .[19]

Verdi arrived in London on 7 June. The next day he wrote to the Countess Maffei:

> . . . I can say nothing about London because yesterday was Sunday and I haven't seen a soul. This smoke, however, and the smell of coal upset me. I feel as though I were on a steamboat all the time. In a few moments I'm going to the theatre to find out how my affairs are going. Emanuele, whom I sent ahead of me, has found me such a homeopathic suite of rooms that I can't move about in them. Nevertheless, it's quite clean, like all the houses in London.[20]

His first concern was to attend a performance at Her Majesty's Theatre in which Jenny Lind, the 'Swedish Nightingale', was appearing, for he had never heard her sing and had delayed writing her arias until he could hear the voice for which he was to compose. The famous soprano was singing, during the season, in Donizetti's *La figlia del reggimento*, Bellini's *La sonnambula* and Meyerbeer's *Robert le diable*. Muzio described her, and it is safe to assume that his opinion echoed Verdi's:

> She is magnificent in all three operas. In *Robert le diable* she is incomparable. Her voice is a trifle harsh at the top, and weak at the bottom, but by hard work she has succeeded in making it sufficiently flexible in the upper register to execute the most formidably difficult passages. Her trill is incomparable. Her agility is unsurpassed, and to show off her virtuosity she is inclined to make the mistake of using excessive fioritura, turns and trills, things that were admired in the last century, but not in 1847. . . .[21]

Jenny Lind's qualities are reflected in the music Verdi wrote for her, notably her opening aria, and the cabaletta of her Act II aria. He now had the opera complete in rough draft, from which he had to make a fair copy before orchestrating the entire work. Piano rehearsals with the singers began while the orchestration was being completed. 'This humid, heavy air', complained Muzio, 'reacts strongly on his nervous system and makes him more eccentric and melancholy than usual.'[22] Verdi had been in London for six weeks when on 17 July he wrote again to Clarina Maffei:

> You will be surprised to hear that I am still in London, and that the opera has not yet been staged. But the smoke and the fog are to blame, as well as this diabolical climate which robs me of all desire to work. But now, at last, everything is finished, or almost finished, and on Thursday 22nd the opera will definitely be staged. I have had two orchestral rehearsals, and if I were in Italy I would know by now whether the work was good or not,

but here I understand nothing. Blame the climate, blame the climate! As you can imagine, I want to leave London as soon as possible and stay in Paris for a month. So you can address your letters to me in Paris, poste restante. For the rest, I'm quite pleased at the state of my health, although if I survive London this time I'm not likely to come back again. Still, it's a city that in some extraordinary way I like.

It's true that they have offered me 40,000 francs for another opera, but I have not accepted. Don't be surprised, however, because that's not really an exorbitant sum, and if I have to come back here I shall ask for much more.[23]

Muzio's descriptions of London and the Londoners in his letters to Busseto are considerably entertaining, and not entirely inaccurate. 'On Sundays not a soul is seen in the streets,' he assured Antonio Barezzi. 'They are all in church, where they have their sermons. Many, however, stay in bed almost all day, from what one hears, and others go into the country and the environs of London, for amusement and debauchery. The English say that on Sundays only dogs and Frenchmen are seen in the streets of London, and it is true that those one sees are all travellers and foreigners.'[24]

In London, Muzio and Verdi worked unceasingly on *I masnadieri* during the daytime. 'We get up at five in the morning and we work until six in the evening (supper time). Then we go out to the theatre for a while, and return at eleven and go to bed so as to be up early next morning.' At the theatre, Muzio was intrigued by the behaviour of London audiences:

> . . . The English are a formal and thoughtful people, and never give way to enthusiasm like the Italians, partly because they don't understand very well, and partly because they say educated people shouldn't make a noise. The English go to the theatre to show off their riches and luxury. When an opera that has already been printed is performed, they have the score in their hands, and follow with their eyes what the singer does, and if, according to their ideas, the singer does well, they applaud, and sometimes call for an encore; but they never insist as we do. I often went to hear the famous Rachel, the leading tragic actress. I saw some Englishmen sitting with the printed play in their hands, not looking at the actress, but following to see if she said all the words.[25]

The impresario Lumley had placed at Verdi's disposal a box at Her Majesty's Theatre, and whenever he used it he was the centre of attention. The ladies, one newspaper reported, 'devoured poor Verdi with their opera-glasses'. Although it was June, the weather was foul (it rained eight times on 28 June, Muzio noted), and Verdi complained bitterly of the rain, mist and smoke. After he had left London, he wrote to Emilia Morosini:

> Although the London climate was horrid, I took an extraordinary liking to the place. It isn't a city, it's a world. Its size, the richness and beauty of the streets, the cleanliness of the houses, all this is incomparable. One stands amazed and feels insignificant when, in the midst of all this splendour, one surveys the Bank of England and the Docks. Who can resist the people? The surroundings and the country outside London [he had been to Lumley's house in the country] are marvellous. But I do not like many of the English customs, or rather they do not suit us Italians. How ridiculous it looks when people in Italy imitate the English. [26]

Needing to concentrate on the completion and rehearsal of his opera, Verdi had accepted no social invitations during his weeks in London, refusing even to meet Queen Victoria who had expressed, through the bass Luigi Lablache, a desire to meet him. It was by command of the Queen that the opera had its premiere on 22 July, the day on which Parliament ended its session, and as the date approached London society became increasingly excited. Verdi was the first of the great nineteenth-century Italian composers to write an opera specifically for London, and the social occasion at Her Majesty's Theatre in the Haymarket promised to be a memorable one. At first reluctant to conduct the premiere himself, Verdi agreed to do so on being petitioned by the Russian ambassador and a deputation of English noblemen. Muzio described to Barezzi the scene on the first night:

> The opera created a furore. From the Overture to the Finale there was nothing but applause, *evvivas*, recalls and encores. The Maestro himself conducted sitting on a chair higher than the others, with baton in hand. As soon as he appeared in the orchestra pit, applause broke out and continued for a quarter of an hour. Before it had finished, the Queen and Prince Albert her consort, the Queen Mother and the Duke of Cambridge, uncle of the Queen, the Prince of Wales, son of the Queen, and all the royal family and a countless number of lords and dukes had arrived. It suffices it to say that the boxes were full of elegantly dressed ladies, and the pit so crowded that no one could remember having seen so many people there before. The doors had been opened at half-past four, and the crowd had burst in with an enthusiasm never previously seen. . . . The Maestro was cheered, called onto the stage, both alone and with the singers, and pelted with flowers. All you could hear was '*Evviva* Verdi! *Bietifol*' [beautiful].[27]

Maffei's version of Schiller's play tells the story of Carlo, son of Count Moor, from whose house he has been banished by the intrigues of his brother, Francesco. Carlo forms a band of brigands. His betrothed, Amalia, repulses Francesco's advances, flees from Count Moor's household, and, by accident, is reunited with Carlo. Francesco has been plotting to kill Count Moor, but Carlo rescues his father and kills his evil brother. When his followers, the brigands, refuse to release him from his oath of loyalty to them, Carlo stabs Amalia to death rather than have her dishonoured by a life with him and the brigands. Despite its unevenness, *I masnadieri* is one of the most interesting and one of the most inspired of the operas which emerged from those much-maligned years in which Verdi obsessively chain-composed. He responded to Schiller's extremely Byronic hero more strongly than to the authentic Byronic protagonist of his next opera, *Il corsaro*, and dressed Carlo and the other principal characters in the most glorious melodies.

The press was, in general, complimentary, *The Times* critic remarking that Verdi's writing had placed more emphasis on the ensemble than on the soloists, and the *Illustrated London News* claiming that 'the music is dramatic in the extreme and somewhat excels the masterpieces of Meyerbeer and other composers of the German romantic school'. One voice, however, that of Henry Chorley, dissented. In *The Athenaeum* he wrote: 'We take this to be the worst opera which has been given in our time at Her Majesty's Theatre. Verdi is finally rejected. The field is left open for an Italian composer.'[28]

Far from being rejected, Verdi was again beseeched by Lumley not only to write one opera a year for ten years but also to become the musical director of Her Majesty's Theatre. But assuming the direction of an entire season was not something which appealed to Verdi, who eventually answered Lumley from Paris proposing to write one opera a season for three years, and to conduct all the other operas of the season for an inclusive sum of 90,000 francs per season. Lumley's response to this was cautious, perhaps because, despite its successful premiere, *I masnadieri* had been performed only four times, as the season had but three weeks to run. He proposed discussing the matter further with Verdi during a forthcoming visit to Italy.

Verdi had conducted the second performance before handing the baton over to Michael Balfe (the composer of *The Bohemian Girl*) and departing for Paris. The public had enjoyed his opera, but Queen Victoria's journal entry for 22 July reveals that she had not:

> Went to the Opera, where we saw the production of Verdi's *I masnadieri* in 4 acts, which is the same subject as *I briganti* by Mercadante. In this new Opera by Verdi based on Schiller's *Die Räuber* the music is very inferior & commonplace. Lablache acted the part of Maximilian Moor, in which he looked fine, but too fat for the starved old man. Gardoni acted the part of Carlo Moor & was beautifully dressed. Lind sang and acted most exquisitely as Amalia & looked very well & attractive in her several dresses. She was immensely applauded.[29]

It is probable that Verdi's main purpose in lingering in Paris on his way back to Italy was to be with Giuseppina Strepponi. But within a few days of his arrival, he had signed a contract with the Paris Opéra to adapt the music of *I lombardi* to a new libretto which would be written in French by Alphonse Royer and Gustave Vaëz. This kept him in Paris for the next four months, adapting his *lombardi* score, composing new music, and supervising rehearsals of the opera which, under the title of *Jérusalem*, was produced in Paris on 26 November.

That Verdi's romantic liaison with Giuseppina Strepponi began at this time in Paris is suggested by the fact that, in one scene of the manuscript of *Jérusalem*, the dialogue was written, alternately, by both of them. The following exchange can be read:

IN STREPPONI'S HAND:	Alas! Hope is banished. My glory has faded! Family, fatherland, all I have lost!
IN VERDI'S HAND:	No, I am still left to you! And it will be for life!
STREPPONI:	Angel from heaven! May I die in the arms of a husband!
VERDI:	Let me die with you! My death will be –
STREPPONI:	– sweet.

Royer and Vaëz had produced a libretto for *Jérusalem* which was no mere translation of the original Italian. Although the period remained the end of the eleventh century, the Italian Crusaders from Lombardy became French Crusaders from Toulouse. The plot was altered, though as much as possible of its shape and psychological development was retained in order to minimize musical changes. Despite this, Verdi's revision was by no means confined to occasional changes of key or alterations to the scoring. He wrote a new orchestral introduction to replace the brief prelude to *I lombardi*, and composed a

The child Verdi
instructing a piano
pupil (perhaps
Margherita Barezzi)

The church at Le
Roncole, where Verdi
played the organ

Margherita Barezzi, Verdi's first wife

Verdi at the age of thirty-two. The inscription is to the Countess Morosini

Antonio Barezzi, Verdi's benefactor and father-in-law

Verdi's friends: the Countess Clarina Maffei and her husband, Andrea Maffei

Cover of the vocal score of Verdi's first opera, *Oberto* (1839)

Giuseppina Strepponi, with the score of
Nabucco, 1842

Verdi at the age of forty

Cover of the vocal score of *La traviata* (1853), showing Violetta and Giorgio Germont in
costumes of the early eighteenth century

Verdi leading a delegation to Vittorio Emanuele in 1859, to ask for the union of Parma with Piedmont

An 1859 cartoon, probably referring to *Simon Boccanegra*. The caption read: 'Supplies of musical doctrine necessary for the public who wish to enjoy the new style of Verdi's music.'

Verdi's librettists: *top left*, Francesco Piave; *top right*, Antonio Somma; *above left*, Temistocle Solera; *above right*, Antonio Ghislanzoni; *opposite, top left*, Eugène Scribe

Three generations of Verdi's publishers: *top right*, Giovanni Ricordi, founder of the firm (1785–1853); *above left*, Tito Ricordi (1811–88); *above right*, Giulio Ricordi (1840–1912)

Verdi in St Petersburg for the premiere of *La forza del destino*, in 1861 or 1862 (aged forty-eight or forty-nine)

'Viva Verdi' is scrawled on walls in Rome in 1859. The letters of the composer's name formed an acronym for 'Vittorio Emanuele, Re D'Italia'

great deal of new music, including one entire scene as well as the ballet which was obligatory for Paris. He described his working conditions in a letter to Giuseppina Appiani on 22 August:

> I owe you a number of letters, but you are sure to excuse me when I tell you all that I have had to do here. It's different from the Opera in London. Just think: you find yourself all day between two poets, two impresarios, two music publishers (they always go in twos here) trying to engage a prima donna, devise an idea for the libretto etc., and I tell you it's enough to drive you out of your senses. However, I don't wish to be driven out of my senses, and I face up to the whole of the theatrical world, all the Parisians, all the newspapers – those for me and those against me – and the comic pieces in *Charivari* and *Entre-Acte*. Apropos *Entre-Acte*, they published a quite funny article about me. I think Emanuele has taken it to Milan, so ask him for it.
>
> I shall be here until about the 20th November, but by the end of that month I shall be admiring the cupola of the Duomo.
>
> Though my health is better here than in London, I don't like Paris as much as London, and I have an extreme antipathy to the boulevards (quiet, don't let anyone overhear such blasphemy).
>
> You ask me about Donizetti, and I shall tell you frankly, although it is not a pleasant story. I have not seen him yet, as it was thought ill-advised, but I assure you I very much want to, and if the opportunity presents itself for me to see him without anyone knowing of it, I certainly shall. His physical appearance is good, except that his head is constantly bowed over his chest and his eyes kept shut. He eats and sleeps well, but says hardly a word, and when he does it's very indistinct. If someone goes up to him, he opens his eyes for a moment. If they say, 'Give me your hand,' he extends it, and so on. Apparently this is a sign that his mind has not completely gone, although a dear friend of mine who is a doctor tells me that he does these things simply out of habit, and that it would be more encouraging if he were animated or even violently mad. There may perhaps be hope, but in his present condition it would take a miracle to improve him. Still, he is no worse now than he was six months ago, or a year ago. No better, either. So that's the truth about Donizetti's condition. It's distressing, simply too distressing. If his condition improves, I shall let you know immediately.[30]

The two poets to whom Verdi refers are the librettists Royer and Vaëz, the two impresarios are Charles Duponchel and Nestor Roqueplan of the Paris Opéra; the two music publishers are his French publishers, the Escudier brothers. Giuseppina Appiani had been a close friend of Donizetti and was understandably anxious to have news of the composer, who was at this time living in a sanatorium at

Ivry, outside Paris, suffering from general paralysis of the insane, the final stage of his syphilis. A month after Verdi wrote his letter to Giuseppina Appiani, Donizetti was taken back to Italy, to his home town of Bergamo where, the following April, he died at the age of fifty.

Rehearsals for *Jérusalem* began on 22 September, two months before the first night, a much longer rehearsal period than was normal in Italy, and the opera was given its premiere on 26 November. The principal singers were Julian Van Gelder (soprano) as Hélène, Gilbert Louis Duprez (tenor) as Gaston, and Adolphe Alizard (bass) as Roger. *Jérusalem* was reasonably successful, though press notices were mixed, some of them striking a characteristically French note of chauvinism. The critic of the *Coureur des Spectacles* thought that, despite its poor (Italian) score, the opera was almost saved by the fact that Verdi had 'conceived the happy idea of composing some pieces on our inspiring soil. From that moment,' the critic observed, 'the prospects began to appear brighter; and from a downright bad Italian programme, swamped in notes no better than it deserved, there emerged a French piece adequate for the occasion.'[31]

Perhaps what most pleased this very French critic was the substitution of Roger, Count of Toulouse for *I lombardi*'s Pagano, Hélène for the earlier opera's Giselda, and Gaston, Viscount of Béarn for Oronte, son of the tyrant of Antioch. That it is more complex than the plot of *I lombardi* is due to the fact that the French librettists were concerned to accommodate as much of Verdi's existing music as possible, while making what they felt were certain essential alterations to Solera's libretto. The new pieces composed by Verdi for *Jérusalem* make their mark in the opera, sufficiently to justify one's considering it as a separate entity from *I lombardi*.

Verdi agreed to allow his Italian publisher Ricordi to have *Jérusalem* translated into Italian: *Gerusalemme* was performed at La Scala on 26 December and was sufficiently different from *I lombardi* for both operas to circulate around various Italian theatres for some years. On the same night as *Gerusalemme*'s Italian premiere, Verdi's London opera *I masnadieri* was also staged for the first time in Italy, simultaneously in Bergamo, Trieste and Verona. The composer was not present at any of these performances, having stayed on in Paris where his relationship with Giuseppina Strepponi had developed significantly. At some point during the year, perhaps now in Paris, he composed a song, '*Il poveretto*', to a poem by Manfredo Maggioni.

He had still to fulfil his commitment to write *Il corsaro* for that 'most odious and indelicate gentleman Lucca',[32] and this he proceeded to do in Paris during the winter of 1847–48.

He had been in possession of Piave's libretto for *Il corsaro* for some time, and since he had first begun to consider Byron's play *The Corsair* as a subject four years earlier he had no doubt accumulated a number of musical ideas for it. On 12 February 1848, he was able to send the completed score to Emanuele Muzio in Milan, requesting him to deliver it to Lucca. In return for the fee agreed upon, Verdi assigned all rights in the opera, for performance and publication, to Lucca. It was as though he simply wished to be rid of the work. When, in October 1848, the opera was staged in Trieste, Verdi remained in Paris. He had hoped that Muzio would conduct the opera in Trieste, but as a result of the political situation in northern Italy Muzio had fled to Switzerland. He and Verdi were not to meet again for many years.

There is no doubt that Verdi wrote *Il corsaro* hastily, indulging in none of his usual tantrums with his librettist, indeed without any contact with Piave during the entire period of composition. It would be difficult to refute the charge that he appeared to be completely uninterested in the opera, and was composing it merely to rid himself of an irksome obligation. But there had been a time when Verdi certainly did want to compose it. He chose Byron's poem himself when he first agreed to write an opera for London, and *The Corsair* seems a not unlikely choice for the composer to have made when one recalls how popular the poem was with the patriotic Italians. A romantic Greek pirate fighting the wicked Turks could easily be seen as a gallant Italian opposing the Austrians. Corrado, the corsair, might have been their own Garibaldi.

The opera follows the exploits of the pirate or corsair Corrado, who leaves his mistress, Medora, on his Aegean island while he leads his followers against the Pasha Seid in the Turkish city of Coron. Taken prisoner by Seid, Corrado is helped to escape by the Pasha's favourite slave, Gulnara, who accompanies him back to his island where they arrive to find Medora dying. In despair, Corrado throws himself into the sea.

Verdi had actually begun work on *Il corsaro* as early as the summer of 1846. On 27 August of that year, in the course of a letter resisting Piave's request for the return of the libretto, Verdi had written:

> You ask me to return *Il corsaro*? *Il corsaro* which I have so cherished, which causes me such concern, and which you yourself turned into verse with

greater care than usual? . . . It is true that *Il corsaro* had been agreed for London, but although the London venture has come to nothing I still have to write the opera for Lucca. And, almost without noticing it, I was gradually composing this *Corsaro*, for which I've sketched some of the pieces I like best – the prison duet and the final trio.[33]

That he by no means disowned the opera which he appears to have thrust out into the world in an uncharacteristically off-hand manner is revealed by a letter Verdi wrote to the soprano Marianna Barbieri-Nini, who was to sing the role of Gulnara in *Il corsaro*. About three weeks before the Trieste premiere, he replied from Paris to her request for advice:

You ask for some advice about your pieces. Well, the cavatina is easy to perform: it must be sung simply, and this you can do. Sing the adagio softly, and broadly. And do not take the cabaletta too quickly either, but quicken the tempo only at the final flourish. I think this cavatina will be most effective. See to it that the finale [of Act II] is well staged. The first agitato, if not well staged, could cause laughter. The adagio should be broadly declaimed, and the stretta not too quick.

The first section of the duet with the bass [i.e. baritone] should be declaimed, sostenuto. Think more about the words than the notes. Sing the cabaletta briskly, but not too fast.

The bass has the first phrase – let him declaim it at the top of his voice, but you should sing softly throughout. (Remember your mezza voce in *Macbeth*.) You know better than I that anger is not always best expressed by shouting, but sometimes with a stifled voice – which is how it should be here. So, sing the entire final section sotto voce, with the exception of the last four notes. Wait until the bass has almost left the stage, and then burst into a cry which should be accompanied by a terrifying gesture, as though foretelling the crime you are about to commit.

As for the duet with the tenor, I can recommend both the drama and the music: this is certainly the least bad number of the entire opera. When you enter, do so slowly, and deliver the recitative sotto voce and slowly. The first section should be moderato, and you should try to express the words with all your being. The beginning of the adagio should be sung equally slowly and sotto voce. Then, from the words '*Ah, fuggiamo*', let your voice expand and sing the rest passionately. When you make your exit, do so hastily, and when you return pale and shocked, take each step virtually as the music indicates, until the moment when you can no longer stand on your feet. . . . The drama of this entire duet is, as you can see, stupendous.

In the final trio, do not forget that you have killed a man. Let your remorse be evident in all the words you sing, even when you are consoling

Medora. . . . If everyone sings with extreme passion, I am certain it will be a success. A final warning: the opera should be divided into two acts only: the first act should close at the end of the finale, the second with the trio [i.e. with a single interval, after the second of the three acts]. The whole opera will thus gain in brevity and interest.[34]

For some reason, Verdi had seemed not to care whether *Il corsaro* was successful at its premiere. His usual practice of completing a final version only during the rehearsal period, and with the singers who were to perform it, was this time abandoned. What he sent off to Lucca was what would normally have been, for him, a first draft, and it was this first draft which was performed in Trieste. Not surprisingly, it was a failure. Two of the numbers were well applauded, but at the end of the evening only the scene designer took a curtain-call. After its third performance, *Il corsaro* was removed from the repertoire in Trieste. It was produced, to no great effect, in Milan, Venice, Malta and Naples in the next few seasons, but after 1854 it disappeared completely for more than a century, re-emerging in Venice in 1963. It is now occasionally performed, for there is no longer any opera by Verdi which is not. Musically and dramatically it leaves much to be desired; but number by number much of the music is enjoyable to hear, though the whole mysteriously adds up to less than the sum of its parts.

Chapter Seven

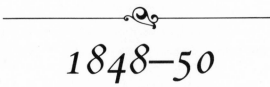

1848–50

It may seem odd that the composer whom we now associate so firmly with Italian aspiration to independence from Austria should during the year 1848, in which war broke out between his homeland and its overlords, have remained abroad in Paris except for a visit in the spring. But it was Giuseppina Strepponi who kept Verdi in Paris, though they did not begin living together openly until the summer, when they took a house in Passy, in those days a quiet residential area a mile or two from the centre of Paris. This was the year in which revolutions broke out spontaneously in a number of European countries, and the Parisians rebelled against their 'citizen king' in February. At the first signs of violence, Louis Philippe prudently abdicated and retired to England, paving the way for the Second Republic. 'Since February 24', Verdi wrote to Giuseppina Appiani two weeks later,

> nothing has happened. The procession that accompanied the funeral of those killed to the memorial column of the Bastille was imposing, indeed magnificent, and although there were neither troops nor police guards to maintain order, the whole thing passed without the slightest trouble. The big National Assembly to choose the government will meet on April 20. I still can't understand why it was not called earlier: I am too hard-hearted or perhaps too malicious. One hears no talk at all about Thiers [Adolphe Thiers, who was to be leader of the new government] but, who knows, perhaps his snout will suddenly pop up. . . . If nothing important calls me to Italy, I shall stay here for the whole of April to see the National Assembly. I have seen everything that has happened so far, both serious and comical (please believe that by 'seen' I mean with my own eyes), and so I want to see April 20.[1]

On 18 March Austrian troops were unwise enough to fire upon a crowd in Milan, precipitating a revolution in that city. For five days there was fighting in the streets. Barricades were put up, the entire city rallied and, after skirmishes in all parts of the town, the Austrians were driven out, their forces under General Radetzky retreating to fortresses at Mantua, Peschiera, Legnago and Verona. When this news reached Verdi in Paris, he immediately returned to Milan, arriving early in April after peace had been restored. 'I left the moment I heard the news,' he replied on 21 April to Piave who had written to him from Venice,

> but I could see nothing but these gigantic barricades. Honour to these brave men! Honour to all Italy, which at this moment is really great! Be assured, her hour of liberation has come. It is the people who demand it, and there is no absolute power that can resist the will of the people. They can agitate and intrigue as much as they like, those who want to achieve power at all costs, but they won't succeed in robbing the people of their rights. Yes, a few more months, and Italy will be a free, united republic. What else could it be?
>
> You speak to me of music? What's come over you? . . . Do you imagine I want to bother myself now with notes, with sounds? . . . There is and there must be only one kind of music welcome to the ears of Italians in 1848: the music of the cannon! . . . I would not write a note of music for all the gold in the world. I would feel immense guilt in using the music paper which is good for making cartridges. Bravo, Piave! Bravi, all the Venetians! Banish all parochial thoughts, let us extend a fraternal hand, and Italy will become the finest nation in the world.[2]

Despite that patriotic outburst, Verdi had not left Paris and Giuseppina Strepponi merely to express his solidarity with the citizens of Milan. In fact, his prime reason for visiting Italy seems to have been to buy a property, the Villa Sant' Agata, near Busseto, where in due course he was to set up house with Giuseppina. When he had completed his business in May, he returned to Paris.

The fact that the Austrians, rather than destroy the entire city, had allowed themselves to be driven out of Milan did not, of course, lead to the immediate withdrawal of Austria from northern Italy. The Milanese appealed to their neighbour state of Piedmont to come to their aid, and the Piedmontese reluctantly declared war on Austria. The various Italian states, however, far from being united, began to quarrel among themselves over allegiances and pledges. The war continued, and in the following year the revolutionary movement collapsed. Austria was to remain in control of northern Italy for a further ten years.

Meanwhile, back in France where he spent the summer months with Giuseppina at Passy, Verdi and nine other eminent Italians residing in Paris wrote in June, at the request of the Milanese Foreign Minister, a letter to General Louis Cavaignac, who, following some of the bloodiest street-fighting Europe had seen, had become temporary dictator of France. The letter called upon France to come to the aid of Italy in its struggle with Austria for independence. 'Do not', it ends, 'permit the cry to arise from the delirium of suffering, and with a semblance of reason, "Unhappy are those peoples who place faith in the promises of France!"'[3]

A few days after the premiere of *Macbeth* the previous year, Verdi had received a letter from the poet Giuseppe Giusti, one of the supporters of the liberal and nationalist political movement, castigating him for having turned away from subjects relevant to contemporary life and politics in order to bury himself in Shakespeare. Giusti exhorted Verdi to find a subject that would inflame the hearts and minds of his fellow-countrymen and unite them in the cause of freedom:

> You know that it is the chord of sorrow which finds the readiest echo in our breasts. Sorrow, however, assumes different aspects depending on the time and nature and condition of this or that nation. The kind of sorrow that now fills the minds of us Italians is the sorrow of a race that feels the need of a better destiny, the sorrow of one who has fallen and wishes to rise, the sorrow of one who repents and waits, longing for regeneration. Accompany, my Verdi, this high and solemn sorrow with your noble harmonies. Do what you can to nourish it, to strengthen it and direct it to its goal.[4]

Verdi had replied sympathetically:

> Yes, you put it very well. 'It is the chord of sorrow which finds the readiest echo in our breasts.' You speak about art like the great man you are, and I shall certainly take your advice, for I understand what you are saying. Oh, if only we had a poet who knew how to produce a drama of the kind you mean! But unfortunately, you yourself will admit it, if we want anything at all effective we are forced, shamefully, to accept foreign things. How many subjects are there in our own history![5]

There spoke Verdi the patriot. Verdi the composer, on another occasion, spoke differently:

The artist must give himself completely to his own inspiration and, if he has real talent, he will feel and know better than anyone else what he needs. I should set to music with perfect confidence any subject that moved me, even if it had been condemned by every other composer as unsuitable for music.[6]

No doubt Verdi would like to have found more Italian subjects, but the fact remains that, of his twenty-six operas, twenty-one have their provenance in non-Italian literary or dramatic works. After *Il corsaro*, he began to look for a patriotic Italian subject. As he had written to Giusti, it was difficult to find young poets capable of writing libretti. In his view there were no new talents on the scene. The youngsters, he complained, thought they had attained perfection if they could claim to write like the successful librettists of the day, like Romani or Cammarano. What Verdi sought was a poet who would not write like his predecessors, but who would produce an operatic text with scope, power, variety, novelty and freedom from convention. With the possible exception of Boito many years later, he was never really to find such a paragon of all the dramatic virtues.

During the troubles of 1848, Verdi placed his talent specifically at the disposal of the patriotic cause. At the request of the revolutionary leader Giuseppe Mazzini, whom he had first met in London the previous year, he composed a song of battle on a poem, '*Suona la tromba*', by the young romantic poet of the *Risorgimento*, Goffredo Mameli, who was to die in the fighting in Rome the following year at the age of twenty-two. When he sent the music to Mazzini in October 1848, Verdi expressed the hope that it would 'soon be sung on the plains of Lombardy, amid the music of the cannon'.[7] By this time, however, the fighting on the battlefields of Lombardy was over.

When he wrote his patriotic song, Verdi was in the middle of composing his patriotic opera, *La battaglia di Legnano*. His contractual obligations were still somewhat complicated. He was negotiating with two publishers, Ricordi and Lucca, and more than two theatre managements. He had agreed to write, for Naples, an opera on a libretto to be provided by Cammarano, though by the time he came to compose the opera he had lost patience with the Naples impresario, Flauto; in due course the opera was performed instead in Rome. The patriotic subject which, urged by Giusti and others, Verdi had been seeking was actually suggested by Cammarano. In July Verdi had attempted to prise a libretto out of his ex-collaborator Piave. 'The subject', he wrote, 'would have to be Italian and free, and if you can't find anything better I would suggest *Ferrucio*, a terrific character, one of the greatest martyrs of Italian freedom. Guerrazzi's *Assedio di Firenze* could provide you with some great scenes, but I would prefer you to stick to history.'[8] However, nothing came of this, and it was Cammarano's suggestion of *La battaglia di Legnano* that Verdi accepted.

The battle of Legnano in 1176, in which the forces of the German Frederick the First had been defeated by the Lombard League, was a subject, Cammarano argued, which would stir every man with an Italian soul in his breast. He cunningly and characteristically proposed stealing his plot from a French play written in 1828, *La Bataille de Toulouse* by Joseph Méry (who many years later was to be co-librettist of Verdi's *Don Carlos*). Méry's play sets a personal story of a woman and two men against the background of Napoleon's Peninsular War in Spain. Cammarano changed the locale from nineteenth-century Spain to twelfth-century Italy and increased the patriotic fervour, providing Verdi with a taut and effective melodrama, and one that was even more effective after the composer had made a number of suggestions. He was confident enough now to treat Cammarano almost as though he were Piave. 'At the beginning, outside the church of Saint Ambrose,' he wrote,

> I should like to combine two or three different melodies. For example, I should like both the priests inside and the people outside to have words in the same poetic metre, and Lida to have a song in a different metre. Leave the task of combining them to me. You might even, if you think it a good idea, give the priests some Latin verses. Do whatever you think best, but be sure that the situation is dramatically effective.[9]

Cammarano carried out Verdi's instructions, even when these were expressed in very general terms:

> Since the woman's role seems to me not to have the importance of the other two, I should like you to add, after the funeral chorus, a great agitated recitative in which she expresses her love, her despair at Arrigo's imminent death, her fear of being discovered and so on. After a beautiful recitative, let the husband arrive and give them a moving little duet. Have the father bless his son, or something of the kind. And so on.[10]

The opera, with its exalted patriotic sentiments and its violent action, was composed in an atmosphere in which international intrigue was in the forefront of people's thoughts. From Paris on 24 August, Verdi wrote to Clarina Maffei:

You want to know French public opinion about the events in Italy? Good Lord, what can I say to that? Those who are not against us are indifferent: I must say further that the idea of a united Italy frightens these little nobodies who are in power. It is certain that France will not intervene with arms unless some unforeseen event occurs to force it in that direction. Anglo-French diplomatic intervention can be nothing but unfair, shameful for France and ruinous for us. Indeed, such intervention would tend to make Austria abandon Lombardy and content itself with Venetia. If Austria could be persuaded to give up Lombardy (at present this seems possible, though perhaps she would sack and burn everything before leaving), that would be a further dishonour for us, the devastation of Lombardy, and one more prince in Italy. No, no, no: I have hopes neither of France nor of England. If I have hopes of anything, it is, can you imagine? of Austria: of confusion within Austria. Something serious must be emerging there, and if we knew how to seize the moment and wage the war that should be waged, the war of insurrection, Italy could be free again. But God save us from having to rely on our kings or on foreign nations.

Italian diplomats are arriving here from all over the place: Tommaseo yesterday, Picciotti today. They will achieve nothing: it seems impossible that they should still hope for anything from France. To put it briefly, France does not want to see a united Italy.

So there's my opinion, but don't attach any importance to it, for, as you know, I don't understand politics. For the rest, even France is in the abyss, and I don't know how she will get out of it. The inquisition which followed the events of May and June is the most wretched and disgusting thing that exists. What a miserable, puny age, even in its crimes! I believe that another revolution is imminent: you can sense the odour of it everywhere. And another revolution will completely finish off this poor republic. Let us hope it will not happen, though there are good reasons for fearing that it will.[11]

By the middle of December, Verdi had completed *La battaglia di Legnano* except for the orchestration, and on 20 December he left for Rome to begin rehearsals. On 27 January 1849 the opera had its premiere at the Teatro Argentina, conducted by the composer, with Teresa de Giuli-Borsi (soprano), Gaetano Fraschini (tenor) and Filippo Colini (baritone) in the leading roles. The political situation in Rome was tense. The Pope, Pius IX, had refused to send any help to Lombardy in its struggle with Austria, and this had led to the murder of his chief administrator by local republicans. The Pope had been besieged for two days in his Quirinal Palace by an armed mob of some thousands, but had escaped to Gaeta, a seaside town south of the Papal State. The republicans called an election which, since the Pope forbade Catholics to exercise their vote, they won with an over-whelming majority. The newly elected Assembly was due to meet in February (and when it did, it declared Rome a republic), so the atmosphere in the packed Teatro Argentina on 27 January was tense with excitement.

The opera was short, simple to understand and full of stirring music. For the first time Verdi had deliberately set out to appeal to his audience's patriotic feelings. He succeeded triumphantly, his music rousing the entire house to a frenzy of enthusiasm. When the first words of the opera's opening chorus were sung, '*Viva Italia! Sacro un patto/ Tutti stringe i figli suoi*' (Long live Italy! A sacred pact binds all her sons), there were hysterical cries from the audience of '*Viva Verdi*' and '*Viva Italia*'. At the end of the third act, when the hero, Arrigo, leaps from a balcony to rejoin his regiment as it leaves, a soldier in a box in the fourth tier of the theatre was so overcome with emotion that he flung his sword, his coat and his epaulettes on to the stage, followed by all the chairs in his box. The opera's brief fourth act was encored, not only on the first night, but at every subsequent performance of the season.

Catching the mood of the movement, the story combines love and patriotism. In northern Italy in the year 1176, the fighters of the Lombard League defeat the Emperor Barbarossa and his invading army. Two of the Lombardian leaders, Arrigo and Rolando, quarrel over Lida who, formerly Arrigo's betrothed, has during his absence married Rolando. *La battaglia di Legnano* is an opera with a purpose. Parts of Verdi's earlier operas had frequently been taken up by the fighters for a united Italy, but this time the composer had given the movement its own opera. It was his contribution to Italy's future as a unified nation; it was also a valid work of art.

The success of *La battaglia di Legnano* was immediate, but it was not lasting. 'Verdi in this work has soared to the sublime,' wrote the critic of *La Pallade*,[12] but other opera houses were slow to take up a work which would doubtless have encountered censorship problems in a number of towns. Even with its plot and characters changed with Verdi's consent, the opera failed to make much headway as *L'assedio di Arlem* (The Siege of Harlem), though it won a rousing reception when, cheekily re-titled *La disfatta degli Austriaci* (The Defeat of the Austrians), it was staged in Parma shortly after the Italian victories of 1869.

Within a week or so of the Rome premiere, Verdi returned to Paris where he began to plan his next opera. He was composing it for Naples, for the sake of Cammarano alone, in order to ease the Neapolitan librettist's position with Vincenzo Flauto and the San Carlo Theatre. His own relationship with Naples at the time of *Alzira* had not been particularly agreeable, and were it not for Cammarano, with whom he enjoyed collaborating, it is unlikely that he would have succumbed to the pressure from Flauto to provide a second opera for that city. In correspondence with Cammarano the previous September while they were still at work on *La battaglia di Legnano*, Verdi had stipulated that their next opera, if they should find themselves compelled to write one in order to fulfil Cammarano's contractual obligations to Naples, should be 'a short text, full of interest, movement and, in particular, passion', [13] which, he claimed, would make it easier for him to set to music.

Cammarano suggested a number of subjects; Verdi had himself become intrigued with Guerrazzi's *Assedio di Firenze*, which he had proposed to Piave, and had actually begun to sketch a brief scenario for a libretto to be based on Guerrazzi. Composer and librettist appear to have agreed to proceed with this, but the dilatory Cammarano, who had promised to send Verdi his detailed synopsis, failed to do so. While he was still in Rome rehearsing *La battaglia di Legnano*, Verdi wrote at least twice to the librettist. A note of justifiable acerbity began to be apparent in his tone: 'If you would send me, before I leave, the synopsis of the opera I am to write for Naples, I shall be grateful. Do remember that I am going to compose this opera only to oblige you, so if you don't want me to proceed with it, I shan't.'[14]

In February and March 1849, Verdi and Cammarano, the composer in Paris and his librettist in Naples, took the matter of *L'assedio di Firenze* much further in correspondence. But in April Cammarano had to report that the censorship authority in Naples considered the subject inopportune, given the political situation at the time, and that he, Cammarano, thought they could do no better than revert to an earlier suggestion which Verdi had made: that they write an opera based on Schiller's play *Kabale und Liebe* (Intrigue and Love). Verdi agreed, Cammarano forwarded to him a detailed synopsis of the libretto, surprisingly within a few days, and the composer reacted in a letter of 17 May, incorporating some detailed suggestions for improvement:

I have just received your scenario, and I confess to you I should have preferred two prima donnas, and I should also have preferred more emphasis on the prince's mistress, exactly as in Schiller. There would have been a contrast between her and Eloisa, and Rodolfo's love for Eloisa would have been more beautiful. I do realize, however, that I cannot always have what I want, and I am very pleased with it as it is. It seems to me, however, that all that devilish intrigue between Walter and Wurm, which dominates the whole of the play, doesn't here have the same colour and force that it has in Schiller. Perhaps in verse it will be different, but in any case let me know yourself whether you think I am right or not. Finally it seems to me that, when Eloisa is compelled by Wurm to write the letter, instead of saying she was Wurm's mistress it could have been more meaningful, also more natural and credible, if she had said she was in love with someone else – anyone except Wurm.

Deal with these remarks of mine in any way you wish, but let me say that, in the first act finale, I am against having a stretta or cabaletta. The situation doesn't require one, and a stretta would probably lose all its effect in this position. The beginning of the piece and the ensembles you can deal with as you wish, but at the end you should stick as closely as possible to Schiller.

RODOLFO: Through death! Go back, I entreat you, I implore you etc.
WALTER: Wretched fellows? Do you hesitate?
ROD: Father, if he goes to prison, your son goes with him.
WALT: Do it!
ROD: I shall draw my sword on you –
WALT: Do it!
ROD: Ah, my father, I would pierce you through the heart rather than –
WALT: Do it!
ROD: God is my witness etc. etc. . . . . how you became Lord Walter.
    (*He rushes out desperately*)
WALT: Let that woman go, and follow me. Rodolfo! Rodolfo!
    (*He goes*)

Here a general exclamation from everyone, and the curtain falls.

You can make this finale as long as you like; since I don't have to repeat the piece (or rather cannot), the length does not matter.

In the second act, take great care with the duet between Wurm and Eloisa. Make a strong contrast between Eloisa's terror and desperation and Wurm's diabolical frigidity. It seems to me that if you can give to the character of Wurm a slightly comic touch, the situation will become even more terrifying. After the other duet between Walter and Wurm, are you having a quartet? I think you need one here, for unaccompanied voices.

I think you should do an aria for Rodolfo's scene. The first part of the piece is all right, but I have the impression that the end will be cold. To lower the curtain on two people alone, after having had a grand finale in the first act: think about this. I believe we'll have to find something here.

The third act is superb. Try to develop further the duet between father and daughter: make it a duet to bring tears to the eyes. The duet which follows is superb and tremendous, and I think it will be necessary to end with a trio with the father.

When Walter enters, he should have as few lines as possible. If, in order to develop these two pieces, you find it necessary to make them a little longer, do so. In the piece for the three basses, I think the principal part should be that of Eloisa's father, so make it a good part. Then Walter, and finally Wurm. Don't forget, in the part of this last character, to keep a certain comical something which will serve to give greater emphasis both to his manners and his villainy.

All I have to say to you now, in a loud voice, is to send me your verses as soon as possible. Farewell, farewell.[15]

Verdi's father–daughter duets, which occur throughout his *oeuvre* from *Oberto* (1839) to *Aida* (1871), were always to reveal the composer writing with great intensity of feeling. Father and son (as in *Les Vêpres siciliennes*) or mother and son (as in *Il trovatore*), were parent and child relationships he also characterized with deep feeling, but there is a special quality about Verdi's fathers and daughters in their moments of intimacy. His own first child, a girl, had died at the age of seventeen months. Did he grieve, throughout his life, because he had not been allowed to know and to love her?

The active role which Verdi took in the shaping, and often the actual writing, of his libretti suggests that he might easily, in different conditions, have become his own librettist, as his German contemporary Richard Wagner already was. With regard to this, there is an interesting comment in one of Cammarano's letters to Verdi during the composition of the Schiller opera, whose title was finally to become *Luisa Miller*:

> If I were not afraid of being described as Utopian, I would be inclined to say that to achieve the greatest possibility of perfection in opera, one single mind should be responsible for both words and music. From this thought, it clearly follows, I think, that where there are two authors, their collaboration must be close and amiable. Poetry must not be either the slave or the tyrant of music. Convinced of this maxim, I have always adhered to it in my own work, and have always, when necessary, consulted with the composers with whom I have collaborated.[16]

At the end of July Verdi and Giuseppina Strepponi left Paris to return to Italy together. Verdi settled in his town house, the Palazzo

Dordoni in Busseto, while Giuseppina went first to Florence to put her own affairs in order. Her principal task was to arrange for the artistic education of her eleven-year-old son, Camillo, in whom the sculptor Lorenzo Bartolini had taken an interest. (The father of Giuseppina's three children – Camillo, born in 1838, Giuseppa, born in 1839, and Adelina, born in 1841 – was most probably the tenor Napoleone Moriani.) From Florence, Giuseppina wrote to Verdi on 3 September:

> I shall have finished my business by Wednesday and shall perhaps leave for Parma on the same evening. Don't come to fetch me, however, because I should be sorry if you had to wait for me in vain in Parma. When I tell you who has charged himself with Camillino's artistic education, you will be astonished! It must suffice for now that I kissed the hands of the famous man, who said to me: 'Will you entrust him to me?' I have seen only a few people in Florence, but they have worked with zeal and, be it noted, they are mere acquaintances. No aristocrats, of course. In truth, sometimes one finds a heart where one expects only indifference, and *vice versa*.
>
> Farewell, my joy! Now that I have almost finished my business, business too important to be neglected, I should like to be able to fly to your side. You speak of the unattractive country, the bad service, and furthermore you tell me: 'If you don't like it, I'll have you accompanied (NB I'll *have you* accompanied!) wherever you like.' But what the devil! Does one forget to love at Busseto, and to write with a little bit of affection?
>
> I'm not there yet, so can still write what I feel, which is that the country, the service and everything else will suit me very well, as long as you are there, you ugly, unworthy monster!
>
> Farewell, farewell. I have scarcely time to tell you that I detest you and embrace you.
>
> PEPPINA
>
> PS. Don't send anybody else, but come yourself to fetch me from Parma, for I should be very embarrassed to be presented at your house by anyone other than yourself.[17]

Verdi's parents had moved into the farmhouse at Sant'Agata and were looking after the livestock. 'Almost all the cows calved happily: there is still one that will calve in the next few days, and then I will organize the stables,'[18] Carlo Verdi wrote to his son. It was not until two years later that Verdi and Giuseppina moved into the Villa Sant' Agata, Verdi having by then moved his parents to a house in Vidalenzo. He and Giuseppina spent the summer of 1849 at the Palazzo Dordoni in Busseto, where Verdi busied himself with the completion of *Luisa Miller*. By the beginning of October the opera was finished except for the scoring, and on 3 October, Verdi and his ex-father-in-law, Antonio Barezzi, left for Naples, while Giuseppina went to visit her mother in Pavia.

It took Verdi and Barezzi more than three weeks to reach Naples. The first part of the journey, by coach across the Apennines to Genoa, was straightforward enough, but their intention to continue by sea was thwarted for some reason; after lingering in Genoa for two or three days, they went on to Rome by coach, arriving on 13 October. They found the Holy City in the middle of a cholera epidemic and had to remain there in quarantine for two weeks, Verdi's attempt to have the quarantine regulations circumvented by the Naples impresario Flauto proving completely unsuccessful.

Eventually, Verdi and Barezzi arrived in Naples. Here, Verdi discovered that the first instalment of his fee for the new opera was not ready for him, though, according to the terms of his contract, it should have been. He had been warned by Cammarano that the theatre was in financial difficulties, so he immediately issued an ultimatum: if the management did not deposit with a third party approved by Verdi the entire sum eventually due to him, he would consider the contract dissolved. The San Carlo management reacted by threatening to have the composer arrested if he attempted to leave Naples without handing over his score. Verdi refused to be intimidated, and declared that he would take himself and his opera on board one of the French warships in the bay of Naples and demand that France protect him from the Kingdom of the Two Sicilies.

How peace between Verdi and the San Carlo was restored is not known, but the situation somehow resolved itself, and *Luisa Miller* went into rehearsal. Before it did, however, Verdi and Barezzi found the time to see a number of the sights of Naples. They visited the classical sites of Herculaneum and Pompeii, the island of Ischia, and several other places of interest. Perhaps because of the time it had taken them to get to Naples, Barezzi had to return home before the opera's first night, and therefore missed a ridiculous episode involving a local composer, Vincenzo Capecelatro. Capecelatro was said to have the 'evil eye' and kept trying to waylay Verdi, whose friends felt constrained to keep constant guard over him. (According to them, it was Capecelatro who had been responsible for the failure of Verdi's *Alzira* in Naples four years earlier.) On the first night of *Luisa Miller*, the *mal occhio* Capecelatro managed to get backstage, and it was his presence which, according to the superstitious Neapolitans, caused part of the scenery to collapse, narrowly missing Verdi.

Despite Capecelatro, the premiere was a huge success. But Verdi had had quite enough of the Neapolitans. Although he had originally agreed to write another opera for the San Carlo's next season, he decided to compose the work without worrying about where it was to be staged. He left the city five days after the *Luisa Miller* premiere, vowing that he would never compose another opera for Naples. (Nor did he, although he was to enter into what turned out to be abortive negotiations with the San Carlo on more than one occasion.) From Busseto at the end of December he wrote to a Neapolitan friend, Cesare de Sanctis:

> I hear from Naples that there are schemes afoot to make a failure of *Luisa Miller*, and that one of the artists at the Opera is, for political reasons, a party to the plot. I am not inclined to believe this, though it may be true. However, it is of no importance. What fools!!! Do they imagine that their sordid intrigues can prevent an opera, if it is good, from going the rounds of the musical world?[19]

The plot of *Luisa Miller* is a simplified and altered version of Schiller's *Kabale und Liebe*. Luisa, daughter of an old soldier, Miller, living on the estate of Count Walter, is loved by the Count's son, Rodolfo. The Count, however, intends that Rodolfo shall marry Federica, Duchess of Ostheim. Count Walter orders the arrest of Miller, and sends one of his followers, Wurm, to force Luisa to write a letter to Rodolfo confessing that she is in love with Wurm. Only if she does so will her father be released from prison. Luisa unwillingly complies. When Rodolfo receives the letter, he pretends to agree to marry Federica, but visits Luisa and poisons both her and himself. Luisa, as she dies, tells Rodolfo the truth, and Rodolfo kills Wurm before he himself dies.

Though it is inadequate as an adaptation of Schiller's excellent play, Cammarano's libretto is, in its own right, a fine piece of work. Verdi's opera, his first attempt to portray something of bourgeois 'respectability' on the stage, is a direct predecessor of *La traviata*, which deals with, among other things, bourgeois hypocrisy. The nature of the plot of *Luisa Miller* calls for a more intimate style of vocal writing than was appropriate for the larger-scale tragedies which had comprised the majority of Verdi's earlier operas, and the composer comes some distance towards providing it, at least in the latter part of the opera.

Back in Busseto, Verdi began to correspond with Cammarano about possible subjects for their next opera. Two of these were in due course to become *Rigoletto* (though with a libretto by Piave) and *Il trovatore*. Among Verdi's suggestions, however, was the subject which had for long continued to intrigue him: Shakespeare's *King Lear*. He and Cammarano must have discussed *Lear* during the weeks that Verdi was in Naples, for the composer now produced his own complete scenario which, on 28 February 1850, he sent to the librettist. The thought that Verdi came very close on at least two occasions – of which this was the first – to composing his *King Lear* is so tantalizing, his scenario is so detailed and impressively put together, and his concept of the opera so exciting that the full text of Verdi's letter and the scenario which accompanied it are well worth reproducing:

King Lear at first sight is so vast and intricate that it seems impossible one could make an opera out of it. However, on examining it closely, it seems to me that difficulties, though no doubt immense, are not insuperable. You realize that there is no need to make *King Lear* into the usual kind of drama we have had up until now: rather, we must treat it in a completely new manner, on a large scale, and without regard for mere convenience. I believe the roles could be reduced to five principal ones: Lear, Cordelia, the Fool, Edmund, Edgar. Two secondary female roles: Regan and Goneril (though perhaps the latter would have to be made a second leading lady). Two secondary bass roles (as in *Luisa*): Kent and Gloucester. The rest, minor roles.

Would you agree that the reason for disinheriting Cordelia is rather infantile for the present day? Certain scenes would definitely have to be cut, for instance the one in which Gloucester is blinded, the one in which the two sisters are carried onto the stage etc. etc., and many others which you know better than I do. The number of scenes can be reduced to 8 or 9: let me draw your attention to the fact that in *I lombardi* there are 11, which has never been any bar to performance. [There are also 11 in Verdi's *Lear* synopsis which follows.]

ACT I SCENE I

Great stateroom in Lear's palace. Lear on his throne. Division of the Kingdom. Demonstration by the Earl of Kent. Rage of the King who banishes the Earl. Cordelia's farewell.

SCENE II

Edmund's soliloquy. Gloucester enters (without seeing Edmund) and deplores the banishment of Kent. Edmund, encountering Gloucester, tries to hide a letter. Gloucester forces him to reveal it. He believes that Edgar is plotting. Edgar enters; and his father, blind with fury, draws a sword against him. Edgar flees, after trying to assuage his father's anger with soothing words.

SCENE III

Hall (or vicinity) of Goneril's castle. Kent is seen dressed as a beggar. Lear arrives and takes him into his service. Meanwhile, the Fool with his bizarre songs mocks Lear for having trusted his daughters. Goneril enters, complaining of the insolence of her father's knights, whom she refuses to allow to stay in the castle. The king erupts with anger when he realizes his daughter's ingratitude. He fears he will go mad, but, remembering Regan, he calms himself and hopes to be treated better by her. The arrival is announced of Regan, who has been invited by her sister. Lear approaches her and tells how Goneril has wronged him. Regan cannot believe this and says he must have offended her. The sisters unite to persuade Lear to disperse his followers. Then Lear, realizing his daughters' heartlessness, cries: 'You think I'll weep; no, I'll not weep.' He swears vengeance, exclaiming that he will do terrible things, 'what they are yet' he knows not, 'but they shall be the terrors of the earth.' (The noise of a tempest begins to be heard.) The curtain falls.

ACT II SCENE I

Country. The tempest continues. Edgar, a fugitive, banished and accused of an attempt on his father's life, laments the injustice of his fate. Hearing a noise, he takes refuge in a hut. – Lear, Fool and Kent. – 'Blow, winds, and crack your cheeks. . . . Rumble thy bellyful! Spit, fire! Spout, rain! Nor rain, wind, thunder, fire are my daughters. I tax you not, you elements, with unkindness; I never gave you kingdom, call'd you children!' The Fool (still joking): 'O, nuncle, court holy-water in a dry house is better than this rain-water out o' door.' He enters the hut and is frightened when he sees Edgar, who feigns madness and utters cries of woe. Lear exclaims: 'What, have his daughters brought him to this pass? Couldst thou save nothing? Didst thou give them all?' (magnificent quartet). Someone bearing a torch approaches. It is Gloucester who, in defiance of the decree of the daughters, has come in search of the king.

SCENE II

Hall in Goneril's castle. Huge chorus (in various verse metres): 'Do you not know? Gloucester transgressed the command! . . . Well then? A terrible punishment awaits him!! What? . . . to have his eyes put out!! Horror, horror!! Wretched age, in which such crimes are committed.' The events relating to Lear, Cordelia, Kent, Gloucester etc. are recounted, and finally all fear a horrifying war which France will wage against England to avenge Lear.

SCENE III

Edmund: 'To both these sisters have I sworn my love; each jealous of the other, as the stung are of the adder. Which of them shall I take? Both? one? or neither?' etc. etc. Goneril enters and, after brief dialogue, offers him command of the army, and gives him a token of her love.

SCENE IV

A poor room in a cottage.

Lear, Kent, Edgar, the Fool, and peasants. The Fool asks Lear, 'Whether a madman be a gentleman or a yeoman.' Lear replies: 'A King, a King!!' – Song – Lear, in a state of delirium, continually obsessed with the idea of the ingratitude of his daughters, wishes to set up a court of justice. He calls Edgar 'most learned justicer', the Fool 'sapient sir' etc. etc. Extremely bizarre and moving scene. Finally, Lear tires and finally falls asleep. All weep for the unhappy king. End of second act.

ACT III SCENE I

The French camp near Dover.

Cordelia has heard from Kent of her father's misfortune. Great sorrow on Cordelia's part. She sends messenger after messenger to see if he has been found. She is willing to give all her possessions to whoever can restore his reason; she invokes the pity of nature etc. etc. The doctor announces that the king has been found, and that he hopes to cure him of his madness. Cordelia, intoxicated with joy, thanks heaven and longs for the moment of vengeance.

SCENE II

Tent in the French camp.

Lear asleep on a bed. The doctor and Cordelia enter very quietly. '[He] sleeps still. . . .' After a brief dialogue, very sweet sounds of music are heard behind the scenes. Lear awakes. Magnificent duet, as in the Shakespeare scene. The curtain falls.

ACT IV SCENE I

Open country near Dover. The sound of a trumpet from afar.

Edgar appears, leading Gloucester: moving little duet in which Gloucester recognizes that he has been unjust to his son. Finally, Edgar says: 'Here, father, take the shadow of this tree for your good host; pray that the right may thrive.' (Exit) Sound of trumpet nearer, noises, alarm; finally the signal to assemble is given. Edgar returns: 'Away, old man; give me thy hand; away! King Lear hath lost, he and his daughter ta'en.' (March) Edmund, Albany, Regan, Goneril, officers, soldiers etc. enter in triumph. Edmund gives an officer a letter: 'If thou dost as this instructs thee, thou dost make thy way to noble fortunes.' An armed warrior with lowered vizor (Edgar) enters unexpectedly and accuses Edmund of high treason: in proof, he offers a letter to Albany. A duel takes place. Edmund is mortally wounded: before he dies he confesses all his crimes, and tells them to hurry to save Lear and Cordelia. . . . 'For my writ is on the life of Lear and on Cordelia – nay, send in time.'

FINAL SCENE

Prison. Moving scene between Lear and Cordelia. Cordelia begins to feel the effects of the poison: her agony and death. Albany, Kent and Edgar rush in to save her, but too late. Lear, unconscious of their arrival, takes Cordelia's corpse in his arms, and exclaims: 'She's dead as earth. Howl! Howl!' etc. Ensemble in which Lear must have the leading part. End.[20]

Verdi's synopsis makes it clear that his understanding of Shakespeare's play was deep, and no mere superficial response to its operatic possibilities. Curiously, two other Shakespeare projects were simultaneously being considered by him. Replying to a suggestion from his French publisher Marie Escudier that he compose for London an opera based on *The Tempest*, Verdi replied that two or three months was not sufficient time for him to deal with so vast a subject, but added: 'I do plan to compose *The Tempest*, and indeed I plan to do the same with all the major plays of the great tragedian.'[21] In June, the composer replied to his friend Giulio Carcano, dramatist and translator of Shakespeare, who had written to suggest that they collaborate on an opera to be based on *Hamlet*:

Unfortunately these huge subjects require too much time. I have had to put *King Lear* aside at the moment, and commission Cammarano to work on the play whenever convenient. But, if *King Lear* is difficult, *Hamlet* is far more so. I am caught between two contracts, and if I am to fulfil these obligations I must choose easier and shorter subjects. But I do not abandon the hope of one day being able to discuss with you the possibility of our working together on this masterpiece of English theatre. I should be proud to clothe your verses with my music, and thus enrich the musical theatre with a fine, poetic work.[22]

Did Verdi, perhaps, sense in 1850 that he was not yet ready for *Hamlet*, *The Tempest* and *King Lear*? He had written a superb Shakespeare opera in *Macbeth* three years earlier, but that was an easier play to interpret in musical terms. (He was to make significant improvements to his *Macbeth* when he revised it for a Paris production in 1865.) With *Luisa Miller* he had broken new ground, proving to himself that he could write as confidently about domestic subjects as about the fabled heroes of mediaeval romance. He was soon to compose the three great operas of his middle period, *Rigoletto*, *Il trovatore* and *La traviata*, and in fact had already begun to discuss the first two of these subjects with Cammarano. *King Lear* was a long-standing obsession with Verdi, but it is difficult not to suspect that he was now beginning to look for excuses not to grapple with Shakespeare's immense tragedy.

Chapter Eight

1850–51

The two commitments which Verdi had to honour in 1850 were to write operas for his publisher Ricordi and for the Teatro La Fenice in Venice. The opera for Ricordi was required by the autumn, and it was to be the publisher's responsibility to place it with a theatre. This presented no problems, as any Italian opera house would have been delighted to procure a new work by the leading composer of the day. The composer himself seems not to have cared which theatre Ricordi offered the opera to, as long as it was not La Scala!

It was in March that Verdi accepted a commission to provide an opera to be staged the following year at the Teatro La Fenice. When he signed his copy of the contract on 28 April, however, the subject of the opera had not been chosen. The Venetian Piave was to be the librettist, and he suggested some subjects, among them a French play, *Stiffelius*, and Dumas's *Le Comte Herman*. Verdi knew *Le Comte Herman* and considered it unsuitable for opera. *Stiffelius* was unknown to him, so he asked Piave to send an outline of the play. He personally thought it unlikely that they would discover anything better for their purposes than *Gusmano il Buono*, an adaptation of a Spanish play. 'However,' he continued,

> I have another subject which, if the police would allow it, would be one of the greatest works of art in the modern theatre. Who knows! They allowed *Ernani*, so they might allow this one too, and there would be no conspiracy scenes in this one.
>
> Try it! The subject is great, immense, and it contains a character who is one of the greatest creations to be found in the theatre of all countries and all times. The subject is *Le Roi s'amuse*, and the character I speak of is Tribolet which, if Varesi is under contract, couldn't be better for him or for us.

PS. As soon as you receive this letter, get moving. Run all over the town and find some influential person who can obtain permission to do *Le Roi s'amuse*. Don't doze. Stir yourself. Hurry. I expect you in Busseto, but not now, not until the subject is chosen.[1]

Piave immediately sent Verdi a synopsis of *Stiffelius*, a play he had seen, which was an Italian translation of *Le Pasteur*, a drama by two French playwrights, Emile Souvestre and Eugène Bourgeois. This modern play about a Protestant minister whose wife commits adultery intrigued Verdi, who wrote to Piave on 8 May:

> *Stiffelius* is good and interesting. It wouldn't be difficult to involve the chorus in it. . . . Transpose the action to wherever you like, though he should remain a Lutheran and the leader of a sect. By the way, is this Stiffelius a historical figure? I don't recall his name in any history that I have read.

But, although he was interested in *Stiffelius*, it was Victor Hugo's *Le Roi s'amuse* that had really captured Verdi's imagination. His letter to Piave continues:

> Oh, *Le Roi s'amuse* is the greatest subject and perhaps the greatest drama of modern times. Tribolet is a character worthy of Shakespeare!! *Ernani* can't be compared with it, this is a subject that cannot fail. You know that, six years ago when Mocenigo suggested *Ernani* to me, I exclaimed: 'Yes, by God . . . that one can't go wrong.' Now, as I was reflecting on various subjects, *Le Roi* came back to my mind like a thunderbolt, an inspiration, and I said the same thing: 'Yes, by God . . . that one can't go wrong.' So then, get the President of the theatre interested, turn Venice upside down, and force the Censorship to allow this subject. What does it matter if la Sanchioli isn't the right singer? If we were to pay attention to this, no more operas would be written. For that matter, no offence to anyone, but who is there who is reliable among the singers of today? What happened on the first night of *Ernani* with the leading tenor out of tune? What happened on the first night of the *Foscari*, with one of the most highly regarded companies of the day? Singers who can make successes by their very presence – singers like Malibran, Rubini, Lablache etc. etc. – they no longer exist.[2]

Excited at the prospect of composing his Victor Hugo opera for Venice, Verdi decided upon *Stiffelius* as the work he would write for Ricordi. This was to be staged in the autumn at the Teatro Grande in Trieste, so it became now the more pressing obligation. Piave produced his libretto very quickly, and Verdi spent the summer months writing the opera whose title became *Stiffelio*. By the end of September, when he had to travel to Bologna to supervise a production of *Macbeth*, *Stiffelio* was virtually complete except for the orchestration. Verdi expected to get this done between *Macbeth* rehearsals, but on his return to Busseto he told Ricordi, 'It is strange that in fifteen days I was only able to orchestrate one piece, but the rehearsals in Bologna were horribly fatiguing.'[3] Towards the end of October, he made his way to Trieste, picking up Piave *en route* in Venice. Ricordi had conveyed to Verdi the offer of hospitality in Trieste, but Verdi had replied to the effect that, though he was grateful for the kindness which people wished to show him, he preferred his independence and would stay in a hotel.

With an opera about the marital difficulties of a Protestant clergyman – Stiffelio, the clergyman, discovers that his wife Lina has been unfaithful, in due course forgives her, but not before his father-in-law has killed her seducer in a duel – neither Verdi nor Piave expected censorship problems. However, they reckoned without the church. The Reverend Lugani in Trieste felt obliged to protest strongly, although the libretto had already been passed by the Imperial and Royal Directorate of Police. Lugani's attitude was satirized in the Trieste newspaper *La Favilla*:

> . . . Signor Lugani, either after reading Piave's libretto or attending the first rehearsals of the opera, felt twinges in his most catholic bowels; he felt his senses reel, and Lutheran, heretical, republican and red crowded around him as the evil spirits did around St Anthony, filling his devout soul with pious horror. Afterwards he was seen running in great agitation through the San Nicolò quarter to the house of His Highness the Director, where he must have spoken in a manner that would have put the most experienced missionary to shame, for His Highness the Director himself finally had to agree that the Imperial and Royal Directorate of Police had made a huge mistake, and that *Stiffelio* could not be produced in its present form without danger to public morals and to Roman Catholic Apostolic doctrine.[4]

What most offended the Reverend Lugani was the idea of a priest being a married man and subject to the desires of the flesh. Stiffelio, therefore, could not be described as a preacher (*ministro*). He became merely sectarian (*settario*). Lines which referred to his evangelical status were altered, and the final scene, which takes place in a church with the congregation assembled to hear Stiffelio, their pastor, preach a sermon, was severely bowdlerized. The church was made to look as though it was not a church, with the cross, the pulpit and the pews removed, and the congregation was forbidden to kneel in prayer. Stiffelio's quotation from the Sermon on the Mount as he publicly forgives his wife her adultery was, of course, also forbidden. Earlier in the opera, when Lina addresses Stiffelio not as her husband but as her minister with the words '*Ministro, ministro, confessatemi*' (Minister, minister, hear my confession), this had to be changed to '*Rodolfo, Rodolfo, ascoltatemi*' (Rodolfo, Rodolfo, listen to me).

All of this no doubt weakened the effect of the first performance of the opera on 16 November. Nevertheless, *Stiffelio* was warmly received by the public and by the press, though the critics tended to have a little fun at the expense of Piave whose libretto had been so savagely mauled. A review in *Il Diavoletto* on 19 November concluded:

> The composer was honoured by being repeatedly called onto the stage, and in the second act finale, which is a marvellous piece of work, sonnets and a crown of laurel were thrown. The sight of the laurel seems to have so delighted the librettist that, although no one had had him in mind, the audience nevertheless had the pleasure of seeing him appear at Verdi's side.[5]

The critic of the *Gazzetta Musicale* wrote: 'This is a work at once religious and philosophical, in which sweet and tender melodies follow one another in the most attractive manner,'[6] but *Il Diavoletto* thought the subject an unsuitable one: 'It is true that we tolerate monks, nuns, the organ, church bells, the exterior of a church, a chorus of people praying, but one should never overstep these bounds.'[7] Although the theatre was sold out for several performances, the offending church scene was omitted at three of them, and *Stiffelio*'s progress through the other opera houses of Italy was not an unimpeded one. When it was staged in Rome, Florence, Catania, Palermo and Naples, it was re-titled *Guglielmo Wellingrode*, with its principal character no longer a nineteenth-century preacher but the Prime Minister of a German principality at the beginning of the fifteenth century! The opera is distinguished by much imaginative writing for the orchestra as well as a number of fine arias. It is also one of the most unusual of Verdi's pre-*Rigoletto* works – clearly a little too unusual for the Italian audiences of its time.

When, some weeks after the Trieste premiere, Verdi heard that La Scala wished to produce *Stiffelio*, he wrote to Giovanni Ricordi:

If it absolutely must be given, the censors must convince themselves that the libretto contains nothing offensive to politics or religion. They should leave the libretto as it is, with all the text and its requisite staging intact. Nothing should be changed, nothing emasculated, and everyone should endeavour to do his best for it. It should be especially observed that the effect of the final scene depends on how the chorus is arranged on the stage. There must be not just the usual single stage rehearsal, but ten or, if necessary, twenty. Unless these conditions are met, I cannot permit *Stiffelio* to be given at La Scala. And remember that, if it should fail in its effect through poor performance, I shall hold you, Signor Giovanni Ricordi, responsible for any damage which may result. Farewell, farewell. PS. I cannot possibly come to Milan to stage *Stiffelio*.

. . . If the censor does not allow the original libretto, with the words '*Ministro, confessatemi . . . Ah Stiffelio io sono!*' the effect becomes impossible to achieve, and in that case it would be better to wait until I have the time to refashion the final scene, without setting it in a church. I shall then go and stage it myself in a theatre and with a cast that suits me. Farewell.[8]

Verdi was to take the opportunity to re-write *Stiffelio* six years later. Meanwhile, there was the more immediate and exciting prospect of the Victor Hugo opera for Venice, *Le Roi s'amuse*, to engage his attention. The opera was given the name of its principal character, the hunchback Tribolet, at first Italianized to *Triboletto*, and finally changed to *Rigoletto*.

Immediately after the Trieste performances of *Stiffelio*, Verdi made his way with Piave to Venice to obtain formal approval from the Venice censorship authority for the libretto of *La maledizione* (The Curse), which at this stage was *Rigoletto*'s working title. This approval, however, was not immediately forthcoming, and Verdi continued his journey home to Busseto, leaving Piave to deal with the situation in his own home town. Some days later, Verdi was informed that the libretto would not be passed for performance. He immediately wrote to C.D. Marzari, the President of the Teatro La Fenice:

The letter which arrived with the decree completely banning *La maledizione* was so unexpected that I almost went out of my mind. In this matter, Piave was at fault: completely at fault! He assured me in several letters, written as long ago as May, that approval had been obtained for it. This being so, I set to music a large part of the play, working with the greatest zeal in order to finish at the time agreed. The decree forbidding it drives me to desperation, because now it is too late to choose another libretto. It would be impossible, absolutely impossible, for me to set another subject to music this winter. This was the third time I was granted the honour of writing for Venice, and the management knows with what punctuality I have always carried out my duties. It knows that when I was almost dying I gave my word I would finish *Attila*, and I did so. Now I repeat on my oath that it is impossible for me to set a new libretto, even if I were to slave away to the point of endangering my health. Nevertheless, to demonstrate my good will, I offer the only thing that I can do. *Stiffelio* is an opera new to Venice. I suggest presenting it, and I would myself come to produce it at whatever time the management thinks opportune, during the carnival season of 1850–51. There is, in this opera, one very great difficulty (also due to the censor), and that is the final scene. It cannot be staged as it is; but if it is not possible to obtain permission from Vienna to do it as I intended, I would be willing to change the ending which would thus be completely new for Venice. I request the management to accept this proof of my goodwill, and to believe that the damage and the displeasure I am caused by this prohibition are greater than I have words to describe.[9]

Piave, meanwhile, had rewritten his libretto and submitted it to the censor again on 9 December under a new title, *Il duca di Vendôme*. On 20 December the Venetian censor approved the new version, but by this time Verdi had seen it as well and he did not approve. He wrote again to Marzari on 14 December:

In order to reply immediately to yours of the 11th, let me say I have had very little time to examine the new libretto. I have seen enough, however, to know that in its present form it lacks character, significance and, in short, the dramatic moments leave one completely cold. If it was necessary to change the characters' names, then the locality should have been changed as well. You could have a duke or prince of some other place, for example a Pier Luigi Farnese, or put the action back to a time before Louis XI when France was not a united kingdom, and have a Duke of Burgundy or Normandy etc. etc., but in any case an absolute ruler. In the fifth scene of Act I, all that anger of the courtiers against Triboletto doesn't make sense. The old man's curse, so terrifying and sublime in the original, here becomes ridiculous because his motive for uttering the curse doesn't have the same significance, and because it is no longer a subject who speaks in so forthright a manner to his king. Without this curse, what scope or significance does the drama have? The Duke has no character. The Duke must definitely be a libertine: without this there is no justification for Triboletto's fear that his daughter might leave her hiding-place, and the drama is made impossible. What would the Duke be doing, in the last act, alone in a remote inn, without an invitation, without a rendezvous? I don't understand why the sack has gone. Why should a sack matter to the police? Are they worried about the effect? But let me say this: why do they think they know better than I do about this? Who is playing the Maestro? Who can say this will make an effect and that won't? We had this kind of difficulty with the horn in *Ernani*. Well, did anyone laugh at the sound of that horn? With that sack removed, it is improbable that Triboletto would talk for half an hour to a corpse, before a flash of lightning reveals it to be his daughter. Finally, I see that they have avoided making Triboletto an ugly hunchback!! A hunchback who sings? Why not? Will it be effective? I don't know. But, I repeat, if I don't know, then they who propose this change don't know either. I thought it would be beautiful to portray this extremely deformed and ridiculous character who is inwardly passionate and full of love. I chose the subject precisely because of these qualities and these original traits, and if they are cut I shall no longer be able to set it to music. If anyone says to me I can leave my notes as they are for this new plot, I reply that I don't understand this kind of thinking, and I say frankly that my music, whether beautiful or ugly, is never written in a vacuum, and that I always try to give it character.

To sum up, an original, powerful drama has been turned into something ordinary and cold. I am extremely sorry that the Management did not reply to my last letter. I can only repeat and beg them to do what I asked them, because my artist's conscience will not allow me to set this libretto to music.[10]

On the same day, Verdi wrote sharply to Piave, who had attempted to placate him by running errands: 'I thank you for the powder and the biscuits, for which you can send me a bill. Don't bother to procure the fish, because I could not have it collected from Cremona.'[11] He informed Piave that he was writing to Marzari about the proposed new libretto, but that he did not intend to pay Piave the 200 Austrian lire he was owed, because the opera would not be composed and, in any case, *Le Roi s'amuse* had been commissioned from Piave on the understanding that the librettist would be able to obtain the censorship authority's permission.

Poor Piave hastened to Busseto, accompanied by the Fenice's secretary, Guglielmo Brenna, in order to persuade Verdi to compromise: they had both participated, together with the Fenice's President, in a meeting with the General Director of Public Order, and that august personage had apparently made a number of substantial concessions. Piave and Brenna arrived in Busseto on the morning of 30 December; they and Verdi must have spent most of the day in discussion, for the document which all three men signed was sent off to Marzari in Venice later the same day. It listed six points on which agreement had been reached:

1   The scene shall be changed from the French court to that of an independent Duke of Burgundy or Normandy, or to the court of a minor absolutist Italian state, preferably that of Pier Luigi Farnese, and in the period most suitable for scenic and dramatic effect.

2   The original characters of the drama *Le Roi s'amuse* by Victor Hugo shall be retained, but other names shall be found for them, dependent on the period chosen.

3   The scene in which Francesco appears determined to use the key in his possession to enter the room of the abducted Bianca shall be omitted. It shall be replaced by another which preserves the decencies but does not detract from the interest of the play.

4   The King or Duke shall come to the rendezvous in Magellona's tavern as the result of a pretended invitation brought to him by the Triboletto character.

5   In the scene in which the sack containing the corpse of Triboletto's daughter appears, Maestro Verdi reserves to himself the right to make such changes as he considers necessary.

6   The above-mentioned changes require more time than was originally supposed. Therefore Maestro Verdi declares that the new opera cannot be performed before 28 February or 1 March.[12]

The General Director of Public Order in Venice was now satisfied, and Verdi proceeded to compose the opera very quickly, completing his score by 5 February, although, as he had informed Marzari, much of it had been written some months earlier. Throughout January he bullied Piave, demanding verses in a decasyllabic metre here, 'six fine lines which express the joy of revenge' there, and calling for a hendecasyllable in a piece of tenor recitative. Piave's replies to Verdi's letters are full of excuses for not having done this, that or the other: 'I have not yet been able to change those verses you asked me for,' he wrote on 20 January, 'however much I hammer my brains. I have written some lines, but none that would satisfy you, so I don't think there's any point in my sending them to you.'[13]

Whether or not Piave sent those particular verses, Verdi was able to inform his librettist on 5 February that the opera was now complete. All that remained for him to do was to make fair copies of the second act and the final duet in Act III which he had composed at the end of January. As usual he planned to do the orchestration during the rehearsal period: he estimated that it would take him five or six days. On 19 February he arrived in Venice and began rehearsing *Rigoletto*, the first performance of which he conducted at the Fenice on 11 March. (He also found time to flirt with a certain 'Angel', a friend of

Piave's who, after Verdi's departure, addressed letters to him *poste restante* at Cremona.)

The title role of the hunchback was sung at the premiere by the baritone Felice Varesi (Verdi's Macbeth of four years earlier). Years later, Varesi's daughter recalled the first night of *Rigoletto*:

> How many times I have heard tell of the emotions of that Venetian premiere. My father, ashamed and timid in his ridiculous buffoon's costume, did not know how to pluck up courage to appear before the public, for he feared their derision; and at the very last moment it was Verdi himself who, giving him a shove to get him on stage, made him stumble over the planks behind the scenes and flung him out on to the stage, staggering all over the place. The audience thought this an inspiration for a buffoon's entry and were enraptured.[14]

Though the names of the characters were changed, the plot follows Victor Hugo's play closely. At the court of the licentious Duke of Mantua, the Duke's jester, Rigoletto, a hunchback, insults Monterone, a nobleman whose daughter had been seduced by the Duke. The Duke and Rigoletto are in turn cursed by Monterone. Disguised as a student, the Duke has also been paying court to Rigoletto's daughter, Gilda, whom her father keeps hidden in his house away from the court. The courtiers, most of whom have felt the lash of the jester's tongue, trick Rigoletto into helping them to abduct Gilda, and they carry her off to the Duke's palace.

By the time Rigoletto finds his daughter at the palace, she has been raped by the Duke. Rigoletto hires an assassin, Sparafucile, to kill him, but Sparafucile is persuaded by his sister, Maddalena, to spare the Duke, whom she finds attractive, and to kill instead the first stranger to enter their inn. Overhearing this, Gilda sacrifices her life for the Duke, whom she still loves. When Rigoletto arrives to claim the body of the Duke, he is horrified to discover that it is his own daughter who has been assassinated. He remembers Monterone's curse as he collapses across Gilda's lifeless body.

Rigoletto is undoubtedly one of Verdi's greatest works. It also marks the beginning of his second or middle period. It was the opera which impelled Rossini to remark that at last he could recognize Verdi's genius. The use of the orchestra is masterly, the delineation of the minor characters brilliant, and the melodic invention prodigious. Verdi also reveals a remarkable insight into character motivation and, in the role of the jester Rigoletto, has created an absolute gift to an intelligent baritone with acting ability.

Rigoletto was a great popular success, a success which increased at each performance in Venice; it has remained one of Verdi's most popular operas. Most of the critics, too, were enthusiastic, though some aspects of the opera puzzled them. On the morning after the premiere, the *Gazzetta Privilegiata di Venezia* gave an immediate reaction:

> An opera like this cannot be judged in a single evening. Yesterday we were almost overwhelmed by its originality: originality, or rather strangeness, in the choice of subject; originality in the music, in the style, in the very form of the numbers; and we could not form a complete view of it. Nevertheless, the opera had the most complete success, the composer being applauded, called for and acclaimed after almost every number. Two pieces had to be repeated. The skill of the instrumentation is true, admirable and stupendous: the orchestra speaks to you, weeps, and conveys passion to you. Never was the eloquence of sounds more powerful.
>
> It seemed to us at a first hearing that the vocal part was less splendid. It is quite distinct from the style previously used, since it lacks great ensembles, and you scarcely notice a quartet and a trio in the last act in which the musical thought was not completely grasped.[15]

The quartet which the critic 'scarcely noticed' is the famous '*Bella figlia dell' amore*' (usually referred to thus, although the quartet properly begins forty-eight bars earlier, with the words '*Un dì, se ben rammentomi*' [One day, if I remember well]). This is one of the highlights not only of *Rigoletto* but of all Italian opera. The four characters, Rigoletto, Gilda, the Duke and Maddalena, voice their widely differing feelings in themes which, each individually suitable and distinct, blend into a beautiful and harmonious whole. When Victor Hugo, author of the original play on which the opera was based, saw *Rigoletto* in Paris in 1857, he exclaimed of the quartet: 'If I could only make four characters in my plays speak at the same time, and have the audience grasp the words and the sentiments, I would obtain the very same effect.'[16]

Other critics who were present at the premiere found *Rigoletto* totally confusing. One thought Verdi had returned to the style of Mozart, another considered that the opera totally lacked invention or originality. When it was staged in London in 1853, Chorley (who had described *I masnadieri* in 1847 as 'the worst opera' by anyone) contented himself with calling *Rigoletto* Verdi's weakest opera!

At the first performance of the opera, the role of Gilda was sung by Teresa Brambilla. The soprano whom Verdi had wanted was Teresa de Giuli-Borsi, who had created the role of Lida in *La battaglia di Legnano*. When, the following year, de Giuli-Borsi was engaged to sing Gilda in another production, her husband Carlo Antonio Borsi had the temerity to write to Verdi requesting him to compose an additional aria for her. Verdi replied scathingly:

> If you could be persuaded that my talent was so limited that I did not know how to do better than I have done in *Rigoletto*, you would not have requested of me an aria for this opera. Miserable talent, you may say, and I agree. But there it is. Then, if this *Rigoletto* can stand as it is, a new aria would be superfluous. And where would one put it? Verses and notes can be provided, but unless they are at the right time and in the right place, they will never make any effect. We may know of a place, but God forbid! We should be flayed alive. Is there any need to show Gilda with the Duke in his bedroom? Do you understand me? Whatever one did there, it would have to be a duet. A magnificent duet! But the priests, the monks and the hypocrites would all cry scandal. Oh, how happy were the times when Diogenes could say in the public square to those who asked him what he was doing: 'Hominem quaero!!' etc. etc.
>
> As for the cavatina in the first act, I do not understand where you find any agility in it. Perhaps you have not understood the tempo, which should be an *allegretto molto lento*. At a moderate tempo, and sung quietly throughout, it should not be difficult. But to return to your first proposition, let me add that I conceived *Rigoletto* without arias, without finales, as a long string of duets, because this was how I wanted it. If anyone adds: 'But one could do this here, and that there' etc. etc., I reply: 'That would be fine, but I did not know how to do any better.'[17]

Opinions differ about Verdi's pre-*Rigoletto* operas. *Nabucco* and *Macbeth* are generally accepted as being first-rate works, and each of the others (with perhaps one or two exceptions) has its defenders. But there can be no argument about *Rigoletto*, which is undoubtedly one of his masterpieces. What is most remarkable about the work is its sustained level of inspiration. As in his two following operas, *Il trovatore* and *La traviata*, companion-pieces to *Rigoletto* in this great flowering of his genius, an uncanny psychological acumen is allied with a wonderfully spontaneous outpouring of melody. From *Rigoletto* onwards, each of Verdi's operas was to have its own individual flavour, its own orchestral colour. During rehearsals of *Rigoletto*, Verdi had said to Varesi that he never expected to do better than the quartet in the last act. In a sense, he was right. Neither he nor anyone else could do better. Verdi continued to do differently.

Chapter Nine

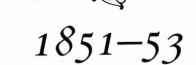

1851–53

Verdi was back in Busseto a few days after the *Rigoletto* premiere, his thoughts already turning to his next opera. He and Cammarano had been in correspondence about the choice of subject for a work which, it was at this point assumed, they would write for Naples. By this stage in his career, however, although he continued to accept commissions, Verdi was beginning to be much more concerned with each opera itself as an artistic entity. It was no longer necessarily a question of writing an opera for Venice or an opera for Naples, but sometimes of writing an opera and then deciding which city had the company best suited to perform it. So, although he and Cammarano may have expected that their next opera would be for Naples, Verdi discussed the possibilities with his librettist without reference to the Naples impresario, Flauto.

Cammarano, at Verdi's instigation, had ceased to do any detailed work on *King Lear*. 'I have thought several times about *King Lear*,' he wrote to Verdi in December 1850, while the composer was still composing *Rigoletto*, 'but speaking honestly, and considering the necessary urgency, another subject, as you propose, would suit me better.'[1] The subject which Verdi then proposed, in a letter of 2 January 1851, was '*El Trovador*, a Spanish drama by Gutiérrez. This seems to me very beautiful, imaginative, and full of strong situations. I should like there to be two female roles: the principal one is the gipsy, a woman of very special character.'[2]

How Verdi first encountered Gutiérrez's play is not known. It had not been produced on the Italian stage, but a singer returning from an engagement in Spain may have brought him a copy, in which case it was probably then translated for him by Giuseppina. When he had not had any response from Cammarano after nearly three months, Verdi wrote to their common friend in Naples, Cesare de Sanctis:

> I am really furious with Cammarano. He has absolutely no regard for time, which to me is a precious commodity. He has not written one word to me about this *Trovatore*: does he like it, or doesn't he? . . . You are his friend, so please urge him not to waste another moment. Although I am angry, give Cammarano a kiss from me. . . .[3]

Within days, Verdi and Cammarano were corresponding about the opera which was to become *Il trovatore*. Cammarano expressed certain doubts about the play, a romantic melodrama with implausible characters, and suggested a few changes which Verdi was reluctant to concede. 'You don't say a word to me about whether or not you like the play,' he complained to the librettist. 'I suggested it to you because it seemed to me to offer some fine dramatic moments, and above all a general quality both singular and original. If you did not share my opinion, why didn't you suggest some other subject? For this kind of thing it is helpful if poet and composer are in agreement!'[4]

What Verdi was drawn to in the play were its strong theatrical situations, and the intensity of the passion conveyed by the characters: the gipsy woman, Azucena, torn between conflicting feelings of love and revenge; the Count di Luna, driven by desire to acts of crazed violence; the manic energy of the troubador, Manrico. What Verdi wanted from Cammarano, and did not in the end get, was a libretto whose verse forms were new and bizarre. He did not need, as he put it, 'cavatinas or duets or choruses or finales'; indeed, he would be happy if the entire opera consisted of 'one single number'. In his instructions to Cammarano, he might almost have been concocting the recipe for *Tristan und Isolde*.

Before he had even received Cammarano's outline for the libretto, Verdi had decided that this opera would not be composed for Naples. When the outline arrived, the composer was disappointed with it, and said that it would be better to give up the idea if, in their opera, they could not retain 'all the novel and bizarre characteristics' of the Spanish play. He sent the librettist his own suggestions for a synopsis, but ended:

> My first suspicion that this play didn't appeal to you is probably true. If this is so, there is still time for us to change our minds rather than do something you don't like. I already have another subject, simple but affecting, which can be said to be almost finished. If you like, I'll send it to

you, and we'll think no more of *Trovatore*.[5]

It is usually assumed that the 'simple but affecting' subject to which Verdi refers is the novel *La Dame aux camélias*, by Alexandre Dumas *fils*. But it is more likely that Verdi's interest in this subject, which was to furnish the plot of *La traviata*, was first aroused by the stage adaptation, also by Dumas, which he and Giuseppina saw in Paris the following year. Whatever the alternative subject to *Il trovatore* may have been, Verdi and Cammarano decided to persevere with the Spanish play, work on which proceeded fitfully throughout 1851.

In any case, Verdi now had other things on his mind. In the spring, he and Giuseppina took up residence at the Villa Sant' Agata, where they were to live for the rest of their lives. They had been living together openly in Verdi's house in Busseto. In Milan this would have caused little or no comment in musical and artistic circles, but Busseto was a small country town whose inhabitants were easily shocked. They considered Giuseppina Strepponi a loose woman, much to Verdi's disgust. The death of his mother on 28 June also distracted the composer from *Il trovatore*. He was deeply upset: Muzio had to see to the funeral arrangements. Unable to concentrate on composition, Verdi went to Bologna for a few days in October, where he directed performances of *Macbeth* and *Luisa Miller* at the Teatro Comunale. On 19 November, for the tenor Giovanni Severi (who had sung in *I lombardi* in 1843), he wrote '*Fiorellin che sorge appena*', a barcarole to words by Piave.

In December he and Giuseppina took themselves off to Paris for the winter, to escape the bleak weather that the Lombardian plains would suffer until the end of March, and no doubt also to avoid the gossip in Busseto. While they were in Paris, Verdi received a letter from his old benefactor Antonio Barezzi, taking him to task for not having legalized his union with Giuseppina. He replied on 21 January, addressing Barezzi as 'Dearest Father-in-law':

> After waiting such a long time, I hardly thought I would receive from you a letter so cold, and containing, if I am not mistaken, so many wounding phrases. If this letter had not been signed Antonio Barezzi, whom I wish to think of as my benefactor, I should have replied most strongly, or not have replied at all. But since it is signed by that name which I shall always consider it my duty to respect, I shall do everything possible to persuade you that I do not merit such a reproof. In order to do this, it is necessary for me to refer to things in the past, to speak of other people, of our native

district, and so my letter will be somewhat prolix and boring, though I shall try to be as brief as possible.

I do not believe that, of your own accord, you would have written a letter which you knew could only cause me displeasure. But you live in a district that has the bad habit of continually interfering in other people's affairs, and disapproving of everything which does not conform to its own ideas. It has never been my habit to interfere in other people's business unless asked to, precisely because I require that no one should interfere in mine. This is why there has been gossip, whispering and disapproval. This liberty of action, which is respected even in less civilized communities, I claim as a right in my own vicinity. You be the judge, and be a judge severe, yet calm and dispassionate: what harm is done if I live in isolation, if I prefer not to make visits to titled people, if I don't take part in festivities, in the pleasures of others, if I manage my own property because it pleases and entertains me? I repeat, what harm is done? In no instance has anyone else suffered any damage.

That said, I come now to a sentence in your letter: 'I understand very well that I am not a man for commissions, because my time is already past, but for little things can I not be useful?' If by that you mean to say that I used to give you important commissions, while now you serve me only in small things, alluding to the letter enclosed in yours, I can find no excuse for this, and though I should do the same for you in similar cases, I can only say I have learnt my lesson for the future. If your sentence is meant as a reproof because I have not entrusted you with my affairs during my absence, permit me to ask you: how could I ever be so importunate as to place heavy burdens upon you, who never even set foot in your own farmyards because your business affairs are so pressing? Should I have commissioned Giovannino? [Giovanni Barezzi, one of Antonio's two sons.] But is it not true that last year, while I was in Venice, I gave him full power of attorney in writing, and that he never once set foot inside Sant'Agata? Not that I am complaining of him, he was perfectly right. He had his own affairs which were sufficiently important, and so he could not take care of mine.

This has revealed to you my opinions, my actions, my wishes, my so-to-speak public life, and since we are making these revelations, I find no difficulty in raising the curtain which veils the mysteries hidden within my four walls, and speaking to you about my domestic life. I have nothing to hide. In my house there lives a lady, free and independent, who, like myself, prefers a solitary life, and who has a fortune capable of satisfying all her needs. Neither I nor she is obliged to account to anyone for our actions. But who knows what our relations are? What affairs? What ties? What rights I have over her, or she over me? Who knows whether she is my wife or not? And if she is, who knows what the reasons may be for not publicly announcing the fact? Who knows whether that is a good or a bad thing? Might it not be a good thing? And even if it is a bad thing, who has the right to ostracize us? I will say this to you, however: in my house she is entitled to as much respect as myself, more even. And no one is allowed to forget that, for any reason. And finally she has every right, both because of her conduct and her character, to that consideration she habitually shows to others.

With this long chatter, all I have meant to say is that I claim my freedom of action, because all men have a right to it, and because my nature rebels against mere conformity. And to say too, that you, who are fundamentally so good, so just and so kind-hearted, must not let yourself be influenced, must not absorb the ideas of a community which – it really needs to be said – at one time did not even consider me worthy to be its organist, and is now complaining and gossiping about me and about my business. This cannot continue. But if it should, I am a man who can look after himself. The world is big enough, and the loss of twenty or thirty thousand francs would never prevent me from finding somewhere else to live.

There can be nothing offensive to you in this letter, but, if anything in it displeases you, then consider it not written, because I swear to you on my honour that I have no wish to displease you in any way. I have always considered you my benefactor, and still do. I consider this an honour and I boast of it. Farewell, farewell, in our customary friendship.[6]

Presumably Barezzi's response to this was conciliatory; he was, at any rate, soon on excellent terms with Giuseppina Strepponi.

While Verdi and Giuseppina were in Paris news arrived from Naples that Cammarano was ill. Work on *Il trovatore*, which had been proceeding at a snail-like pace, now entirely ceased for a time. But, in any case, Verdi's attention had been distracted by another subject. In February, he and Giuseppina attended a performance of the play *La Dame aux camélias*, which Alexandre Dumas *fils* had adapted from his own novel. The story of the courtesan who attempts to lead a respectable life with the man she loves, but who leaves him at the request of his father in order not to bring scandal upon the family, may have seemed to Verdi to have piquant parallels with his own present situation. In any event, he responded immediately to the work's possibilities as a subject for opera, which he began to discuss with Piave. Throughout 1852, he was simultaneously concerned with both *Il trovatore* and *La Dame aux camélias*.

In March he and Giuseppina returned to the Villa Sant' Agata. Verdi was still waiting for Cammarano to recover and resume work on *Il trovatore*, and he was being asked by the opera houses of Milan, Venice and Bologna to undertake commissions. Early in May, he agreed to compose for Venice the opera which turned out to be the Dumas subject, now called *La traviata*. In July, Cammarano died in Naples. 'I was thunderstruck by the sad news of Cammarano,' Verdi wrote to Cesare de Sanctis. 'I can't describe the depth of my sorrow. I read of his death not in a letter from a friend, but in a stupid theatrical journal. You loved him as much as I did, and will understand the feelings I cannot find words for. Poor Cammarano. What a loss.'[7]

Cammarano had died leaving *Il trovatore* unfinished. The last words he had written, eight days before he died (according to de Sanctis), were those of the tenor aria '*Di quella pira*', which brings the curtain down on Act III. Verdi paid the poet's widow six hundred ducats instead of the agreed five hundred, and through de Sanctis engaged a young Neapolitan poet, Leone Emanuele Bardare, to complete the libretto and make any necessary revisions. Having agreed to finish the opera in time for it to be performed at the Apollo Theatre, Rome, early in the following year, the composer made certain stipulations: that he be convinced of the excellence of the company's leading soprano, Rosina Penco; that another strong female singer be found to play the role of the gipsy; and that the censorship approve Cammarano's libretto before he, Verdi, proceeded any further with the composition of the opera. He learned from de Sanctis that Signora Penco had a somewhat piercing voice but was very pretty, and this apparently satisfied him. Communicating with Bardare through de Sanctis, he resumed work on the opera, which was finished by mid-December.

Meanwhile, in August, the composer had received a visit from Léon Escudier. The French Emperor, Napoleon III, had made Verdi a Chevalier of the Legion of Honour, and had sent Escudier to Italy to present the honour to him. 'I found Verdi about to go to table', Escudier recalled in his memoirs:

There was also present a man with a frank, open, likeable face, a magnificent presence, his age about twice Verdi's; his simple manners, his sweet and affectionate language, his broad shoulders, struck me; he had on me the effect of a patriarch. It was Verdi's father-in-law. His name is Antonio. We soon made acquaintance, and a quarter-hour later I was calling him familiarly Papa Antonio. . . .

At the dessert, I stood up a moment and came back with a little box in my hand.

'Dear Maestro,' I said to Verdi, setting the box before him, 'here is a token of the affection of the French government and, I should add, of the French public.'

Verdi frowned, opened the box, and found the Chevalier's cross, with two or three metres of red ribbon which I had taken care to add to it.

He tried to dissimulate his emotion; at heart, he felt a lively satisfaction, and firmly clasped my hand.

But it was Papa Antonio who remained stunned. He wanted to speak, and it was impossible for him to articulate a word. He waved his arms, stood up, flung himself on Verdi's neck, clasped him to his bosom, embraced me in turn, then his eyes flooded and he wept like a baby.[8]

In December, final adjustments were made to *Il trovatore*, after Verdi had written not only the music but also virtually all of the words of Act II, scene II. He courteously gave his new collaborator, Bardare, a chance to alter them, but the young librettist either did not want or did not dare to suggest any changes. On 20 December Verdi left Sant' Agata for Rome, with Giuseppina accompanying him only as far as Livorno, where she stayed for a few days before proceeding to Florence. It would seem that the reason Giuseppina did not go on to Rome was that the composer was concerned to avoid gossip. She wrote to him from Livorno on 3 January:

I am delighted that you find yourself lost without me, and I wish for you such boredom that you will abandon this barbarous idea of leaving me isolated like a saint in the Thebaid! My dear Magician, your heart is that of an angel, but your head, when it is a question of gossip and such things, has a cranium of such thickness that, if Gall were alive, he would add some odd observations to his treatise on craniology.[9]

Rome was in a state of anticipatory excitement about Verdi's new opera, and on 19 January the first performance of *Il trovatore* was given at the Apollo Theatre to wild acclaim. The next day, crowds surged through the streets around the theatre shouting 'Long live Verdi'. The opera was quickly taken up by other Italian theatres and, in due course, by the civilized world; Verdi's melodies were transcribed and arranged for all kinds of instruments and ensembles, and were soon to be heard on barrel-organs throughout the length and breadth of Italy, and eventually in England and America as well.

Il trovatore's effects are indeed broad and immediate. The wealth of melody, the passionate melancholy of Leonora's music, the dark beauty of the orchestral colouring, the almost brutal vigour and speed of the entire opera, whose characters, as the Viennese critic Hanslick said, arrived on the stage as if shot from a pistol: these are some of the ingredients that have ensured the opera's popularity since its first performance. *Il trovatore* is the veritable apotheosis of the bel canto opera, with its demands for vocal beauty, agility and range. It is as though Verdi had decided to do something which he had been perfecting over the years, and to do it so beautifully that he need never do it again.

In *Il trovatore* he was saying goodbye to the fabled world of high romance. The opera is set in fifteenth-century Spain during a period of civil war. The royalist Count di Luna and the troubador Manrico, a rebel leader, are rivals for the hand of Leonora, who gives her love to Manrico. Di Luna and Manrico are unaware that they are brothers, since Manrico has been brought up by Azucena, a gipsy whom he believes to be his mother. She has moments in which her mind wanders, during one of which she reveals that her own mother had been burned as a witch by the father of the present Count di Luna. She recalls how, in her hysteria, intending to throw the Count's brother into the flames, she had killed her own child by mistake.

Leonora, believing Manrico killed in battle, is about to enter a convent when di Luna attempts to abduct her, but he is foiled by the sudden arrival of Manrico. Preparations for the marriage of Leonora and Manrico are in hand when Manrico learns that Azucena, whom he still thinks is his mother, has been captured by di Luna. He rushes off to save her, but is himself captured and imprisoned by the Count.

In order to procure the release of Manrico, Leonora offers herself to di Luna, and then takes poison rather than submit to him. When Manrico learns the price of his freedom, he curses Leonora, but realizes he has wronged her when she collapses and dies in his arms. The Count orders Manrico's execution. As he dies, Azucena announces to the Count that he has killed his own brother. At last, she has avenged her mother's death, though at a cruel cost to herself, for she loved Manrico as though he were her son.

At the premiere the leading roles had been sung by Rosina Penco (Leonora), Emilia Goggi (Azucena), Carlo Baucardé (Manrico) and Giovanni Guicciardi (di Luna). Penco and Baucardé were the only well-known singers, but apparently all four performed superbly.

The *Gazzetta Musicale* described the opera the next day as 'heavenly' and continued:

The composer deserved this splendid triumph, for he has here written music in a new style, imbued with Castilian characteristics. The public listened to each number in religious silence, breaking out into applause at every interval, the end of the third act and the whole of the fourth arousing such enthusiasm that their repetition was demanded.[10]

Verdi was blasé about the success of *Il trovatore*, writing later to Clarina Maffei that 'they say this opera is too sad, and that there are too many deaths in it. But after all, everything in life is death! What else is there?'[11]

A few days after the premiere he was back at Sant' Agata and immersed in *La traviata*. Very little of it had been composed before the *Trovatore* opening, so he was now writing against time.

Piave arrived to be on hand to make any adjustments to the libretto. The story centres around Violetta, a high-class Parisian courtesan. Alfredo Germont falls in love with her, not knowing that she is dying of consumption. She goes to live with him in the country, but leaves him at the request of his father to avoid bringing scandal upon the Germont family. She returns to her former protector but is publicly insulted at a party by Alfredo, who fights a duel with his rival. Alfredo returns to Violetta when he learns the truth about her sacrifice, but arrives only a short time before she dies.

Verdi was worried that the Venice company might not be good enough to do justice to the opera, so one of Piave's tasks during his visit was to try to persuade him that Fanny Salvini-Donatelli, the Fenice's prima donna for the season, would make a suitable Violetta. Verdi was insisting upon a soprano who was young, with a good figure and able to convey passion. Salvini-Donatelli, he maintained, fulfilled none of these requirements. He recommended Rosina Penco from *Il trovatore*. Piave reported back to the Fenice president, Marzari, that the composer was in 'an infernally bad mood, perhaps because of his indisposition, but more likely because he has no faith in the company'.[12]

Piave returned to Venice, and Verdi wrote to him there on 16 February:

Here are two more numbers, a tenor aria and a bass aria [i.e. the baritone aria, '*Di Provenza il mar, il suol*'] and that's the second act finished. In the cabaletta of the tenor aria, you will have to re-write the third and the seventh lines, to get the stress right. In the scene where Giuseppe comes in to say that Violetta has left, Annina cannot have returned, so Violetta and Annina could not leave together. I have patched it up, in order to write the music, but you will have to write some better verses.

I received the tenor cabaletta today. It says absolutely nothing. I shall be in Venice on Monday evening. Have my usual apartment prepared for me at the Europa, with a good piano, properly tuned. Also, I should like you to find, either from a carpenter or by borrowing it, a writing-stand, so that I can write standing up. Make sure that everything is ready, because I intend to begin the orchestration immediately, the evening I arrive.

I've received an anonymous letter from Venice which says that if I don't make them change the soprano and the bass [baritone] it will be a complete fiasco. I know, I know. I'll show it to you.[13]

On 21 February Verdi arrived in Venice and began the orchestration. Giuseppina, who had not been well, was left at Sant' Agata, and on 23 February she wrote to him:

As I promised, I am writing to tell you that I am neither better nor worse than on Sunday. However, Frignani assures me that with today's powders I shall have a notable and prompt improvement. He has forbidden me meat and green vegetables, prescribing a diet of soup and eggs to be eaten tepid. As long as it's tepid, he also allows me black coffee, and as you know, that's my only little weakness – at table. All I ask and hope is to be completely well again by the time you return. You can't imagine how upset I was, those last few days, seeing you, my poor Magician, working like a black and, on top of that, having the sight of my illness! But I shall be well again, and with my good humour I shall try to make you forget past annoyances. You are so good to your Livello [an affectionately derogatory pet-name], and I am desolate at not being able to reward you for what you do for me. . . . And to think that lofty soul of yours came spontaneously to lodge itself in the body of someone from Busseto! One needs the faith of St Thomas to believe it. It is still my opinion that an exchange took place when you were a child, and that you came into being as the result of some charming lapse of two unhappy and superior beings! Write to me when you can, hurry on the rehearsals, and return to your den. Our youth is over, but we are still the whole world to each other, and we watch with lofty compassion all the human puppets bustling about, climbing, slipping, fighting, hiding, reappearing, all in order to put themselves at the head, or near the top, of the social masquerade.[14]

The scoring of *La traviata* was completed by the beginning of March, and the opera had its premiere at the Teatro La Fenice on 6 March 1853, with Fanny Salvini-Donatelli as Violetta, Lodovico Graziani as Alfredo Germont and Felice Varesi as the elder Germont, Alfredo's father. Verdi's laconic note to Emanuele Muzio, written the following day, is well-known: 'Dear Emanuele, *Traviata* last night – a fiasco. Was it my fault or the singers'? Time will tell.'[15]

The first night had indeed been a fiasco. According to the *Gazzetta*

Privilegiata di Venezia, the first act had gone well, mainly because of the disdained Salvini-Donatelli who, as Violetta, had the lion's share of the music to sing. Verdi was called onto the stage several times. The rot had set in with Act II, in which the tenor and the baritone had performed execrably, and in the final act the audience laughed at the stout Salvini-Donatelli's attempts to portray a woman dying of consumption.

Verdi's letters to Muzio, and other friends to whom he wrote on 7 March in similar terms, were sent before the press reviews appeared. The reviews revealed, somewhat unusually, that the new opera had been appreciated at its true worth by the critics rather than by the public, who seemed prevented by the shortcomings of the singers from enjoying either the drama or the music. The critical view was that Verdi was not well served by his singers, with the exception of the miscast soprano, and that judgment should be reserved until the opera could be heard in an adequate performance. It seems clear that the tenor, Graziani, was in poor voice; and the baritone, the renowned Varesi, apparently sulked his way through the performance as he considered that the composer had written him a part unworthy of his capabilities.

Varesi, who had been fortunate enough to be allowed to sing the title roles in the premieres of *Macbeth* in 1847 and *Rigoletto* in 1851, wrote after the third performance of *La traviata* in March 1853 to his friend, the publisher Lucca, complaining of his role in the new opera and attempting to justify his poor showing:

> I am taking advantage of the kindness you showed me during your brief stay in Venice, and in giving you some information about Verdi's opera *La traviata*, I beg you to defend me against the impudent article in the *Gazzetta di Venezia* which has made even Verdi's idolators indignant.
>
> I will refer you to reliable witnesses from Milan, among them Ariolo, Giulini and Vittadini, with whom you can speak in Milan in a few days. They will tell you how I sang in *La traviata* and whether I was in good voice: besides, the most powerful proof is that, when the third performance was cancelled because Graziani was ill, and they put on *Il corsaro* instead, I created such an effect and won such applause that the public declared I was unrecognizable from one opera to the other. I do not mean to set myself up as judge of the musical merits of *La traviata*, but I certainly maintain that Verdi did not succeed in exploiting the gifts of the artists at his disposal. In the whole of Salvini's part, only the cavatina ['*Ah, fors'è lui*'] lies well for her. In Graziani's part, little or nothing. In mine, the adagio of

an aria [*'Di Provenza il mar, il suol'*]. This caused much strong feeling among the Venetian public, which expected me to have something that suited me really well, since Verdi had already created for me the colossal parts of Macbeth and Rigoletto with such success; and also because, before the premiere, it was known that the Maestro was very pleased with me.

Here is the story of last night, the third performance, a benefit performance for the poor. A very sparse audience. Some applause for the brindisi, and much for Salvini's cavatina, with two calls. In the big duet between Salvini and me [in Act II] some applause both after the adagio and after the cabaletta. Applause at the second act finale, and two calls for the Maestro and the artists. In the third act, no applause, and one call to say goodbye to the Maestro who was known to be leaving the next morning.

I shall be most grateful to you if you would make some mention of this, for the sake of my self-respect which was so affected by the article in the *Gazzetta*. That article attempted to put the weight of responsibility for the public's displeasure on my shoulders. If that were true, however, they would not have applauded me in the few passages that were suited to my abilities.[16]

This is highly unconvincing. Though the character of Germont may have seemed to Varesi, after the tragic stature of Macbeth and Rigoletto, to give him too few possibilities to rise to dramatic heights, the role is a gift to an intelligent baritone with acting ability, and it presents no difficulties musically. It is not surprising that when Varesi conveyed his condolences to Verdi at the end of the first performance, the composer replied, 'Make your condolences to yourself and your companions, who have not understood my music.'[17] Verdi was not, however, disappointed in the orchestral playing, for on 9 March he wrote to the first violinist at the Teatro La Fenice: 'As I cannot do so personally, may I ask you in my name kindly to convey my warmest compliments to the professors of the orchestra for the devotion and care with which they performed this poor *Traviata*.'[18]

One of Verdi's reasons for having made an opera of Dumas's play was his fascination with the idea of using a contemporary subject and showing characters from modern life on the stage. Some Verdi commentators have suggested that the first-night Venetian audience may have been disconcerted at seeing modern dress on the operatic stage. But this is not what they saw. Someone at the Fenice theatre had taken fright, and the period and costumes were those of Louis XIV, early eighteenth-century. It was not until 1853 itself had become a bygone age that *La traviata* began to be seen in the costumes of the mid-nineteenth century.

Despite the failure of *La traviata* in Venice, impresarios in other Italian cities were keen to be allowed to stage it. The composer, however, was cautious: he did not want it performed again until he could be certain that the right cast was available. The conductor Angelo Mariani wanted to stage it in Genoa with two of the Venice singers, but this, of course, Verdi refused to allow. His friend Cesare de Sanctis suggested a production at the San Carlo in Naples, to which the composer replied: 'Ah, so you like my *Traviata*, that poor sinner who had such bad luck in Venice. One day I shall make the world do honour to her. But not in Naples, where your priests would be horrified to see on the stage the kind of things they themselves do at night on the quiet.'[19] He considered travelling to Rome to produce *La traviata* there himself, but again was not satisfied as to the suitability of the singers.

When *La traviata* did reach the stage again, it was in Venice, the city of the opera's unfortunate premiere, though not at the Teatro La Fenice. Antonio Gallo, who was in charge of the San Benedetto theatre, a less prestigious Venetian opera house, sought Verdi's permission for a revival of the opera, using the sets and costumes from the original production but with a completely different cast. Piave would be engaged to stage the opera, and there would be as many rehearsals as the composer thought necessary. The principal singers would be the soprano Maria Spezia, the tenor Francesco Landi, and the baritone Filippo Coletti, who had created the baritone roles in *Alzira* and *I masnadieri*.

Verdi gave his approval, revised five numbers of the score with which he had not been completely satisfied at the premiere, and made adjustments to the baritone role of Germont *père* to suit Coletti's range, which was lower than that of Varesi. *La traviata* was staged at the San Benedetto theatre on 6 May 1854, fourteen months after its Fenice premiere. Verdi did not attend any of the performances, for by then he was in Paris where he was composing a new work for the Paris Opéra, but he was delighted to hear from his publisher Tito Ricordi (who had become head of the firm on the death of his father, Giovanni) that *La traviata* was being received in Venice with the wildest enthusiasm. It was now thought to be a most beautiful opera, and the majority of people who had heard it claimed to have thought it a beautiful opera the previous year as well! Verdi wrote to de Sanctis:

> You ought to know that *La traviata* which is being performed at the San Benedetto theatre is the same, exactly the same as the opera performed last

year at the Fenice, except for one or two transpositions of key and a few alterations to notes which I did to make it fit better the capabilities of these particular singers. These will be printed in the score, because I consider the opera as having been written for the present cast. Apart from that, not a single piece has been altered, not one number added or taken out, not one musical idea altered. Everything which was there at the Fenice is there at the San Benedetto. Then, it was a fiasco. Now it has caused a sensation. Draw your own conclusions.[20]

Certainly, *La traviata* is now seen not only as one of Verdi's finest and best-loved operas but also as one of the world's great music-dramas. Perhaps it was not immediately recognized as such because of its melodic wealth: it must have seemed hardly fair that a superb music dramatist should also be able to invent such a prodigality of tunes and such beautifully expressive writing for the strings. Each of his great middle-period operas has its own distinctive sound, and in *La traviata* the dark, melancholy hues of *Il trovatore* have given way to a warmer string sound. This is an opera in which all of Verdi's finest qualities are to be perceived: his technical mastery, his clarity, his humanity, his psychological penetration and his unerring taste.

Chapter Ten

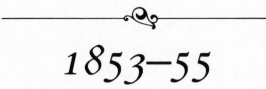

1853–55

After the initial performances of *La traviata* Verdi returned to Sant'
Agata. Cesare de Sanctis tried to interest him in a Neapolitan librettist
named Domenico Bolognese as a possible successor to Cammarano,
and Bolognese suggested one or two subjects to Verdi, among them
Faust, but none appeared to excite the composer's imagination. 'I
adore *Faust*,' Verdi told de Sanctis, 'but I wouldn't want to make an
opera of it. I've studied it a thousand times, but I don't find the
character of Faust musical; that is, musical in the way I think of
music.'[1]

If Verdi was uninterested in the subjects being proposed to him, this
may well have been because *King Lear* had begun actively to engage
his attention again. In April, the well-known playwright Antonio
Somma had written to him, suggesting that they collaborate on an
opera. Somma, a lawyer by profession, was the author of a number of
successful tragedies, and for seven years in the 1840s had been the
Director of the Teatro Grande in Trieste. In his reply Verdi set forth
some of his thoughts concerning the theatre and opera. His attitude,
he said, had changed over the years, and he would no longer be
interested in setting to music such subjects as *Nabucco* and *Il due Foscari*
because, although dramatic, they lacked variety. For the same reason,
however elevated the classical Greek and Roman playwrights might
be, his preference was for Shakespeare whom he admired above all
others. Ten years previously, he told Somma, he would not have
risked composing *Rigoletto*, but in fact,

as far as dramatic effectiveness is concerned, it seems to me that the best
material I have yet put to music (I'm not speaking of literary or poetic

worth) is *Rigoletto*. It has the most powerful dramatic situations, and it has variety, vitality and pathos. All its dramatic developments result from the frivolous, licentious character of the Duke. Hence Rigoletto's fears, Gilda's passion, and so on, which give rise to many dramatic situations, including the scene of the quartet which, as far as effect is concerned, will always be one of the finest our theatre can boast.[2]

Verdi ended his letter by suggesting that Somma take a look at *King Lear*. 'I shall do the same,' he added, 'since I've not read it for a long time.' It was three years since he had discussed *Lear* with Cammarano and had written his own synopsis. He now re-read the play, and found himself again being drawn into its world. Soon he and Somma were engaged in a detailed correspondence, its subject the creation of an opera to be based on Shakespeare's play. Verdi's creative genius was now ready to grapple with the demands of this, perhaps the greatest of Shakespeare's tragedies, and it seemed that, this time, *Il re Lear* by Giuseppe Verdi would finally be brought to birth. 'The choice suits me,' Somma wrote to the composer after they had both re-read *Lear*, 'not only because of what the great drama is in itself, but also because it is different from any of the subjects you have so far set. If you decide to do it now, I would gladly agree to write the libretto.'[3]

Somma proceeded to make an outline in five acts, but Verdi suggested reducing it to three or, at the most, four. 'Keep in mind the need for absolute brevity,' he advised his newly acquired librettist. 'The public is easily bored.'[4] Towards the end of June, Somma produced his revised outline, and Verdi accompanied his notes on it to the librettist with a letter:

Do whatever you think right with the notes I have jotted down on your outline. There are two things about this project which have been concerning me. First, it seems to me that the opera is becoming excessively lengthy, especially the first two acts. So, if you can find anything to cut or to condense, do so: the effect will be all the greater. If this isn't possible, at least do your best to say things as briefly as possible in the less important scenes. The second thing is that I think there are too many changes of scene. The one thing that has always prevented me from making greater use of Shakespearian subjects has been precisely this necessity of changing scenes all the time. When I went to the theatre, it annoyed me immensely; it was like watching a magic lantern. In this, the French are right: they plan their dramas so that they need only one scene for each act. In this way, the action flows freely without hindrance, and without anything distracting the audience's attention. I completely understand that in *Lear* it would be impossible to have only one scene for each act, but if you could manage to dispense with some of them, that would be helpful. Think it over, and when you've put a few scenes into verse send them to me.[5]

Throughout the summer, Antonio Somma worked on his libretto, sending it to Verdi scene by scene, and in return receiving the composer's suggestions and criticisms. Though an experienced verse playwright, Somma had never before written an opera libretto, and Verdi was able to instruct him in the special requirements entailed in writing verses for music. 'Everything can be set to music, it is true,' the composer wrote,

but not everything can prove effective. To compose music, one needs stanzas for writing cantabiles, stanzas for writing ensembles, stanzas for composing largos, allegros, etc. etc., and all varied, so that none of it proves cold and monotonous. Let me examine this poetry of yours. I shall not mention Edmund's aria, though it shifts too abruptly from adagio to allegro. It can stay as it is. In the following duettino, you've given me nowhere for a melody or even a melodic phrase, but since it's brief it can stand, if you add a stanza of four lines in the same metre for Edmund, and the same for Edgar.

The following part which, musically speaking, would be the finale of the act produces problems. The Fool's stanzas are very good, but from the moment Goneril enters there's no knowing what to do. Perhaps you intended those six-line stanzas as an ensemble, but you have written those stanzas as dialogue, so the characters must answer one another, and consequently their voices can't be united. Then for the same reason, one would have to make another ensemble with the eight-line stanzas when Regan enters. At the end, you have Goneril and Regan exit, and Lear ends the act on his own. This is all right in a tragedy, a spoken drama, but in music the effect would be, to say the least, cold.[6]

Verdi then proceeded to suggest ways in which the scene could be made more effective. By the end of the summer, he had received two acts of the libretto from Somma, which he took with him to Paris where he and Giuseppina were to spend the next two years, for Verdi had committed himself to the composition of a new work for the Paris Opéra, which was to be staged in December 1854.

They had first intended to spend the winter of 1853–54 in Naples, for in September Verdi asked de Sanctis if he could find an apartment there for two people, well situated and facing the sea, and if a lady, accompanying him with her passport in order, would suffer any annoyance from the police. He added that he did not want to hear any operas, or proposals for operas! De Sanctis assured him that there would be no problems, but in October the composer and his inamorata left Sant' Agata not for Naples but for Paris. Verdi continued to correspond with Somma about *King Lear*, although he did not at any time consider making it his Paris opera. It would be too vast a subject and its form too novel and daring for Paris, he told Somma, for the French 'only understand melodies which have been repeated for twenty years'.[7]

Somma was in Venice, continuing to work at his libretto. 'If there are any lines of recitative that you can shorten or cut out', Verdi wrote to him there in March 1854, 'it will be so much gained for the opera as a whole. In the theatre, lengthy is synonymous with boring, and the boring is the worst of all styles.' He assured Somma that he could not wait to begin composing *Lear*, with which he hoped to accomplish something 'not quite as bad as my other works'.[8]

At this time, Piave too was busy in Venice, staging the second production of *La traviata* at the Teatro San Benedetto. 'I wish Verdi were here,' he wrote to Tito Ricordi, 'instead of breaking his balls, combatting that rich Jew of a Meyerbeer. He renounces the throne offered him by Italy, to sit on a bench in France!'[9] (The Paris–based composer Giacomo Meyerbeer was Verdi's only serious rival in France.) When Somma wrote with welcome news of the success of *La traviata*, in which Maria Spezia was proving a much more believable Violetta than the creator of the role, Verdi replied, 'I hear marvellous things about la Spezia. Would she be a good Cordelia? Let me know.'[10]

It was not until the following year, 1855, that Somma was able to send Verdi the final two acts of his *King Lear* libretto. By this time, Verdi had composed his Paris opera, *Les Vêpres siciliennes*, and it was within weeks of being performed. For the time being, thoughts of *King Lear* were put aside.

Verdi had not begun composing his opera for Paris immediately upon his arrival in October 1853, for he did not receive the libretto until the end of December. The librettist was the famous and extraordinarily prolific French playwright, Eugène Scribe, who had made a fortune with his plays and libretti which he had been turning out regularly for more than forty years. A hack writer *par excellence*, Scribe usually worked with collaborators to create romantic plots with cardboard characters, unconvincing dialogue, and an abundant opportunity for spectacle. He had provided libretti for most of the leading composers of his day, among them Meyerbeer, Auber, Donizetti and Gounod.

For Verdi, Scribe lazily resuscitated a libretto which he and Charles Duveyrier had written in 1839 for Donizetti. At that time it was entitled *Le Duc d'Albe*, and was about the Flemish uprising against their Spanish masters in the sixteenth century (a subject Verdi was to deal with years later in *Don Carlos*). But Donizetti left the opera unfinished; completed by Matteo Salvi, it was to have its first performance in an Italian translation in Rome in 1882. In 1853, Donizetti having been safely dead for five years, Scribe changed the names of the characters of *Le Duc d'Albe*, set the action in thirteenth-century Sicily, and engaged Duveyrier to make what changes he thought necessary. 'Instead of the Flemish, who want to massacre the Spaniards, and can't, we shall have the Sicilians, furious, outraged and vindictive, who do massacre the French,' Scribe instructed his collaborator.[11] (Scribe told Duveyrier that he had acquainted Verdi with the provenance of the libretto. Nearly thirty years later, however, Verdi claimed that he had always imagined Scribe's *Les Vêpres siciliennes* to be an original work, written expressly for him in 1853.)

The final libretto was indeed set against the historical events of 1282 when the Sicilians rose against the French in an act of wholesale slaughter. There is a fictional plot involving the love of Hélène, a Sicilian patriot, for Henri, who unknown to her is the son of the French governor of Sicily. The opera ends with the massacre, known as the Sicilian Vespers because the signal to attack was the ringing of the vesper bell.

Verdi began working on the opera in January 1854, but at a very slow pace. This was not quite the first time that he had composed music to a French, instead of an Italian, text, for he had written a certain amount of new music for *Jérusalem*, the French version of *I lombardi*, seven years earlier. It was, however, his first attempt at French grand opera, a somewhat grandiose genre virtually invented by Meyerbeer, and he was not completely at home with its con-ventions or its format. 'I write very slowly,' he confessed to Giuseppina Appiani in a letter written on 25 February. 'In fact, it may be that I shall not write. I don't know why, but I know that the libretto is there, still there in the same place.'[12]

To the Countess Maffei, on 2 March, he wrote:

Shall I write for La Scala? No. If I were asked my reason, I would find it embarrassing to reply. I could say I have little desire to write, or better still that I loathe signing contracts. But it is not, as people have said, because I have obligations here until after '56; I have no other commission after I finish the opera I am writing. Nor is it the desire (as people have also said) to *put down roots here*!! Put down roots? That's impossible! And, in any case, what would be the point of it? What purpose would it serve? Fame? I don't believe in it. Money? I make as much, and perhaps, more in Italy. And even if I wanted to, I repeat, it's impossible. I'm too much in love with my desert and my own sky. I don't raise my hat to counts or marquesses, or to anyone. Finally, I haven't got millions, and the few thousand francs I have earned through my own labours I shall never spend on publicity, on claques and such filth. And they seem to be necessary here for success! A few days ago, even Dumas wrote in his newspaper about Meyerbeer's new opera: 'What a pity that Rossini did not give us his masterpieces in 1854! It is also true to say that Rossini never had that German vivacity which knows how to bring a success to the boil six months before the event in the cauldrons of the newspapers, and thus time the explosion of interest precisely for the first night.' That is very true. I was at the first performance of this *Etoile du Nord*, and I understood little or nothing, while the good public here understood everything, and found it all beautiful, sublime, divine! And this same public, after 25 or 30 years, has not yet understood *Guillaume Tell*, and so it is performed in a bungled fashion, mutilated, with three acts instead of five and in a production unworthy of it! And this is the world's leading opera house.

But, without realizing it, I am talking to you of things which cannot interest you. So I shall finish by telling you I have a fierce desire to return home. I say this to you, secretly, because I am sure you will believe me. Others will believe it an affectation on my part. But I have no interest in saying what I do not feel. Our Milanese *lions*, however, have such an exaggerated idea of what goes on in Paris! Well, so much the better. Good luck to them! The season was beautiful during the three days of carnival, and after that crowds on the boulevards.[13]

One cannot help suspecting that Verdi was being extremely disingenuous in assuring Clarina Maffei that he longed to return home, for he continued to reside in France with Giuseppina for another twenty-one months. They spent the disappointingly cold summer of 1854 at Mandres, where Verdi continued fitfully to work on *Les Vêpres siciliennes*. By the end of September it was complete, and at the beginning of October they were back in Paris for Verdi to begin rehearsals. A letter the composer wrote to Giuseppina Appiani on 21 October marks the sad ending of his friendship with her. The

Countess Appiani had evidently offended Giuseppina, presumably by addressing a letter to 'Giuseppina Strepponi' instead of to 'Madame Verdi', although Strepponi was not then entitled to the use of Verdi's name:

> It was by chance, by pure chance, that your letter reached Peppina. As the address you chose to put on it is unknown at the door of this house, your gracious letter was in danger of being lost if, I repeat, I had not by chance run into the postman who, seeing a name ending in 'i', asked me about it. I retrieved it and carried it to its destination. Peppina said to me that, having renounced letters and the arts, and keeping up a correspondence only with her family and a few very intimate friends, she would be grateful if I would make her apologies and reply to so *spirituelle* a letter. And here am I, who cannot write like you or like Peppina, in the greatest embarrassment at having to reply to a letter so well written, so fine, and, I repeat, so *spirituelle*. My rough style does not allow me to make a show of wit or of spirit, so I shall tell you briefly that we are in a great hurry to pack our bags, that Cruvelli's flight from the Opéra has obliged me to ask to be released from my contract, which I hope will happen, that I shall go straight to Busseto but stay there for only a few days. Then, where shall I go? I can't say. Now that my bag of news is empty, I press your hands.[14]

'Cruvelli's flight from the Opéra' referred to the sudden disappearance of Sophie Cruvelli, the singer who had been rehearsing the leading female role in *Les Vêpres siciliennes*. A German soprano who had Italianized her name from Crüwell, she was a beautiful though eccentric young woman in her late twenties, with a superb voice and great dramatic talent, who had made her debut in Venice in a revival of *Attila* in 1847. A fine performer of Verdi's soprano roles, she appeared in *Ernani* and *Nabucco* in London in 1848, and in *Luisa Miller* in Milan in 1850. She first sang in Paris in *Ernani* in 1851, and became a great favourite in that city in the title roles of Bellini's *Norma* and *La sonnambula*, Beethoven's *Fidelio* and Rossini's *Semiramide*.

Engaged to create the role of Hélène in *Les Vêpres siciliennes*, rehearsals for which began on 1 October, she rehearsed with the company for eight days, during which time she was also singing at the Opéra on some evenings. On 9 October the opera to be performed was Meyerbeer's *Les Huguenots* with Sophie Cruvelli as Valentine. However, Madame Cruvelli failed to arrive at the theatre and the performance had to be cancelled.

On 22 October, the day after Verdi wrote his coldly dismissive letter to Giuseppina Appiani, *La France Musicale* announced: 'It is still unknown what has become of Mlle Cruvelli. Her unexpected flight renders impossible for the present the performance of the opera by Messieurs Scribe and Verdi, which was put in rehearsal on the first of this month. In this situation, M. Verdi has declared officially to the administration that he will withdraw his score.'

The soprano's disappearance mystified and intrigued Parisian society for several weeks. Had she been kidnapped? Was she still alive? Had she eloped? At the end of October, Verdi wrote to Piave:

> I hope that by now you are well informed of the musical goings-on here. La Cruvelli has fled! Where? The devil knows! At first this news gave me a pain in the arse, but now, confidentially, I'm amused by it. It's true that I lose a great deal of money, but that doesn't matter: if I were greedy, I would be twice as rich as I am. This defection gives me the right to dissolve my contract, and I have grasped the opportunity to request that, formally.
>
> It's true that the Minister of State has made me a number of offers, to engage anyone else I like, to translate immediately either *Trovatore* or *Rigoletto*, to write straightaway another opera, in three acts, while they make other arrangements to give the grand opera in five acts; but utilizing all the *grâce* you have been able to teach me, I have said no to everything. I have persuaded them that it is not a good idea to make translations, nor to give a short opera, and I cannot give the five-act opera because it was written for la Cruvelli.[15]

Rumours began to circulate that Cruvelli had eloped with her lover, a Baron Vigier, and the scandal of her disappearance became gossip in a number of other European cities. In London, a burlesque called *Where's Cruvelli?* was staged.

In the middle of all this, Verdi received a flattering request from Genoa. A new opera house was being built there, and the management hoped not only that it could open with an opera composed for the occasion by Verdi, but also that he would give his consent to the theatre being called Teatro Verdi. Declining the honour of having a theatre named after him, he was nevertheless willing to compose an opera for Genoa, and Tito Ricordi suggested that *King Lear*, whose libretto was ready and waiting, might be suitable.

However, while Verdi was considering this, Sophie Cruvelli suddenly turned up in Paris, calmly announced that a note she had written to the Opéra management explaining that she intended to take several weeks' leave must have gone astray, and on 20 November she reappeared on the stage of the Opéra as Valentine in *Les Huguenots*, the role she was to have sung on the evening of her sudden flight. At

Valentine's first entry in *Les Huguenots*, the Queen addresses her with the words *'Dis-moi le résultat de ton hardi voyage'* (Tell me the result of your bold journey). The question was so apposite that the audience, which had been disposed to demonstrate its displeasure with Cruvelli, burst into disarmed laughter.

Sophie Cruvelli had merely taken a premature honeymoon in Brussels and Strasbourg with Baron Vigier. Two years later she married him and retired from the stage. Her reappearance in Paris meant that rehearsals for *Les Vêpres siciliennes* could be resumed, and this in turn prevented Verdi from composing *Lear*, or anything else, for the new theatre in Genoa, which, in due course, opened its doors as the Teatro Paganini. 'If la Cruvelli doesn't run off a second time,' Verdi told Cesare de Sanctis, 'I hope the opera can open at the beginning of February.'[16] But the opera did not open at the beginning of February, for relations between composer and librettist, and between composer and musicians, had become strained. Taking a little time off from *Les Vêpres siciliennes*, Verdi conducted *Il trovatore* on 26 December at the Théâtre-Italien. At the beginning of January, he complained in a long letter which he wrote, in French, to François Louis Crosnier, the recently appointed Director of the Paris Opéra:

I feel it my duty to let no more time pass without making a few observations concerning *Les Vêpres siciliennes*.

It is both upsetting and mortifying for me that M. Scribe will not take the trouble to improve the fifth act, which everyone agrees is uninteresting. I fully realize that M. Scribe has a thousand other things to concern him which are perhaps more important to him than my opera! But if I had been able to foresee his complete indifference I should have stayed in my own country where, really, I was not doing so badly.

I had hoped that M. Scribe would find it possible to end the drama with one of those moving scenes which bring tears to the eyes, and whose effect is almost certain, since in my opinion the situation lends itself to that. Please note that this would have improved the entire work, which has nothing at all touching in it except the romanza in the fourth act.

I had hoped that M. Scribe would have been kind enough to appear at rehearsals from time to time, to be on the lookout for any unfortunate lines which are hard to sing, to see whether anything needed touching up in the numbers or the acts and so on. For example, the second, third and fourth acts all have the same form: aria, duet, finale.

Finally, I expected M. Scribe, as he promised me at the beginning, to change everything that attacks the honour of the Italians.

The more I consider this, the more I am persuaded it is dangerous. M.

Scribe offends the French because Frenchmen are massacred, he offends the Italians by altering the historic character of Procida into the conventional conspirator beloved by the Scribe system, and thrusts the inevitable dagger into his hand. Good Lord, there are virtues and vices in the history of every race, and we are no worse than the rest. In any case, I am first of all an Italian, and whatever happens I will not become an accomplice in offending my country.

It remains for me to say a word about the rehearsals in the foyer. Here and there I hear words and remarks which if not actually wounding, are at least inappropriate. I am not used to this, and I shall not tolerate it. It is possible there are people who do not think my music worthy of the Opéra. It is possible there are others who think their roles unworthy of their talents. It is possible that I, for my part, find the performance and style of singing other than I would have wished! In short, it seems to me, unless I am strangely mistaken, that we are not at one in our way of feeling and interpreting the music, and without perfect accord there can be no possible success.

You see that everything I have just said is serious enough for us to stop and consider how to avoid the catastrophe which menaces us. For my part, I see but one means and I do not hesitate to propose it: the dissolution of the contract. I quite realize you will answer that the Opéra has already lost some time and money, but that is little in comparison with the year I have lost here, during which I could have earned a hundred thousand francs in Italy. You will go on to say it is all very well to annul a contract when there is a deficit, to which I reply that I should by now have paid it if my losses and expenses were not already too great.

I know that you are too just and reasonable not to choose the lesser of two evils. Trust my musical experience: given the conditions under which we are working, a success is really improbable. A half-success profits no one. Let each of us try to make up for lost time, try to arrange everything calmly, and we may both gain by it.[17]

Crosnier did not agree to cancel the contract, and rehearsals continued for the astonishingly long period of a further five months. Some adjustments were made by Scribe to the libretto, but the atmosphere at rehearsals was frequently tense. The composer Hector Berlioz, an acquaintance of Verdi, attended a dress rehearsal on 1 June, and the following day wrote to a friend: 'Verdi is at loggerheads with all the people at the Opéra. He made a terrible scene at the dress rehearsal yesterday. I feel sorry for the poor man; I put myself in his place. Verdi is a worthy and honourable artist.'[18]

Finally, on 13 June 1855, *Les Vêpres siciliennes* was given its premiere at the Paris Opéra. In addition to Sophie Cruvelli as Hélène, the principal singers included Louis Gueymard as Henri, Marc Bonnehée as Guy de Montfort and Louis-Henri Obin as Procida. A twenty-one-year-old English student named Charles Santley was in the audience; nearly forty years later, as the distinguished baritone Sir Charles Santley, he recalled the occasion in his memoirs:

> I noticed Verdi's opera, the *Vêpres siciliennes*, was announced for Wednesday, with Sophie Cruvelli in the cast, and I could not resist the temptation of staying one day more in order to have another opportunity of hearing the goddess who had enchanted me a couple of years before. I knew nothing about the distribution of places, and took what was offered me in exchange for my money, in consequence of which I found myself with the crown of my head almost touching the ceiling, planted behind a row of people who, with that French politeness of which I have often heard, but seldom experienced, would insist upon standing, and entirely obstructing my view of the stage. Spite of the discomfort, I enjoyed the performance. Obin, the bass, especially pleased me; I was somewhat disenchanted by my goddess; the tenor I did not like; and the baritone Bonnehée, I liked very much; only, as he did not go down to F, or anywhere near it, I did not take the interest in him I would have done a few years later, when I learned to distinguish between bass and baritone.[19]

As a singer, Santley's interest was in the performers; the quality of the music seemed not to concern him. But the press and public in general appeared to approve of the new opera. Verdi's art, always one of concision and directness, was by its nature ill-suited to the prolix form and empty professionalism of Meyerbeerian grand opera, but he poured much excellent music into this, his first real attempt to compose a French five-act opera, one whose finest pages are those in which his sincerity burns through the deadwood of Scribe's libretto.

'It seems to me that *Les Vêpres siciliennes* is not going too badly,' Verdi wrote to Clarina Maffei two weeks after the first performance. 'The press here has been either moderate or favourable, except for only three writers who are Italian.'[20] The opera also won the approval of French composers, Adolphe Adam declaring that it had converted him to an appreciation of Verdi's music, and Hector Berlioz writing, in *La France Musicale*:

> Without casting a slur on the merit of *Il trovatore* and of so many other moving works by him, it must be agreed that in *Les Vêpres* the penetrating intensity of melodic expression, the sumptuous variety, the judicious sobriety of the orchestration, the amplitude, the poetic sonority of his ensemble pieces, the warm colours glowing everywhere, and that sense of

power, impassioned but slow to deploy itself, that is a characteristic of Verdi's genius, stamp the entire work with a grandeur, a sovereign majesty more marked than in the composer's earlier creations.[21]

Verdi had written to Clarina Maffei that he hoped to be in Italy within two weeks. In fact, he was not to return there until six months later. He and Giuseppina spent the summer at the attractive little thermal spa of Enghien, on the outskirts of Paris, and at some time during the year Verdi made a quick visit to London alone in order to prevent an unauthorized performance of *Il trovatore* which would have deprived him of royalties. A recently promulgated English law denied property rights to dramatic works by non-British citizens except for works which were being presented for the first time in the United Kingdom. Writing to his lawyer in Busseto in October 1855, Verdi claimed that on his two visits to London it had been suggested that he should become a citizen of either England, France, or even Piedmont (since France and Piedmont had signed trade agreements with England). 'But', he continued, 'I wish to remain what I am, that is to say a peasant from Le Roncole, and I prefer to ask my Government [i.e. Parma] to make an agreement with England.'[22]

During the autumn of 1855, Verdi was busy in Paris supervising a French translation by Emilien Pacini of *Il trovatore* for a production at the Opéra, where it was performed in 1857. He assisted Arnoldo Fusinato in translating *Les Vêpres siciliennes* into Italian. The translation was performed in Parma and Turin on 26 December, not, however, under the title of *I vespri siciliani* but, for the usual censorship reasons, as *Giovanna de Guzman*, and set in Portugal. A few days before the first performance of *Giovanna de Guzman*, Verdi and Giuseppina Strepponi had finally left Paris and were now in residence at Sant' Agata.

Chapter Eleven

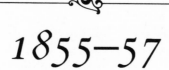

1855–57

An Italian-born French writer, Marc Monnier, included in an article on Verdi a brief but tantalizing mention of an encounter with the composer one evening in 1855, at the Théâtre-Italien in Paris. It was during the interval of a performance of Rossini's *Otello*, and Verdi was standing 'not in the centre of the foyer where celebrities are wont to stand, surrounded by a galaxy of admirers who in turn are flanked by their own satellites; instead he stood to one side, engrossed in his own thoughts. I spoke to him of Rossini, he replied by discussing Shakespeare.'[1] Might those engrossing thoughts during a perform- ance of Rossini's *Otello* have been of an *Otello* which, thirty years later, he would himself create? Or was he, perhaps, contemplating the *King Lear* which, at this time, he was still expecting soon to compose?

King Lear was certainly to occupy his thoughts during 1856. However, on his return to the farm at Sant' Agata, Verdi plunged himself into the role of country gentleman. 'I'll tell you of my affairs,' he wrote to de Sanctis on 7 February. 'They are not very important, and they are reduced to almost nothing. Total abandonment of music, a little reading, a slight occupation with agriculture and with horses. *Voilà tout.*'[2] This was not entirely true, for in January he had gone to Parma to attend a performance of Bellini's *I puritani* and to propose to the Duchy of Parma that the Government should participate in an international treaty on copyright.

On 9 February, Verdi received from the King of Piedmont and Sardinia the title of Cavalier Knight of the Order of St. Maurizio and St. Lazzaro, and in the middle of March he travelled to Venice where the now successful *La traviata* was being staged again at the Teatro La Fenice. He had also, for some months, been in correspondence with

Piave concerning a revision of *Stiffelio*, and towards the end of March Piave arrived at Sant' Agata to discuss this project.

It had always been clear to Verdi that the fortunes of *Stiffelio*, first performed in Trieste in 1850, were being hampered by its libretto. In 1854 he had written to de Sanctis: 'Among my operas which are not in circulation, there are some I must forget about, because their subjects were at fault. But there are two I should not like to be forgotten: they are *Stiffelio* and *La battaglia di Legnano*.'³ In November 1855, he had written from Paris to Piave, who had suggested that Verdi come to Venice and stage *I vespri siciliani*: 'Your proposal that I come to produce *I vespri* could suit me, so long as it doesn't prevent me from revising *Stiffelio*. Why not perform both of them in Venice? I believe that might amuse the management. I would come to Venice soon, first mount *I vespri* and then the revised *Stiffelio*.'⁴

This plan was not to be realized. By the following April, when Piave and Verdi worked on the revision at Sant' Agata, the new version of *Stiffelio* was intended for production in the autumn in Bologna. But when the opera finally reached the stage, it was on the occasion of the inauguration of a newly constructed theatre in Rimini, the Teatro Nuovo Comunale, in the summer of 1857, and the work had a new title: *Aroldo*. By that time, Verdi and Piave had written another opera and had seen it premiered in Venice.

Before Piave came to Sant' Agata, Verdi had written to him on 10 March:

> Before setting out, please obtain all the material necessary for rearranging *Stiffelio*. You know there are not many books here, nor is there any big library nearby. So arm yourself. I have already mentioned to you that I would not like to make Stiffelio a crusader. Something newer and more interesting. Think about it.
> Come quickly then, and, if you can, bring a lion [*leone:* slang for poodle] with you, which you know will delight Peppina.⁵

If Piave brought a dog as a present for Giuseppina, it was probably a Maltese terrier; a male dog of that breed, rather confusingly called Loulou, became an important member of the Verdi household at about this time. As for Stiffelio, Verdi may not have wanted him to become a crusader, but that is precisely what, as Aroldo, he did become. Retaining the plot outline of *Stiffelio*, Piave gave new names and occupations to the characters, whom he transferred from nineteenth-century Germany to twelfth-century Britain. The Protestant preacher Stiffelio became the Saxon knight Aroldo, who returns from the Holy Land to find that his wife (no longer Lina, but Mina!) has been unfaithful to him. Most of the action takes place at a castle in Kent, with a last act, whose music is completely new, set on the banks of Loch Lomond. (Although Verdi spells these names correctly in his autograph score, the printed libretto refers to a castle 'near Kenth' and to Loch 'Loomond'.)

The transformation of *Stiffelio* into *Aroldo* took several weeks, and was finished by the end of May. By then, Verdi had signed a contract to write with Piave a new opera for Venice for the Lent season of the following year, 1857. Before deciding upon a subject, however, he took a brief holiday in Venice with Giuseppina to enjoy the delights of sea-bathing on the Lido. This appears to have been prescribed for Giuseppina by her doctor, who accompanied them. After three weeks they returned briefly to Busseto, before travelling to Paris to dispose of Verdi's house and effects there. While in Paris, Verdi became involved in legal action against an impresario, Calzado, who was threatening to perform *La traviata* and *Rigoletto* from pirated Spanish editions. Due to the primitive state of the laws relating to copyright, Verdi lost his suit.

On the day that he left Sant' Agata for Paris, Verdi had informed Piave that he believed he had found a subject for the opera for Venice, and promised to send the librettist an outline from Paris. This was *Simon Boccanegra*, from a play about the fourteenth-century Doge of Venice by the Spanish playwright Antonio García Gutiérrez, the author of the play on which *Il trovatore* had been based. Piave was instructed to obtain the censors' approval of *Simon Boccanegra* as a subject for the opera. When the librettist promised Verdi a finished script by the end of September, Verdi replied irritably from Enghien:

> What is the point of finishing the story of *Simon Boccanegra* before the end of the month? Don't the police and the directorate have a sufficiently detailed draft? Indeed, it is not a draft but the completely finished drama. There will not be an idea or a word changed in the libretto. What does it matter now whether it is in prose or in verse? And, as you have quite rightly observed, this *Simone* has something original about it. Therefore the layout of the libretto, the numbers and so on, must be as original as possible. This cannot be done unless we get together: at present it would be a waste of time.[6]

Earlier in the year, despite his having said after the premiere of *Luisa*

Miller that he would never write another opera for Naples, Verdi had signed a contract for a new opera to be performed at the Teatro San Carlo. His hope was that this time he could proceed to compose *King Lear*, and with this in mind he began again to scrutinize Somma's libretto. 'I am not sure', he wrote to the librettist,

> that the fourth act of *King Lear* is good in the form in which you sent it to me, but I do know that you cannot impose so many recitatives on the audience, one after another, especially in the fourth act. These are not merely a composer's caprices. I would be willing to set even a newspaper or a letter to music, but in the theatre the public will put up with anything except boredom. . . . I'm not quite sure what it is, but something doesn't satisfy me. It certainly lacks brevity, perhaps clarity, and perhaps truth.[7]

Verdi made it clear to the San Carlo management that he would want 'a really fine baritone' for the role of Lear, a leading soprano ('not a dramatic soprano, but a singer of expressive quality') for Cordelia, a very good contralto for the Fool, two very good secondary performers (presumably for Goneril and Regan), and 'a dramatic tenor with a good voice, for a less important role' (perhaps Edgar?).[8]

The soprano he himself had in mind for Cordelia was the twenty-four-year-old Maria Piccolomini, whom he thought a very fine Violetta in *La traviata*, and who in 1856 was having a triumph in London in that role. From Paris in August he sounded her out. Although the soprano was enthusiastic at the prospect of creating a leading role in a Verdi opera, the San Carlo management failed to conclude an agreement with her, and Verdi refused to accept Rosina Penco, whom they offered him instead. Though he thought Penco an excellent artist, he did not consider her right for Cordelia. 'I cannot agree with the understanding you have come to with Penco,' he wrote to Vincenzo Torelli, who was acting on behalf of the San Carlo management:

> It is not my custom to allow artists to be foisted on me, not even if Malibran were to come back into this world. Not all the money on earth would make me relinquish this principle. I have the greatest esteem for Penco's talent, but I don't want her to be able to say to me, 'Oh, Maestro, give me that role in your opera, I want it and I have a right to it.'[9]

King Lear was, therefore, postponed yet again; Verdi began to consider other subjects for Naples and, meanwhile, began in Paris the composition of *Simon Boccanegra*. He also signed a contract to produce *Il trovatore* in French translation for the Paris Opéra. For this production he composed ballet music for Act III, since it was customary for a grand opera in French to include a ballet in the third act. He also took the opportunity to make a few alterations to his score. *Le Trouvère* had its premiere at the Opéra on 12 January 1857, and on the following day Verdi and Giuseppina left for Busseto and Sant' Agata.

Verdi had almost finished composing *Simon Boccanegra* while he was in Paris. As he was not happy with some of the verses which Piave had sent to him, he had asked Giuseppe Montanelli, an exiled Tuscan patriot living in Paris, to revise them. Montanelli's revisions are quite extensive, and when Verdi sent the final draft of the libretto back to Piave, he accompanied it with the following brusque note:

> Here is the libretto, shortened and altered to just about what it should be. As I said in my other letter, you may put your name to it or not, as you please. If you are upset about what has happened, I am upset too, and perhaps more than you, but all I can say to you is, 'It was a necessity'![10]

In mid-February, Verdi and Giuseppina travelled to Venice, and on 12 March 1857 *Simon Boccanegra* was produced at the Teatro La Fenice. Piave was in charge of the staging, but a letter which Verdi had written him some weeks earlier reveals the extent to which the composer himself always kept the stage picture in mind while composing, and the importance he attached to production and stage effect:

> . . . Be particularly careful with the staging. The directions are precise enough, but nevertheless allow me some observations. In the first scene, if the Fieschi palace is at the side it must nevertheless be completely visible to the entire audience, because they must see Simon when he enters, and when he comes out onto the balcony and detaches the lantern. I am sure I have created a musical effect here, and I don't want it to be lost in the staging. In addition, in front of the Church of San Lorenzo I should like a small practical staircase of three or four steps which, at one moment, Paolo and, at another, Fiesco, could lean against or hide behind.
> . . . The Grimaldi Palace in Act I need not have great depth. Instead of one window, I should have several, reaching down to the floor. There should be a terrace, and a second backdrop with a moon whose rays would reflect on the sea, so that it is visible to the audience. The sea should be a glittering backdrop. If I were an artist, I would try to make it a beautiful scene, simple but extremely effective.
> You must pay particular attention to the final scene. When the Doge orders Pietro to close the entrance to the balcony, the rich illuminations must be visible, with plenty of space so that everyone can see the lights

clearly as they are, little by little, extinguished until, when the Doge dies, everything is in pitch blackness. I think it should be an extremely effective moment, and woe betide you if you do not stage it properly.[11]

The principal singers were Leone Giraldoni (baritone) as Boccanegra, Luigia Bendazzi (soprano) as Maria, Carlo Negrini (tenor) as Gabriele, and Giuseppe Echeverria (bass) as Fiesco. Although they all appear to have acquitted themselves well, *Simon Boccanegra* was not a success. 'The music is of the kind that does not make its effect immediately,' wrote the critic of the *Gazzetta Privilegiata di Venezia*. 'It is very elaborate, written with the most exquisite craftsmanship, and it requires to be studied in detail.' The critic went on to say, however, that, although the music in general was too heavy and dark, lacking variety of colour, 'certain signs of disfavour, all too eloquent and outspoken, did not issue from the lips of Venetians but were spoken by foreigners'. It appears that an organized claque was in operation against Verdi. According to the composer's friend Cesare Vigna, an alienist by profession, 'there were dark and subtle plots laid by certain rich Israelites who were totally committed to acting in support of a certain Maestro Levi (of the ancient tribe), the composer of a *Giuditta* which shared the same fate as Holofernes, yet who, despite this, wants to try his luck again in the theatre.'[12] Vigna also claimed to discern the hand of Meyerbeer in the disappointing reception accorded *Simon Boccanegra*.

Verdi appears not to have given credence to this talk of plots and claques. Writing to Vincenzo Torelli the morning after the premiere, he simply reported that the fiasco of *Boccanegra* had been almost as great as that of *La traviata*, adding: 'I thought I had done something passably good, but apparently I was mistaken. We'll see later who was wrong.'[13]

Much of the published criticism was directed at Piave's libretto. When a rumour began to circulate to the effect that the composer himself had written the libretto, Verdi was furious with Piave, whom he suspected of having spread that story. Piave, however, was able to assure the composer that he had not been responsible, and a somewhat guilty Verdi then felt he should support his loyal collaborator. He wrote to Cesare Vigna, a month after the first performance of *Boccanegra*:

Have the Venetians now calmed down? Who would ever have thought that this poor *Boccanegra*, whether a good or a bad opera, could stir up such a devil of a row? But I remain calm, and not offended by my enemies whether Jews or Christians of past, present or future, and, like you, I find the world fair enough. . . .

The rumour that the libretto was written by me was really the end!!! A libretto that bears Piave's name is judged in advance as the worst possible poetry, but, frankly, I know I would be content if I could write verses as good as '*Vieni a mirar la cerula . . .*' [Come and behold the azure], '*Delle faci fastanti al barlume*' [In the glow of the festive torches], and several others, with many such lines scattered here and there. I confess that, in my ignorance, I could not do so well.[14]

In the opera's prologue, the sea-adventurer Simon Boccanegra, who has had a child by Maria, daughter of the patrician Fiesco, learns simultaneously that he has been elected Doge of Genoa and that Maria has died. The first act of the opera takes place twenty-five years later: Fiesco, who has brought up the child, Amelia, without being aware of her parentage, plots against the Doge with the help of Gabriele Adorno, who is in love with Amelia. Boccanegra discovers Amelia's identity, and he and his daughter are reunited. Gabriele, misunderstanding the nature of their relationship, intends to kill the Doge, but when he learns the truth he joins Boccanegra's faction. Boccanegra is poisoned by his disaffected henchman Paolo. As he dies, he and Fiesco are reconciled. The Doge blesses the union of his daughter and Gabriele, and proclaims Gabriele his successor.

In *Simon Boccanegra* Verdi continued to move away from the old division into self-contained numbers, in the direction of a continuing and dramatically truthful melody. The opera's orchestral colour is almost unrelievedly gloomy, but Verdi was invariably at his best when he allowed his own pessimistic temperament to infiltrate into every corner of a libretto. Nearly a quarter of a century later he was to revise and improve the opera, but this 1857 *Boccanegra* is a fascinating work in its own right.

In the weeks following the premiere, Verdi spent the sunny days of spring in the fields and the woods of his estate with the farm-workers and the animals, finding (or so he told Cesare Vigna) that his nicest companions were the four-legged ones. But he had not completely immersed himself in farming. Early in April, Piave had arrived at Sant' Agata to help make certain revisions to *Simon Boccanegra*, which Verdi had agreed to stage in Reggio Emilia in May. The opera was received favourably there, as it was the following year in Naples when the composer again was in charge of the staging. Elsewhere, however, it fared less well. In Florence a disastrous production was laughed off the stage, and at La Scala, Milan, in 1859 a mediocre cast with an especially poor leading baritone virtually finished the opera off. On that occasion, Verdi wrote bitterly to Tito Ricordi:

The fiasco of *Boccanegra* in Milan had to happen, and it did happen. A *Boccanegra* without Boccanegra!! Cut a man's head off, and then recognize him if you can. You are surprised at the public's lack of decorum? I'm not surprised at all. They are always happy if they can contrive to create a scandal! When I was twenty-five, I still had illusions, and I believed in their courtesy; a year later my eyes were opened, and I saw whom I had to deal with. People make me laugh when they say, as though reproaching me, that I owe much to this or that audience! It's true; at La Scala, once, they applauded *Nabucco* and *I Lombardi*; but, whether because of the music, the singers, orchestra, chorus or production, the entire performances were such that they were not unworthy of applause. Not much more than a year earlier, however, this same audience ill-treated the opera of a poor, sick young man, miserable at the time, with his heart broken by a terrible misfortune. They all knew that, but it did not make them behave courteously. Since that time, I've not seen *Un giorno di regno*, and I've no doubt it's an awful opera, but heaven knows how many others no better were tolerated and even applauded. Oh, if only the public at that time had, not necessarily applauded, but at least suffered my opera in silence, I shouldn't have been able to find words enough to thank them! If they now look graciously upon those operas of mine that have toured the world, then the score is settled. I don't condemn them: let them be severe. I accept their hisses on condition that I don't have to beg for their applause. We poor gipsies, charlatans, or whatever you want to call us, are forced to sell our labours, our thoughts and our dreams, for gold. For three lire, the public buys the right to hiss or to applaud. Our fate is one of resignation, and that's all! But, whatever my friends or enemies say, *Boccanegra* is in no way inferior to many other operas of mine which were more fortunate: perhaps this one needed more care in performance and an audience which really wanted to listen to it. What a sad thing the theatre is!![15]

In May 1857, however, pleased at the successful reception of his own staging of *Simon Boccanegra* in Reggio Emilia, Verdi began to turn his thoughts to the opera he had agreed to write for Naples, the subject of which had not been chosen. *Aroldo*, the revised version of *Stiffelio*, was, of course, finished and was shortly to be given its first performance in Rimini. According to Giuseppina (in a letter to Léon Escudier), Verdi was determined not to accept any firm commitments after the Naples opera: 'He says that he has been chained up too long, and that he is now rich enough to free himself.'[16]

Much of the spring and summer of 1857 was spent by Verdi reading plays in an attempt to find one suitable for operatic purposes. He took time off to supervise the production in Rimini of *Aroldo*, which was to inaugurate the new theatre, arriving in the town on 23 July accompanied by Giuseppina and Piave. As usual, the composer was meticulous in his preparation of the opera's production:

> Accompanied by Piave, he visited the tailor to examine the costumes, which he ordered to be made and re-made, being always hard to please. The sociable librettist chatted with the women in the establishment and told them risqué stories, at one of which the usually gloomy and sulky Verdi smiled broadly. . . . At rehearsals, which he attended regularly, nothing escaped his hawk-like attention. The village bell that was to sound the *'Ave Maria'* in Act IV of *Aroldo* was out of tune, and Verdi worked on it with a file until he obtained the right note.[17]

The conductor was the forty-five-year-old Angelo Mariani, who had already established a good reputation. He was, in fact, one of the earliest professional conductors in Italy: until the mid-nineteenth century, the conductor was either the composer of the music being played, or the first violinist leading the orchestra from his desk. It was only as orchestral scores became more complex and orchestras bigger that the figure of the conductor emerged into the limelight.

Mariani's reputation was in large part founded on his conducting of operas by Verdi. He and the composer had met before the Rimini engagement, but now a close friendship grew between the two men. The story is told that at one of the rehearsals for *Aroldo*, when Mariani was castigating the orchestra for being unable to play the storm music as he thought it should be played, Verdi listened in silence for a time before approaching the conductor and advising him not to persist but to proceed to the next number in the score. After the rehearsal, when Mariani protested to the composer that he would eventually have got the orchestra to play the passage correctly, Verdi smilingly pointed out that it was not the fault of the players. The orchestration, he said, was quite wrong and he would re-do it overnight.

The principal singers in the Rimini premiere of *Aroldo* were Emilio Pancani (tenor) in the title role; Marcellina Lotti (soprano) as Mina; Gaetano Ferri (baritone) as Egberto; and Gian-Battista Cornago (bass) as Briano. Mariani wrote to Tito Ricordi during the rehearsal period:

> As usual, teaching the singers their roles has added years to Verdi's life. If

Pancani is in good form, he should be most effective; Lotti has a superb voice but is lacking in artistry; Ferri is excellent, and Cornago all right. As for the music, this *Aroldo* may turn out to be one of Verdi's finest operas. There are numbers in it which are absolutely certain to make an effect. The fourth act, which is all new, is a magnificent affair. It contains a storm, a pastoral chorus, and an Agnus Dei, treated in canon form, and beautifully composed.[18]

On 16 August 1857, the Teatro Nuovo Comunale was opened with *Aroldo*. At 1 a.m. the following morning, Mariani wrote again to Ricordi:

I have just come from the theatre, or rather from Verdi's hotel, where I left a crowd of people with a band, and wax torches, all cheering and giving him the most frenzied ovation.

Aroldo created a furore. There was not a single number that was not applauded. The Maestro was called on stage an infinite number of times. He is extremely pleased about it, and the performance was good. . . . Also called on stage was our dear Piave who was so happy he could hardly contain himself.[19]

Although the first night was undoubtedly a happy occasion, *Aroldo* appears to have been no more than moderately successful. A more sober account than Mariani's exists:

Rimini was crowded with visitors. Expectation ran high. Portraits of Verdi appeared in shop windows, on walls, in the windows of houses everywhere. Epigraphs were written in praise of this Italian genius. The brilliant Overture was the most popular number in the score, but the rest of the opera failed to excite the audience. Discreet applause greeted the last notes of this 'warmed-up *Stiffelio*', as it was called, and everyone preferred the old version in which there was at least more sincerity, a more coherent style, and more expression and inspiration.[20]

Except for its new final act, the musical differences between *Stiffelio* and *Aroldo* are not of major significance. It might fairly be said, however, that those alterations that Verdi made are improvements. Dramatically, it is another matter. Stiffelio, the Christian preacher, has become Aroldo, the Christian warrior, and what seemed believable behaviour in a nineteenth-century clergyman may well have struck Verdi's audiences as unbelievable in a twelfth-century Crusader. For Stiffelio to swoon with emotion at the sound of a sacred chorus, or to forgive his wife her adultery in the words of the Gospel, is feasible. For the fighter Aroldo to behave similarly must have been considerably less convincing.

In the autumn, *Aroldo* was staged in Bologna and Turin. According to Emanuele Muzio, the Bologna performances were 'a triumph', but Verdi, when he wrote to Ricordi, sounded a more cautious note. Disappointed with the reception his opera had been accorded in both towns, he blamed the singers for the Bologna outcome, and believed that in Turin it was the fault of the production, as well as poor casting of the subsidiary roles. 'It would be as well to take care that the sets for the fourth act are not so ridiculous in other theatres,' he advised his publisher. 'I can assure you that this fourth act is the least poor in the opera, but if the visual aspect is neglected it could compromise the entire work, and we could have another *Stiffelio* on our hands.'[21]

Verdi was right. In 1859, *Aroldo* was a failure in Naples, and, although within the next few years it reached Vienna, Buenos Aires, Lisbon, New York, and a few other cities in the Americas, by the end of the century it had disappeared even from Italian stages. After years of neglect, *Aroldo* was broadcast in Italy in 1951, on the occasion of the fiftieth anniversary of Verdi's death. Since then not only has *Aroldo* been occasionally performed, but also *Stiffelio*, which is now recognized as a separate opera, and by no means an unsuccessful one.

Chapter Twelve

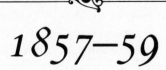

1857–59

When Verdi and Giuseppina returned home from Rimini a few days after the premiere of *Aroldo*, Verdi had still not settled upon a subject for the opera he had agreed to compose for Naples, though he had considered a number of plays. On 9 September, however, he wrote to Vincenzo Torelli in Naples to say that he had chosen a Spanish work, and was already having it adapted. Ten days later he wrote again, having changed his mind:

> I am in despair! In these last months I have read through so many plays (some of them very beautiful), but not one of them is right for my purpose. I settled on a very fine and interesting play, *The Treasurer of King Don Pedro* [*El Tesorero del Rey Don Pedro* by Gutiérrez], which I immediately had translated, but when I made a scenario to reduce it to operatic proportions, I found various difficulties and gave it up. Now I am working on a French play, *Gustave III of Sweden*, a libretto by Scribe which was done at the Opéra over twenty years ago. It's grandiose and huge, and really beautiful, but it's in many ways conventional, like all of Scribe's works for music, which I've never liked but which I now find insufferable. I repeat, I'm in a state of despair, because it's too late now to find another subject, and in any case I don't know where to find one. I'm not inspired by any that I've read. I suggest, therefore, a way of settling the matter in the best interests of the theatre and my own reputation. Let us give up the idea of my writing a totally new opera this year, and substitute *La battaglia di Legnano*, rearranged with a new libretto, with new pieces added where necessary, as I did with *Aroldo*. If we did this, I could come and produce *Boccanegra*, and then, if you like, *Aroldo* as well, and finally *La battaglia*. Thus, instead of one, you would have three operas which I would conduct; and, unless my *amour propre* is deceiving me, one or the other of them would be a success. Let me add that all three operas are perfectly suitable for your company.

If you accept this combination, I shall also, if you wish, agree to write *King Lear* for next year, provided you have the right singers, which you know is imperative. So as not to lose time, and to finish off everything at once, I propose now the following terms. For *King Lear* the contract can remain as it is, except for the changing of the dates. For *Boccanegra*, *Aroldo* and *Battaglia*, which belong to Ricordi, it will be necessary for me to contact him and obtain his agreement. I imagine he will give it, in which case you will have to deal only with me. You will have the performance rights of *Aroldo* and *Boccanegra* for the autumn and carnival season, 1857–58. You could have the rights, for the Kingdom of Naples, of the new version of *Battaglia*. My fee for the rights to *Boccanegra*, and for my staging it, would be 1,500 ducats. Similarly for *Aroldo*. 3,000 ducats for *La battaglia*. Think about this, and then say yes, because I think this is in your interests. I shall lose somewhat by not having parts to sell to publishers, but that doesn't matter. But if you don't like this proposal, I shall have to write *Gustave*, which I'm luke-warm about.[1]

The San Carlo management did not care for Verdi's proposal, and insisted that he fulfil his contract by composing a new opera for their forthcoming season. Half-heartedly, therefore, Verdi prepared to compose *Gustavo III di Svezia*, and asked Antonio Somma to turn Scribe's French libretto into an Italian one. Somma agreed, but added that he would prefer to do it anonymously or pseudonymously, perhaps not wanting to be involved in any trouble with the censors which might arise from an attempt to show on stage the assassination of a reigning monarch.

The story of how a libretto about Gustave III of Sweden eventually became an opera about a Governor of Boston in colonial times is a long and complex one, which it will be interesting to explore in some detail. Even before Somma had finished his first draft of the libretto, Torelli had written from Naples to Verdi, informing him that it was highly unlikely that the subject of Gustave's assassination would be approved by the censors. Verdi must have expected this, for he replied mildly that he thought it should not be too difficult to transfer the locale and change the names of the characters. 'But now that the librettist is hard at work,' he added, 'it is best to let him finish his libretto, and then later we can think about the changing of the subject. It's a shame! To have to give up the pomp of a court like that of Gustave III! And it will be quite difficult to find a Duke of the stature of this Gustave. Poor poets and poor composers!'[2]

Two weeks later, at the end of October, Somma began sending the libretto to Verdi in instalments. Warned that the names of the characters would have to be changed, he appeared not greatly to mind. Verdi responded to the verses he was receiving in his usual fashion, praising this scene, rejecting that, requiring lines to be rewritten in different metres, and constantly reminding his librettist that the quality of the verse was less important than the theatrical effect. Meanwhile, the Neapolitan censorship was becoming more strict in its requirements. On 17 November Somma wrote to Verdi:

> Yesterday, your letter of the 14th reached me, with the memorandum from the Neapolitan censor enclosed. They will allow the action to be placed, it says, anywhere in the north except for Sweden or Norway. But in which century must the action take place? Give me some idea about this. To find a period that will justify a readiness to believe in witches, as requested by His Excellency the Censor, will not be easy. . . . In any case, I can see that to please them, it will be in our best interests to submit.[3]

Somma suggested setting the opera in Pomerania, a region of Prussia, in the twelfth century. However, Verdi replied:

> I really think the twelfth century is a little too remote for our Gustave. It is such a raw and brutal period, especially in those countries, that it seems a serious contradiction to use it as a setting for characters conceived in the French style as Gustave and Oscar are, and for such a splendid drama based on customs nearer our own time. We shall have to find some great prince or duke, a rogue whether of the North or not, who has seen something of the world and caught something of the atmosphere of the court of Louis XIV. When you have finished the drama, you can think about this at your convenience.[4]

The libretto was completed early in December. Over the Christmas holidays Somma visited the composer at Sant' Agata, by which time Verdi had finished a first draft of the music. On 14 January 1858, accompanied by Giuseppina and their Maltese terrier, Loulou, Verdi arrived in Naples to deliver the opera to the management of the Teatro San Carlo; it was now called *La vendetta in domino* and set in seventeenth-century Pomerania. On the evening of his arrival, Verdi attended a performance of *I vespri siciliani*, which was being performed under the title of *Batilde di Turenna*!:

> When he arrived in his box, there was a general murmur in the vast auditorium of the San Carlo, and all eyes and opera-glasses were turned in his direction. . . . After Coletti's aria the audience broke into clamorous applause, cheering Maestro Verdi who, touched and grateful, modestly acknowledged the ovation several times.

But after the magnificent duet for Fraschini and Coletti, the applause became quite unrestrained, and the Maestro was prevailed upon by his friends, as well as by his feelings of gratitude, to come down and appear upon the stage where he was called forth, several times with the others, and then alone. In homage to him, the orchestra chose to repeat the overture, following which the celebrated Maestro was called forth two more times, amongst warm, unanimous and resounding applause. Thus the Italian genius, great and sublime, was hailed here in the seat of harmony and song, where Rossini flowered, where Donizetti was crowned with laurel, where Bellini gave his sad melodies to the world. . . .[5]

Behind the scenes, however, trouble was brewing for the new opera. The censors were not satisfied with the fictitious names given to King Gustave III and his assassin, Captain Ankarstroem, or the change of country and century. In Paris, a bomb had been thrown at Napoleon III on his way to the Opéra, an incident which increased the nervousness of the Neapolitan monarchy and its censors. They were most reluctant to approve the subject of the opera, however much its provenance was disguised. This had been known to the management of the San Carlo theatre for many weeks, but it was not until Verdi had been in Naples for several days, wondering why the management was avoiding him, that the impresario found the courage to break the news to the composer. From Naples on 7 February Verdi wrote to Somma:

I'm drowning in a sea of troubles. It's almost certain the censors will forbid our libretto. I don't know why. I was quite right to warn you to avoid every sentence, every word which could offend. They began by objecting to certain phrases and words, and then entire scenes and finally the whole subject. They made the following suggestions but only as a special favour:

(1) Change the hero into an ordinary gentleman, with no suggestion of sovereignty.

(2) Change the wife into a sister.

(3) Alter the scene with the fortune-teller, and put it back to a time when people believed in such things.

(4) No ball.

(5) The murder to be off-stage.

(6) Omit the scene of the drawing of the name.

And so on, and so on, and so on!!

As you can imagine, these changes are out of the question, so no more opera. So the subscribers won't pay the last two instalments, so the government will withdraw the subsidy, so the directors will sue everyone, and already threaten me with damages of 50,000 ducats. What hell! Write and give me your opinion of all this.[6]

An understandable note of slight acerbity is discernible in Somma's reply. 'You ask me for an immediate opinion on the deplorable situation you are in,' he wrote,

> a situation which I had heard about from other sources two days ago. But what sort of opinion do you want from me, I wonder, and on what? A legal opinion about the law suit which the management threatens? But the matter is extremely simple, and your line of defence is self-evident. If the censor, as we both know, approved the first draft of the libretto subject to modifications which were then complied with in our libretto, and if later he forbids the libretto without giving a reason, you cannot be held responsible to anyone at all. But is it possible that you want my opinion on how to revise the libretto, when you tell me that the opera will not be given since the changes asked for by the censor are out of the question?
>
> I am therefore led to believe that your letter is asking me something else, which is not an opinion. Very well, my friend: I will sacrifice all my author's vanity, if this will serve to reconcile you with the San Carlo and the censor.
>
> Make whatever use of my poetry seems best to you. Delete and revise as the censor requires, if there is time, retaining what they permit, and rewriting scenes and dialogue when the censor demands it. Do whatever is necessary to please those gentlemen: *but I insist on two things*: one, that instead of my name on the title page there should appear that of someone else; merely to remain anonymous is no longer sufficient for me, after it has been announced by everyone that I am the author of the libretto; two, that the opera be no longer entitled *La vendetta in domino*, but something else, whatever you like.[7]

Meanwhile, Verdi had been making his own feelings known to the San Carlo management. To the theatre's secretary, Vincenzo Torelli, he wrote on 14 February:

> To you, Secretary to the management of the Royal Theatres, the sole person with whom I have been in correspondence both before and since this ill-fated contract, I address myself, so that you, the principal member of the team of management, will kindly reach some decision concerning our regrettable contretemps. Further changes in the libretto are proposed, and then others, and then others again (it seems to be a joke, not to say a mockery), changes which do nothing but eliminate its character and destroy its effectiveness, after having been already approved, which approval you, in turn, communicated to me.
>
> Put the action back five or six centuries?! What an anachronism! Cut out the scene where the name of the assassin is chosen by drawing lots?! But this is the most powerful and original situation in the drama, and you

expect me to give it up? I have already told you, I will not commit the monstrosities that were committed here with *Rigoletto*. Such things happen because I cannot prevent them. Nor is it any use talking to me about success. If one or two or three numbers, here and there, are applauded, that is not enough to make an opera. On artistic matters I have my ideas, my convictions, which are very clear and very precise, and I cannot, indeed must not, renounce them.[8]

In an attempt to solve the problem, the San Carlo management prepared an altered libretto which met the censor's requirements, called *Adelia degli Adimari* and set in fourteenth-century Florence. Verdi regarded this as a total mutilation of the drama, and thus of his music:

La vendetta in domino consists of 884 verses; in *Adelia* 297 have been changed, many have been added, and a great many have been deleted. I ask further if, in this drama written by the management, there exists, as there does in mine,

The title?	No.
The librettist?	No.
The period?	No.
The place?	No.
The characters?	No.
The situations?	No.
The drawing of lots?	No.
The ball?	No.

No composer who respects his art and himself could or should dishonour himself by accepting, as a subject for music which was written to a completely different plot, these oddities which distort the most obvious principles of dramaturgy and constitute an outrage to the artist's conscience.[9]

The San Carlo threatened legal action against Verdi, whose lawyer issued a counter-claim. The case was settled out of court, with Verdi the winner in that the contract was dissolved, and he was allowed to retain *La vendetta in domino* as his own property to offer elsewhere. In return, he agreed to produce *Simon Boccanegra*, an opera new to Naples, in the autumn.

On 23 April Verdi left Naples and made his way home to Sant' Agata via Genoa and Piacenza. On 12 May he wrote to Clarina Maffei:

I have been back from Naples for the last ten or twelve days, and I would have written to you immediately if I had not had to make a couple of trips to Parma and to Piacenza. Now I am here and, after the excitements of Naples, this deep peace is more dear to me than ever. It is impossible to find an uglier place than here, but on the other hand it is impossible for me to find a place where I can live with greater freedom. Then there is the silence, which gives me time to think. And the absence of uniforms of any colour is also a good thing. I had thought of going to Venice for the bathing season, but they have invited me to write an opera there, and so to avoid being pestered I shall stay at home. I may return to Naples in the autumn, and perhaps go to Rome at carnival time if the censorship there will allow me to stage the opera that I wrote for Naples. If not, so much the better, for then I would not compose anything, not even next carnival. Ever since *Nabucco*, you could say I have not had an hour's peace. Sixteen years in the galleys!

Dear Clarina, tell me all your news, and let me know that you are well. Write to me about what is happening in Milan, and what life is like there now. It has been ten years since I last saw that city, which I loved so much, and where I spent my youth and began my career! How many memories, both cherished and sad!! Who knows when I shall see it again![10]

Verdi had already been in touch with Rome regarding the possibility of staging *La vendetta in domino* there. He had, in fact, offered his opera to the Teatro Apollo while the Neapolitan lawyers were still arguing. Having remembered that Scribe's play *Gustave III* had been performed in Rome, and that the subject was therefore presumably acceptable to the censorship authority there, Verdi had written to his friend the sculptor Vincenzo Luccardi to ask for a copy of the placard announcing Scribe's *Gustave III*. His first intention had been to use this as evidence of the innocence and harmlessness of Scribe's libretto, but when it became clear that the Neapolitan authorities would not be moved, he approached, through Luccardi, the Rome impresario Vincenzo Jacovacci and offered the opera to him for his Teatro Apollo. Before he left Naples, Verdi had signed a contract with Jacovacci to have *La vendetta in domino* staged in Rome.

However, all was not yet plain sailing. Jacovacci must have miscalculated the weight of his influence with the Vatican censors, who now made it clear that they objected to aspects of the opera's libretto. 'In Rome, *Gustave III* is allowed as a spoken drama, but the same subject is not allowed as an opera libretto!!!', Verdi wrote angrily to Jacovacci. 'This is really very strange! I respect your superiors, and have nothing to say against them. But, if I have refused to stage the opera in Naples with an altered libretto, I can hardly allow it in Rome, if they, too, want to alter the libretto.'[11] His immediate reaction was to suggest an annulment of his contract with Rome.

Jacovacci managed to persuade Verdi not to act precipitately. He gave the composer precise details of the changes required by the censor, and Verdi passed these on to Somma who was, by now, thoroughly disenchanted with the entire business:

> In your letter, you ask me if I can write other verses with these changes in mind, but in a manner that will not offend the susceptibilities of the Roman censor. How can I do this? As long as a change has some element of reason, whatever its motive, some kind of compromise might be found to satisfy the censor. But when, instead of reasonable change, there is capriciousness, ignorance, and a mad desire to upset everything, then in all honesty I can only give up any hope of succeeding.[12]

Somma ended by again telling Verdi to do as he wished with the libretto provided that the librettist's identity was suppressed, and Verdi, unusually for him, decided not to continue the struggle against censorship. He would, he told Somma, prefer the opera to be staged rather than not staged, and Rome was, in his view, preferable to other cities. The censor had now approved the subject and most of the details of the plot, but was insisting that the action be set somewhere outside Europe. 'What would you think of North America at the time of the English domination? Or, if not America, then some other place, the Caucasus perhaps?' Verdi asked his librettist,[13] who wearily agreed to the action being set at the end of the seventeenth century in Boston, Massachusetts, a colony where the Salem trials of 1692 clearly showed that belief in witches was then still alive.

There were still, however, several of the censor's queries to be dealt with. On 6 August Verdi wrote to a now completely exasperated Somma:

> Arm yourself with courage and patience. Particularly with patience. As you will see from the enclosed letter from Vasselli [Antonio Vasselli, Donizetti's brother-in-law, who lived in Rome], the censor has sent a list of all the lines he disapproves of. If, on reading this, you feel a rush of blood to the head, lay it down and try it again after you have eaten and slept well. Remember that, under present conditions, our best plan is to present the opera in Rome. The lines and expressions deleted by the censor are numerous, but it could have been worse. In any case, it is better like this, since now we know how to proceed, what we can leave in, and what must go. Also, a great many lines would have had to be changed, since the King is now only a Governor. Don't worry about the gallows in Act II, I'll try to obtain permission for it. Cheer up, alter the lines marked, and try to arrange that you have fifteen or twenty days free during the carnival season so that you can come to Rome where I hope we shall have a good time together.[14]

In September Somma sent Verdi a revised libretto with all the required changes made. Gustave III of Sweden was now Riccardo, 'Conte di Warvick' [*sic*] and Governor of Boston, and his assassin was no longer a Swedish army officer but Riccardo's secretary, Renato, a Creole. The fortune-teller was a negress, and the conspirators, Counts Horn and Ribbing, became Samuel and Tom, enemies of the Governor. The opera took its new title, *Un ballo in maschera*, from the sub-title of Scribe's original libretto, *Gustave III ou Le bal masqué*. The libretto was now finally approved by the censors, and Verdi put the finishing touches to his score in the second half of September before departing with Giuseppina for Genoa, and proceeding by sea via Rome, to Naples, where he was to fulfil his promise to produce *Simon Boccanegra*. Cesare de Sanctis was instructed to find an apartment in Naples with a view of the sea (required by Giuseppina) in a quiet location (required by Verdi) and with a courtyard or garden (required by Loulou, the Maltese terrier).

During the few hours he spent in Genoa waiting for the ship, Verdi took the opportunity to reply frankly to Léon Escudier, who had enquired if he would be interested in writing another work for the Paris Opéra:

> You speak to me of the theatre? . . . and of composing for the Opéra?!! . . . You?! . . . Let us speak openly, and let me say everything I feel.
> 1. I am neither sufficiently rich nor sufficiently poor to write for your principal theatre. Not sufficiently poor to need those meagre earnings; not sufficiently rich to lead a comfortable life in a country whose living expenses are very high.
> 2. For the Opéra, I wrote *Vespri* and had two other operas translated, with an outcome neither too hostile nor too favourable. If they hope for, or expect, anything better from me, they are mistaken. Now, as then (I tell you in confidence, in your ear), I have some facility in making up *tunes*, but it would seem that this is not the right merchandise for the Opéra. Later, perhaps, I will no longer have the ability to make them up, then I too will write some orchestral *frum frum*. You shall see! In *Vespri* there are two or three real *tunes*, whether good or bad ones. Perhaps this is the reason the score lies dormant. I don't say this as a complaint (Heaven forbid!) . . .[15]

After the successful performance of *Boccanegra* in Naples, Verdi and Giuseppina remained in the city for some weeks, enjoying the mild Neapolitan winter, until 10 January when they left for Rome and rehearsals of *Un ballo in maschera*. Verdi was now at the height of his fame. Abroad, his operas were being performed all over Europe as well as in the New World, while in Italy he was revered as the greatest living composer and as the voice of Italian independence. In Naples, his barber sold locks of the composer's hair; in Rome, they scrawled on public walls the words 'Viva Verdi', the composer's name an acronym for '*Vittorio Emanuele, Re D'Italia*'. (Vittorio Emanuele II was King of Piedmont–Sardinia, but it was the hope of most liberals that he would become the first king of a united Italy.)

The sea journey from Naples to Civitavecchia in January 1859 was a rough one. 'We spent an infernal night', Verdi wrote to de Sanctis on 10 January, 'and we reached harbour this morning at ten-thirty, that is almost nineteen hours at sea! Peppina was very ill; the great Loulou also suffered; I alone gave nothing to the sea. But what *illness*, and those sixteen hours in a berth, unable to move! Raging, cold wind, and water everywhere.'[16]

After resting for a day, the shaken travellers went on to Rome by coach, and Verdi immediately plunged into rehearsals for *Un ballo in maschera*. Luccardi had rented for them a house which Giuseppina described in a letter to de Sanctis as ugly. She also predicted a poor performance of the opera, the singers being in her view for the most part mediocre, and she claimed that Verdi was tired of the theatre and wanted only to be rid of the present opera which had been occupying him for nearly eighteen months.

At the premiere on 17 February 1859, the leading roles were sung by Eugenia Julienne-Dejean (Amelia), Gaetano Fraschini (Riccardo), Leone Giraldoni (Renato) and Zelinda Sbriscia (Ulrica, the fortune-teller). The opera was a huge success despite some shortcomings in performance, and it has remained one of Verdi's most popular works. In recent years, producers have begun to stage it in its proper setting, eighteenth-century Stockholm, with the original historical characters, Gustave III and his enemies. (The character of Amelia, the assassin's wife and Gustave's lover, has no basis in historical fact: the king's extra-marital activities were predominantly homosexual.)

The opera as performed in Rome in 1859 tells the story of Riccardo, Governor of Boston at the end of the seventeenth century, who falls in love with Amelia, wife of his secretary and close friend, Renato. His love is returned, but Amelia's conscience troubles her and she consults Ulrica, a black sorceress, who sends her to gather at midnight a certain herb which will cause her to forget Riccardo. Overhearing Amelia's conversation with Ulrica, Riccardo follows her to the spot where she is to gather the herb, by the gallows outside the city. Renato, who has come in search of Riccardo to warn him of the approach of conspirators, is requested by the Governor to escort the veiled lady back to the town without attempting to discover her identity. Riccardo leaves, but Renato and Amelia find themselves surrounded by the conspirators and Amelia's identity is revealed. Renato swears vengeance on his friend Riccardo, and joins the plot to assassinate him. At a grand masked ball, Riccardo is stabbed by Renato. As he lies dying, Riccardo declares Amelia innocent and forgives Renato.

Out of all the censorship difficulties, the alterations, reworkings and compromises, one of Verdi's finest operas was born. *Un ballo in maschera* shows, musically and dramatically, none of the scars one might in the circumstances have expected to find. It is one of the composer's middle-period masterpieces, a work whose characters are rich in humanity, and whose melodies combine the warmth and vigour of the old Verdi with the lightness and elegance that had entered his work with *La traviata*. Somma's libretto, if one forgets history and King Gustave III of Sweden, is tautly constructed and ripe for music, though flowery in style and less direct in manner than the work of Verdi's more professional collaborators such as Piave and Cammarano. The music which clothes the libretto is not only sumptuously scored but also perfectly attuned to the style of its subject and impeccable in character. In addition to the drama of the events, there is a great deal of laughter in the score, ranging from the quick gaiety of Oscar, the page, through Riccardo's amused irony, to the mocking taunts of the conspirators, all depicted with Verdi's characteristic melodic prodigality.

Chapter Thirteen

1859–61

Three days after the premiere of *Un ballo in maschera*, the Accademia Filarmonica Romana elected Verdi as an honorary member. He and Giuseppina remained in Rome for a further three weeks, during which time the impresario Jacovacci attempted to persuade the composer to sign a contract for another new opera. Verdi was now forty-six years of age; he had composed twenty-three operas during the previous twenty years, his 'years in the galleys', and he was tired. He could now afford to retire and live the life of a gentleman farmer, and this he felt inclined to do. He announced, if not to the world at large then at least to his friends and business acquaintances, that he had finished with composition. He was to live for another forty-two years, but during those years he wrote no more than five operas (three of them for theatres outside Italy), and all five had to be virtually dragged out of him. Italy's greatest composer for the theatre had, it seems, lost interest in the theatre.

Verdi's first announcement of his intention to retire seems to have been made at a dinner party in his Rome apartment on 11 March 1859, the eve of his and Giuseppina's departure from the city. Their guests at dinner that evening included Giuseppe Cencetti, a theatrical producer and journalist who, some days later, published this account of the occasion under the title 'Maestro Verdi and the impresario Jacovacci':

> The morning before the day fixed for his departure from Rome, Verdi graciously invited to dinner the impresario Vincenzo Jacovacci, who gladly appeared at the appointed hour at Verdi's house, believing perhaps that such a show of kindness augured well for the future of his theatrical plans. The only people Jacovacci found present at the illustrious Maestro's farewell banquet were, apart from the latter's dear spouse, the conductor

Emilio Angelini, that fine sculptor Vincenzo Luccardi (an intimate friend of Verdi's) and the undersigned producer. We spent part of the dinner happily discussing the dearth of good singing-actors, and the difficulty of finding libretti with impact and dramatic situations, despite the abundance of fine poets in Italy. Contrary to his custom, Jacovacci did not speak, and contributed only monosyllabically to the discussion; he seemed to be quite engrossed in the victuals when suddenly he put down his fork, stared with his sparkling eyes at his distinguished host who sat opposite, and exclaimed: 'Maestro, I shall send you as many blank contracts as you need to form a good company of singers, and you shall engage the artists you prefer for any new opera you compose.'

This unexpected apostrophe was followed by a prolonged exclamation of 'Splendid!' which issued simultaneously from the lips of the three other guests, and was soon repeated by Verdi himself, who added: 'The scheme is splendid and does you honour, but – but I no longer compose.'

'But Maestro,' came Jacovacci's unflustered reply, 'these are cruel words for the audiences who so yearn for and applaud your music.'

'I am most grateful to them, but I no longer compose.'

'But Maestro, this is a terrible thing for us poor impresarios who won't know which way to turn to – '

'Make money,' the other guests interrupted in chorus.

'I am sorry,' replied Verdi, 'but I no longer compose.'

'Take care that I don't have this barbaric decision of yours printed in the press,' added the impresario, casting me a meaningful glance.

'Go ahead, Cencetti,' replied the Maestro, who had noticed Jacovacci's glance, 'but I no longer compose.'

'This is most distressing,' Jacovacci murmured, and sighed; but he soon recovered his good humour and was not the least witty of the small gathering, so that the dinner ended as happily as it had begun. Taking leave of the illustrious composer, Jacovacci shook his hand with warmth and respect, saying: 'I wish you a long and happy life, and I shall pray that the balmy air of Busseto's fields might soothe your mind, relieving it of a melancholy which, if not prejudicial to your fame (since that is now immortal), is inflicting serious damage on opera houses and – '

'There is no point in proceeding, since I – '

'No longer compose! I've understood perfectly! Yet since "Wise men change their thoughts when changing house" I beg you to remember the need for my project.' And with these words the zealous impresario, bowing deeply, walked to the door. As he brushed past me, I whispered in his ear: 'Don't lose heart, true genius is inexhaustible and cannot resist the call of inspiration.'

'I know, I know,' Jacovacci grinned. 'When I speak, there's always a reason!' And, rubbing his hands like a satisfied man, he took his leave of the celebrated Maestro.[1]

Verdi and Giuseppina arrived home at the Villa Sant' Agata on 20 March. Verdi may have busied himself with crops and livestock for a few weeks, but on 29 April international politics intruded. Cavour, the Prime Minister of Piedmont, had for some time been working towards the unification of the Italian states under King Vittorio Emanuele, and as part of his tactics he had been trying to provoke Austria into attacking Piedmont. In January a defensive alliance between Piedmont and France had been signed. On 23 April Austria delivered an ultimatum, calling on Piedmont to disarm. Cavour rejected the ultimatum on 26 April, Napoleon III sent French troops to Piedmont under the terms of the alliance, and on 29 April war broke out between Piedmont and Austria when the Austrian forces crossed the river Ticino and invaded Piedmont, which was precisely what Cavour had hoped they would do.

The battle raged only a few miles from Sant' Agata; cannon fire could be heard from Piacenza, eighteen miles away. In June, Verdi initiated a subscription fund for the wounded and for the families of those killed.

The battle of Solferino on 24 June, in which more than 300,000 men were engaged, proved indecisive, but the Austrian army was in better condition than the allied forces of France and Italy, and on 12 July Napoleon III signed a secret treaty with Austria, under the terms of which Austria and France agreed to favour the creation of a confederation of Italian states with the Pope as honorary President. Austria would cede Lombardy to France on the understanding that France would in turn hand it over to Piedmont, but Austria would continue to maintain its dominion over Venice.

When this treaty, arranged between France and Austria, was presented to Vittorio Emanuele, Cavour attempted to dissuade the King from signing it. However, Vittorio Emanuele really had no option. He signed, and Cavour offered his resignation which was accepted. To most Italian states, with the exception of Milan, what had happened seemed a terrible betrayal on the part of their allies and their rulers. This was a time of great confusion, and of bickering among the various Italian states. In August, Verdi's district, the Duchy of Parma, joined with neighbouring Modena and announced an election, with universal male suffrage, for an Assembly in Parma.

Also in August, another event of some importance to Verdi occurred. On the 29th, he and Giuseppina were married secretly in the Piedmontese village of Collonges-sous-Salève, near the Swiss border of the province of Savoy. (The following year, Collonges and the whole of Savoy became part of France.) They had gone to Geneva to meet the Abbé Mermillod, the rector of the church of Notre Dame, who then accompanied them in a carriage from Geneva to the parish church at Collonges where, as Verdi wrote later, the local priest was sent for a walk and the marriage solemnized by the Abbé.

This event was not mentioned by Verdi in any of his correspondence at the time, and, from the tone of a letter he wrote nine years later when he was attempting to establish that the marriage was valid under Italian law, the ceremony seems to have meant little to him. Why, after they had been living together for twelve years, Verdi and Giuseppina Strepponi should have felt the need to be legally united, is not known. The uncertainty of life during a time of war may have been a contributing factor, but it is more likely that, knowing that he might soon be entering public and political life, Verdi thought it prudent to accept the conventional moral view and legalize his union.

In the election for the Assembly in Parma, Verdi was asked to represent Busseto and agreed to do so: not surprisingly, he was elected. 'The honour which my fellow citizens have conferred upon me as their representative at the Assembly of the provinces of Parma makes me both proud and extremely grateful,' Verdi wrote to the Mayor of Busseto the day after the election. 'Though my meagre talents, my studies, and the art which I profess do not make me very suitable for this kind of office, I hope I shall be fortified by the great love I feel, and have always felt, for our noble and unhappy Italy.'[2]

The Assembly met in Parma on 7 September, and five days later voted unanimously in favour of Parma's annexation to Piedmont. On 15 September a delegation whose members included Verdi presented a petition to King Vittorio Emanuele II in Turin, calling for the annexation. It was during this visit to Turin that Verdi met the statesman Cavour through the British minister, Sir James Hudson. From Busseto some days later, Verdi wrote to Cavour, confessing how moved he had been at their meeting, and calling Cavour 'the supreme citizen, he whom every Italian will have to call father of our country'.[3] It was Cavour's support of the King which had led Verdi from being a republican to being, as he now was, a loyal subject of the King, in whom he saw the only hope for a united and independent Italy.

There was still unrest in the Parma region where, in the city itself, a reactionary colonel had been killed by the mob. Local communities were setting up armed guards, and Verdi found himself involved in ordering 172 rifles from Genoa for the use of the Parma militia. When the rifles failed to arrive, he enlisted the aid of Angelo Mariani, who was in Genoa conducting opera, in checking the initial order, tracing the whereabouts of the rifles, and examining them to ensure that they were the right kind of weapon for the purpose.

Verdi's interest in guns in the winter of 1859–60 was not limited to rifles for purposes of civil defence. In February he wrote to Léon Escudier in Paris:

Since I no longer manufacture notes, I plant cabbages and beans, etc. etc., but, as this occupation no longer suffices for me, I have taken up shooting!!!!!! In other words, when I see a bird, *Bang*! I shoot. If I hit it, that's fine. If not, forget it. I have a supply of good Saint-Etienne guns, but now I've decided I would like a double-barrelled *Le Faucheux*, Double System, in other words the *old system* loading with powder and shot, as well as the so-called *Le Faucheux system*, with cartridges. . . . Good hunters shoot straight, even with poor weapons, but a Master of Music needs a gun that shoots straight by itself.[4]

The worst weeks of the winter, from 3 January to 11 March, were spent by the Verdis in Genoa, where they stayed at the Hotel Croce di Malta in Via Carlo Alberto, Mariani having failed to find a suitable house or apartment for them. When they left to return to Busseto, Mariani was enjoined to continue the search for a permanent winter home for them in Genoa. Verdi and Giuseppina were by now close friends of the distinguished conductor, and Verdi was never unwilling to make great demands on the time and energy of his friends. ' Dear Mariani,' he wrote from Busseto on 21 March,

When you were only a musician, I would not have dared write you a letter like this one, but now that you have become a capitalist, a speculator and a usurer, I am giving you several commissions for which I shall reimburse you in a few days (only a few days), on which you will have to spend a few hundred francs, which you will receive back with interest, broker's fee, discount charges and similar thieveries etc. etc.

First of all, go and get my portrait, and pay everything according to the terms of the letter I enclose.

Secondly, make Maestro Cambini take you to that particular gardener, and buy 10 *Magnolia Grandiflora*, about one and a half metres high, but in no case less than one metre. They are to be well packed in straw, but not until the day before departure.

Thirdly, go to Noledi, and ask him if he will exchange my St Etienne rifle for his Liège, the one I like which is a 13–14 calibre. You know the one, and I'll also give him four gold napoleons. You can assure him that my rifle is as good as new, for I have only used it during part of December, and both the wood and the iron look as good as new. But if Noledi should wish to see it first, write to me immediately, so that I can put it in a little box and send it by train. I should like you, however, to try out the Liège rifle for me and make sure that it shoots straight and doesn't kick. It will need to be tested with bullets five or six times.

The snow has all gone. However, if you wait a few days more, the ground will have dried and we can go into the woods.

Bring everything with you, and put it all on the train as luggage. You will take a ticket to Piacenza, and then from Piacenza to Borgo San Donnino. You will leave at ten in the morning, and arrive at Piacenza and be in Borgo after four. You will find a carriage for Busseto, but, as this waits for the coach from Parma, it thus leaves Borgo very late. You can wait for the Borgo coach, or take an express carriage which will bring you to Sant' Agata, or write to me the day before and I shall come to Borgo, or send my horses. Is that clear?

Please take care with everything, particularly the rifle, and if, when you test it, it seems to be really superior, don't worry about spending a little more money on it.[5]

Poor Mariani did his best to satisfy Verdi, shopping around in Genoa to find the cheapest magnolias of the right size, collecting the statuette of the composer, and discovering that the gun Verdi wanted had already been sold. Unfortunately, the magnolias were too tall for the luggage compartment of the train, and Mariani was advised by the station master to take them to the goods station the next morning before seven and have them put on an open truck covered with tarpaulin to prevent the straw wrappings catching fire from the sparks of the engine. At this point, Verdi increased his order of magnolias from ten to twelve!

Mariani despatched the magnolias and the statuette to Verdi, as well as a box which had arrived in Genoa from Naples, containing books and pictures from the apartment Verdi and Giuseppina had occupied there, and in due course the conductor himself arrived at Sant' Agata to join Verdi in a spot of shooting. Giuseppina was sceptical of the prowess of both men. 'Mariani is coming to Sant' Agata after Easter,' she wrote to a friend, 'and then Verdi and he will start their walks in the woods near the Po, after the game. However, if we eat woodcock, pheasant etc. at home, it will be because I have been able to find some to buy in the market.'[6]

On 12 March the citizens of Parma voted again for annexation to Piedmont, and the Busseto Town Council agreed to demonstrate their devotion to King Vittorio Emanuele by presenting him with a cannon. 'I wish', wrote Verdi to the councillors, 'that every town in Italy would imitate your example, for it is not with celebrations and illuminations but with arms and with soldiers that we will become strong and respected masters in our own house.'[7] He regretted, however, that he could not accede to their request that he compose a patriotic hymn on the poem he had been sent, not only because he felt unsuited to this type of composition, whose usefulness he doubted, but also because he did not wish to give offence to the city governments of Turin and Milan, whose similar requests he had refused.

In January 1860, Cavour had been recalled to power by Vittorio Emanuele. When Cavour had met Napoleon III secretly in 1858, the two men had reached agreement that in return for support against Austria, the French were to be given Savoy, and perhaps Nice as well. On 24 March 1860, Savoy and Nice were duly annexed to France; in May, Garibaldi with a band of a thousand men began his own contribution towards the unification of Italy by invading Sicily and, four months later, Naples, thus paving the way for Vittorio Emanuele to become King of Italy in 1861.

Meanwhile, Verdi continued to show no interest in returning to composition, busying himself instead with making improvements to Sant' Agata. These were costly, so he wrote to Tito Ricordi in May in order to extract some of the royalties he was owed:

> For several years I have lived in the country in a hut in such poor condition, so humble, so indecent I would almost say, that I am ashamed to allow even my most intimate friends to see it. You, who have seen it, will know I am telling the truth. For three years, I have been wanting to have it renovated, not to turn it into a palace or a villa but simply a decent and habitable home.
>
> So far, various circumstances have prevented me from carrying out this plan of mine, but work began on it some days ago (modest work which will not cost me more than a few of the more than 10,000 francs you owe me), and I would not like now to suspend it, nor could I, because of the commitment I have already made to the workmen. So you see that I cannot do without this 10,000 francs. All I can suggest is that you pay it to me, not all at once, but in four equal instalments on the first of each month, beginning on June 1.[8]

In response to good wishes sent by Piave for his birthday in October, Verdi wrote to his old collaborator:

> I was unable to answer your very dear letter because I had rheumatism in my right arm. Now, if I am not well, I am at least better, and I thank you very, very much for your birthday wishes on 9 October, and somewhat less for your congratulations on the success of *Ballo* [which had been staged in Bologna]. You know, I have never been very much affected by this kind of business, and now I feel so indifferent it is unbelievable. If people knew, they would call for me to be crucified, and they would accuse me of being ungrateful, or of not loving my art.
>
> But no, I have adored and I do adore this art, and when I am alone and occupied with my notes, then my heart throbs, tears stream from my eyes, and my emotion and pleasure are indescribable. But when I think that these poor notes of mine must then be flung before beings without intelligence, before a publisher who sells them to serve for the amusement and the sport of the mob, oh, then I no longer love anything! Let's not talk about it. . . . Write to me often, and love me. . . .[9]

Verdi was, perhaps, beginning to feel restless away from the ceaseless activity of the opera house, the quarrels with managements and censors, the rush to meet deadlines. At the beginning of December he travelled alone to Genoa, leaving Giuseppina to cope with the upheaval of rebuilding at Sant' Agata. He planned to be away for about two months, but in fact returned after five days, perhaps because Giuseppina had not been in good health.

In January he left Sant' Agata again, to visit Cavour in Turin. Cavour had decided that the time had come for elections to be held for Italy's first national parliament, and it was widely rumoured that Verdi, one of the best-loved and most important citizens of the country, would be obliged to stand for election to the Chamber of Deputies. It was in order to avoid doing anything of the kind that Verdi wished to see Cavour. He intended to explain that his only value was as an artist and that he had no head for politics. However, he was persuaded by Cavour that it was his duty to add lustre to the first Italian parliament by his presence.

While Verdi was away, Giovanni Minghelli-Vaini, member of a liberal family from Modena and an acquaintance of the Verdis, wrote to enquire if Verdi intended to stand for election, as he, Minghelli-Vaini, wished to represent Busseto. He was assured by Giuseppina that Verdi had no intention of putting himself forward, and was disconcerted later to find that this was not the case. He wrote a somewhat aggrieved letter to Verdi, who replied:

It was not between one glass and the next, but at that time when one drinks at most a cup of coffee that the business, unsought by me, of my nomination to parliament was discussed. My journey to Turin had no other purpose than my desire to free myself of it, which you know. I did not succeed, and I am most desolate, particularly since you are so much more used to parliamentary battles than an artist who has nothing in his favour but his poor name.

I proposed you, and spoke warmly for you in Busseto, in the knowledge that I would be procuring for my country a real Italian, an honest man, and a Deputy whose enlightenment would help our good cause. I have not put myself forward, I shall not put myself forward, nor make any move to have myself nominated. Although the sacrifice will be a heavy one for me, I shall, however, accept if I am nominated, and you know the reasons that force me to do so. I have definitely decided, however, to resign as soon as I can. This letter, which I authorize you to show to anyone who dares to cast injurious aspersions upon you, must suffice to justify you, and to restore you to a state of perfect calm. As for the remedy you suggest to me, that I should get myself nominated in another electoral district, forgive me, but this is against my principles. If I were to do that, I should be *putting myself forward* for election, and I repeat for the hundredth time, *I may be forced to accept* but I will not put myself forward or offer myself to another district.

If you succeed in winning a majority of votes over me, becoming nominated and thus freeing me from this imposition, I shall not be able to find words sufficient to thank you for this welcome service, and you will be a great acquisition for the Chamber, will give yourself pleasure, and give the very greatest pleasure to G. Verdi.[10]

Verdi was elected on 3 February 1861 by a margin of 339 to 206, and he and Giuseppina went to Turin where the first Italian parliament was to meet on 18 February. Parliament was opened by the King with a speech in which he paid tribute to the part played by Garibaldi, as well as by France, in the unification of Italy. A month later, Vittorio Emanuele, King of Piedmont, was formally proclaimed Vittorio Emanuele, King of Italy. Verdi attended the first sessions of the new parliament regularly, always voting exactly as Cavour did. 'In that way,' he remarked, 'I can be quite certain of not making any mistakes.' The question of whether to continue the Austrian custom of subsidizing theatres and music schools was being considered, and here Verdi was able to speak on a subject in which he was interested and of which he had expert knowledge. He advised that the leading opera houses, those of Rome, Milan and Naples, should have their permanent ensembles maintained by the government. 'Had Cavour lived', Verdi wrote later, 'the plan might have been realized. With other ministers it was impossible.'[11]

On 6 June, Cavour died. Verdi organized at his own expense a memorial service in Busseto at which, as he wrote to his friend Arrivabene, 'The priest officiated without charge, which is quite something. I was present at the sad ceremony in full mourning, but the real mourning was in my heart. Between us, I was not able to restrain my tears, and I cried like a child. Poor Cavour! and poor us.'[12]

The death of Cavour was a disaster for the newly created country of Italy, and for Verdi it meant the personal loss of someone he had always revered. He had entered politics only because Cavour wished him to, and though he served his full time as a Deputy, he became considerably less assiduous in his attendance at sessions of parliament. Four years later, he refused to stand for another term; shortly before announcing this, he had, in February 1865, written to Piave:

> You ask me for news and information about my public life. My public life does not exist. It's true I'm a Deputy, but only by mistake. Nevertheless, I'll tell you the story of my Deputyship. In September 1860 I was in Turin. I had never seen Count Cavour and was most anxious to get to know him. I asked the English Ambassador there to introduce me. Since the treaty of Villafranca the Count had been living on one of his country estates, far removed from public affairs. I think it was at Vercellese, and one fine morning we visited him there. After that time, I had occasion to write to him and to receive a few letters from him, in one of which he exhorted me to accept the candidacy for a Deputyship, which my fellow citizens had offered me and which I had refused. His letter was most amiable, so much so that I did not see how I could answer it simply by saying 'no'. I decided to go to Turin; I visited him one day in December at 6 o'clock in the morning, in 12 or 14 degrees of frost. I had prepared my speech which seemed to me to be a masterpiece, and I said everything that was in my mind. He listened to me attentively; and, when I described my ineptitude for the position of Deputy, and my outbursts of impatience at the long speeches you have to put up with occasionally in the Chamber, I did so in such a bizarre fashion that he uttered a great roar of laughter. Then he began to refute my reasons, one by one, and said to me things which seemed to make sense. So I said, 'Very well, dear Count, I accept, but on condition that I can resign after a few months.' He was agreeable so long as I informed him first.
>
> I became a Deputy, and at first I frequented the Chamber. Then came that solemn sitting in which Rome was proclaimed capital of Italy. I voted, then approached the Count and said to him, 'Now it seems to me time to say farewell to these benches.'

'No,' he replied, 'wait until we go to Rome.'
'Are we going there?'
'Yes.'
'When?'
'Oh, when, when!'
'Well, meanwhile I'm going to the country.'
'Farewell, take care of yourself. Farewell.'

These were the last words he spoke to me. A few weeks later he died. After a few months I left for Russia, then went to London, from there to Paris and back to Russia, then to Madrid, then travelled through Andalusia and returned to Paris where I stayed a few months for business reasons. I stayed away from the Chamber for more than two years, and after that I attended on very few occasions. Several times I tried to offer my resignation, but on one occasion they said it was not a good time to have new elections, at other times there were other reasons, so I'm still a Deputy, without the slightest desire or taste for it, with no aptitude or talent for it, and completely lacking in the patience which is so necessary there. That's all. I repeat, if anyone needed to write about my career as a member of parliament, he would only have to print in the centre of a beautiful piece of paper, 'The 450 are really only 449, for Verdi as a Deputy doesn't exist.'[13]

Chapter Fourteen

1861–63

One of the reasons for Verdi's withdrawal from the Italian opera scene after the premiere of *Un ballo in maschera* in 1859 was undoubtedly his conviction that there was a dearth of good, or at least of suitable singers for the kind of music he wished to compose. Writing some months after the premiere to the Rome impresario Jacovacci, who had apparently gone into print to defend Verdi's opera against attacks in the press, Verdi said it was best not to read the newspapers. 'But you must admit', he continued,

> that if anyone or anything needed defending during the carnival season, it was that wretched company you presented me with. Put your hand on your heart and confess that I was a model of rare self-denial in not taking my score and going off in search of dogs, whose barking would have been preferable to the sounds of the singers you offered me.[1]

When he was not playing the role of the farmer or member of parliament, Verdi's thoughts must have strayed back to the world of opera. During the more boring debates in parliament, he amused himself by scribbling musical jokes on parliamentary paper, and a conversation noted by his fellow-Deputy Quintino Sella, whom Verdi sat next to in the chamber, suggests that he still regarded himself as a composer. When Sella asked Verdi how ideas for music came to him, whether he first thought out the principal theme and later combined it with accompanying voices, the composer did not reply, 'I no longer compose.' Instead he said, 'No, no, the idea presents itself complete, and above all I feel the colour of which you speak, whether it should be the flute or the violin. My difficulty is to write it down quickly enough, to express the musical idea in its entirety as it comes into my mind.'[2]

Even before his election to parliament, Verdi had been considering the possibility of composing another opera. In December 1860, while he was absent in Turin being persuaded by Cavour to allow himself to be nominated, Giuseppina received a letter from an old friend of hers, Mauro Corticelli, who was touring Russia as secretary to the actress Adelaide Ristori. Enclosed with Corticelli's letter was another, addressed to Verdi, from the celebrated tenor Enrico Tamberlick. At the age of forty, Tamberlick was at the height of his career as a dramatic tenor. He appeared regularly abroad, notably in London, where he had sung Manrico in the first English production of *Il trovatore* in 1855, and in St Petersburg where he sang for several seasons between 1850 and 1863. Indeed, after the early years of his career he rarely appeared in his native Italy.

Tamberlick's letter, written from St Petersburg, was an invitation to Verdi, at the behest of Sabouroff, director of the Imperial Theatres, to compose an opera for St Petersburg. 'Here,' Tamberlick wrote,

> the management offers you all the advantages that you can wish for, if you agree to write a work for the coming season. You would be free to choose the subject and the librettist, and to decide on the conditions. The opera would remain your property. The public here adores you, without ever having seen you, and they would be overjoyed to have you here in person. I cannot tell you with what celebrations the artists would receive you.[3]

Giuseppina was somewhat startled to read in Corticelli's letter that the winter temperature at St Petersburg could easily drop to twenty-two below zero, but she promised to try to persuade Verdi 'to expose his nose to the danger of freezing in Russia'. Indeed, she seems to have been excited at the prospect of a winter in the far north, for she told Corticelli, 'If I don't succeed by eloquence, I shall employ a method which I have been assured succeeds even at the gates of Paradise with St Peter: that is, I shall insist, and go on making a nuisance of myself until I get what I want.'[4]

Whether because she was especially persuasive or because he was already missing the theatre and his psychosomatic birth-pangs, Verdi agreed to accept the commission. The subject he chose was Victor Hugo's *Ruy Blas*, but this play about a valet who becomes not only the lover of the empress, but also the prime minister of his country, invested the common man with too great a dignity and nobility to commend itself to the Russian authorities. In Turin for a session of parliament in March 1861 Verdi received a telegram from Tamberlick informing him that *Ruy Blas* was out of the question, despite his having been promised *carte blanche* in the choice of subject. In due course the composer replied to the effect that he had been glancing through play after play in the hope of finding another subject but so far without success. He would not sign a contract until he had found a subject which he liked, and which would be both suitable for the artists available in St Petersburg and acceptable to the authorities. He would go on searching, but as time was running out it would be wise not to expect an opera for the coming season. Verdi ended his letter by suggesting that, if Tamberlick intended to return to Italy after the current season in St Petersburg, perhaps they could meet and discuss the matter. Instead, Tamberlick sent his young brother Achille to Turin in April, empowered to negotiate regarding *Ruy Blas*. The Russians, it seems, were in the last resort willing to accept a subject distasteful to them for the sake of having Verdi compose for their theatre. Giuseppina, who was in Turin with her husband at the time of the younger Tamberlick's visit, wrote to Corticelli:

> He arrived and, seeing the terrain not too favourably disposed, swore to conquer, despite the fact that Verdi, taking advantage of the veto imposed on his subject by that famous telegram, was much more concerned with the Chamber of Deputies than the theatre. He then embarked quietly on his mission, rectifying the telegram's mistake, and declaring with the utmost calm that Verdi could set to music *Ruy Blas* or anything he liked, since he had been instructed to agree to every possible condition Verdi might require, apart from insisting that Tsar Alexander declare a republic in Russia.
>
> Verdi scratched his head, pointing out this difficulty with *Ruy Blas* and that difficulty with other plays he had glanced at, and mentioned that a certain play he had once read, and liked, could not be found. That was enough, and soon we were chasing round the bookshops and second-hand dealers of Turin, leaving no corner unexplored. Nothing! Not to be found! In the end it was granted to Verdi (who, to be fair, was as active as the rest of us, since he saw no right and proper way of avoiding it) to seize by the scruff of the neck a certain person who was going to Milan, the only place where it would be possible to find the play, and from whom in fact he received it after twenty-four hours, to the great relief of Tamberlick who, although he affirmed, with the greatest pleasure in the world, that he liked Turin and would gladly stay there for a month, nevertheless hurried off as soon as the Gordian knot had been untied, and will have stopped, I think, only when he got to Paris.

So now it is ninety per cent certain that Verdi will write for St

Petersburg. This being the probability, I have already begun to have dresses, petticoats, vests and shirts lined with padding and trimmed with fur. I do not consider at all that, before we arrive in Russia, the month of July must be got through here: the idea of the cold we have to suffer next winter puts out of my head the idea of the heat we shall probably have to suffer this summer.[5]

Giuseppina does not mention the title of the play in her letter to Corticelli, but clearly it was *Don Alvaro o la fuerza del sino* (Don Alvaro or The Power of Fate) by Angel Perez de Saavedra, Duke of Rivas, which in due course was turned by Piave into the libretto of *La forza del destino*. A contract naming *Don Alvaro* as the subject of the opera was prepared in Paris in June, and by mid-July Piave was in Busseto to discuss and work on the opera with Verdi.

The contract which Verdi signed reads as follows:

The Management of the Imperial Russian Theatres engages Maestro Chevalier Verdi to write an opera for the Imperial Theatre of St Petersburg on the following conditions:

1   Monsieur Verdi must be in St Petersburg to rehearse the opera in time for the first performance to take place at the beginning of January 1862, new style.

2   The Management accepts the libretto *Don Alvaro or La forza del destino*, or any other that Monsieur Verdi may think suitable.

3   Monsieur Verdi will have his choice of the artists engaged at St Petersburg for the casting of the roles in his opera.

4   The costumes and decor will be completely new, and as is usual a dress rehearsal will be given which is equivalent to a first performance.

5   The Imperial Management of St Petersburg will have the right to have a copy made of the score, rights in which will be acquired for the entire Russian Empire.

6   It is understood that Monsieur Verdi will retain the rights for all other parts of the world.

7   Monsieur Verdi will be paid sixty thousand francs in gold in three equal instalments, the first on his arrival in St Petersburg, the second at the first orchestral rehearsal, and the third at the dress rehearsal.

The Management undertakes to pay Monsieur Piave either two or three thousand francs for the libretto.

[The following paragraph is added in Verdi's handwriting:]

This contract being from this moment in full force, Monsieur Verdi, should he fail to fulfil his obligations (other than by reasons of illness or force majeure) will pay an indemnity of sixty thousand francs to the Management of the Imperial Russian Theatres.[6]

Piave stayed in the town of Busseto, and not at the Villa Sant' Agata, during his summer visit to work on the libretto, for Verdi considered that the operations of the workmen had rendered his house temporarily uninhabitable. As was his custom, especially when working with Piave, Verdi made his own first draft of the libretto in prose, planning the shape of the work and the distribution of scenes, and requiring his librettist merely to turn it into verse. Piave made several trips to Busseto and Sant' Agata after his first visit in July; when he was not there he was continually receiving written criticisms and admonitions from Verdi. In one letter, written on 5 August, Verdi threatened to call in Andrea Maffei (as he had done with *Macbeth*) should Piave's work prove unsatisfactory. 'For God's sake, my dear Piave,' Verdi concluded, 'let's think this over carefully. One can't go on like this, it's absolutely impossible with this drama. The style must be tightened up. The poetry can and must say everything that the prose says, but with half the words. So far, you're not achieving that.'[7]

While Verdi was at work on the composition of the opera at Sant' Agata, a comical scene rather like something out of Rossini's *Barber of Seville* was enacted in the autumn in his town house in Busseto. Some of his workers, pressing grapes in the courtyard of the house, sang so noisily that the police and the National Guard arrived and forcibly silenced them. 'Is there a law that prohibits you from singing in your own house?' the composer asked his parliamentarian friend Piroli. 'And if there is, ought one not to be warned with some degree of civility before it is imposed by armed force? Tell me what can be done, after you have questioned my agent carefully. I am disgusted, and reluctant to swallow this insult (and it is not the first) from my amiable fellow citizens.'[8]

Throughout the autumn, Verdi worked 'day and night', as he told his lawyer. 'My angel, you've also finished Act III!!!', Piave wrote excitedly on 11 November. 'It's no good, you were born to command even inspiration. You are a real tyrant.'[9] Ten days later the opera was complete except for the scoring, and on 24 November Verdi and Giuseppina left Busseto for Russia, travelling by way of Paris, presumably to avoid going through Austria. They stayed for two days in Paris, which enabled Verdi to collect the new evening suit he had ordered and also to see Léon Escudier. On 30 November the Verdis left Paris for Berlin, finally arriving in St Petersburg on 6 December. They were met with freezing weather: according to Verdi it was twenty degrees below zero outside, and only fourteen above inside. They were met, too, with the illness of Emma La Grua, the singer who was to have sung the leading soprano role. The opera therefore had to be postponed.

Giuseppina had been making elaborate preparations for the journey for several months. Large quantities of wine, pasta, cheese and salami had been sent in advance to St Petersburg, and these no doubt helped to keep the worst rigours of the Russian winter at bay. Giuseppina wrote to Verdi's friend, the writer and patriot Count Opprandino Arrivabene:

> . . . This terrible cold has not bothered us in the least, thanks to our apartment. One sees the cold but doesn't feel it. But, be quite clear, this curious contradiction is a benefit only to the rich, who are able to shout, 'Hurray for the cold, the ice, the sleighs and other joys of this world.' But the poor people in general, and the coachmen in particular, are the most miserable creatures on earth. Just think, dear Count, many of the coachmen stay sometimes all day and some of the night sitting still on their boxes, exposed to freezing cold, waiting for their masters who are guzzling in beautifully warm apartments while some of these unhappy beings are freezing to death. Such horrible things happen all the time. I shall never get used to the sight of such suffering.[10]

By the end of January it was clear that *La forza del destino* was not going to be staged until the following winter. After spending a few days in Moscow, the Verdis travelled by train back to Paris, via Berlin. 'Here I am in Berlin,' Verdi wrote to the tenor Tamberlick,

> after a trip with no sinister events except the appalling cold from Dunaberg to Kovno. We travelled three or four miles in an open train in thirty-three degrees of cold to join the train of a Grand Duke who had stopped at the fort. It is a terrible thing to be at the disposition of others, even a Grand Duke! Now I understand the meaning of cold, and there was one moment when I seemed to feel all the swords of the Russian army in my head. If I could believe in another world, an inferno of ice as Papa Dante calls it, I should begin tomorrow to recite the Rosary and Miserere, and ask for pardon for all my sins of commission and omission. The railway carriages that took us from Dunaberg to Kovno were unheated, and even the wine – a good one at five roubles a bottle – turned to ice![11]

The Verdis arrived in Paris on 24 February 1862. Their intention had been to see friends and relax for a few days before continuing their journey to Italy, but instead Verdi found himself engaged in irksome composition. An International Exhibition was to be held in London in the spring, and composers from several countries were being commissioned to write pieces for performance. Meyerbeer was to represent Germany; Auber, France; and William Sterndale Bennett, England. Rossini had first been approached to represent Italy, but had replied that he was too old and infirm. Verdi reluctantly agreed in his stead and, discovering that Meyerbeer and Auber were producing orchestral works, decided to compose a cantata with a solo tenor part for Enrico Tamberlick on the theme of international peace and friendship. He commissioned a text from a twenty-year-old Italian music student, a protégé of Clarina Maffei temporarily resident in Paris. The young student's name was Arrigo Boito: twenty years later Verdi and Boito were to collaborate more memorably.

Satisfied with Boito's text, Verdi rewarded the young man with a gold watch, and proceeded to compose quickly a not unattractive piece for tenor, chorus and orchestra, lasting about a quarter of an hour in performance, and utilizing in its final section the national anthems of France ('The Marseillaise'), Italy (Novaro's 'Fratelli d'Italia') and England ('God Save the Queen'). Verdi and Giuseppina then left Paris at the end of March. Giuseppina proceeded directly to London, to await Verdi who first spent two weeks in Turin attending sessions of parliament, and a few days in Busseto, before proceeding to London where he was to conduct his *Inno delle nazioni* (Hymn of the Nations).

Arriving on 20 April, Verdi discovered that his Hymn had been rejected by Michael Costa, the musical director of the Exhibition, on the ground that it did not fulfil the terms of the commission. Perhaps not displeased at being given an opportunity to complain, the composer sent an indignant letter to *The Times* from his London address, 43 Alpha Road, Regent's Park:

> Having just arrived in London, I hear that, in one of your articles which appeared on the 19th inst., it is reported that, of the four composers who were each commissioned to write a piece of music for the opening of the International Exhibition, I am the only one who has not yet delivered his composition. Permit me to say that this is not the case. On the 5th inst., a person [Giuseppina] designated by me wrote to the secretary, Mr Sandford, that my composition was in his possession, completely finished, and at the disposal of Her Majesty's Commissioners. I have not

composed a march, as was first agreed, because Auber told me in Paris that he was composing one for the same ceremony. Instead I composed a cantata for solo voice and chorus, which Tamberlick kindly offered to sing. I thought that this change would not have displeased the Royal Commissioners. However, they have intimated that twenty-five days (sufficient time to learn a whole new opera) were not enough to learn this short cantata, and they have refused to accept it. I wish this fact to be known, not in order to give importance to a transaction of no consequence, but only to correct the mistake that I did not deliver my composition. I should be most grateful if you would publish this letter in your most esteemed newspaper.[12]

To Léon Escudier in Paris Verdi wrote that he was delighted at the rejection of his cantata, for he detested all such occasional pieces. He soon, however, regretted having written to *The Times*, for, when his Regent's Park address was revealed in the newspaper, the next day's post brought 'a hail of letters saying God-awful things about the Commissioners and Costa, and also requesting autographs, left, right, and centre, in a very odd and thoroughly English manner'.[13] Verdi attended the opening of the Exhibition and heard the music of Sterndale Bennett, Meyerbeer and Auber. To Escudier he wrote: 'What carried the day was the march by Auber, to whom please give my regards, and also my thanks, because without him I would have composed a march which would have been performed, and which would have bored the balls off me and everybody else.'[14]

The London newspapers took Verdi's side against the organizers of the Exhibition. The *Morning Post* on 25 May hoped that the composer realized the profound indignation felt by the London public at the spurning of his cordial and friendly collaboration. It concluded that Verdi

probably believed that the Exhibition Committee was gifted by Providence with common-sense, and with some ability to appreciate art and the intentions of the artist. We are sorry for Signor Verdi, the most widely esteemed composer in Europe, and for ourselves as Englishmen and compatriots of that anything but gentlemanly Committee, to find that in these two perfectly legitimate hopes he has been entirely deceived.[15]

It would appear that ill-will towards Verdi on the part of Michael Costa, the musical director of the Exhibition, director of the opera at Covent Garden, and a Neapolitan conductor and composer, played a part in the rejection of the *Inno delle nazioni*, for when a rival impresario, Colonel Mapleson, arranged to have Verdi's cantata performed at Her Majesty's Theatre, Costa refused to release Enrico Tamberlick from his Covent Garden obligations, and Verdi was obliged to adjust the solo part to suit the soprano Therese Tietjens, who took part in the first performance of the work on 24 May, Queen Victoria's birthday. The *Hymn of the Nations* (conducted by Luigi Arditi, known today as the composer of the song '*Il bacio*') was received with great enthusiasm, and Verdi took six curtain calls. Most press notices were favourable, though *The Times* had reservations about the propriety of including 'The Marseillaise', and also referred to the 'somewhat bombastic stanzas of the poetaster' Boito.[16] Four further performances were given during the following week.

While she and Verdi were in London, Giuseppina took the opportunity to improve her English, occupying much of her spare time in studying the language. This *jeu d'esprit* to Mauro Corticelli is a fair example of the style of several letters she wrote from London in English:

Well! Very well! You have some good aptitude for commercial style, and I shall employ you as a Secretary when I shall be able to open a Cheesemonger Shop. But, you must submit yourself (before I put you in possession of such a noble charge) at an experiment with closed doors.

You are right in giving all your mind and time to your important *things*. I am not so silly to pretend, that a future Cheesemonger's Secretary, ought to occupy himself with trifles: but I am very glad to know it, because things being so, I shall buy some trifle in London myself.

I beg your pardon, for every error that I am sure, you shall find in my letter. Be indulgent, and think, Mister Secretary, that I am *all alone* without hope today to see some English person able to correct it.[17]

On 31 May the Verdis left London, spending a few days in Paris and a week in Turin on the way back to Busseto where, in July, a domestic tragedy occurred. Verdi wrote of it to the conductor Mariani who had wanted to pay a visit to Sant' Agata in the company of the British diplomat Sir James Hudson:

A very grave misfortune has struck us and made us suffer terribly. Loulou, poor Loulou is dead! Poor creature! The true friend, the faithful, inseparable companion of almost six years of life! So affectionate, so beautiful! Poor Loulou! It is difficult to describe the sorrow of Peppina, but you can imagine it. Fraschini [the tenor Gaetano Fraschini], who was here for five or six days during the illness of that poor animal, must have been very bored with us, and saddened. And now you want to come with the Minister? Heaven knows how happy and honoured I would feel to receive in my house someone whom I love and revere so, and you know I speak sincerely. But, my dear Mariani, in my house now there is desolation.[18]

Giuseppina wrote that she and Verdi had cried like babies 'to see those beautiful eyes shut, eyes which had gazed at us with such love'. They buried their beloved little friend under a willow tree in the garden, and the composer erected a headstone with the inscription 'To the memory of one of my most faithful friends'. Verdi was distressed, for he had been used to carrying Loulou under his cloak in the winter months during his walks around the estate. The little dog had even accompanied his master and mistress on their travels abroad and had been given a passport! Giuseppina was heartbroken at the loss of Loulou; fortunately she was able to occupy herself in the preparations for departure again for St Petersburg. Verdi spent most of August orchestrating *La forza del destino*, and they both set out towards the end of the month, spending some time in Paris and eventually arriving in St Petersburg on 24 September 1861.

Before beginning rehearsals for *La forza del destino*, the Verdis spent a week in Moscow, where *Il trovatore* was being performed at the Bolshoi Theatre. Verdi planned to attend a performance incognito, but the word spread that he was in the audience and he had to allow himself to be dragged on stage. As soon as he appeared, the audience rose to its feet, greeting him with cheers and interminable applause. The following day, the performers gave a sumptuous banquet for him.

In St Petersburg, rehearsals went well, and shortly before the first night the Tsar awarded Verdi with the Cross of the Royal and Imperial Order of St Stanislaus. On 10 November *La forza del destino* was given its first performance at the Imperial Theatre; Verdi reported to Ricordi that it had been a success, and praised what he described as an excellent performance with extremely lavish sets and costumes.

The principal roles were sung by Caroline Barbot (Leonora), Constance Nantier-Didiée (Preziosilla), Enrico Tamberlick (Alvaro), Francesco Graziani (Carlo), Gian-Francesco Angelini (Padre Guardiano), and Achille de Bassini (Melitone). De Bassini, a forty-three-year-old baritone, had created three important leading roles in Verdi operas: the Doge in *I due Foscari* (1844), Seid in *Il corsaro* (1848) and Miller in *Luisa Miller* (1849). Although de Bassini had no reputation in buffo roles, Verdi had apparently written the comical Melitone specifically with him in mind. 'I have a part for you,' he had written to the baritone, 'if you are willing to accept it. It's comical and very charming, that of Fra Melitone. It will suit you perfectly, and I've almost identified it with you personally. Not that you are a clown, but you have a certain vein of humour which fits perfectly with this character I've written for you, assuming that you approve.'[19] Another Verdi veteran in the cast, in the very small role of the mayor, was the bass Ignazio Marini, who had created the title roles in *Oberto*, Verdi's first opera (1839) and *Attila* (1846).

The critic of the *Journal de St Pétersbourg* wrote, immediately after the premiere:

> It is midnight. We have just left the first performance of the new opera which Maestro Verdi has written expressly for the Italian Theatre of St Petersburg. We should not want this issue of the paper to go to press without mentioning the brilliant success of this beautiful work.
>
> We shall speak again at leisure about this beautiful score and about the evening's performance; but for the moment we wish to report the composer's victorious success and the ovations for the artists who, in order to comply with the insistent demands of the entire audience, had on several occasions to drag the celebrated composer on to the stage, to the sound of wild cheering and prolonged applause.
>
> It is our opinion that *La forza del destino*, of all Verdi's works, is the most complete, both in terms of its inspiration and the rich abundance of its melodic invention, and in those of its musical development and orchestration.[20]

After the third performance, a group of supporters of the Russian nationalist school of composers staged a demonstration against the opera, but this merely had the effect of inciting a vast majority of the audience to a counter-demonstration of enthusiastic applause. Prevented by bronchitis from attending the premiere, the Tsar came to the fourth performance, at which, according to Giuseppina, after having applauded Verdi 'and called him out himself by name, [he] wanted his Minister to introduce him into his box, and there, so to speak, he was buried under an avalanche of compliments especially from the Tsarina who was very cordial and astute in everything she said'.[21]

The first Italian production of *La forza del destino* was staged in Rome three months later under the title of *Don Alvaro*, with some alterations made to appease the Roman censor, who considered the work 'immoral, impolitic, and a sordid compound of modern corruption'.[22] Verdi was not present; having left Russia on 9 December, he and Giuseppina were in Paris for Christmas, and on 5

January they proceeded to Madrid, where Verdi was to conduct the Spanish premiere of the opera. This was his only visit to Spain. From Madrid on 13 January 1863, he wrote to his friend, the Roman sculptor Luccardi, to demand news of the Rome production:

> If you always address your letters so badly, no wonder I never receive them. This one has reached me only because it fortunately went to Sant' Agata and my steward has sent it on to me.
>
> I have been in Madrid for two days now, and I'm here to stage *La forza del destino*. I can't tell you anything about this city yet, but I shall write to you about the works of art I see, and about my opera. You, however, shall write to me frequently about this opera, the rehearsals and the performance. For the rest, I'm not worried about the musical performance, but about the various changes that have been made in the libretto. It's an opera of huge dimensions, and it needs great care. Enough, we shall see. I shall write in any case, and the plain, unadulterated truth.[23]

On 17 February, having heard of the outcome in Rome, Verdi wrote again to Luccardi:

> Many thanks for the telegram you sent me, and for the letter I have just this moment received. The opera went well enough in Rome, but it could have gone a thousand times better if Jacovacci had for once got it into his head that, to have a success, you need both operas suited to the singers and singers suited to the operas. It's true that in *La forza del destino* the singers don't have to know how to do *solfeggi*, but they must have soul, and understand the words and express their meaning. I'm sure that with a sensitive soprano the duet in the first act, the aria in the second, the romance in the fourth and, in particular, the duet with the Father Superior in the second act, would all have been successful. There you have four numbers spoiled in performance. And four numbers are quite a lot, and can affect the fate of an opera! The role of Melitone makes its effect from the first word to the last. Jacovacci has now seen the need to replace this singer, but as an old impresario he should have seen it from the beginning. For the rest, let's thank our good fortune that the singers and, in particular, the impresario didn't completely ruin the opera by their shortcomings. I thank you, too, for your affectionate friendship and for the solicitude you have shown in sending me your comments.
>
> The opera will be produced here on Saturday, and on Sunday morning I shall send you news of it. Rehearsals are going reasonably well.[24]

The Madrid premiere of *La forza del destino* on 21 February 1863 was successful with the public, but less so with the press: one of the critics accused the composer of having desecrated a Spanish masterpiece. The Duke of Rivas, author of the play on which the opera was based, was present in the audience on the first night and apparently shared this view. Verdi thought the occasion a success, considered the Spanish chorus and orchestra admirable, the soprano and tenor good, and the rest 'zero or bad'.[25]

Before leaving Spain, Verdi and Giuseppina went on a tour of Andalusia which he, at least, found long, uncomfortable and tiring:

> The Alhambra, *in primis et ante omnia*, the cathedrals of Toledo, Cordoba, Seville, deserve their reputation. The Escorial (forgive me this blasphemy) I do not like. It is a mass of marble, there are very rich things in the interior, and some very beautiful, including a fresco by Luca Giordano which is marvellously beautiful, but on the whole good taste is lacking. It is severe, terrible, like the fierce sovereign who built it.[26]

That final sentence is a fascinating comment from someone who four years later, in the opera *Don Carlos*, was to compose so formidable a musical portrait of that sovereign, Philip II.

In the middle of March Verdi and Giuseppina left Spain for Paris, where Verdi was to supervise a revival of *Les Vêpres siciliennes*. But he had not finished, creatively, with *La forza del destino*. Dissatisfied especially with the final scene, he allowed the opera to be performed in Italian theatres but delayed its French production until he could adjust the score and the libretto to his satisfaction. The opera was, by Verdian standards, a long one, but he did not wish to shorten it. Though he tinkered with the score on several occasions, it was not until the question of a revival at La Scala for the carnival season of 1869 came up that he was to undertake a major revision.

The plot of *La forza del destino* is somewhat rambling. When the Marquis of Calatrava attempts to prevent the elopement of his daughter, Leonora, with Don Alvaro, son of an Inca princess, Alvaro accidentally kills the Marquis. Cursed by her father as he dies, Leonora seeks the help of the Father Superior of a monastery, who arranges for her to live the life of a hermit in a cave close to the monastery. Leonora's brother, Don Carlo, pursues Alvaro in search of vengeance. The two men meet as fellow-officers in the army, but when his true identity is revealed to Carlo, Alvaro refuses to fight him and decides to enter a monastery. Eventually he is found by Carlo, who taunts him to such an extent that Alvaro forgets his Christian vows and the two men rush out of the monastery to fight, their duel taking place close to Leonora's retreat. Alvaro mortally wounds Carlo, and calls to the hermit to help the dying man. When the hermit appears, Alvaro is astonished to discover that it is Leonora. Before he dies, Carlo stabs his sister. As she dies, her prayer for Alvaro's redemption is answered.

Often referred to as a flawed masterpiece, *La forza del destino* is as tuneful a work as *Il trovatore*. Despite this, and despite the fact that the Spanish plays on which the two operas are based have much in common, *La forza del destino* is not at all like the earlier opera. In fact, it is not very like anything else in Verdi's *oeuvre*. Much of it betrays the circumstances of the Russian commission: the choral writing, the almost Dostoevskian monks with their dark bass voices, the sprawling formlessness of the action, the military scenes. And much of the opera, particularly the character of Melitone and the chorus scenes, influenced the Russian composer Mussorgsky when he came to write *Boris Godunov* six years later.

Chapter Fifteen

1863–67

After their tour of Andalusia in February and March 1863, Verdi and Giuseppina proceeded to Paris, where Verdi was to rehearse *Les Vêpres siciliennes*, which was being revived at the Opéra. This proved to be an unhappy experience, mainly because of the poor standards and lack of discipline in the Opéra orchestra under its chief conductor Pierre Dietsch, who two years earlier had been responsible for a disastrous performance of *Tannhäuser* and had been described by Wagner as an 'orchestral castrato'. Matters came to a head two days before the first night of the revival, which Verdi had been rehearsing diligently with the singers at the piano for three and a half months. There had, however, been only two orchestral rehearsals when Verdi called for a complete run-through of the opera with singers and orchestra. Léon Escudier, who was present, described the scene in an article in *L'Art Musical*:

> During the first number the Maestro thought he noticed a little ill-will among the strings; very politely he remarked on this, but they took no notice. They then exaggerated the nuances that Verdi had called for to such an extent that the players' intention could no longer be in doubt. The Maestro approached one of these gentlemen and remarked, without the slightest bitterness, that he could not understand what had caused the orchestra's ill-will. The reply was very odd:
> 'This rehearsal is a waste of time; we could have done without it.'
> 'But,' said Verdi, 'if I asked for it, it was because I thought it was necessary.'
> 'Each of us, you see,' said the musician in question, 'has other business to attend to.'
> 'Ah! you have other business to attend to!' replied the Maestro. 'I

thought that your business was here. It seems that I was mistaken.'

Whereupon Verdi summoned the conductor, M. Dietsch, and expressed his amazement at the behaviour of his musicians. 'After such a demonstration, which I consider most unseemly, I have nothing else to do here. I shall leave.' Verdi then picked up his hat and left.[1]

The composer of *Les Vêpres siciliennes* attended neither the dress rehearsal nor the first performance of the revival. But Dietsch was summarily dismissed from his position, and Georges Hainl, conductor of the opera house at Lyons, was immediately engaged to replace him. Hainl conducted the third performance of the opera, which, with mediocre singers, failed to excite audiences. Verdi and Giuseppina returned to Italy, and Verdi swore to himself that he would avoid any future dealings with the Paris Opéra.

There were sessions of parliament to be attended in Turin at the end of July, but by the beginning of August the Verdis were at Sant' Agata for the rest of the summer. Even here there were to be aggravations, this time involving the young poet and musician Arrigo Boito and his friend Franco Faccio, a young composer who was another protégé of Clarina Maffei. In reply to a letter from her recommending both young men, Verdi wrote:

> Last year in Paris I saw Boito and Faccio often, and they are certainly two young men of great intelligence, but I can say nothing of their musical talent, because I have not heard anything by Boito and only a few things by Faccio which he came to play for me one day. For that matter, since Faccio is shortly to produce an opera, the public will pronounce its sentence. These two young men are accused of being very enthusiastic admirers of Wagner. There is nothing wrong with that, provided that admiration does not degenerate into imitation. Wagner is already made, and there is no point in remaking him.
>
> Wagner is not a fierce beast, as the purists would describe him, nor is he a prophet as his apostles would like to think. He is a man of great intelligence who takes delight in doing things the difficult way because he cannot find the easier and straighter paths. The young should not deceive themselves; there are very many who believe they have wings because they really lack the legs to stand on their own feet.
>
> Let Faccio put his hand on his heart and, paying attention to nothing else, write at its dictation. Let him have the courage to attempt new ways and to face opposition.[2]

Clarina Maffei communicated Verdi's words to Faccio, and the young composer was encouraged and moved by them. In November

Faccio's opera *I profughi fiamminghi* (The Flemish Fugitives) was given its premiere at La Scala with moderate success, and the composer wrote an effusive letter to Verdi, thanking him for his advice and encouragement. Unfortunately, a few days later some friends of Faccio's gave him a celebratory dinner at which Boito read a poem he had written in praise of his friend, which was subsequently published, and which were interpreted by Verdi as referring offensively to himself and to his music. Italian art was exhorted to escape from the grip 'of the old and the cretinous' ('*dalla cercia del vecchio e del cretino*'), and Faccio is seen as a young saviour who will cleanse the altar of art, now 'stained like the wall of a brothel' ('*bruttato come un muro di lupanare*'). 'Dear Clarina,' Verdi wrote to the Countess Maffei:

> For a fortnight I've been whirling about here and there like a lunatic, doing nothing as usual, simply for the sake of boring myself and wearying any friend I came across, and this is why I've replied neither to your letter nor to Faccio's. Moreover, I can say to you with my customary frankness that Faccio's letter has caused me some embarrassment. How can I reply to it? A word of encouragement, as you have done, perhaps; but a word of this kind given by me would be made known to the public. The matter, however, is already discussed in public, so any word would be useless. I know that there has been much talk of this opera, too much in my opinion, and I have read a newspaper article in which I found such big words as Art, Aesthetics, Revelations, the Past, the Future etc. etc. I confess that (great ignoramus that I am!) I understood none of it. On the other hand I am acquainted with neither Faccio's talent nor his opera. And I don't want to know it, so that I can avoid discussing and giving judgment, things which I detest because they are the most useless in the world. Discussions do not convince anyone, and judgments are usually wrong. Finally, if Faccio, as his friends say, has found new paths, if Faccio is destined to restore art, currently 'as ugly as the stink of a whore-house', to its altar, so much the better for him, and for the public. If he is led astray, as others assert, then let him put himself back on the right road, if he believes in it, and if it seems right for him.[3]

Verdi was offended by what he perceived to be Boito's low opinion of him. The young man seemed to him to be suggesting that Verdi was, to put it bluntly, no artist but a commercial purveyor of entertainment, soiling the altar of the art of music. Nothing could have been further from the truth, for almost single-handedly Verdi had transformed Italian opera from an industry into an art. The evidence of his concern with the staging of his operas as dramatic works exists in hundreds of his letters, though in this, as in most matters concerning his profession, the composer's common sense never deserted him. 'I know that you are almost exclusively concerned with the *mise-en-scène*,' he once had occasion to write to Léon Escudier. 'That's fine, but I wouldn't want it to be too much. I am an enemy of excess, and I don't always admire your productions because they can be too contrived.'[4] Verdi expected his singers to be singing-actors, and considered that orchestral playing, lighting, costumes and scenery were all aspects of the total work of operatic art. As he told Tito Ricordi:

If artists would learn to read and understand, impresarios learn to stage, and orchestras and choruses knew how to perform *piano* and *forte* and to keep together, the effects would be different from what they are. And note that I am not asking for extraordinary or impossible things, I am merely asking for what is absolutely necessary. It is as though a painter asked for a little light to see what he was painting.[5]

The year 1864 began quietly for Verdi. He and Giuseppina spent much of the winter in Genoa, and he attended some of the sessions of parliament in Turin. Throughout the year he continued to concern himself with ways of improving the dénouement of *La forza del destino*, but rejected a suggestion from Tito Ricordi (made in December 1864) that he should consult the Spanish playwright Gutiérrez. He thought it a poor idea

to write to Gutiérrez, when in Madrid there is the Duke of Rivas [author of the play on which the opera was based], to whom I can write whenever I wish. But neither Gutiérrez nor the Duke would think of anything. For a thousand reasons, it would be a mistake to turn to Ghislanzoni or Marcello, and Boito would not do. I shall find something eventually, you'll see. Meanwhile, lease out the opera as it is.[6]

In June Léon Escudier visited Verdi in Genoa, and it was probably then that the question of a Paris production of *Macbeth* was first mentioned. The impresario of the Théâtre Lyrique had asked Escudier, as Verdi's Paris representative, if the composer would be willing to compose ballet music for insertion into the opera. In October, whether or not he had broached the subject earlier, Escudier wrote formally to Verdi about this, and the composer's reply indicated that he would not only be interested in composing ballet music for the opera he had written eighteen years earlier, but would also want to take the opportunity to subject the entire work to a thorough revision:

> I have glanced through *Macbeth* in order to do the ballet music, but alas! I have found a few things in it that must be changed. In short, there are certain numbers which are weak or, even worse, lacking in character. This is what will have to be done:
> 1 Write an aria for Lady Macbeth in Act II.
> 2 Various cuts to be reconsidered in the vision scene of Act III.
> 3 Completely rewrite Macbeth's aria.
> 4 Touch up the first scenes of Act IV.
> 5 Do a new last act finale, deleting Macbeth's death scene.
> To do all this, as well as the ballet, will take time, and you must try to convince Carvalho to renounce any thought of producing *Macbeth* this winter. Discuss this with him, and then reply to me. I am leaving tomorrow for Turin where I shall stay for eight or ten days.[7]

On 7 November Verdi returned to Busseto from Turin and began his revision of *Macbeth*. By early January he had sent Escudier the first three acts and had given detailed instructions regarding the staging of the banquet scene as well as the ballet, and also made suggestions regarding the translation. He told Escudier:

> In the first act duet between Lady Macbeth and Macbeth, it is the first part that makes the most effect, and in it there is a phrase containing the words '*follie, follie che sperdono i primi rai del dì*'. The French translation must use the equivalent '*folie, folie*', for it is perhaps in this word and in Lady Macbeth's secret derision that the whole effect of this piece lies.[8]

At the beginning of February 1865, Verdi was able to write to Escudier that the revision was finished:

> Today I have sent to Ricordi the last act of *Macbeth*, absolutely complete. The whole of the chorus which opens the fourth act is new. The tenor aria is revised and re-orchestrated. Then all the scenes after the baritone's romanza to the end are new, i.e. the description of the battle and the final hymn. You will laugh when you hear that, for the battle, I have written a fugue!!! I, who detest all that reeks of the academy. But I can assure you that in this instance that particular form works well. The racing about of subjects and counter-subjects and the dissonant clashes can express the idea of battle very well. Ah, if you only had our trumpets, which sound so bright and full-toned. Your *trompettes à piston* are neither one thing nor the other. Nevertheless, the orchestra will enjoy itself. As soon as possible I

shall send you my notes on the whole of the fourth act. Have you received the third?

On Sunday I leave for Turin, and then Genoa where I shall stay for the rest of the winter. From Genoa I shall write at length, and you can answer me there. I see that the newspapers have begun to talk already about this *Macbeth*. For the love of God, *ne blaguez pas trop*.[9]

With the revision of *Macbeth* completed, Verdi turned his attention again to *La forza del destino*, and to ways of improving its finale. He was distracted by the illness of his eighty-year-old father, whom he visited twice in February, and by the need to travel frequently to Turin to attend meetings of parliament.

Five weeks before the premiere of his revised *Macbeth*, Verdi sent some instructions for Escudier to pass on to Amélie Rey-Balla, the soprano who was to sing the role of Lady Macbeth:

And now for the sleepwalking scene – the most important scene of the opera. Anyone who has seen Ristori knows that it must be performed with a minimum of gesture, or rather with one single gesture: that of erasing a blood-stain she imagines to be on her hand. Each movement must be slow, and each step should be barely visible: her feet must steal over the ground, as if she were a statue or a ghost. Her eyes should be glazed, her appearance corpse-like; she is on the point of death and will die immediately afterwards. Ristori emitted a rattle – a death-rattle. This should not and cannot be done in music, just as there should be no cough in the last act of *La traviata* and no laughter in 'È scherzo od è follia' in *Un ballo in maschera*. In the sleepwalking scene, a lament from the cor anglais is an excellent substitute for a death-rattle, and more poetic. The scene must be sung with the utmost simplicity and a hollow voice (she is dying), but the voice must on no account sound as though it comes from the stomach. There are a few moments where the voice may open out, but these must be the briefest of flashes, and are marked in the score.[10]

Verdi did not go to Paris for the premiere on 21 April 1865, but received news of its success in telegrams from Escudier and the impresario Carvalho. The latter's message was fulsomely worded:

Maestro, I write you under the effect of one of my greatest musical emotions. *Macbeth* has just obtained at the Théâtre Lyrique an immense success. Thank you, dear Maestro, for the faith you had in me. . . .[11]

Escudier was both more terse and more informative: '*Macbeth* immense success. Finale first act, Brindisi encored. Admirable performance. Marvellous production. General enthusiasm. Am writing by post to Busseto.'[12] But Verdi, when he saw the French reviews for himself, realized that the success of *Macbeth* had been only partial. He wrote to Escudier:

> In some French newspapers I have noticed sentences which would admit of doubt. Some draw attention to one thing, and some to another. Some think the subject sublime, and others say it is not suited to music. Some say that I did not know Shachspeare [*sic*] when I wrote *Macbeth*.
>
> In this they are completely wrong. I may not have interpreted *Macbeth* well, but that I do not know, do not understand and feel Shachspeare, no by God, no. He is one of my favourite poets, whom I have had in my hands from my earliest youth, and whom I read and re-read continually.
>
> I would like to know what has happened since, and I shall be obliged to you if you will tell me sincerely and frankly. Please also do me the favour of sending me, whatever they may say, the *Débats*, the *Siècle*, and all the leading newspapers.[13]

In the summer of 1865, Verdi found himself feuding with the town of Busseto. For the previous six years a municipal theatre had been under construction; it was now almost completed, and the mayor and town council had taken it for granted not only that their local composer Giuseppe Verdi would allow the theatre to be named after him but also that he would use his influence to help them engage some of the most famous singers of the day for the opening performance. In a letter to Barezzi written in 1845 when the idea was first mooted, Verdi had written jocularly of the project, but in 1861, while the theatre was actually being built, he had suggested that work on it should be suspended and the funds contributed to the national cause, as war seemed imminent again. Nevertheless, now that the theatre was complete except for its interior decoration, the municipality looked again to Verdi.

Feeling that he was being coerced, Verdi reacted by refusing to have anything to do with the theatre, which brought accusations of ingratitude from the town council, who reminded him of the help he had received from the town at the beginning of his career. This, of course, infuriated Verdi, who dictated to Giuseppina a letter, presumably addressed to the municipal authority, in which he threatened to leave the district and live elsewhere. 'I am liberal to the utmost degree,' he ended irrelevantly, 'without being a Red. I respect the liberty of others, and I demand respect for my own. This town is anything but liberal. It makes a show of being so, perhaps out of fear, but its tendencies are clerical.'[14]

The outcome of the affair was that in August Verdi grudgingly accepted the dedication of the theatre, and presented the municipality with a cheque for the amount (a generous one in those days) of 10,000 lire. When the theatre eventually opened three years later, a box was put at the permanent disposal of the composer who, however, made a point of never setting foot inside the building.

Loulou's successor in the Verdi household was a dog named Black (spelled 'Blach'), and the composer's correspondence with his friend Opprandino Arrivabene was often carried on through their two dogs. 'Greetings,' wrote Black to Ron-Ron on 28 August 1865:

> It was very bad of you, my dear brother, not to come and see me, for I would have welcomed you with open paws and wide-open jaws, and my four teeth biting into your hairy cheeks. In short, I would have shown you all my fraternal canine affection. . . . My majordomo, factotum and secretary, the blunderer, provides me with everything. The macaroons continue to pour into my mouth, all the large bones are for me, the soup is ready when I awaken, the entire house is at my disposal and, now that the heat is so oppressive, I change rooms and beds every other minute, and woe to anyone who tries to stop me. In my happier moments I am kept busy educating a young kitten, with whose progress I am quite satisfied. If it doesn't end up being choked, it will leave behind it the reputation of being a very clever thief.
>
> So you see, my dear brother, everything here is progressing well, thanks to my suggestions and my commands; and if you should arrive, my paws, teeth and tail are all ready to receive you in a manner befitting a most worthy relative. My male secretary and my lady secretary send you their greetings. À propos the first, I've read in some newspaper that he's on the verge of making a new blunder. . . .[15]

Verdi's blunder was probably that he had signed, that same day, a contract to give a revised version of *La forza del destino* at the Paris Opéra, and also to compose a new work for that theatre, despite having vowed to have nothing further to do with it after the *Vêpres siciliennes* contretemps of two years earlier.

In September he finally abandoned politics, resigning his seat as a Deputy. For some time he had been decidedly less than assiduous in his attendance at sessions, and he had become increasingly disgusted by the venal behaviour of so many of his colleagues in parliament. Before he left, Verdi interested himself in ensuring that his successor should be both a liberal politician and an honest man, for he felt keenly the lack of worthy and serious minds in government.

On 20 November 1865 Verdi and Giuseppina left Busseto and, after spending some days in Genoa, arrived in Paris on 1 December. On New Year's Eve, Verdi wrote to Arrivabene ('Dear Arrivabene. Dog, dog, dog!', the letter begins):

> I roam through the length and breadth of Paris, and I examine carefully the new part which is truly beautiful. How many boulevards, how many avenues, how many gardens, and so on, there are. A pity the sun doesn't shine more frequently! I have been to the Opéra four times!!! and once or twice to all the musical theatres, and I was bored everywhere. *L'Africaine* is certainly not Meyerbeer's best opera. I have also heard the Overture to *Tannhäuser* by Wagner. He's mad!!! You know that I came here to stage *La forza del destino* straight away, and to write a new opera for the end of '66. But there was too much work to be done on *Forza*, and it was impossible for me to undertake it in the space of a year, so we have agreed to begin with the new opera, which will be *Don Carlos* taken from Schiller. The librettist will be Méry. Once things have been properly settled with the librettist I shall return to Sant' Agata to work in peace, and shall come back here again towards the end of August or early in July.[16]

The librettist Joseph Méry, whose play *La Battaille de Toulouse* had been used as the basis of Verdi's *La battaglia di Legnano* eighteen years earlier, was already confined to his bed with the illness which was to cause his death; most of the work on the adaptation of Schiller's *Don Carlos* was done by Camille du Locle, son-in-law of the Director of the Opéra. Verdi remained in Paris until 17 March, by which time he had composed the first act of *Don Carlos* which was to be a grand opera in five acts. During this time, he and Giuseppina continued to frequent the theatres and to do a little entertaining. After moving house three times during their first month in Paris, they settled into an apartment at 67 Avenue des Champs-Elysées, where they gave a supper party for the unveiling of a bust of Verdi by the sculptor Jean-Pierre Dantan. Adelina Patti was among their guests. They also visited the elderly Rossini, and Giuseppina later confided to her diary, '*Madame Rossini plus désagréable que d'habitude*'. Rossini sent Verdi a note, addressed to 'M. Verdi, Célèbre Compositeur de Musique, Pianiste de la 5me Classe!!!' and signed 'Rossini, Ex-Compositeur de Musique, Pianiste de la 4me Classe'.

Verdi wrote to Arrivabene in February:

> Have no doubt – I am alive! and I know I am because I feel the tedium of all the boring pricks [*cazzi*] who inundate Paris, scourging poor humanity. It makes no difference whether one is in the middle of the Champs-Elysées,

three miles from the centre, or at the Hôtel de Bade right in the middle of the Boulevard des Italiens. The most curious thing is that, with so much going on, you find when you get to bed at night that the twenty-four hours of the day have passed without your having done anything![17]

Nevertheless, he and Giuseppina stayed on in Paris until 17 March. On their way back to Italy they stopped off in Nice to visit the ailing Méry (who died several weeks later). After spending a few days in Genoa, the travellers arrived back in Busseto, and Verdi immersed himself in *Don Carlos*. By mid–May he had completed a draft of Act II; and, by early June, Act III.

In April, Italy and Prussia had signed a treaty, and both countries were preparing to go to war with Austria. On 19 June Italy declared war on Austria, and at Sant' Agata Verdi felt too close to the firing line for life to be comfortable. 'I expect any moment to hear cannon,' he had written to Léon Escudier in May, 'and I am so close here to the army's camps that it wouldn't surprise me one fine morning to see a cannonball roll into my room.'[18] In June he wrote to an old friend, Giuseppe Piroli:

> I am still here, but at the first cannon shot I shall leave, because the very idea that the Austrians might put in an appearance here would make me run a thousand miles without stopping for breath, if only to avoid seeing those ugly faces. For the moment I shall go to Genoa, and shall stay there till the very last moment before I must or should leave for Paris.[19]

Verdi was really in two minds as to what he should do. He felt it would be unpatriotic to leave Italy at such a time, yet he did not want to endanger the lives of Giuseppina and himself by remaining at Sant' Agata. At the beginning of July the Verdis moved to Genoa where they rented an apartment at the Palazzo Sauli on the Carignano hill. (This was to be their winter residence for the next eight years.) Verdi had by now not only completed a draft of Act IV of *Don Carlos* but had also orchestrated all four acts. Only Act V remained to be composed. When the war ended suddenly and badly for Italy, he and Giuseppina departed for Paris, leaving their friend the conductor Mariani to supervise the furnishing of their Palazzo Sauli apartment.

Arriving in Paris on 24 July, Verdi began to work on the final act of *Don Carlos*. Escudier had been instructed by letter some days earlier to go to the house in the Champs-Elysées, which was still being rented by Verdi, and make arrangements for the carpets to be thoroughly beaten because dust affected the composer's throat badly. On 11

August Verdi had his first rehearsal with some of the principal singers, but a week later he and Giuseppina left Paris to spend three weeks at Cauterets, a spa in the Pyrenees, where Act v of the opera was finally completed. They returned to Paris on 12 September, and later in the month rehearsals began at the Opéra under Verdi's direction, although until early December he was still intermittently working on the orchestration (probably of Act v).

As always in that bureaucratic institution, rehearsals at the Paris Opéra were an irritating and frustrating business. After more than ten weeks of rehearsals, on 10 December Verdi wrote to Arrivabene: 'I hope that the first performance will take place not later than mid-January. You see what a lousy place this Opéra is. Things go on interminably!'[20] Giuseppina told her friend Mauro Corticelli:

> *Don Carlos*, if it pleases God and the tortoises of the Opéra, will receive its premiere at the end of January! Good gracious! How a composer is punished for his sins by having a work staged in that theatre with its machinery of marble and lead! Just think! I am burning with impatience to go to Genoa to put in order and enjoy our apartment, and at the Opéra they argue for twenty-four hours before deciding whether Faure or la Sass is to raise a finger or a whole hand![21]

In fact, the premiere did not take place until 11 March. That Verdi's difficulties at the Opéra were not unique is clear from an article which appeared in *La France Musicale*:

> There has been talk of incidents and a curious anecdote concerning the preliminary rehearsals for Verdi's new opera. The composer's patience has been most sorely tried; but finally, thanks to the ever conciliatory intervention of Perrin [Director of the Opéra], all difficulties have been resolved, and we are assured that all the artists are now satisfied. It has to be admitted that the composers who work for the Opéra do not always tread on rose-strewn paths. More often than not, alas, they encounter thorns instead of flowers. Happy are they who can reach their goal without losing patience and having to fight some great battle.[22]

A fascinating though somewhat over-written account of Verdi rehearsing at the Opéra was given in *Le Figaro* by a journalist who had hidden in the theatre and listened to the third act of *Don Carlos* at one of the eight dress rehearsals:

> The chandeliers were extinguished, the great auditorium was plunged into darkness and seemed quite devoid of life apart from the stage and the orchestra whose number had been especially increased for this opera.

Above the players' heads, above the violins and the sparkling brass instruments, stood Georges Hainl [the conductor who had been appointed four years earlier to replace the unsatisfactory Dietsch], with his ruffled hair and bristling moustache. Baton in hand, like a colonel before the attack, he contemplated his soldiers huddling in the trenches.

Opposite, almost mesmerizing him with his flashing eyes, sat Verdi, his large white hands resting on his knees, motionless like some Assyrian God, musing, listening with all his being, completely absorbed in this music which had emerged vibrant and living from the depths of his soul.

The composer is tall, thin yet solidly built, with shoulders like those of Atlas which look capable of supporting the weight of mountains. His long, luxuriant thick hair is thrown forward on to his brow in heavy locks, his beard is jet-black, but white below the chin. There are two deep lines across his cheeks, his face is gaunt, his eyebrows thick, his eyes bright and shining, his mouth large, bitter and disdainful. His appearance is proud and manly, his attitude that of a defiant opponent. . . .

Verdi listens. His entire being, the whole might of his sturdy temperament strains towards a single goal. His sense of hearing is doubly, triply acute. He questions everything. In this tumultuous harmony he can hear the quietest of notes. He can hear everything simultaneously: the chorus, the brass, the aria, and everything that happens on and off the stage. He stands, leaps about, valiantly spurring on all these groups, shouting in an Italian accent which gives a certain charm to his speech:

'*Il y a un trou là! Allons! Vite!*'

Some of the music is being sung at the front of the stage, but he now addresses the chorus at the back, almost leaping towards them:

'*Eh! Eh! Il y a un accent sur cette note-là!*'

In one direction, he shouts, '*Allons, presto!*' and in another, '*Piano! Con amore!*'

He gets up, beats time, snaps fingers, and this strident, bright, sharp sound like castanets is heard above the orchestra and the chorus, goading them on, driving them forward as though lashed by a whip. Then he claps his hands. He radiates harmony from head to toe, he measures himself against his ideal, he instils his artistic genius into these men and women, kindling them with his fire, stamping on the floor with his heels, running to the back of the theatre, stopping the singers and re-discovering his original conception among the chaos from which an ordered world will emerge.[23]

On 16 January Verdi's father, who had been in poor health for some years, died in Busseto. As Verdi was busy with the preparations for *Don Carlos*, Giuseppina had to deal with the funeral arrangements. Carlo Verdi left a sister, aged eighty-three, and a great-niece, aged seven, for whom Verdi and Giuseppina made themselves responsible. They took the girl, Filomena Maria Verdi, grand-daughter of the composer's Uncle Marco, into their household, and although they never formally adopted her she became Verdi's heiress. In 1878, at the age of eighteen, she was to marry Alberto Carrara, son of a notary who looked after Verdi's affairs. Filomena, known as 'Fifao', inherited the Sant' Agata property, where her descendants, the Carrara-Verdis, still live.

One of the final dress rehearsals of *Don Carlos*, a complete run-through of the opera, began at 7 p.m. but did not end until midnight. Subsequently, Verdi was informed that he would have to make cuts, it being the custom in Paris for performances to end before midnight as the last trains for the outer suburbs and surrounding districts departed around twelve-thirty. Performances could not begin earlier than seven because people would still be dining at that hour. Though Verdi's opera was extremely long, which was unusual for him, it contained no music that could be cut without damage to the work, except, of course, for the ballet which, however, was sacrosanct to Parisian audiences. Reluctantly, Verdi made the necessary excisions before the first public performance. (The material he cut has, in recent years, been discovered in the archives of the opera house, since when more than one production of the complete, uncut *Don Carlos* has been staged.)

On 11 March 1867, the opera was given its premiere at the Paris Opéra, the leading roles being sung by Marie-Constance Sass (Elisabeth), Pauline Gueymard (Eboli), A. Morère (Don Carlos), Jean-Baptiste Faure (Rodrigue), and Louis-Henri Obin (Philippe II). Among the chorus of six Flemish deputies, comprised of students from the Conservatoire, was a nineteen-year-old baritone, Victor Maurel, who was to become one of the greatest singers of his time, creator of the roles of Iago and Falstaff in Verdi's last two operas.

'Last night, *Don Carlos*,' Verdi wrote to Arrivabene the following day. 'It was not a success. I don't know what will happen now, but I shouldn't be surprised if things were to change. Tonight leave for Genoa.'[24] Forty-three performances of the opera were given during the season, after which it disappeared from the stage of the Paris Opéra until recent years.

The plot of *Don Carlos* stays reasonably close to the Schiller play. In order to secure peace between Spain and France, Philip II of Spain marries Elisabeth de Valois who had been engaged to his son, the

Infante Don Carlos. Carlos is urged by his friend Rodrigue, Marquis of Posa, to try to secure freedom for the Netherlands from Spanish misrule, but when Carlos confronts the King, Philip orders his arrest. The Princess Eboli, a former mistress of the King, but now in love with Carlos, is led by jealousy to intrigue against Carlos and Elisabeth. Rodrigue sacrifices his life helping Carlos to escape from prison, but when Carlos and Elisabeth meet secretly to say farewell, they are discovered by the King and the Grand Inquisitor, and Carlos is saved from the Inquisition only by the intervention of the ghost of his grandfather, Charles v, who escorts him to safety. (Schiller's play ends differently. The King hands his son over to the Grand Inquisitor, with the chilling words, 'Cardinal, I have done my duty. Now do yours.')

French critical reception of the opera was mixed. Verdi read the reviews in Genoa, whither he had fled; when he discovered that the influence of Wagner had been discerned by more than one of the critics, he wrote at once to Escudier:

> My dear Léon, we really are a bunch of lunatics. I ask you, was it necessary to travel up and down the railway in order to relieve one's mind after eight months at the Opéra? In short, one never comes to the end, and one would never have a minute's time to write operas again if it were not for rehearsals!
>
> I have read in Ricordi's *Gazzetta* the account of what the leading French newspapers say of *Don Carlos*. So then, I am an almost perfect Wagnerian. But if the critics had paid a little more attention they would have seen that there were the same intentions in the trio in *Ernani*, in the sleepwalking scene in *Macbeth*, and in many other pieces of mine. But the question is not whether *Don Carlos* is composed to this or that system, but whether the music is good or bad. That question is clear and simple and, above all, the right one to ask.[25]

Modern critical opinion perceives *Don Carlos* to be one of Verdi's most impressive works, though it was not appreciated by the French composers of the day. The young Bizet, for example, thought it very bad, with neither melody nor style. Rossini, however, wrote to Ricordi that, in his opinion, Verdi was the only composer capable of writing grand opera.

Don Carlos has now come to be highly regarded by lovers of Verdi's music. Its dark orchestral colouring, its rich, complex musical characterization, and indeed (*pace* Bizet) the quality of its melody, combine to make it one of the most rewarding and stimulating of operas to be encountered in the theatre. It is, admittedly, the one opera in which Verdi can be said to have forsaken his customary sharp conciseness, but this is to a large extent a consequence of its being written as a five-act, Parisian grand opera. *Don Carlos* can hardly be called prolix, and it glows with its composer's humanity, which he has been able to breathe into characters who, on the printed page, must have seemed to him at first acquaintance to be frigidly formal.

Chapter Sixteen

1867–69

Returning to Genoa in mid-March after the *Don Carlos* premiere, Verdi and Giuseppina took possession of their new apartment. On 24 April the city conferred honorary citizenship on the composer, and on 1 June *Don Carlo*, an Italian translation of *Don Carlos*, was given its first performance, not in Italy, but in London, at the Royal Opera House, Covent Garden. 'So it was a success in London?' Verdi wrote to Escudier. 'And, that being so, what will the gentlemen of the Opéra say when they realize that in London a score can be rehearsed in forty days, when they need four months?'[1]

The Genoa apartment had been purchased by Verdi at Giuseppina's instigation. As she wrote to their friend Clarina Maffei:

> The sun, the trees, the flowers and the immense variety of birds that make the country so alive and so beautiful for the greater part of the year, leave it sad, desolate and mute in the winter. Then I no longer love it. When the snow covers these immense plains, the trees with their naked branches look like bare skeletons, and I can't bear to raise my eyes to look outside, I curtain the windows as high as a man's head, and I feel an endless melancholy, a strong desire to run away and reassure myself that I am among living beings and not ghosts in the silence of a huge cemetery. Verdi, with his character of iron, still loves the country even in winter, and would have succeeded in discovering pleasures and occupations suited to the season. But in his kindness he took pity on my isolation, and after much wavering we have pitched our tent for the winter, close to the sea and the mountains, and I am now furnishing the fifth and certainly the last apartment of my life.[2]

Giuseppina was mistaken about that, for seven years later she and Verdi moved to an apartment in another Palazzo. However, in the spring of 1867 she was busy decorating the new apartment, and in May travelled to Milan to look for furniture. While she was there, Giuseppina was introduced by Clarina Maffei to Alessandro Manzoni, the elderly and distinguished author of *I promessi sposi*, the most famous Italian novel. Verdi, who revered Manzoni, was amused, astounded and moved when Giuseppina returned to Sant' Agata and, with pretended nonchalance, said to him, 'If you go to Milan, you must introduce yourself to Manzoni. He is expecting you. I was at his house with Clarina the other day.' 'How I envy my wife having seen that Great Man,' Verdi wrote to Clarina:

> But I don't know if, even if I were to come to Milan, I would have the courage to present myself to Him. You know very well how great and how deep is my veneration of that Man who, in my opinion, has written not only the greatest book of our time but one of the greatest books ever to emerge from the human mind. And it is more than a book, it is a consolation to mankind.[3]

Verdi's old benefactor, Antonio Barezzi, had been seriously ill for some months. He lingered on until the summer and died on 21 July 1867. When the end came, Verdi and Giuseppina were with him. Barezzi was in bed, weak and hardly able to speak, but he raised his eyes longingly to the piano which stood in a corner of his room. Verdi understood that the old man was asking for his favourite tune from *Nabucco*, so he sat and began to play '*Va, pensiero*'. Barezzi raised a hand, murmured '*O, mio Verdi! Mio Verdi!*', and died peacefully.

The Verdis made a visit to Paris in the summer in the company of the conductor Angelo Mariani, who wanted to attend a performance of *Don Carlos* there before conducting the Italian premiere of the opera in the autumn. Verdi and Giuseppina stayed in Paris from mid–August until the end of September, but, although they were back in Italy in October, they did not attend Mariani's first Italian performance of *Don Carlo* at the Teatro Comunale, Bologna, on 27 October. During the month Giuseppina's friend Mauro Corticelli, the theatrical agent, who was back in Italy and unemployed, was offered the position of bailiff at Sant' Agata for as long as he wanted it; he accepted it gratefully.

. In December Verdi's faithful librettist Piave suffered a stroke which deprived him of speech and movement. He remained alive for a further eight years, and Verdi helped him financially, arranged to provide an income for the librettist's young daughter, and also organized the publication of an album of six songs for Piave's benefit. He solicited compositions from five other composers with whom Piave had been associated: Auber, Cagnoni, Mercadante, Federico Ricci and Ambroise Thomas. Verdi's own contribution to the album was a light-hearted little song, '*Tu dici che non m'ami*' (You say you do not love me).

A glimpse of the domestic life of the Verdis is afforded by Giuseppina's diary entries at the very beginning of 1868. New Year's Day, 'apart from the fairly serious quarrel yesterday about the house in Genoa', passed fairly happily, and Verdi gave his wife a New Year's present, 'for he is a grand seigneur and generous'. 2 January was peaceful: 'The dinner met with approval. I am happy. He is calm.' On 3 January Verdi and Giuseppina played billiards, which they did quite frequently, and the composer busied himself 'acting as carpenter and locksmith, and playing the piano'. Giuseppina's entry for that day ends:

> It would be so easy to be happy, when one has one's health and a little property. Why isn't he always like that, instead of finding fault with all that I do, which I do only with the single intention of making his life comfortable, agreeable and peaceful?

The following day 'the clouds are back', and Giuseppina notes: 'Verdi becomes irritated at tones of voices that are too soft or too lively, so that I wonder what might be the happy medium that would suit him!' She continues:

> I wanted to become a new woman to respond worthily to the honour I received in becoming his wife, and the good that I receive constantly from that man, who, to be perfect, is lacking only a bit of sweetness and charm.

Later, she writes: '2.30 p.m. Now he is playing the piano and singing with Mariani.'[4]

In mid-January, hearing of the imminent premiere of Ambroise Thomas' *Hamlet* at the Paris Opéra, Verdi wrote to Escudier: 'Is it true they've inserted two ballets? Hamlet and dance tunes!! How incongruous! Poor Shakespeare!'[5] When Escudier sent him a libretto of the opera, Verdi commented, 'Impossible to do worse. Poor Shakespeare! How they've ill-treated him. Only the scene between Hamlet and the Queen succeeds: it is both theatrical and suitable for setting to music. For the rest – Amen!'[6]

It is in February 1868 that with hindsight one catches a first hint of

Verdi's future involvement with Egypt and the creation of *Aida*. Camille du Locle, the young French librettist who had completed the libretto of *Don Carlos* after the death of Joseph Méry, was travelling in Egypt, and wrote to Verdi from Thebes. In his reply, Verdi expressed a polite interest in hearing, on du Locle's return, of 'the wonders you have seen, and the beauty and ugliness of a country which once had a greatness and a civilization I have never been able to admire'.[7] How extraordinary that, two years later, Verdi was so vividly to recreate in music that past Egyptian civilization for which he felt such a lack of admiration.

At this time Verdi seems to have been flirting with the possibility of writing a comic opera, his first since the unsuccessful *Giorno di regno* of nearly thirty years earlier, for there exists at Sant' Agata a detailed scenario in French, in the composer's handwriting, of a libretto based on Molière's *Tartuffe*. The first sentence reads: 'One may note in *L'Imposteur* [the alternative title of *Tartuffe*] that diversity of persons, that variety of character so propitious to those conflicts and contrasts in which music excels, because by its very nature this art can present them better than any other.'[8] Unfortunately, nothing came of this project; it was not until a quarter of a century later, near the end of his life, that Verdi was to make his triumphant return to comic opera.

In May Verdi was made a Commendatore of the Order of the Crown of Italy. However, he did not keep his decoration for long. The Minister for Public Instruction, Emilio Broglio, had written, in a letter to Rossini which was made public, that since Rossini, who had given up composition forty years earlier, there had been nothing worth discussing except four operas by Meyerbeer. Always quick to take offence, Verdi wrote to the Minister:

> I have received the diploma naming me a Commander of the Crown of Italy. This order was established to honour men who have done some service to Italy in the army, or in literature, science or art.
>
> Yet although, as you yourself said and believed, you are not at home in music, a letter addressed by Your Excellency to Rossini expressed the opinion that no opera has been written in Italy for the last forty years. Why, then, is this decoration sent to me? Surely there must have been some mistake in the address. I return it.[9]

Still concerned to improve the ending of *La forza del destino*, and no longer able to enlist the aid of the opera's original librettist, Piave, who, though conscious, was unable to speak or move, Verdi turned to

Antonio Ghislanzoni, a poet, playwright, novelist, baritone and
erstwhile political activist, who in his mid-forties had become editor
of the *Gazzetta Musicale di Milano*. Ghislanzoni, who had met the
composer only once previously at a dinner in Milan in 1846, visited
Sant' Agata for several days in the spring of 1868 to discuss *La forza del
destino*, and subsequently published in his magazine an account of his
visit which contains a lively description of the villa and its inhabitants:

Maestro Verdi is now fifty-five years of age. Tall, strong, slender,
endowed with robust health and a robust, energetic character, he promises
to keep his vigour for ever. When I met him for the first time twenty years
ago, his entire appearance presented alarming symptoms. Whereas then
his frail frame, pale face, sunken cheeks and deep-set eyes aroused ominous
fears, today you find nothing in that countenance but the glowing health
and stability of a man destined for a long career.

And, like his appearance, his character also seems to have changed for
the better. No one could be more receptive, genial, expansive. What a
difference between my taciturn table companion of 1846 and my lively and
often high-spirited host of 1868! I have known artists who, in their youth,
were light-heartedly and extravagantly cheerful and affable, and then
became, with the veneer of glory and decorations, impenetrable and
virtually intractable. Verdi, on the other hand, may be said to have
proceeded through a career of triumphs, and discarded, after each, one part
of that hard and rough exterior which characterized him in his younger
years.

The villa at Sant' Agata is where Maestro Verdi still prefers to live. His
prodigious physical and mental activity can develop here more freely than
elsewhere. At five in the morning he walks along the avenues of his estate,
visits the fields and farms, and amuses himself sailing up and down the lake
in a small boat which he navigates skilfully. He does not pause a moment.
As respite from music, Verdi reads poetry; he finds an outlet for his strong
emotions by seeking refuge in history and philosophy. There is no branch
of human knowledge which his restless mind, avid for culture, does not
research with rapture.

Signora Giuseppina Strepponi, his wife, who has an excellent mind and
an affectionate heart, is as cultured as she is lovable, and shares with this
Attic and gifted artist the pleasurable domestic duties. Harmony reigns in
both their hearts and all that one sees around them.

And meanwhile, messages arrive from every corner of the civilized
world, begging for operas, offering incredible sums of money, promising
honours and triumphs. How long can Maestro Verdi resist such tempting
offers of wealth and glory? I do not consider it possible for the composer of
Don Carlos to exhaust the effervescence of his own genius, that over-

bearing need to express himself, which always spurs him on. The volcano has its moments of inactivity, but its latent fire must sooner or later erupt.[10]

Clarina Maffei, whom Verdi had not seen for twenty years although he had kept up his correspondence with her assiduously, paid a surprise visit to her old friend at Sant' Agata towards the end of May by arrangement with Giuseppina. 'He received me like a sister,' Clarina told a friend. 'He knew me at once, but didn't believe his eyes. He gazed at me in astonishment; then he blurted out exclamations and embraced me.'[11] She stayed for a week, and Verdi promised her that he would go to Milan and visit the great novelist Manzoni.

That visit took place on 30 June 1868. 'What can I say to you of Manzoni?' Verdi wrote to Clarina Maffei on his return to Sant' Agata:

How to explain the extraordinary, indefinable sensation the presence of that saint, as you call him, produced in me? I would have knelt before him if men could be worshipped. They say it must not be done, and so be it; although we venerate on altars many who lacked the talent or the virtues of Manzoni, and who indeed were downright rascals. When you see him, kiss his hand, and convey to him all my veneration.[12]

The summer months were spent by Verdi and Giuseppina at Sant' Agata, with occasional visits to Genoa, except for three weeks from late August when they took the thermal cures at Tabiano, about thirty kilometres west of Parma. Verdi was no doubt displeased when, at the opening of the new Teatro Verdi in Busseto on 15 August, a performance of *Rigoletto* was preceded by one of his juvenilia – a *Capriccioso* which he had composed at the age of twelve. (He did not, of course, attend the performance.)

On 13 November Rossini died in Paris. 'A great name has disappeared from the world,' Verdi wrote to Clarina Maffei. 'His was the most extensive, the most popular reputation of our time, one of the glories of Italy. When the other [Manzoni] who still lives has gone, what will we have left?'[13] He conceived a plan to honour the great composer's memory, and on 17 November wrote to Tito Ricordi a letter which Ricordi published in his *Gazzetta Musicale*:

To honour the memory of Rossini, I should like to ask the most distinguished Italian composers (headed by Mercadante, if only with a few bars) to compose a Requiem Mass to be performed on the anniversary of his death.

I should like not only the composers but also all the performers, in addition to giving their services, to offer a contribution towards the expenses.

I want no foreigner, or anyone outside the world of music, to help in this, however powerful they may be. Otherwise, I should immediately dissociate myself from the project.

The Mass should be performed in the church of San Petronio, in the city of Bologna, which was Rossini's true musical home.

This Mass should be an object neither of curiosity nor of speculation. Once it has been performed, it should be sealed and placed in the archives of the Music Academy of that city, whence it should never be removed. An exception could perhaps be made for future anniversaries of his death, should posterity wish to celebrate them.

If I were in the good graces of the Holy Father, I would beg him to allow, at least this once, women to take part in the performance of this music, but since I am not, it would be best to find a person more suitable than I to achieve this end.

It would be a good idea to set up a committee of intelligent men to take charge of the arrangements for the performance, and especially to choose the composers, assign the movements, and supervise the general form of the work.

This composition, however good its individual numbers may be, will necessarily lack musical unity; but though it may lack in this respect it will serve, nevertheless, to show how greatly we all venerate that man whose loss the entire world laments.[14]

An organizing committee was set up in Milan to carry out Verdi's suggestion. The composers, chosen by lot from a larger list, were (in alphabetical order) Antonio Bazzini, Raimondo Boucheron, Antonio Buzzola, Antonio Cagnoni, Carlo Coccia, Gaetano Gaspari, Teodulo Mabellini, Alessandro Nini, Carlo Pedrotti, Enrico Petrella, Pietro Platania, Federico Ricci and Verdi. In due course the committee handed out assignments to them, Verdi being asked to contribute the final movement, the 'Libera me'. Before then, however, he had at last completed the revision of *La forza del destino* that he had been contemplating ever since the opera's St Petersburg premiere in 1862, and had directed his revised version at La Scala.

The initiative for the *Forza* revision had come from Tito Ricordi who, realizing that Verdi would be unlikely to concentrate his energies sufficiently on the task of reshaping the opera until a definite occasion or deadline presented itself, had arranged for La Scala to announce *La forza del destino* for the 1869 carnival season. 'By all means let *La forza del destino* be announced,' Verdi agreed, 'though without mentioning any changes, since there might very well not be any.'[15] He had, in fact, already begun to discuss the matter with Antonio

Ghislanzoni, one of whose suggestions was that the gipsies of the military camp scenes might be brought back at the end of the opera, 'so that, when the curtain falls, the stage should not be entirely crowded with monks'.[16] But this did not commend itself to Verdi, and it was the composer himself who hit upon the idea of replacing Alvaro's suicide with a final trio in which, his soul redeemed, Alvaro submits to the will of God. Presumably Verdi's agnosticism had prevented him from arriving at this solution earlier. Though dramatically it is not really an improvement on the original ending to the opera, musically it provides a far superior resolution, for the trio which Verdi composed is one of his finest and, in its context, most affecting.

Though the Scala performances were conducted by Franco Faccio, the production was directed by Verdi. 'I will come myself to Milan to take the rehearsals I consider necessary for *La forza del destino*,' he wrote from Genoa to Ricordi on 15 December, 'changing the last finale and various other passages here and there throughout the opera. I want nothing to do with the management of La Scala. I don't want my name to be on the posters, and I shall not stay for the premiere....'[17] However, he did stay for the premiere on 27 February 1869, which Giuseppina also attended. From Genoa, two days later, Verdi wrote to Arrivabene:

> I returned here last night from Milan at midnight, dead tired from work. I shall need a fortnight's sleep to recover. By now you will have heard about *La forza del destino*; the performance was good and it was a success. La Stolz and Tiberini were superb, the others good. Chorus and orchestra performed with indescribable precision and energy. They had the devil in them. Good, very good.[18]

'La Stolz and Tiberini' were the dramatic soprano Teresa Stolz and the tenor Mario Tiberini. Teresa Stolz was a thirty-five-year-old Bohemian, who had been performing in Italy for the previous four seasons and had sung Elisabetta in the Bologna production of *Don Carlo* in 1867 conducted by Angelo Mariani, to whom she had become engaged. Verdi's friendship with Mariani began to cool at about this time and, although disagreements regarding the arrangements for the Requiem Mass for Rossini were a contributing factor, it may well be that Verdi's growing admiration for Teresa Stolz was the principal cause. The composer's relations with the Teatro alla Scala, on the other hand, now began to take a turn for the better after nearly twenty-five years.

Immediately upon his return to Genoa from the Milan premiere, Verdi wrote to his friend Senator Giuseppe Piroli, who was now a Deputy for the constituency of San Donino. After informing him of the success of the performance, and the excellence of the leading singers, Verdi continued:

Orchestra and chorus divine. What fire and enthusiasm they all had. It's a shame, a shame that the government ruthlessly refuses help to this art, and to this theatre which still has so many good aspects. You may ask why they cannot get on without government subsidy. It's not possible. La Scala Opera House has never been as well attended and as active as it is this year, but, despite this, if the management cannot achieve fifteen performances of *Forza* with nightly receipts of over 5,000 lire, they are lost. I don't believe it will be possible for them to give so many performances, so they will have to close the theatre with a deficit before the season is over. A shame, a shame![19]

In July, Verdi was made a Knight of the Savoy Order of Civil Merit. This carried with it an annual pension of 600 lire which he donated to the town of Busseto so that two prizes of 300 lire each could be awarded to those children from poor families who gave the best proof of their intelligence and industry in the school examinations. He stipulated that one prize was to go to a boy, and one to a girl.

On a more dramatic level, a letter from Giuseppina to Clarina Maffei, dated 18 July 1869, reveals that she and Verdi were nearly drowned, that month, in their lake:

God be thanked that it's over now – it's thus unnecessary for me to attempt to give you a palpitatingly tragic description of it; but all the same, I can tell you that the puddle, the infamous puddle, nearly became our tomb. The ancient proverb is right when it says that still waters should never be trusted. Verdi was in the boat, holding out his hand to help me in. I had one foot in the boat, but in setting down the other the boat capsized, and down we both went to the bottom – the very bottom of the lake! Verdi, thank God, chance, or his presence of mind, feeling the boat brush against his head, was able, by raising an arm, to thrust away that sort of coffin lid. This movement somehow helped him to get onto his feet, and in that position he was able, with incredible strength and promptitude and with the help of Corticelli [Giuseppina's friend the theatrical agent], to pull me out of the water, where I was unable to move, caught by my dreadfully distended silk garments, virtually unaware of my predicament, and thus making no attempt to save myself. I shall not describe the alarm, the despair of my poor sister who ran away crying 'Help!' or the fright of all who saw us in that terrible moment. I hadn't had time, so to speak, to take fright, since losing my balance and finding myself with two fathoms of water over my head had all occurred in a flash. I was about to faint, when I opened my eyes and found myself supported by the arm of Verdi, who was standing bolt upright with water up to his throat, and I thought he must have hurled himself in on purpose to save me. It was only later that I learned how things had happened, and then I was seized with terror, thinking of Verdi and the consequences which that sorry involuntary bath could have had for him and art.[20]

By mid-August, Verdi had completed the 'Libera me' for the projected Mass for Rossini. However, it proved impossible to organize a performance. Verdi had hoped that a chorus from Pesaro, conducted by Mariani, could be used, but either Mariani proved unco-operative or, as seems more probable, Verdi chose to think him so. Giulio Ricordi, Tito's son who was now working in the family firm, suggested postponing the performance, but Verdi could see no point in this. His idea had been to have the Mass performed on 13 November, the first anniversary of the composer's death. 'Given the circumstances,' he wrote to Ricordi,

there is, in my opinion, only one course the committee can take. That is to announce to the public that the trouble taken to obtain the means to perform this Mass has proved to be in vain, and at the same time to give back to each composer his piece of music, with expressions of gratitude for the interest he has shown. The expenses incurred up to now by the committee should be, as is only natural, my concern. Send me the bill and let's talk no more of it.[21]

Chapter Seventeen

1869–71

In the summer of 1869 Verdi received a letter from Paul Draneht, general manager of the Cairo Opera, informing him that a new theatre was to be opened in Cairo to celebrate the construction of the Suez Canal, and inviting him to compose something for the occasion. The composer replied: 'Although I deeply appreciate that you wanted to give me the honour of writing a hymn to mark the date of the opening, I regret that I must decline this honour, because of the number of my current activities, and because it is not my custom to compose occasional pieces.'[1]

Since one still sometimes reads that *Aida* was composed for the opening of the Suez Canal, it is important to set out the real facts clearly. There was never any question of Verdi composing an opera for the opening of the new Cairo Opera House, which was in-augurated on 1 November 1869 with a performance of *Rigoletto*, conducted by the composer's old friend and former pupil, Emanuele Muzio. Later in the month, on 17 November, the Suez Canal was officially opened. Camille du Locle, who had visited Egypt the previous year, was in correspondence with Verdi, hoping to persuade him to write another opera for Paris. In December 1869 Verdi wrote to du Locle from Genoa:

> Thanks for *Froufrou*, which I read in one go. If, as the Revue says, all of it had been as distinguished and original as the first three acts, this play would be extraordinarily fine: but the last two, although they are greatly effective, fall into the commonplace. Still, however good *Froufrou* may be, if I had to write for Paris I should prefer a cuisine, as you call it, finer and more piquant than that of Meilhac and Halévy. Sardou, for instance, with du Locle to write the verses. But alas, it's neither the fatigue of writing an

opera nor the judgment of the Parisian public that prevents me; it's the certainty of never being able to have my music performed in Paris as I want it.

It's very strange that a composer must always see his ideas altered and his concepts misrepresented. In your opera houses there are too many wise men (that is not meant to be an epigram). Everyone wants to pass judgment according to his own ideas, his own taste, and, which is worst of all, according to a system. They do not take into account the character and individuality of the composer. Everyone wants to give an opinion or express a doubt; and if a composer lives for too long in this atmosphere of doubt, he cannot escape having his convictions shaken a little, and begin to correct and adjust, or, to put it better, to look askance at his own work. Thus, in the end, you have not a work in one piece, but a mosaic. That may be fine, if you like it, but it's still a mosaic.

You may reply that the Opéra has produced a string of masterpieces in this manner. They may be masterpieces, but allow me to say that they would be even more perfect if this pieced-together feeling and these adjustments were not so obvious at every point. No one, surely, will deny the genius of Rossini. All right, but despite all his genius, his *Guillaume Tell* has about it this fatal atmosphere of the Opéra; and sometimes, although more rarely than in the work of other composers, you feel there's too much here, not enough there, and that it doesn't move with the honesty and security of *Il barbiere*. By this, I don't mean to disapprove of the way you work; I only mean to say that I really can't crawl once again under the Caudine yoke of your theatres, when I know it's impossible for me to have a real success unless I write as I feel, free from other influences, and without having to remember that I'm writing for Paris and not for the world of the moon. What is more, the singers would need to perform not in their fashion but in mine. The chorus, which certainly is very capable, would have to do likewise. In short, I would have to control everything. One will alone would have to prevail: mine. That may seem somewhat tyrannical to you, and perhaps it is. But if the opera is one whole, then the idea is a unity, and everything must work together to form this unity.

Perhaps you will say that there is nothing in Paris to impede one from achieving this. No. In Italy it can be done, at least I can always do it, but in France, no. For example, if I arrive in the foyer of an Italian theatre with a new opera, no one would dare to express an opinion of it, or a judgment, before having understood it properly, nor would anyone make silly requests. The work and the composer are respected, and judgment is left to the public. In the foyer of the Opéra, on the contrary, after four chords you hear everyone whispering, '*Olà, ce n'est pas bon . . . c'est commun, ce n'est pas de bon goût . . . ça n'ira pas à Paris!*' What do such poor words as '*commun*', '*bon goût*', '*Paris*' signify, if you are dealing with a real work of art which should be universal?

The conclusion of all this is that I am not a composer for Paris. I don't know whether I have any talent or not, but I know for certain that my ideas of art are quite different from yours. I believe in inspiration, while you believe in workmanship. For the purpose of discussion I accept your criterion, but I require the enthusiasm that you lack in feeling and in judgment. I want art in whatever form it is manifest; not entertainment, artifice and the system, which is what you prefer.

Am I wrong? Am I right? Whatever the answer, I am right to say that my ideas are quite different from yours and, what's more, that my backbone isn't pliable enough for me to give way and deny my profound convictions which are deeply rooted. Also, I should be extremely upset if I were to write for you, my dear du Locle, an opera which you perhaps would have to withdraw after a dozen performances as Perrin [Director of the Opéra] did with *Don Carlos*. If I were twenty years younger, I would say to you, 'Let us see if, later, your theatrical affairs take a turn which will bring them closer to my ideas.' But time passes quickly, and at present it's not possible for us to understand each other, unless something unexpected occurs, which I can't imagine.

If you come here, as you have led my wife to hope you will, we shall speak more of this at length. If you don't come, it's probable that I shall be in Paris at the end of February. If you come to Genoa, we shall not be able to offer you the ravioli again, for we no longer have our Genoese cook. Still, you won't die of hunger, and, what is certain, you will find two friends who think well of you, and to whom your presence will be a real delight.[2]

It was during du Locle's visit to Genoa later in December that he informed Verdi of the wish of the Khedive (or Viceroy) of Egypt to have Verdi write an opera for the Cairo Opera House. The composer was not interested. He asked du Locle to send him from Paris a volume of the essays of Wagner, and on 23 January 1870 had occasion to remind him: 'Most wretched du Locle! You have forgotten to send me Wagner's literary writings. You know that I want to acquaint myself with this aspect of him, and so I ask you to do what you have failed to do.'[3]

Du Locle replied immediately:

Do not accuse me of negligence. The works by Wagner that you want have never been translated into French; those that I have read have been mainly in newspapers so old that it has been impossible for me to find the dates. . . . The only piece by Wagner that can be produced is his famous preface to his librettos (I believe I saw that volume in your house). As for the others, 'Art and Music', 'Politics and Music', 'The Jews and Music', they have not been translated. To make certain, I had someone write to M. Wagner himself, without telling him, of course, who wanted those translations.[4]

In March, Verdi visited Paris, travelling between Genoa and Marseilles by steamer, and du Locle took the opportunity again to place the offer of the Khedive Ismail Pasha before him. Verdi still was not interested; he took more seriously du Locle's request that he compose an opera for the Paris Opéra-Comique, the theatre of which du Locle was about to become co-director. Verdi much preferred this theatre, which he referred to as *'la petite boutique'*, to the Opéra, to which he had given the scornful appellation *'la grande boutique'*. But his previous experience in Paris had made him more cautious than ever, and he refrained from committing himself. He stayed in Paris until 20 April, seeing as many plays and operas as possible, finding the soprano Adelina Patti 'marvellous' in *Rigoletto* and *La traviata*, the rest of the singers 'dreadful', and musical standards everywhere worse than mediocre, 'except for the Opéra-Comique, where there is a good chorus and especially a delightful orchestra'. At a meeting with Victorien Sardou, the dramatist, and Emile Perrin, Director of the Opéra, Verdi argued with the Frenchmen about their leading opera house, 'myself saying that the Opera *est une affreuse boutique*, they insisting that it is the only possible imaginable theatre of times past, present and future. . . . The pretensions of the French have no limits!'[5]

It was not until Verdi received from du Locle a scenario of an Egyptian subject on his return to Sant' Agata that the composer's interest in writing an opera for Cairo began to be aroused. The scenario had been prepared by an old friend of du Locle, Auguste Mariette, an Egyptologist in the employ of the Khedive. An adaptation of a story, 'La fiancée du Nil', by Mariette, it became the basis of the libretto of *Aida*, for Verdi responded positively to the scenario, which he thought well constructed, with two or three 'very beautiful' situations. 'Who did it?' he asked du Locle, adding, 'Now let us hear the pecuniary conditions of Egypt, and then we shall decide.'[6] Du Locle replied that the synopsis was 'the work of the Viceroy and of Mariette Bey, the famous archaeologist', which was untrue; it had been written by Mariette alone. The Viceroy (or Khedive) was involved only because he was very keen to have Verdi write an opera for Cairo, and was displeased that his approaches to the composer had so far been unsuccessful. Through Mariette he authorized du Locle to approach Gounod or Wagner should Verdi prove recalcitrant. 'I shall not hide from you the fact that H.H. the Viceroy is extremely annoyed and chagrined by the idea of foregoing the collaboration of M. Verdi, whose talent he holds in the highest esteem,' Mariette had written to du Locle.[7]

Verdi, however, did not continue to prove recalcitrant. On 2 June he wrote to du Locle:

> Here I am at the Egyptian business; and first of all I must be allowed to set aside time to compose the opera, because this is a work of vast dimensions (as though it were for the *grande boutique*), and because the Italian poet must first find the thoughts to put into the mouths of the characters, and then write the verses. Assuming that I am able to manage all this in time, here are the conditions:
> 1   I shall have the libretto done at my expense.
> 2   I shall, also at my expense, send someone to Cairo to rehearse and conduct the opera.
> 3   I shall send a copy of the score, and will grant rights only in the Kingdom of Egypt, retaining for myself the rights in libretto and music for all other parts of the world.
> In compensation, I shall be paid the sum of 150,000 francs, payable at the Rothschild Bank in Paris, immediately the score is delivered.[8]

Verdi's terms were accepted by telegram from Mariette in Cairo to du Locle in Paris on 10 June, and du Locle wired the news to Verdi on the same day, following this three days later with a letter:

> The Viceroy cares about this business more than you can imagine. He has sent word to me that he will write to the Emperor [of France] to get permission for me to go down there, in your absence, for the last rehearsals of the production. Imagine the Emperor's astonishment when he receives such a letter! Thank God it's none of his business.[9]

Verdi, unwilling to undertake a long sea journey, had made it clear that there was no possibility of his travelling to Cairo to direct the opera himself. He suggested Emanuele Muzio as conductor, but when he discovered that Muzio was about to become conductor at the Théâtre-Italien in Paris, he withdrew the suggestion, for he did not want Muzio to forego (as that faithful friend would have done) an engagement in Paris which would be much more useful to him. 'Dear Emanuele,' he wrote to his ex-pupil on 20 June,

I am glad that your business with Bagier [Director of the Théâtre-Italien] is concluded. It's a position that you have earned, and now it's up to you alone to keep it. Bring honour to yourself and show your worth. Now that you are appearing before the public, your fortune and your future depend on you alone. Even if Bagier should go, and his theatre should close, there will be ten other theatres that will want you once you are known as a man of ability. Respect others, and insist on respect for yourself. Don't be unjust, and don't be weak. Treat the highest exactly the same as the lowest; don't show partiality to anyone. Reveal neither sympathy nor dislike, and don't be afraid even to curse occasionally.[10]

On 19 June du Locle arrived at Sant' Agata, and in a few days he and Verdi had fashioned, from Mariette's synopsis, a libretto with dialogue in prose. On 25 June, after du Locle's departure, the composer wrote to Giulio Ricordi:

I have studied the synopsis once more, and I have made, and am still making, further changes. We must now think of the libretto, or rather of versifying it, for all we need now is to put it into verse. Can Ghislanzoni do this work for me, and would he wish to? . . . Explain to him clearly that it is not a question of producing an original work, but merely of putting this into verse.[11]

Antonio Ghislanzoni was engaged to turn the libretto into Italian verse, but it is clear, not only from the above but also from the correspondence between Verdi and Ghislanzoni during the following months, that *Aida*'s composer was the opera's real librettist. Early in July Ghislanzoni and Ricordi visited Verdi to discuss a schedule and method of work; by mid-July Verdi had received a versified Act 1 from Ghislanzoni and was able to begin composing the opera. His imagination was excited by the ancient Egyptian subject, and he was concerned to achieve the greatest degree of historical accuracy consonant with his aesthetic intent. He asked du Locle to gather information from Mariette about the sacred dances of Egyptian priestesses, and was duly told that

they performed in long robes and to a slow and solemn rhythm. The music that accompanied it was probably a kind of plainsong, which constituted the bass part, with a very high upper part performed by young sopranos (boys). The instruments that accompanied these dances were twenty-four stringed harps, double flutes, trumpets, timpani, and smaller drums, enormous castanets (rattles), and cymbals.[12]

The opera had to be written in six months at the most, since the

Khedive had stipulated that it was to be performed at the Cairo Opera House in January 1871. In July 1870, while he was still writing Act I, Verdi was already concerning himself with the scenery and costumes, and was also demanding information about ancient Egyptian instruments. Most of all, however, he worried away at the libretto. He had always maintained that, given a fine libretto, an opera was virtually made, and he continued to polish that of *Aida* until it was exactly what he required down to the last syllable. Great, or even good, poetry was not necessarily what he was seeking. He looked for the 'theatrical word' (*parola scenica*), as he explained in a letter to Ghislanzoni on the subject of the Aida–Amneris duet in Act II, scene I:

> There are some good things at the beginning and end of the duet, which is nevertheless too lengthy and distended; it seems to me that the recitative could be managed in fewer lines. The verses are fine until '*A te in cor desto*'. But then, when the action warms up, I feel it lacks the 'theatrical word'. I don't know if I can explain what I mean by 'theatrical word', but I think I mean the word that most clearly and neatly brings the stage situation to life.
>
> For example, the lines
>
> > *Involto gli occhi affisami*
> > *E menti ancor se l'osi:*
> > *Radames vive . . .*
>
> are less theatrical than the words
>
> > *. . . con una parola*
> > *strapperò il tuo segreto*
> > *Guardami t'ho ingannata:*
> > *Radames vive . . .*
>
> although these may be uglier.
>
> Similarly, the lines
>
> > *Per Radames d'amore*
> > *Ardo e mi rivale*
> > *– Che? voi l'amate? – Io l'amo*
> > *E figlia son d'un re*
>
> seem to me less theatrical than the words '*Tu l'ami? ma l'amo anch'io, intendi? La figlia dei Faraoni e tua rivale.*' – Aida: '*Mia rivale? E sia: anch'io son figlia*' etc.
>
> I realize that you will say to me, 'But what about the verse, the rhyme, the stanzas? I don't know what to say, except that, if the action calls for it, I would immediately abandon rhythm, rhyme and stanza. I would use blank verse in order to be able to say clearly and distinctly what the action requires. Unfortunately, it is sometimes necessary in the theatre for poets and composers to have the talent not to write either poetry or music.

The duet ends with one of the usual cabalettas, which I think is too long for the situation. Anyway, we shall see what can be done with the music. Aida's words, however,

> *Questo amore che t'irrita*
> *Di scordare la tentero*

don't seem very effective to me.

Send me this rewritten duet as soon as possible, with the finale which follows, because I shall have to work on it if I am to finish in time.[13]

When he received the revised verses, Verdi wrote again to Ghislanzoni:

I received the finale yesterday, and today the duet; the duet is fine, except for the recitative, which in my opinion (forgive me) could be said with still fewer words. But, I repeat, it could very well stand as it is.

This isn't the time to write to Mariette, but I have already thought of something for the consecration scene. If it doesn't seem right to you, we can try again. But, in the meantime, it seems to me that we could make a rather effective musical scene of this. The piece would consist of a litany intoned by the priestesses, to which the priests respond; a sacred dance to slow and sad music; a short recitative, powerful and solemn like a biblical psalm; and a prayer in two stanzas, sung by the priest and repeated by all. I should like it to have a sad, quiet character, particularly the first stanza, to avoid similarity with the other choruses in the finale of the introduction and in the finale to the second act, which both sound a little like the Marseillaise.

It seems to me that the litanies (and, for the thousandth time, forgive my boldness) should be in short stanzas of one long line and one five-syllabled line, or – and perhaps this would be better, in order to get everything said – two eight-syllabled lines. The five-syllabled line could be the *Ora pro nobis*. So there would be short stanzas of three lines each. That makes six, and that will be more than sufficient to make up one musical number.

Have no doubt, I am not averse to cabalettas; but I must have a situation that gives a reason for them. In the duet in *Un ballo in maschera*, there was a magnificent reason. After that entire scene, if I may say so, an outpouring of love was necessary.[14]

By mid-September the first two acts of the opera, which was to be in four acts, were finished. In July the Franco–Prussian war engineered by Bismarck had broken out. Verdi was upset by the French defeats and fearful of a victorious Prussia. At the battle of Sedan on 2 September the Prussians captured most of the French army and the Emperor Napoleon III himself. This led to the bloodless uprising of 4 September in France and the beginning of the Third Republic. On 20

September Pope Pius IX and his troops were bombarded by the Italian army in order, King Vittorio Emanuele had explained, to prevent a revolutionary uprising. This proved the end of the papal state: it was a great day for most Italians. Of the Prussians Verdi wrote gloomily and, one might consider, presciently to his old friend the Countess Maffei:

> This French disaster fills my heart with despair as it does yours. It's true that the blague, the impertinence, the presumption of the French was, and is, despite all their misfortunes, insupportable. Nevertheless, France gave liberty and civilization to the modern world; and, if she falls, let us not delude ourselves, the liberty and the civilization of us all will fall. Our men of letters and our politicians may praise the knowledge, the science, and even (God forbid them) the art of these conquerors, but, if only they would look a little below the surface, they would see that the old blood of the Goths still flows in their veins, that they are terribly proud, hard, intolerant, scornful of everything that is not German, and of a rapacity without limit. Men of intellect, but lacking in heart, a strong race but uncivilized. And that King [William I of Prussia] who is always talking about God and Providence, with the aid of whom he is destroying the greater part of Europe! He believes himself destined to reform the customs and punish the vices of the modern world!!! What a splendid missionary!
>
> The old Attila (another such missionary) stopped before the majesty of the capital of the antique world, but this one is about to bombard the capital of the modern world. And, now that Bismarck wants to make us believe Paris will be spared, I fear more than ever that it will be at least partly destroyed. Why? I don't know how to say it. Perhaps so that there will no longer exist so beautiful a capital; for they will never be able to create its equal. Poor Paris, which I saw looking so gay, so beautiful, so splendid last April![15]

By mid-November Act IV of *Aida* had been completed in draft, except for the final duet for Radames and Aida. 'At the end', Verdi told his librettist,

> I should like to avoid the usual death agonies, and not have words like 'I'm failing, I'm going before you. Wait for me. She is dead. I'm still alive' etc. etc. I should like something sweet, other-worldly, a very short duet, a farewell to life. Aida should then fall calmly into the arms of Radames. Immediately, Amneris, kneeling on the stone of the vault, should sing a *Requiescant in pacem* etc. I shall write the scene down to explain myself better.[16]

And he did so, actually giving Ghislanzoni the words of the final duet, and asking him to improve them. Some days later, Verdi wrote:

I have received the verses which are beautiful, but they don't seem quite right for me. Since you were so late in sending them to me, I have written the piece already, in order not to lose time, using the monstrous verses I sent you.[17]

In addition, therefore, to composing the music of the beautiful final duet, 'O terra, addio', Verdi also wrote the '*versi mostruosi*' which are, in fact, not at all monstrous but simple, sincere and, in their context, extremely moving.

Ghislanzoni visited Sant' Agata for a few days towards the end of November to help with final adjustments, and by the end of the year the opera was completely finished. However, the Franco–Prussian war prevented the Cairo premiere from taking place as scheduled in January, for Paris was under siege and the scenery which had been constructed there could not be shipped to Egypt. Consequently it was delayed by eleven months, and *Aida* did not reach the stage until Christmas Eve 1871. The first Italian performance, which, contractually, could not be given until after the Cairo premiere, was consequently also postponed.

Meanwhile, Verdi turned his attention to other matters. The composer Mercadante had died on 17 December 1870, and Verdi was invited to succeed him as Director of the Naples Conservatorium. He considered the invitation seriously, for he was extremely interested in teaching methods, about which he held firm views, some of which he set forth in a letter which he wrote to Francesco Florimo, librarian of the Conservatorium, reluctantly refusing the appointment. His main reason was that, to put his methods into practice, he would have to supervise the teaching to such an extent that he would have no time for his other business affairs. He told Florimo, however, that what he would like to have said to the young students was:

Practise the fugue constantly, tenaciously, to satiety, until your hands are strong enough to bend the notes to your will. Thus you will learn to compose with confidence, will dispose the parts well, and will modulate without affectation. Study Palestrina, and a few of his contemporaries. Then skip until you come to Marcello, and direct your attention especially to his recitatives. Go to very few performances of modern operas, and don't let yourself be fascinated by beauties of harmony and instrumentation, or the chord of the diminished seventh, that rock and refuge to all of us who don't know how to compose four bars without a half-dozen of these sevenths.[18]

'Let us turn to the past,' Verdi concluded. 'That will be progress.' In mid-February he visited Florence for a few days to discuss reform of the Italian schools of music with the Minister of Education, and early in the following month, again in Florence, he presided over a commission to study the question and to report to the Minister. Later in the month, in Genoa, he spent some time drafting a document with recommendations.

Now that Verdi had completed *Aida*, Giulio Ricordi was anxious to involve him in thinking about his next opera rather than lapsing into retirement again. Ricordi wanted to create a partnership between Verdi and Arrigo Boito, the poet and composer with whom Verdi had briefly collaborated on the *Inno delle nazioni* nine years earlier, but who shortly afterwards had displeased the composer with his poem in which Verdi discerned an insulting reference to himself.

Ricordi's hope was that he could persuade Verdi to write an opera using Boito as his librettist. Verdi had apparently told Ricordi that he was interested in the possibility of composing an opera about Nero, but Boito had announced his intention of composing such an opera and was in the process of writing his own libretto. According to Ricordi, Boito was willing to abandon his project if Verdi would consent to use his libretto. (Boito had also written a *Hamlet* libretto for his friend Franco Faccio; Ricordi sent Verdi a copy of this libretto, and the composer expressed his admiration of it.)

Verdi was interested in Ricordi's proposal but, as always, was reluctant to commit himself. Also, he was involving himself in arrangements for the Italian premiere of *Aida* in Milan, and did not want to think ahead to future engagements. 'I have not the courage to say "Let's do it", nor do I dare renounce such a beautiful project,' he wrote to Ricordi. 'Tell me, my dear Giulio, could we not leave this matter on one side for a time, and consider it later?'[19] He busied himself during the spring and summer of 1871 considering singers for the Milan *Aida*, and in late September visited the city for meetings with Gerolamo Magnani, who was to design the production. It was during this visit that Verdi also planned a new seating arrangement for the Scala orchestra, intended to improve both the orchestral sonority and the audience's view of the stage. On his return to Sant' Agata, he wrote to the Mayor of Milan concerning this:

> The double-basses form a kind of barrier which, in certain places, prevents the spectator from having a good view of the performance. This is due to the way the old stalls were constructed. But it would be deplorable, and I

should be particularly sorry, if we were forced to put the double-basses back in their old place. If this were done, it would spoil my plan to group the orchestra so that the sound is fuller, and weak and hesitant performances thus avoided. We should have gone to a great deal of trouble, without having obtained any certain results.

There may be a remedy. When I examined the stalls, I saw, as did all the others, that the flooring is in so bad a condition that, in a little time, it will be beyond repair and will have to be completely replaced. Since this necessity will soon become imperative, and the expense will have to be undergone, would it not be possible, dear Mr Mayor, to put the work in hand immediately, lowering the floor so that, taking its height at the entrance as zero, it would be about fifty centimetres lower when it reaches the stage?

The orchestra would naturally be lowered, and the difficulty about the double-basses as I have indicated it would not exist. The stage would be higher and, with the slope of the stalls which is common to all theatres, the spectators would get a better view of the performance.[20]

The first Italian performance of an opera by Wagner, an event of considerable importance in the Italian musical world, was given when Mariani, thereafter considered by Verdi to be a defector, conducted *Lohengrin* at the Teatro Comunale, Bologna, on 1 November 1871. Verdi attended a later performance on 19 November. When he arrived at the Bologna railway station, he ran into Mariani who was meeting someone else from the train. 'I went to greet [Verdi]', wrote the conductor to a friend the next day, 'and tried to relieve him of the burden of his case, but he wouldn't allow me. I realized that he was not pleased that I had seen him arrive.'[21] At the theatre that evening, after the second act of Wagner's opera, Verdi was recognized in Box 23 of the second tier and, though he refused to show himself, was applauded solidly for a quarter of an hour.

Verdi had taken with him a vocal score of *Lohengrin* in which, throughout the evening, he scribbled comments on the music and its performance. At the end, he summed up:

Impression mediocre. Music beautiful, when it is clear and there is thought in it. The action, like the text, moves slowly. Hence boredom. Beautiful instrumental effects. Too many held notes, which makes for heaviness. Mediocre performance. Much verve but no poetry or refinement. In the difficult passages, always wretched.[22]

After the performance, in the waiting room of the railway station at about 3 a.m., Verdi encountered Boito, whom he had not seen since their first meeting in Paris ten years earlier. Their conversation, however, was mainly about the difficulty of sleeping in railway carriages.

Some days later the principal singers of the forthcoming Italian premiere of *Aida* came to Genoa to rehearse with the composer. Among them was Teresa Stolz, who was to sing the title rôle. She had by now broken her engagement with Mariani, and was fast becoming a close friend of both Verdi and Giuseppina. Verdi visited Milan in mid-December to attend rehearsals at La Scala of a revival of *La forza del destino*, but by 23 December was back in Genoa where the *Aida* principals met again to rehearse. (It was at this time that Verdi composed a full scale overture to *Aida*, to replace the prelude of the Cairo score. However, after rehearsing it with the Scala orchestra, he decided against using it: it remained unplayed until Arturo Toscanini, hearing of its existence, had the score and parts copied from the manuscript, which is still in the possession of the Carrara-Verdi family at Sant' Agata, and performed it in a radio concert in New York in 1940.)

On 24 December 1871, the world premiere of *Aida* took place at the Cairo Opera House, conducted by Giovanni Bottesini. The principal roles were sung by Antonietta Pozzoni (Aida), Eleonora Grossi (Amneris), Pietro Mongini (Radames) and Francesco Steller (Amonasro). Mariette's synopsis had been expanded by du Locle and Verdi into a gripping story of love and patriotism in the Egypt of the pharaohs. It tells of the love of Radames, a captain in the Egyptian army, for Aida, a slave who is really the daughter of the king of Ethiopia. Radames is chosen to lead the army against the Ethiopians: during his absence the pharaoh's daughter, Amneris, discovers that her slave, Aida, loves Radames. She is roused to a jealous fury, as she herself is in love with him.

Radames returns victorious, bringing many prisoners, among whom is Amonasro, Aida's father. Tricked by Amonasro into revealing the present position of the Egyptian troops, Radames is arrested and condemned to be buried alive. When his tomb is sealed, he discovers that Aida has concealed herself within it so that she may die with him. As the lovers prepare for death, above the tomb Amneris prays to the gods to grant repose to the soul of Radames.

The Khedive had invited several of the French and Italian music critics to Cairo, and one of them, Filippo Filippi, was misguided enough to contact Verdi in advance, offering to undertake commissions for him or to be at his disposal in any way the composer might require. Verdi told Giulio Ricordi that he felt 'so disgusted, so revolted, so irritated' by Filippi's offer that he 'would a thousand times set fire to the score of *Aida* without a sigh'. He wanted 'no *réclames*, no machinations . . . no *Lohengrinades*. . . . Rather the fire!'[23] To Filippi he made his feelings equally plain:

> You in Cairo? That would be the most powerful publicity imaginable for *Aida*! It seems to me, however, that art treated in this fashion is no longer art, but a trade, a pleasure trip, a hunt, something which one trails around after, something one wants to make, if not successful, at least notorious at all costs! The feeling this inspires in me is one of disgust and humiliation! I always remember joyfully my first years when, almost without a single friend, without anyone to talk to me, without preparations, without any kind of influence being exerted on my behalf, I presented my operas to the public, ready to exchange shots, and extremely happy if I managed to make an occasional favourable impression. Nowadays, what an apparatus accompanies each opera! Journalists, soloists, chorus, conductors, players etc. etc., all must carry their stone to the edifice of publicity, to build up a framework of wretched gossip which adds nothing to the merit of an opera but merely obscures its real value. This is deplorable, deeply deplorable!!
>
> I thank you for your kind offers for Cairo, but I wrote yesterday to Bottesini about everything concerning *Aida*. All I want for that opera is good and, above all, intelligent singing, playing and stage production. For the rest, *à la grâce de Dieu*. That's how I began my career, and that's how I wish to end it.[24]

The premiere was a glittering success. Filippi, in an article in the Milan journal *La Perseveranza*, described the occasion:

> The curiosity, the frenzy of the Egyptian public to attend the premiere of *Aida* were such that, for a fortnight, all the seats had been bought up, and at the last moment the speculators sold boxes and stalls for their weight in gold. When I say the Egyptian public, I speak especially of the Europeans; for the Arabs, even the rich, do not care for our kind of theatre: they prefer the miaouing of their own chants, the monotonous beatings of their tambourines, to all the melodies of the past, the present and the future. It is a perfect miracle to see a fez in the theatres of Cairo.
>
> On Sunday night the theatre was crowded from top to bottom long before the performance began. Ladies occupied the boxes in great numbers, and one's attention was distracted by their unseasonable chattering or by the rustling of their garments. Speaking generally, I found much beauty and elegance, particularly among the Greeks and foreigners of high extraction who are numerous in Cairo. I ought also to say, from

love of truth, that by the side of the handsomest and the best dressed were to be seen every evening the faces of Copts and Jews, with strange headgear, impossible costumes, colours which clashed so violently that nothing worse could be imagined. As to the ladies of the harem of the Court, no one could see them; they occupied the first three boxes to the right, on the second tier, and a thick white muslin hid their faces from indiscreet looks.

For this splendid Italian creation, the Khedive had the satisfaction not only of the excellent outcome, but also of seeing how all the public which crowded into the theatre on Sunday evening recognized immediately what a debt of gratitude art and civilization owe to this rare prince, unique in his intelligent munificence. The applause for him, universal, long and frenzied, soon exploded. At the end, the soft, high last notes of the violins had hardly died away when a cry of 'Long live the Khedive' was heard reechoing throughout the theatre. . . .[25]

One immediate consequence of the enormous success of *Aida* was that Verdi was made a Commendatore of the Ottoman Order.

Chapter Eighteen

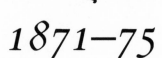

1871–75

Verdi regarded the first European production of *Aida* at La Scala, Milan, as of greater significance than the Cairo premiere. That Teresa Stolz should sing Aida was taken for granted, but the mezzo-soprano role of Amneris was of equal importance, and its casting greatly exercised the composer. The Viennese Maria Waldmann was favoured by Giulio Ricordi, but the fee she asked was enormous. 'I think we should put it straight to la Waldmann,' Verdi told Ricordi. 'Either she desists from her ridiculous demands, or negotiations will cease.'[1] When Ricordi suggested auditioning other singers for the role, Verdi replied:

> You know the libretto of *Aida*, and you know that the role of Amneris requires an artist of great dramatic feeling who can really hold the stage. How can one hope to find this quality in someone who is almost a newcomer? Voice alone, however beautiful (and that's difficult to judge in an empty room or theatre), is not enough for this role. So-called vocal finesse means little to me. I like to have roles sung the way I want them, but I can't provide the voice, the temperament, the '*je ne sais quoi*' that one might call the spark. It's what is usually understood by the phrase 'to be possessed by the devil'.

After listing his requirements regarding orchestra, chorus and conductor, and producing a sketch to indicate how the orchestra should be seated, he continued:

> This arrangement of the orchestra is much more important than is usually believed, for the instrumental colouring, for the sonority, and for the effect. These small improvements will open the way to other innovations that will certainly come one day. One of them will be the removal of the

spectators' boxes from the stage, thus enabling the curtain to come right up to the footlights. Another improvement would be to make the orchestra invisible. This idea is not mine, but Wagner's, and it's a very good one. It's incredible nowadays that we should tolerate seeing horrid white ties and tails, for example, between us and the costumes of Egyptians, Assyrians or Druids etc. etc. and, in addition, see the whole of the orchestra, which should be part of a fictitious world, almost in the middle of the stalls among the crowd as it hisses or applauds. Add to all this the annoyance of seeing the tops of harps and contrabassoons as well as the flailing arms of the conductor waving about in the air.

Answer me, then, categorically and decisively because, if I cannot be given what I require, then there is no point in our continuing these negotiations.[2]

As late as 26 December, two days after the Cairo premiere, Verdi was still worried about his Milan Amneris. 'La Waldmann frightens me,' he told Ricordi:

She has such a curious accent, pronunciation and sameness of sounds that she can produce the most unpleasant effects. . . . I am transcribing for you a lengthy telegram from the Bey (obviously the Khedive paid for it), from which you will see the importance of Amneris and, therefore, how much study la Waldmann will need: 'Maestro Verdi, Genoa: First performance *Aida* triumphant success. First, second finales, two duets soprano and tenor, grand march, council scene, total fanaticism. Enthusiastic audience applauded absent Maestro. Congratulations, thanks, Draneth.'[3]

On 2 January Verdi arrived in Milan to begin rehearsals at La Scala, staying, as he now usually did, at the Grand Hotel et de Milan, Via Manzoni 29, where he occupied a small suite consisting of bedroom and drawing-room. (The Scala season had opened on 26 December with a revival of *La forza del destino* in which Teresa Stolz sang Leonora and Maria Waldmann the role of Preziosilla, which did not suit her.) Verdi was responsible for the staging of *Aida*, but did not conduct the orchestra, leaving this to Franco Faccio. On 13 January he wrote to Arrivabene:

I have begun rehearsals for *Aida*. The devil has stuck his horns in, making Capponi ill, and I have had to be satisfied with Fancelli: beautiful voice, but a blockhead. In any case, if they aren't too hard, I'll do all I can to break this devil's horns.

You will say I am presumptuous! No, no. I have good elements in the chorus and orchestra; I have la Stolz and Pandolfini; la Waldmann is intelligent; so something should come out of it. I shall write to you about it, and shall tell you the truth. *La forza del destino* is going well; I do not listen to the applause, but I look at the full houses.[4]

That Giuseppe Fancelli, the tenor whom Verdi had to accept as a replacement for Giuseppe Capponi, was indeed a blockhead, is confirmed by Giulio Ricordi's account of an incident which occurred during rehearsals:

> There wasn't a day on which the Maestro did not occupy himself with him, illustrating even the words and the moods of the role. His time and breath were wasted. On one bad morning Verdi could no longer control himself. Having made Fancelli repeat the same phrase over and over without obtaining any result, Verdi rose to his feet, seized the tenor by the back of his neck, and, while repeatedly pounding the man's forehead on the keyboard, burst out: 'When will anything ever get into your head? Never!' With that, he furiously left the room.
>
> Fancelli did not react and did not utter a word. But the moment Verdi was gone, he turned to the rest of us who were dumbstruck, and looking at all of us, one after the other, mumbled with a desolate expression: 'A great Maestro, yes, sir! I agree. But he wants the impossible! He wants people to read his music as he wrote it, and to sing on pitch and in tempo, and even to pronounce the words! How can you do all that stuff at the same time? I couldn't, even if I were Almighty God himself.'[5]

It was not only his leading tenor who incurred the composer's wrath. At the first dress rehearsal, while the ballet was in progress Verdi suddenly jumped to his feet, shouting, 'Get rid of those ballerinas! Get rid of those people. There's too much movement!' He climbed quickly onto the stage, ordering immediate modifications to the ballet, despite the protests of the choreographer.

Aida was given its first Italian performance on 8 February 1872 with Teresa Stolz in the name part, Maria Waldmann (Amneris), Giuseppe Fancelli (Radames), Francesco Pandolfini (Amonasro), a chorus of 120 and an orchestra of ninety. It was a great occasion with the theatre full to overflowing – it was said that the ticket prices had been a matter of speculation on the stock exchange! The reception was wildly enthusiastic, and with one or two exceptions critical reaction was extremely favourable. The next morning Verdi reported as usual to his friend Arrivabene:

> Last night *Aida*. Very good. Performance of ensemble and soloists excellent, production also. Stolz and Pandolfini very good. Waldmann good. Fancelli beautiful voice but nothing else. The others good, and the

orchestra and chorus fine. As for the music, Piroli will speak to you about it. The audience liked it. I don't want to play modest with you: this is by no means the worst thing I've written, and time will give it the place it deserves. In short, it's a success and will pack the theatre. If I'm wrong, I'll write to you. Meanwhile, farewell in haste.[6]

The last of the *Aida* performances, all of which had played to full houses, was given on 31 March. On that day, Verdi wrote sarcastically to Giulio Ricordi:

So this evening will be the last for *Aida*!! I can breathe again!! There'll be no more talk about it, or at least no more than a few final words. Perhaps some new insult, accusing me of Wagnerism, and then . . . *Requiescant in pacem!*

And now, will you be kind enough to tell me what sacrifices this opera of mine has imposed upon the management? Don't be stupefied by the question: there must obviously have been sacrifices, since none of these gentlemen, despite all the work I have done and the thousands of lire I have expended, has said so much as 'Thank you, dog!' Or should I perhaps thank them for having accepted and produced this wretched *Aida*, whose twenty performances earned 165,000 lire, not counting the subscribers and the gallery? . . .[7]

The success of *Aida* was world-wide. Every Italian opera house wanted to produce it as soon as possible, though many were thwarted by Verdi's determination to ensure that only first-class productions would be mounted. He was less concerned about performances abroad, realistically accepting that there was little he could do to influence standards in other countries. Within a few seasons the opera had been produced in Buenos Aires, New York, Berlin, Madrid, Vienna, Budapest, Warsaw, St Petersburg, Prague, Paris, London, Kiev, Rio de Janeiro, Bucharest, Brussels, Tiflis, Havana, Mexico City, Stockholm and a score of other cities. By the end of the century there can have been very few opera houses anywhere in the world which had not staged *Aida*.

Verdi himself directed productions of the opera in Parma and Naples. He travelled to Parma on 3 April to begin rehearsals with Teresa Stolz, Maria Waldmann and Giuseppe Capponi, the tenor who had been prevented by illness from participating in the Milan premiere. After only seventeen days' rehearsal *Aida*, conducted by Giovanni Rossi, was given its first performance in Parma on 20 April to great acclaim. However, the following month, Verdi received a letter from a dissatisfied customer who lived in nearby Reggio Emilia:

On the 2nd of this month I went to Parma, drawn there by the sensation made by your opera *Aida*. So great was my curiosity that half an hour before the commencement of the performance I was already in my seat, no. 120. I admired the scenery, I heard with pleasure the excellent singers, and I did all in my power to let nothing escape me. At the end of the opera, I asked myself if I was satisfied, and the answer was 'No'. I started back to Reggio, and listened in the railway carriage to the opinions of my fellow travellers, nearly all of whom agreed in considering *Aida* a work of the first order.

I was therefore seized with the idea of hearing it again, and on the 4th I returned to Parma. I made unprecedented efforts to get a reserved seat. As the crowd was enormous, I was obliged to spend five lire to witness the performance in any comfort.

I came to this conclusion about it: it is an opera in which there is absolutely nothing thrilling or exciting. Without the pomp of the spectacle, the public would not sit through it to the end. When it has filled the theatre a few more times, it will be banished to the dust of the archives.

You can picture to yourself, my dear Signor Verdi, my regret at having spent on two occasions thirty-two lire. Add to this the aggravating circumstance that I am dependent on my family, and that this money preys on my mind like a frightful spectre. I therefore address myself frankly to you in order that you may send me the amount. The account is as follows:

Railroad – one way	2.60 lire
Railroad – return	3.30
Theatre	8.00
Detestable supper at station	2.00
	15.90
Twice	×2
	31.80

Hoping you will deliver me from this embarrassment, I salute you from my heart.

PROSPERO BERTANI[8]

Amused by the letter, Verdi sent it on to Ricordi with a covering note:

You may well imagine that to protect the son of a family from the frightful spectres which pursue him, I shall willingly pay the little bill which he sends me. I therefore beg you to forward by one of your representatives the sum of 27.80 lire to this Signor Prospero Bertani, Via San Domenico, No. 5, Reggio. It isn't the entire sum that he demands, but – to pay for his supper too! – certainly not! He could very well have eaten at home!!!!! It is understood that he must send you a receipt, and a note in which he must undertake to attend no new opera of mine, thus avoiding for himself that threat of spectres, and sparing me further travelling expenses.[9]

Signor Bertani received his 27.80 lire and gave the required undertaking to expose himself to no further operas by Verdi.

The summer of 1872 was spent by the Verdis at Sant' Agata and Genoa, with a week's visit at the beginning of August to Tabiano, near Parma, for the thermal baths. On 24 August Verdi had occasion to write one of his impolite letters about the Paris Opéra, in reply to Olivier Halanzier-Dufrenoy, Director of the Opéra, who hoped to stage *Aida* in a French translation which had been prepared by Camille du Locle and Charles Nuitter:

> I thank you very much for the courteous manner in which you have proposed to enter into business relations with me. I am also specially flattered that you have thought the score of *Aida* worthy of the Opéra. But, in the first place, I am too imperfectly acquainted with the personnel of the Opéra; and, secondly, permit me to confess, I have been so little satisfied each time that I have had anything to do with your great theatre, that I am not disposed to risk a new attempt.
>
> Possibly later, if you preserve your good intentions towards me, I may change my mind. But at present I have not the courage to face again all the trickery and opposition which rule in that theatre, of which I have preserved a painful recollection.
>
> Excuse me, sir, if I have explained my ideas with perhaps too much frankness; but I was desirous of speaking to you with candour, so as to leave no uncertainty. This does not prevent me from having for you, sir, personally, a feeling of gratitude for the courteous expressions with which you have been good enough to honour me in your letter.[10]

Early in November, accompanied by Giuseppina, Verdi travelled to Naples where he was to direct productions of *Don Carlo* and *Aida*, with Teresa Stolz and Maria Waldmann appearing in both operas. He slightly revised the score of *Don Carlo* for this occasion, turning to Ghislanzoni to supply the necessary alterations to the libretto. Rehearsals for *Aida* had to be postponed when Teresa Stolz became indisposed: the opera was finally staged at the Teatro San Carlo on 30 March 1873. Meanwhile, Verdi had made use of what he described to Arrivabene as his moments of idleness in Naples during March to compose his first and only string quartet, which was given a private performance before an audience of seven or eight friends in his suite at the Albergo delle Crocelle on 1 April. His audience liked it so well that they demanded an immediate encore of the entire work. 'I don't know whether this quartet is beautiful or ugly, but I do know that it's a quartet,' the composer told Arrivabene.[11] Five years later, when the Mayor of Parma requested his permission to have it played at a concert, Verdi replied:

> I have given no further attention to the quartet I wrote for mere amusement when I was in Naples some years ago. . . . This is to tell you that I have never attached any importance to this piece, and for the present at least I do not wish to have it brought forward in any way.[12]

The quartet (in E minor) is a delightful work, excellently laid out for the instruments and formally satisfying, combining in its old-fashioned style something of Haydn's fluent gracefulness with the vigour of early Beethoven. Verdi's attempted suppression of it may have been connected with his feeling that the Italian musical genius was for opera, and that chamber music ought really to be left to the Viennese school. Eventually he was forced by constant requests from professional and amateur music societies to allow Ricordi to publish the quartet, after which it began to be played at public concerts. An impresario in London wanted to have it performed by a huge string orchestra of eighty, an idea which appealed to Verdi!

On 22 May 1873 the composer's hero, the novelist Alessandro Manzoni, died in Milan at the age of eighty-nine, two weeks after he had slipped on the steps of the church of San Fedele and been carried home unconscious. Verdi was greatly affected by Manzoni's death. 'I am deeply saddened by the death of our great man,' he wrote to Giulio Ricordi. 'But I shall not come to Milan tomorrow, for I haven't the heart to attend his funeral. I shall come in a little while to visit his grave, alone and without being seen, and perhaps (after further reflection, and after I have weighed up my strength) to propose some way of honouring his memory.'[13]

Manzoni's funeral was took place on 29 May. Four days later Verdi travelled to Milan to visit the grave, and the following day, having thought carefully about how he could most effectively honour Manzoni's memory, he wrote again to Ricordi:

> I would like to compose a Mass for the Dead, to be performed next year on the anniversary of his death. The Mass would have rather vast dimensions, and in addition to a big orchestra and a big chorus it would also require (I cannot be specific as yet) four or five principal singers.
>
> Do you think the City would assume the expenses of the performance? The copying of the music I would have done at my expense, and I myself would conduct the performance, both at the rehearsals and in church. If you think this is a possibility, speak of it to the Mayor. Give me an answer as soon as you can, for you can consider this letter of mine binding.[14]

On behalf of the city, the Mayor of Milan accepted the composer's offer. Manzoni's death was being mourned all over Italy, and his funeral in Milan had been a huge public ceremony, but some of the obituary notices in Catholic newspapers seemed to Verdi to be distinctly ungenerous in tone. One paper had accused Manzoni of being a bad Catholic, another found 'a fine poison' in his books. 'I have read many of the newspapers,' Verdi wrote to Clarina Maffei, 'and not one of them speaks fittingly of him. Many words, but none of them deeply felt. No lack of stinging remarks, however. Even about him! Oh, what an ugly race we are!'[15]

Manzoni's liberal ideas were anathema to the church, but there is no doubt that throughout his lifetime he considered himself a Christian believer and a Catholic. The composer who contemplated honouring Manzoni's memory with a Requiem Mass was, however, not a believer but an atheist, willing in his more contemplative moments to soften his attitude to one of agnosticism, but implacably opposed to organized religion. In 1872, in a letter to one of Verdi's friends, Dr Cesare Vigna, a specialist in mental diseases, Giuseppina had occasion to touch upon Verdi's attitude to religious matters. Vigna had sent to Sant' Agata a pamphlet he had written on the subject of science and religion, and in acknowledging receipt of it Giuseppina wrote:

> Verdi thinks too highly of you not to believe your words and, despite the fact that you are a doctor, to number you among the believers in spiritual things. But, between ourselves, he presents the strangest phenomenon in the world. He is not a doctor, but an artist. Everyone agrees in saying that there fell to his lot the divine gift of genius. He is a jewel among honest men; he understands and feels himself every delicate and elevated sentiment. And yet this brigand permits himself to be, I won't say an atheist, but certainly very little of a believer, and that with an obstinacy and calm that make one want to beat him. I exhaust myself in speaking to him about the marvels of the heavens, the earth, the sea, etc. etc. It's a waste of breath! He laughs in my face, and freezes me in the midst of my oratorical periods and my divine enthusiasm, by saying: 'You're all crazy.' And unfortunately he says it in good faith.[16] [Giuseppina, in drafting this letter, had written: 'This brigand permits himself to be an atheist with an obstinacy and calm . . .', but altered the sentence before transcribing the letter from her notebook.]

Verdi was, by nature and by profession, a musical dramatist. Composing a religious work, therefore, on the highly dramatic text of the Catholic Mass for the Dead posed for him problems not essentially different from those he had faced in writing music to be sung by the Jews of the Old Testament in *Nabucco*, the Egyptian worshippers of Amon the Sun God in *Aida*, or the pagan Attila the Hun and his Ostrogoths in *Attila*. In June 1873, he and Giuseppina left to spend the summer months in Paris, where Verdi began to write his *Requiem* for Manzoni, making use of the 'Libera me' he had composed five years earlier as his contribution to the aborted *Requiem* for Rossini.

By mid-September he and Giuseppina were back in Italy. After travelling by train through the recently opened Mt Cenis tunnel, Verdi wrote enthusiastically from Turin to Camille du Locle: 'The tunnel is really sensational! Splendid gas illumination inside, and profound darkness outside. Fresh air, without being suffocated by the smoke – it's a most beautiful thing. And then, three thousand metres of earth and rocks above your head!!'[17]

Perhaps because he was now deeply involved in the creation of the *Requiem*, Verdi responded with an uncalled-for irascibility to an invitation from the president of the theatre in Trieste to attend the first performance of *Aida* there. His reply is just within the bounds of politeness, but to Giulio Ricordi he complained, 'By God in heaven, I must be thought of as a charlatan, a clown who enjoys displaying himself like a Tom Thumb, a Miss Baba, an orang-utan, or some other freak!! Poor me! Poor me!'[18] Returning to Busseto, he continued to work on the *Requiem* throughout the autumn and winter. By April 1874 the score was complete, and at the beginning of May the composer went to Milan to begin rehearsals for its performance on 22 May, the first anniversary of Manzoni's death, at the Church of San Marco, which he had chosen as having the best acoustics.

The soloists in the *Requiem* were four singers who had been closely and successfully associated with *Aida*: Teresa Stolz (soprano), Maria Waldmann (mezzo-soprano), Giuseppe Capponi (tenor) and Ormondo Maini (bass). The performance of the *Requiem*, conducted by the composer with a chorus of one hundred and twenty and an orchestra of one hundred drawn from the leading Italian opera houses, was an enormous success, and the work was proclaimed a masterpiece by an audience which included music-lovers, musicians and critics from all over Europe. Three days later, Verdi had to conduct a second performance at La Scala, and Franco Faccio conducted a further two as the composer had to leave Milan to prepare a chorus and orchestra in Paris for performances of the work there. That from the beginning this agnostic, dramatic and popular Mass was received by audiences as a musical rather than as a religious experience is clear from the description in a Milan journal, *Il Sole*, of the performance at La Scala:

> When the dial of the theatre clock pointed to nine o'clock, the four artists entrusted with the solos, Mesdames Stolz and Waldmann, Messrs Capponi and Maini, came onto the stage. Madame Stolz wore a becoming costume of blue silk, trimmed with white velvet, and Mademoiselle Waldmann was dressed all in pink. The appearance of these redoubtable artists was the first signal for applause, which became formidable when Verdi appeared. But the latter, grave as usual, taking his position at the desk in the centre of the stage, and facing the four singers, who were near the orchestra, gave the signal of attack, and the applause ceased as if by enchantment.
>
> To follow the movements one by one would be quite impossible; but we will say, nevertheless, that all were applauded with rapture. The 'Dies Irae', with all the episodes which it comprises, was received with extraordinary favour. But at the 'Offertorium', the enthusiasm knew no bounds, and the public insisted on the repetition of this admirable quartet with chorus. . . . They also encored the 'Sanctus', a fugue for double chorus, which was performed wonderfully. The magic wand of Verdi seemed to have electrified all the performers.
>
> At the 'Agnus Dei', the applause grew louder, and suppressed shouts broke out during the performance, so powerful was the inspiration which it revealed. The public, although they had exacted the repetition of the two preceding pieces, and although consideration for the artists warned them not to insist upon it in this case, could not refrain from unanimously crying out, 'Bis!' It was so overwhelming a demonstration that Verdi could do no less than obey with courtesy.
>
> After the 'Offertorium' had been repeated, a silver crown was presented to Verdi on an elegant cushion, whilst the public applauded with rapture.[19]

It is perhaps not surprising that the German conductor Hans von Bülow, who happened to be in Milan on the day of the first performance, should have described the *Requiem* (before hearing it) as 'Verdi's latest opera, in ecclesiastical dress'. There is some justification for his comment, though Brahms, when he heard of it, declared, 'Bülow has made a fool of himself. This is a work of genius.' Naturally, the language of Verdi's *Requiem* is dramatic: that was his métier. He had set out to express the emotional meaning and implications of the liturgical text, just as in his operas he was concerned to express the meaning of the words and situations with which he was presented by his librettists. The only significant difference was that this time he was unable to bully a librettist into altering the words!

After the enormously successful Milan performances, Verdi conducted seven performances of the *Requiem* at the Opéra-Comique in Paris, most of them with his Milan soloists, and then, at the end of June, paid a four-day visit to London to explore the possibility of presenting the work there. He attended a Handel Festival concert at the Crystal Palace, finding its 'three or four thousand performers . . . an immense humbug',[20] and, as on his previous visits to the city, thought London both curious and exciting. After arranging for the *Requiem* to be performed the following year at the Royal Albert Hall, he returned, via Paris, to Sant' Agata where he and Giuseppina spent the summer. In September, Giuseppina busied herself in Genoa supervising the moving of furniture from their apartment in the Palazzo Sauli on the Carignano hill to a new one on the top floor of the Palazzo Doria, a magnificent palace on the sea-front. In November, Verdi was named Senator of the Kingdom of Italy. He was expected to go to Rome to take the oath at a Royal Session of parliament, but politely declined: *Aida* was being performed there at the Teatro Apollo and, as he told his friend Senator Piroli, 'If I came to Rome, it would be quite difficult for me to avoid those musical bores, and I don't want to meddle in performances of *Aida* at this time.'[21]

Verdi continued to react angrily when invited to attend perform-ances of *Aida*. 'Just think,' he complained to Ricordi, 'there isn't a village where *Don Carlos*, *Forza* or *Aida* is given to which I am not invited to attend a performance, so that I can do four pirouettes on the stage!'[22] He was more interested in promoting, and indeed conduct-ing, performances of the *Requiem*: a European tour of the work in the spring of 1875 was arranged by Ricordi on which Verdi and his four soloists would perform it in Paris, London, Berlin and Vienna, with local choruses and orchestras, the soloists consisting of Teresa Stolz and Maria Waldmann from the initial performances, with a new tenor (Angelo Masini), and a bass (Paolo Medini) who had created the role of Ramfis, the High Priest, in *Aida* in Cairo.

The following year, Maria Waldmann was to retire from the stage upon her marriage to Count Galeazzo Massari. 'Goodbye, then, to our beautiful Eboli and Amneris, who now has no equal in those roles,' Verdi wrote to Ricordi.[23] He had composed for Waldmann a new solo setting of the 'Liber scriptus' for insertion in the *Requiem* to replace the choral fugue of the first performances. However, he advised the singer against including it in the Paris performances on the tour, for the work had been heard in Paris the previous year, 'and even if that piece were effective, everyone would say "It was better as it was before." This would be the thanks you and I would surely have.'[24]

Before setting out on the tour, Verdi indulged in an acerbic exchange of correspondence in March with Ricordi on the subject of the Rome production of *Aida*. 'I hear that *Aida* is being torn to shreds in Rome,' he declared on 21 March,[25] making it clear that he held the firm of Ricordi responsible, since they were supposed to be acting in his interests and should not have allowed a mediocre staging. Four days later, having been given more information about the performances by his Roman friend Vincenzo Luccardi, Verdi wrote again to Ricordi:

Dear Giulio,

Performance!!!!

Nicolini [the tenor] has always omitted his piece!!!
Aldighieri [the baritone] has omitted the third act duet at various times!!
Even the second act finale was cut one night!!!!!!

In addition to transposing the romanza ['*Celeste Aida*'] down, they changed several bars.

A mediocre Aida!!
A soprano for Amneris!!

And, what's more, a conductor who takes the liberty of changing the tempos!!! . . . We don't need conductors and singers to discover new effects; for my part, I declare that no one has ever, ever, ever been able to draw out all the effects conceived by me. No one!!! Never, never, neither singers nor conductors!! But it is fashionable now to applaud even conductors, and I feel sorry for the few I esteem; even more, I feel sorry for those who pass on indecencies in the opera house from one to the other without end. At one time we had to endure the tyranny of prima donnas; now we'll also have to endure that of conductors! . . . Let me finish by asking you to tell the House of Ricordi that I cannot tolerate the above-mentioned improprieties. If it wishes, the House of Ricordi can withdraw my last three scores (and that would give me great pleasure), but I cannot allow them to be subjected to alterations. . . .[26]

Ricordi must have sent a telegram with assurances that nothing of this kind would occur again, for Verdi returned to the attack the following day: 'I received the telegram. You have taken care of the future, but what about the past?'[27] Ricordi continued to make excuses, but this particular exchange of views came to an end with an angry and bitter outburst from the composer on 4 April:

Excuse me if, in spite of all your arguments, I continue to believe that the *Aida* in Rome was performed much worse than in any other place thus far, and that it was done in a *patchwork*. I know quite well that perfection does not exist, and that elsewhere there were very deficient parts. But at least the parts were in place. . . .

You speak to me about the results obtained!!!!!!!!! Where are they? I'll tell you. After an absence of twenty-five years from La Scala, I was booed after the first act of *La forza del destino*. After *Aida*, endless chatter: that I was no longer the Verdi of *Ballo* (of that *Ballo* which was booed the first time they heard it at La Scala); that it would have been terrible if there hadn't been a fourth act (so wrote d'Arcais); that I didn't know how to write for singers; that only the second and fourth acts had tolerable moments (nothing in the third); and finally that I was an imitator of Wagner!!! Fine result after a career of thirty-five years to end up as an imitator!!!

Certainly this chatter does not (and never did) make me budge an inch from what I wanted to do, because I have always known what I wanted. But having arrived at the point where I am now, be it high or low, I am entitled to say, 'If that's the way it is, do as you please.' And when I want to write music, I can write it in my study, without listening to the pronouncements of the scholars and the imbeciles.

I can only take as a joke your statement 'The total salvation of the theatre and of art is in your hands!!' Oh no, have no doubt; there will always be composers. And I repeat what Boito said in a toast to Faccio after his first opera: 'Perhaps he who will sweep clean the altar is already born.' Amen.[28]

On 10 April, Verdi travelled to Milan to rehearse the *Requiem* for the European tour, and on 19 April the first of seven performances was given at the Opéra-Comique. 'The Mass is going really well in every respect,' the composer wrote to Piroli from Paris on 6 May. 'The quartet of singers has gained much because this year we have a tenor who has a delightful and true voice. Oh, if only he were an artist!'[29] (Verdi suffered chronically from tenors.)

While he was in Paris, Verdi was made a Commander of the Legion of Honour. Also, while he was in Paris, a twenty-three-year-old American student of singing, Blanche Roosevelt (who was to make her stage debut in London the following year in *La traviata* under the name of Blanche Rosavella), contrived to interview him in his rooms at the Hôtel de Bade and published an account of the occasion in the Chicago *Times*. Most of the conversation, as Miss Roosevelt reported it, was no more than small talk, but she included a description of Verdi as he appeared in his sixty-second year which brings the composer's features to life more graphically than the somewhat frozen photography of the period has managed to do:

His personal appearance is not striking; he is small, but very broad-shouldered, with a full, generous chest, and well-built body. He has large, laughing gray eyes, eyes that flash and change colour every instant. The face is strong, and shows very few lines for a man of his years. The features are large, the cheek-bones high, and the lower part of the jaw rather sunken; the chin and side of the face are covered with a short, heavy beard, once black, but now slightly mixed with gray. The mouth is large and pleasant, but it is almost totally concealed by a dark moustache, which gives the face a very young look. The forehead is very broad and high, denoting great character and quickness of perception; the eyebrows are heavy, also gray and black. The hair is very long, lying lightly on the forehead; it, also, is slightly mixed with gray. There is a wonderful firmness and hidden strength in Verdi's countenance, which made me think of a picture I had once seen of Samson.

In one way I was disappointed in his looks. He has the air and figure of anything but an ideal composer. I do not know what I expected to find, but certainly he has the frank, social manners of an ordinary individual rather than the exclusive and sometimes painful diffidence characteristic of men of great talent. I cannot say he lacks dignity, but there was so utter an absence of self-consciousness in his bearing, and such a happy, gracious smile on his face, that I was charmed with his whole manner.[30]

On 13 May the Verdi troupe left Paris for London, where on 15 May the composer conducted the first of four performances of his *Requiem* at the Royal Albert Hall. The London press was divided in its opinion. The *Pall Mall Gazette* thought the work the most beautiful sacred music since Mozart's *Requiem*, while the *Morning Post* objected to the 'shouting of the chorus in the "Dies Irae" ' and the 'canine vociferation of the "Libera me" '. It continued: 'There is no melody that the mind can receive consonant with the words, and the breaking of those words into short, sharp ejaculations, like a series of barks or yells, is certainly not indicative of reverence.' The *Daily Telegraph* was enthusiastic, dissociating itself from 'Puritans who think all sacred music should conform to English standards.'[31]

Verdi thought Ricordi's arrangements regarding the London performances unsatisfactory, and was inclined to blame the publisher for the fact that the box office receipts resulted in a small loss. Because of this disappointing outcome of the London visit, Ricordi cancelled the projected Berlin performances, to the extreme annoyance of the composer, who had looked foward to showing the Germans what could be achieved by Italian music, albeit with a pair of Austro-Hungarian female soloists. As Giuseppina had noted in her diary three years earlier, when a German and Austrian tour of *Aida* was being considered,

> In this way it would be a veritable artistic event, establishing (I hope) our music well and truly in Germany. Verdi would derive individual glory from the tour, and Italy general glory. The two ladies would be the ones now performing *Aida* in Padua [Stolz and Waldmann], since, not only are they German-speaking, but they have acquired an Italian style, while preserving the German quality of their voices.[32]

From London the tour proceeded via Paris to Vienna, a city Verdi had not visited since 1843. On 7 June he conducted his first rehearsal of the *Requiem*, earlier rehearsals having been taken by Franco Faccio who had preceded him to Vienna. *Die Neue Freie Presse* reported:

> Maestro Verdi appeared at eleven o'clock today at the Hofoperntheater to conduct in person a first full rehearsal of his great *Requiem* for Manzoni. The celebrated composer was welcomed by the entire chorus and the *Akademischer Gesangverein* with ecstatic applause and cries of 'Long live Verdi', which lasted for several minutes. Verdi thanked them courteously and then began the rehearsal, during which the musicians, at particularly striking moments, played the part of audience and broke out into loud applause. Verdi, who mostly speaks French to the musicians, is said to have been highly satisfied with the performance of both orchestra and chorus, and he repeatedly proclaimed that they had exceeded his highest expectations.[33]

The atmosphere, it would appear, was rather different from that which Verdi had grown used to at the Paris Opéra. The first of four performances of the *Requiem* was given at the Hofoper on 11 June in the presence of the Emperor Franz Joseph (who attended three of the four performances), and was greeted rapturously, as were the rest. Verdi was delighted with Vienna. He described the opera house as the best theatre in the world, and, after the first performance, wrote to Vincenzo Luccardi,

> Since you wish it, I can tell you that the success of the *Requiem* was really great. A performance such as one will never hear again! Orchestra and chorus wonderful! The duet for the two men, the 'Offertorium' and the 'Agnus Dei' were all encored![34]

The famous Viennese music critic Eduard Hanslick (he who was caricatured by Wagner as Beckmesser in *Die Meistersinger von Nürnberg*) published an interesting and perceptive review:

Verdi's *Requiem* is a sound and beautiful work, above all a milestone in the history of his development as a composer. One may rate it higher or lower as one pleases: the cry 'We never expected this from Verdi' will never end. In this sense it is a companion piece to *Aida*, which seems still more significant both in invention and execution. How far it is from *Ernani* or *Il trovatore*! And yet [the *Requiem*] is unmistakably Verdi, wholly and completely. The study of old Roman church music shines through it, but only as a glimmer, not as a model.

To be sure, and this must be stated at the outset, the theatre has greater need of Verdi than has the church. If he has shown in the *Requiem* what he can do on foreign soil, he remains, nevertheless, far stronger on his home ground. Not even in the *Requiem* can he deny the dramatic composer. Mourning and supplication, awe and faith, they speak here in language more passionate and individual than we are accustomed to hear in the church. . . .

One must grant Verdi this testament of sincerity: no movement of his *Requiem* is trivial, false or frivolous. He proceeds incomparably more earnestly, more sternly, than Rossini in his *Stabat Mater*, though the kinship of the two works is not to be denied. . . . Verdi, following the better Neapolitan church music, has denied neither the rich artistic means of his time nor the lively fervour of his nature. He has, like many a pious painter, placed his own portrait on his sacred canvas. Religious devotion, too, varies in its expression; it has its countries and its times. What may appear so passionate, so sensuous in Verdi's *Requiem* is derived from the emotional habits of his people, and the Italian has a perfect right to inquire whether he may not talk to the dear Lord in the Italian language![35]

In addition to the *Requiem*, two performances of *Aida* were given on 19 and 21 June at the Hofoper, at the first of which Franz Joseph bestowed upon Verdi the highest Austrian cultural honour, the *Komturkreuz* of the Order of Franz Joseph. Both performances of *Aida*, conducted by the composer, were greeted with immense enthusiasm. Interviewed by *Die Neue Freie Presse*, Verdi spoke admiringly of the recently constructed opera house. (The Vienna Staatsoper of today, it had opened in 1869 with a performance of Mozart's *Don Giovanni*.) He thought the orchestra the best he had ever conducted or heard, was enchanted by the city, which reminded him vividly of northern Italy, and expressed the hope that he might return soon to conduct a new work. (However, he declined an invitation to make a detour to Budapest to conduct his *Requiem* at the National Theatre.) He expressed a qualified admiration for Wagner who, he said, had done opera an incalculable service by freeing it from traditional forms. 'I too have attempted to blend music and drama in my *Macbeth*,' he continued,

> but unlike Wagner I was not able to write my own libretti. Wagner surpasses every composer in his rich variety of instrumental colour, but in both form and style he has gone too far. At the outset he successfully avoided mundane subject matter, but he later strayed from his idealistic aims by carrying his theories to extremes, and committed the very error that he had originally set out to reform: and so the monotony, which he avoided with such success, now threatens to dominate him.[36]

While in Vienna, Verdi visited the Conservatorium, where he asked to see the library's Beethoven manuscripts, which he examined with great interest, especially the Violin Concerto and the 'Eroica' Symphony. He heard performances by the students, professed his astonishment at the quality of orchestral playing, and congratulated a young contralto, Frau Bernstein, who sang some of Azucena's music from *Il trovatore*. He also told the Director of the Conservatorium that he himself owed a great debt to this prestigious school of music where so many artists who sang in his operas with such success had received their training.

The *Requiem* tour ended in July in Venice with five performances at the Teatro Malibran. These were conducted by Faccio, as Verdi and Giuseppina had returned to Sant' Agata. The same cast and conductor also gave four performances in Florence in September. Verdi by now was convinced that the firm of Ricordi had not been entirely honest in its accounts relating to royalties due to him, so he demanded to see all the records and contracts concerning his operas, going back as far as *Rigoletto* a quarter of a century earlier. Tito Ricordi, head of the firm, took himself off to the spa of San Pellegrino, leaving his son Giulio to deal with Verdi, who had sent Mauro Corticelli to Milan to fetch the contracts which Ricordi had made with various theatres. Verdi himself spent several days examining the contracts, and arrived at the conclusion that he had, for many years, been systematically cheated by his publisher. The firm attempted to place the blame on a man named Tornaghi who was in charge of their contracts department, but, as Giuseppina wrote to Giulio Ricordi, 'Who is the proprietor, please? Signor Tito, I believe. Who has been corresponding with Verdi in recent times? You. How, then, could you and your father not know about Tornaghi's actions? And, knowing of them, how could you pass them over?'[37]

Giuseppina's letters of this period reveal her to have emerged from her occasional depressions onto a plateau of serenity and contentment. But, when the Ricordis attempted to enlist her aid in effecting a reconciliation with Verdi, her reply to a letter from Tito Ricordi's wife, though sympathetic, was not encouraging. 'The thought of your moral sufferings and those of your family', wrote Giuseppina,

> really rends my heart. I wish all this were just a bad dream. But think, yourself, for a moment, of Verdi. How could this man, who for so many years has brought riches and honour to your firm, how could this man, I say, imagine that in the House of Ricordi, irregularities were being committed, to his detriment, wounding him thus materially and morally? No (I say it again), no one, no one, you understand, either here or elsewhere, has wished maliciously to influence Verdi against you. Nor is he a man to allow himself to be influenced. In this painful business he has had to surrender to the evidence! . . . I told Giulio, and I repeat to you, that only after a complete examination of the contracts will Verdi take such measures as he thinks just and reasonable. For the moment I am absolutely unable to say more.[38]

The final outcome some months later was that the firm of Ricordi agreed to pay Verdi the sum of 50,000 lire in compensation. 'It is not the entire amount that they owe me,' the composer told Senator Piroli in December, 'but that does not matter. The bad thing is that there will no longer be between us the relationship there used to be.'[39] Eventually, however, it became clear that Verdi's friendship with Tito Ricordi's son Giulio would survive and continue to flourish independently of the composer's suspicions regarding the firm's highly creative accounting methods.

In September, Giuseppina somewhat quixotically purchased from Verdi the Palazzo Dordoni (the present Palazzo Orlandi) in Busseto, where she had lived with him in 1849. Her intention was to restore the house and maintain it as a memorial to the composer who 'from the humblest origins, succeeded by his genius, and by every private and public virtue, in raising himself to the highest social spheres and honouring the town he inhabited for some time and Italy, our common motherland'.[40]

Chapter Nineteen

1875–78

For some time, gossip had been circulating in Italian musical circles about Verdi's relationship with the soprano Teresa Stolz. This reached print in the summer of 1875 when, arising from its account of a quarrel between rival impresarios concerning a forthcoming performance in Florence of the *Requiem* with the soloists who had been on tour with the work, the Florence *Rivista Indipendente* on 22 August promised its readers a revelation of 'certain intimacies of Signora Stolz, with Maestro Mariani and now with Verdi'. The journal then launched, on 4 September, a campaign directed against Teresa Stolz with a denigratory, offensive and highly inaccurate description of the singer's career, preceded by the kind of hypocritically moralistic introduction one can still read in the popular press of today: 'Determined always to conserve the complete independence of our paper, we shall not draw back from the task we have undertaken, but shall tell the truth always, even when the truth is not to everyone's liking.'

Teresa Stolz is characterized as an untalented singer who furthered her career by becoming the *inamorata* of the conductor Mariani, who coached her so remarkably well that, when she appeared under his baton in Bologna in *Don Carlo* ('one of Verdi's minor works [which] in Paris had left few pleasant memories and perhaps been somewhat of a fiasco'), both Verdi as composer and Stolz as interpreter had a great success:

> But la Stolz, this tempting Eve, turned too desirous glances towards the composer .`.` . who, in a moment of weakness, fell at the feet of Cupid of the golden wings. . . . As a result of this painful incident a coldness developed in the relations of Mariani and la Stolz, and the latter, a practised

courtesan, burned incense before the more splendid star, Maestro Verdi.

According to the *Rivista Indipendente*, it was because he had been spurned by Teresa Stolz that Mariani fell ill and died. (In fact, he died of cancer of the bowel from which he had suffered for many years; Verdi, who by then had turned against his former friend, is said to have remarked merely that Mariani's death was a loss to art.) The *Rivista Indipendente* article continued with a story about Verdi's missing wallet:

Staying there [in Milan] by accident or design were Verdi, composer of the *Requiem Mass* written for Manzoni, and for whomsoever instructs his heirs to pay for it, and the celebrated (according to him and to her) Teresa Stolz. They were not (see how modern they are) staying in the same hotel, but that did not prevent Maestro Verdi from going soon to honour the rotund and appetizing soprano with a visit (platonic, we understand). Signor Verdi was received with all the honours and the duties incumbent in such visits, and a little later the amorous couple stretched themselves out, or rather did not stretch themselves out but accommodated themselves or made themselves comfortable, or sat, on a soft sofa. What curious things they did on that sofa, what contests took place, what disputes, why they became so agitated, to tell the truth we do not know, as we were not in the room and the door was shut. But the fact is that, without either la Stolz or Verdi noticing, in the heat of their struggles a wallet containing 50,000 lire slipped out of Verdi's pocket.[1]

Noticing the loss only after he had returned to his own hotel, Verdi, it is claimed, accused his servants of having stolen it. However, one of the waiters, who knew where he had been, made enquiries at Stolz's hotel on the composer's behalf. To Teresa Stolz's embarrassment, Verdi's wallet was found on her sofa.

Though the *Rivista Indipendente* promised further instalments, in fact nothing more was published. A few days after the appearance of the 4 September article, the singer must have written to the Verdis to suggest that perhaps her visits to Sant' Agata might no longer be welcome, for she received a reply from Giuseppina written on 15 September:

Calm down again if you are angry. Assume that I replied to you at once, as I wished to do, and would have done if opposing currents had not drawn me to right and to left, not permitting me to sit down at my writing-desk. By this time you will be in Florence, where I think it best to address this letter. That you love us I know, or rather we know. We believe it, and are glad to believe it, and we are confident that, over you, we shall never suffer disillusionment. That we love you, you know, you believe it, you are glad to believe it, and you are just as sure as we are. For you, we shall be the same as long as we live. So, my dear Teresa, the fear of being in the way, because you saw in me a tinge of sadness, is a fear to set beside that which made you, in dread of disturbing us, go to your room at an early hour with the famous phrase: 'If you'll excuse me, I'll retire.' With us you will never be in the way, as long as you and we remain the honest and loyal persons we are. And with that and a kiss I close the paragraph.[2]

Among earlier biographers of Verdi, those with romantically fertile imaginations have decided that the composer had a love affair with Teresa Stolz, while those determined not to allow the slightest stain on Verdi's high moral character have declared that the composer showed no romantic interest in the singer whom he admired as an artist and accepted as a friend. Proof one way or the other is unlikely to be discovered now, but the truth would appear to be that Verdi was at one time attracted by Teresa Stolz but that he did not have an affair with her.

When the soprano first entered the lives of the Verdis at the time of the 1869 revision of *La forza del destino* at La Scala, she was thirty-five years of age, Verdi was fifty-six, and Giuseppina fifty-four. That Stolz became a close friend is undeniable, and it is true that, on the *Requiem* tour, they lived almost as a *ménage à trois* in the hotels in which they stayed. One of Verdi's letters to Giulio Ricordi requesting him to arrange hotel reservations makes it clear that, although she occupied a separate suite, Stolz took her meals with the Verdis: 'La Stolz needs a bedroom, a parlour, and another room for her maid. We shall take our breakfasts and lunches in the apartment: breakfasts and lunches for three.'[3] However, there is nothing in Verdi's letters to Stolz, or hers to him, to Giuseppina, or to anyone else, to suggest that a clandestine affair existed. It may be that Verdi was flattered by the attentions of the younger woman, or that he flirted lightly with her, but he seems never to have gone out of his way to be alone with her, or to travel to cities where she was appearing in his operas.

The only evidence of an improper relationship, if evidence it is, comes from the correspondence and the notebooks of Giuseppina who, throughout these years, was not in the best of health, and who was subject to moods of depression. A letter of hers to Clarina Maffei in March 1874, written from Genoa where Verdi was finishing the *Requiem*, shows her then to have been at her lowest. Without giving any specific reason for her dejection, she wrote:

Happy you, who believe, who possess and deserve to possess the affection of your old and new friends! I – in profound discouragement I tell you this – I no longer believe in anything or anybody, almost. I have suffered so many and such cruel disillusionments as to become disgusted with life. You will say that everyone has to tread the spiny path of disappointment, but that only means to say that, stronger than I, others have retained some hope and some little faith in the future. Instead of which, now, when anyone tells me they love me, I laugh.[4]

Though she always remained on the most cordial terms with Teresa Stolz, there is no doubt that Giuseppina felt jealous of the singer and of Verdi's attentions to her. In April 1876, when, if there had been anything between Verdi and Stolz, it was by then in the past, there is in Giuseppina's letter-book the partial draft of a letter clearly intended to be addressed to Verdi. One does not know whether he ever saw it:

'It didn't seem to me a fitting day for you to pay a call on a lady who is neither your daughter, nor your sister, nor your wife!' The observation escaped me and I perceived at once that you were annoyed. It's quite natural, this ill humour of yours hurt me, for, as she's not ill and there's no performance, it seemed to me that you could spend twenty-four hours without seeing the said lady, all the more since I had taken the trouble, so as not to fail in attention towards her, of asking her personally how she was; I told you as soon as I reached home again.

I don't know if there's anything in it, or not. I do know that since 1872 there have been [added and erased: febrile] periods of assiduity and attentions on your part that no woman could interpret in a more favourable sense. [erased: I know that I have never failed to show cordiality and courtesy to this person.] I know that I have always been disposed to love her frankly and sincerely.

You know how you have repaid me. [erased: There is no biting word] With harsh, violent, biting words! You can't control yourself. [partly erased: But then I open my heart to the hope that you will see this person and things as they are.]

If there's anything in it, let's get this over. [erased: If you find this person so seductive] Be frank and say so, without making me suffer the humiliation of this excessive deference of yours.

If there's nothing in it, be more calm in your attentions, [added and then erased: don't display such agitation] be natural and less exclusive. Think sometimes that I, your wife, despising past rumours, am living at this very moment *à trois*, and that I have the right to ask, if not for your caresses, at least for your consideration. Is that too much?

How calm and gay I was the first twenty days! And that was because you were cordial.[5]

This was written in Paris, whither the Verdis and Teresa Stolz had travelled for the first French production of *Aida*. (Stolz had spent the winter of 1875–76 in Russia, where she sang in *Aida* and the *Requiem* in Moscow and St Petersburg; Verdi had rejected an offer of 6,000 roubles to conduct the four Russian performances of the *Requiem*.) The three arrived in Paris on 22 March 1876. Giuseppina's draft letter is undated, but it follows an entry for 21 April and, from the evidence of its final paragraph, must have been written more than twenty days after their arrival. On 22 April, *Aida* was given its French premiere at the Théâtre-Italien, sung in Italian. Teresa Stolz and Maria Waldmann were in their usual roles, and the occasion was an immense success, with Verdi conducting the first three performances, and Muzio conducting a further twenty-three. Verdi had quarrelled with Léon Escudier over the production, after he had attended the first stage rehearsal. 'What I said last night in a moment of anger,' the composer wrote on 16 April, 'I now repeat with the clearest head: I will not return to the theatre until I am sure, completely sure, that the indecencies of the scenery in the fourth act have been amended.'[6] Verdi also insisted that the single interval, between Acts II and III, be no longer than twenty minutes.

In a letter written the morning after the *Aida* premiere to Mauro Corticelli, who was managing the Sant' Agata property in their absence, Giuseppina described the occasion:

> In spite of all the bestiality of the stage hands and the stage managers, the opera had one of those frank, enthusiastic successes, which make an epoch in the history of art and especially in the musical–theatrical history of Paris. The singers were acclaimed in the theatre, lauded and censured in the press; but it was Verdi who was really given the crown of glory. In spite of the habitual coldness of the Parisian public, women, men, orchestral musicians, everyone abandoned themselves on this occasion to an expression of enthusiasm that I can't remember being equalled, except in the *Requiem*. But that technical department, and those stage hands! One would think they were being paid to mess everything up; they didn't succeed, however, and that money was wasted, because the success was colossal! Tonight we shall sleep at last.[7]

A French translation of the opera had been prepared by Charles Nuitter for eventual performance at the Paris Opéra: Verdi, who thought it terrible, spent some time with Nuitter during May, rewriting it with him. On 30 May the composer conducted his *Requiem* at the Théâtre-Italien, and on 1 June a performance of his

String Quartet was given to a large invited audience at the Hôtel de Bade. On 7 June Verdi and Giuseppina left Paris to return to Sant' Agata. Two weeks later, on the day after the final performance of *Aida* in Paris, Teresa Stolz wrote to Giuseppina:

> It is a very sad thing to see dear ones leave!! I would have liked to say so many things to you in those last moments, but instead I stood there like a plaster statue, and I didn't say even a word to express my gratitude for all the kindness you did me in allowing me to live in your dear company. These three months were for me delightful, there were some ailments, some artistic emotions, but in the end I felt so happy with you.[8]

Stolz's letter ends with details of a coffee-coloured fabric which Giuseppina had apparently asked the singer to find for her in Paris. Whatever the truth may have been concerning Verdi's relationship with Teresa Stolz, he and Giuseppina continued their friendship with the soprano, and the correspondence between the two women remained amiable. In 1877, Stolz retired from the stage, settled in Milan, and visited the composer at Sant' Agata regularly for the rest of his life.

It was while the Verdis were in Paris that his old collaborator Francesco Maria Piave died, in Milan on 5 March 1876. He was sixty-six, and for years had been living what can only have been a vegetable-like existence. Verdi had been helping to support the librettist and his family throughout his illness, purchasing an annuity for Piave and settling a capital sum on his daughter.

Shortly after his return to Sant' Agata, Verdi wrote to Clarina Maffei:

> At last I am in Italy. I am not emotionally exhausted (as you say), but I am worn out by a number of little annoyances on all sides. This is all over, however, so let's not talk about it any more.
>
> What do I plan to do? It's my duty, you say, to keep composing!! But no, I definitely plan to do nothing. What good would it do, anyway? It would be a useless thing, and I prefer nothing to something useless. I don't want to make any resolutions, but, tell me, of what use was all the trouble I went to, these past few years? Pretentious as I am, I thought of reviving our theatres and, at least, of showing how operas should be done. I began in Milan with *La forza del destino*. At that time, the theatre had a terrible chorus, a poor orchestra, and a *mise-en-scène* that lacked common sense. I changed things a little, and *La forza del destino* was rather well performed. For *Aida* the following year I made improvements in the chorus and orchestra, and *Aida* (although musically I was criticized as though I had

committed a crime, and I was even accused of not knowing how to write for singers, and Filippi dared to suggest that I should change my method of rehearsing) – *Aida*, I repeat, put the theatre back on its feet and made a lot of money for the management. Then what happened? For two years, in spite of an excellent company, they put on dreadful productions and the management lost many thousand lire. . . . So what good does it do to compose? Besides, if I want to, I can do it at home for my own pleasure, but as far as the public and the impresarios are concerned – let's talk about something else.[9]

The Verdis' informally adopted young relation, Maria, graduated from a teachers' training school in Turin in August. Both Verdi and Giuseppina attended the graduation ceremony, after which Giuseppina and Maria took the waters at the spa of Tabiano whence Verdi brought them home at the beginning of September. Teresa Stolz, who had also been at Tabiano, came back to Sant' Agata with them and stayed for some weeks. Whether the *ménage à trois* continued amicably, or whether Giuseppina left the house as a consequence of Stolz's protracted visit, is not known, but Giuseppina did go to stay with her sister in Cremona for at least a few days in October. By then Teresa Stolz had taken herself off to Russia for six months where she made her final appearances in opera. Whether Giuseppina went to her sister before Stolz's departure is not clear. Giuseppina continued to correspond with the soprano: 'I wish you all that you yourself desire,' she wrote at Christmas 1876, 'certain that you will desire only things that are honest, good and worthy of you.'[10] The likelihood is that, if there was a crisis in Verdi's relations with the two women who were closest to him, it was now passing. When Stolz returned to Milan in March of the following year, and publicly announced her retirement from the stage, Giuseppina wrote to her and received an affectionate reply. Their exchanges do not appear to be those of a wronged wife and a mistress.

Verdi and Giuseppina left Sant' Agata on 20 October for their usual winter in Genoa. Before they set out, Verdi wrote a brief note to Clarina Maffei who had recommended to him a comedy by Achille Torelli (the son of Verdi's friend Vincenzo Torelli):

I saw *Color del tempo* in Genoa. There are great things in it, above all a quick-wittedness which is a particular gift of the French. But, *au fond*, there's little there. To copy truth may be a good thing, but to invent truth is better, much better.

There may seem to be a contradiction in these three words 'to invent truth', but you ask Papa [Shakespeare]. It may be that Papa found Falstaff just as he was, but it would have been difficult for him to find a villain as villainous as Iago, and never, never such angels as Cordelia, Imogene, Desdemona etc. etc., and yet they are so true!

To copy the truth is a fine thing, but it is photography, not painting.

What useless chatter. We are leaving today. Bon voyage, you say? I hope so. Wish me well, and farewell.[11]

In January 1877 Verdi received an unexpected invitation from Germany. Ferdinand Hiller, the German-Jewish composer and anti-Wagnerian, wrote in his capacity as Director of the Niederrheinisches Musikfest (the Lower Rhine Music Festival) to ask if Verdi would be willing to conduct his *Requiem* during the 1877 festival. The festival, which was held in rotation in the Lower Rhine cities of Aachen, Cologne and Düsseldorf, was in general devoted to German music; Hiller, a friend of Rossini, was however a firm advocate of Italian music and a devoted admirer of Verdi. The 1877 festival was to be held in Cologne, and Verdi agreed to conduct the *Requiem* there on 21 May. The work had already been performed in Cologne, but the participation of the composer made the festival occasion an important event: when Verdi and Giuseppina arrived in the city in mid-May they were given a magnificent reception. On the day after the performance Verdi wrote to Arrivabene:

I said I was going to write to you before leaving Italy, and I write to you only now, after having been here for eight days. But now I have much to tell you. I can tell you in the first place that I am half-dead from hard work, not only because of the rehearsals but also because of continuous comings and goings, invitations, visits, dinners, suppers etc. etc. I refused as many as I could, but I could hardly refuse to go to a concert given by the Choral Society where I heard various choral works by their greatest masters, which were splendidly performed. The Quartet Society also invited me to hear my quartet, also marvellously performed. I heard rounds, Lieder etc. Finally, last night, the Mass, with a chorus of 300 and an orchestra of 200. A most excellent performance by the chorus, but not by the four soloists [who included a twenty-nine-year-old soprano, Lilli Lehmann, already firmly embarked upon her distinguished career]. A very good success. The ladies of the chorus, trained amateurs of Cologne and nearby towns who sing *gratis*, presented me with a baton of ivory inlaid with silver, to conduct with. The ladies of the city gave me a magnificent crown of silver and gold. On each leaf is engraved the name of one of the ladies. Also the members of the festival presented me with a magnificent album, containing views of the Rhine, all magnificent pictures by one of their best painters: a true work of art. Tomorrow there will be seven bands in the

Gardens to say 'farewell' in music. In short, a fine reception from all points of view. I shall take a short trip to Holland, and then go to Paris for a few days to rest.[12]

The critic of the *Kölnische Zeitung*, who wrote that Verdi had drawn wonderful sound from the strings of the orchestra, also attempted a description of his conducting technique:

To see this man face to face, above all to see him in action, would thrill any music lover. And I do not believe that anyone was disappointed. The fire which burns in the decisive moments of his dramatic music is also revealed undiminished in Verdi's whole being, as soon as he holds the baton in his hand. The singer or orchestral player knows at once: there stands the living interpretation of the work about to be heard. Verdi does not merely beat time, he conducts in the fullest sense of the word, he mirrors the musical ideas in his expression, his stance, and the movement of his baton.[13]

After their visits to Holland and to Paris, the Verdis returned to Busseto and Sant' Agata towards the end of June, and the composer again occupied himself with non-musical tasks. 'I lead my usual peasant's life,' he told Arrivabene some months later,

or rather now I act as bricklayer, because I build, knock down, remodel houses etc. etc., just to be doing something. After Cologne, I nailed up the piano, so to speak, and music seems to me now something from another world. I am not even interested in politics. I read or rather skip through some of the newspapers.[14]

He was not so remote from the musical world, however, that he could not respond when Giulio Ricordi informed him that La Scala had engaged Adelina Patti, a soprano whom Verdi greatly admired:

I don't understand what you write about Patti agreeing to sing Aida. If that is so, you can imagine how pleased I should be. Otherwise, not!

A great success, then! It couldn't have been otherwise! You heard her ten years ago, and now you exclaim 'How she's changed.' You're wrong! Patti was then what she is now: perfectly organized. Perfect equilibrium between singer and actress, a born artist in every sense of the word.

When I heard her for the first time in London [in 1861] – she was eighteen – I was struck dumb not only by her marvellous technique but by certain dramatic traits in which she revealed herself as a great actress. I remember the chaste and modest demeanour with which, in *La sonnambula*, she lay on the soldier's bed, and how, in *Don Giovanni*, she left the libertine's room, corrupted. I remember a certain reaction of hers during Don Bartolo's aria in *Il barbiere* and, above all, in the recitative preceding the quartet in *Rigoletto*, when her father points out her lover in the tavern and says 'And you still love him?', and she replied, 'I love him.' I cannot describe the sublime effect of those words as she sang them. All this, and more, she was able to say and do, over ten years ago. But many people couldn't admit it then, and you did as your public did. You wanted her to be baptized by yourself, as if the entire public in Europe who had gone mad about her knew absolutely nothing! But *'Nun sem nun . . . Milanes . . . el prim teater del mond!'* [Milanese dialect: 'We are what we are. Milan has the finest theatre in the world.'] Doesn't it seem to you that all that bears too close a resemblance to the detested *'chez nous'* of the French? And the leading theatre of the world? I know five or six such leading theatres, and really they're the ones where you frequently hear the worst music. What's more, between ourselves, admit it, what a mediocre orchestra, what a poor chorus you had six years ago. The worst kind of machinery, a horrible lighting system, impossible equipment. Stage production then was unheard of – for better or worse. Today, things are a little better, but not much; in fact, very little![15]

In the autumn of 1877, the Verdis moved from their Genoa apartment on the top floor of the Palazzo Doria to a more palatial one on the first floor, a splendid suite of some twenty rooms opening on to a terrace overlooking a magnificent garden which stretched down to the harbour. This was to remain their winter home for the rest of their lives. In January 1878 King Vittorio Emanuele died of a fever at the relatively early age of fifty-eight, and was succeeded by Umberto I. The following month, Pope Pius IX died at the age of eighty-five, after a reign of thirty-two years, the longest in papal history. Verdi felt the Pope's death more keenly than that of the King. 'Everyone is dying!' he wrote to Countess Maffei:

> Everyone! Now the Pope! Poor Pope! It's true that I am not in favour of the Pope of the Syllabus, but I am in favour of the Pope of the amnesty and of the *Benedicite, Gran Dio, l'Italia*. Without him, who knows where we would be now?
> They accused him of going back on his word, of having lacked courage, and of not having been able to wield a sword like Julius II. How fortunate! If, in '48, he had been able to chase the Austrians out of Italy, what would we have now? A government of priests! Probably anarchy and dis-memberment. It's better as it is! Everything that he did, both good and bad, proved useful to our country. In the final resort, he was a good man, and a good Italian: better than many others who shout nothing but country, country, and . . . So may the poor Pope rest in peace![16]

It must indeed have seemed to Verdi that everyone in the world was dying. Piave had died, as had Solera, another old colleague whom the composer had not seen for years, and also his old friend the sculptor Vincenzo Luccardi. Verdi no longer had a regular librettist to feed him with ideas and he had, in any case, lost the will to compose. He took but a fitful interest in the fortunes of his operas; though, when Adelina Patti visited him in March, and in the course of conversation asked his permission to make a cut in Act III of *Aida*, he resisted. To Patti, he merely said, '*Aida* no longer concerns me. You should speak to the gentlemen in Milan about it'; but to the most important of those gentlemen, Giulio Ricordi, he wrote that there was nothing that could be cut from that act,

> not even the ugly cabaletta of the tenor–soprano duet. It is part of the situation, and it must, or should, remain. If not, there is a hole in the canvas. You know that I am the greatest enemy of cuts and transpositions. It's better not to perform the operas. If la Patti finds this role difficult, why does she do it? What need does she have to do *Aida*? As I have said to her personally, many times, 'Why a new opera when you have so many old ones to choose from?' La Patti has no need for new operas, for *Aida*, or for any other.[17]

It would appear that Patti found the role of Aida too dramatic for her essentially lyrical soprano voice. Teresa Stolz, the most admired interpreter of the role in Italy, no doubt took some pleasure in telling Verdi and Giuseppina, after she had seen Patti's Aida, that 'La Patti interprets certain things tremendously well, but either does not care for others or cannot interpret them. A very strange thing, her high notes are now forced.'[18]

In March, Verdi and Giuseppina took Maria Verdi on a two-day trip to Monte Carlo, visiting the Casino which both intrigued and appalled Verdi, perhaps because he gambled and lost twenty gold napoleons. (Giuseppina lost only five.) 'A Paradise and an Inferno in one,' he wrote to Maria Waldmann. 'Nothing more horrible to me than those gambling halls – a veritable salon of the damned! And nothing more beautiful than that resort and that climate.'[19] In April they spent two weeks in Paris. In May, Teresa Stolz emerged from retirement to sing in performances of Verdi's *Requiem* in Bologna, conducted by Franco Faccio. The following month, Verdi wrote to Clarina Maffei:

> Let me know what our distinguished friend Signora Teresa is doing. It's a century since I heard anything of her. Since the *Mass* in Bologna I haven't

received a word from her! I can quite understand how, living in a great city, in fine apartments, paying and receiving calls, going to theatres and concerts, as I often read in the papers, she doesn't think any more about the old Maestro. (La Waldmann, though, writes to me fairly often.) Give her my regards, and scold her a bit, too, and if she pulls a face take no notice: it means to say she knows she's in the wrong. It could be, however, that I am in the wrong, and haven't replied to her last letter.[20]

Whoever was in the wrong, Teresa Stolz was stirred into action. She wrote, on 27 June: 'Dear Maestro, your kind approach gave me great pleasure. I haven't forgotten you and never shall forget you, as long as I live. I abstained from writing only from fear of being a nuisance.'[21] She declined an invitation to Sant' Agata in July as she had a heavy cold, and suggested that her visit should be postponed until after she had been to Bohemia to see her relatives. Giuseppina wrote to her, conveying the news that young Maria Verdi was soon to be married, and ended her letter, 'Add your own good wishes to ours, keep well, retain a bit of affection for your old friends, and we'll see you again after your trip to Bohemia.'[22] When in October she visited Sant' Agata for the first time in two years, Teresa came as an old family friend, and was accepted as such by both Verdi and Giuseppina.

Maria Verdi married Alberto Carrara, the son of Dr Angiolo Carrara, Verdi's lawyer in Busseto, on 17 October. Giuseppina had described the bridegroom to Teresa Stolz: 'He's a young man of about twenty-seven, without the brilliant qualities that allure at first sight, but of upright mind, severe honesty, and with a very good heart.'[23] The wedding was held in a chapel which Verdi had recently built in the villa. He gave the bride away, and Giuseppina thought the nineteen-year-old Maria looked 'a true symbol of virginity, with a beauty wholly chaste and innocent, full of modest and virginal grace'.[24]

A day or two before the wedding, in response to a letter from Arrivabene, Verdi had occasion to give his opinion of the leading French composer of the time:

Gounod is a great musician, a great talent, who composes excellent chamber and instrumental music in a manner all his own. But he isn't an artist of dramatic fibre. *Faust* itself, though successful, has become small in his hands. *Roméo et Juliette* and this *Polyeucte* [which had been given its premiere the previous week at the Paris Opéra] will be the same. In a word, he always does the intimate piece well, but his treatment of situations is weak and his characterization is bad. The same can be said of many, many others. Don't think me malevolent: I'm giving my sincere opinion to a friend with whom I don't want to be hypocritical.[25]

Towards the end of November 1878, the Verdis visited Paris for eight days to attend the International Exposition, and in December he was elected honorary member of Modena's Accademia di Scienze, Lettere e Arti. He still had no plans to return to composition, and when Franco Faccio reported to him on the success of a performance of *Don Carlo* which he had conducted at La Scala, Verdi seemed less interested in this than in maliciously reminding Faccio of Boito's notorious remark of so many years ago. 'Find operas good or bad (for the moment, I mean),' he wrote, 'just so long as they draw an audience. You will say that is inartistic, that it befouls the altar; no matter, you can clean it afterwards.'[26] Verdi can hardly have guessed that Boito was, before long, to re-enter his life, and to highly dramatic effect.

Chapter Twenty

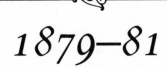

1879–81

Verdi was now sixty-five, in robust health, and still at the height of his mental powers; however, Giuseppina, although two years younger, was ageing more rapidly. She had for some time been troubled by rheumatic pain in her knees which often made walking difficult, and she also complained of 'liverish spots'. The pace of life at Sant' Agata and at the apartment in Genoa was slowing down, and there must have been times when a silence descended upon the household as Verdi's melancholia took hold of him or when Giuseppina was suffering pain. Nevertheless, they occasionally made visits to the opera or to the theatre in Genoa. One evening in March 1879 they attended in Genoa a performance of Boito's opera, *Mefistofele*, which had first been staged eleven years previously in Milan. Giuseppina wrote to Teresa Stolz that the tenor had been indisposed, and that she would therefore prefer to see the opera again before passing judgment on it. Verdi, to Arrivabene, was more forthcoming:

> I had always heard tell, and always read, that the Prologue in Heaven was cast in a single movement, a thing of genius; but I, listening to the harmonies of that piece, based almost always on dissonances, seemed to be, not in heaven certainly! You see what it is not to be any longer *dans le mouvement!*[1]

Boito called to see Verdi at the Palazzo Doria apartment and was received kindly. If he was, at this time, harbouring any hope that he might be allowed to collaborate with Verdi on an opera, Boito was too shy or diffident to say so.

When Verdi was asked, in April 1879, to become President of the newly formed Milan Orchestral Society, he of course refused, not only because of his increasingly reclusive nature but also because he regretted what he called 'the chaos of our ideas into which tendencies and studies contrary to our nature have plunged the art of Italian music'. In this chaos he desired to take no part. He was not averse to Italian composers attempting to excel in symphonic music, but he feared that, in following what he identified as an Austro-German branch of music, Italy was in danger of turning away from, and thus losing supremacy in, that vocal music in which she had over the centuries excelled. 'It is fine to educate the public, as the academics say, to great art,' he told the Society, 'but it seems to me that the art of Palestrina and Marcello is also great art, and it is ours.'[2] Earlier in the year he had, almost surreptitiously, returned to composition for, as he would have put it, his own amusement, with two settings of translations from the Latin by Dante, a 'Pater Noster' which is a piece for unaccompanied five-part chorus, and an 'Ave Maria' for solo soprano and string orchestra. He allowed both of these works to be performed the following year at the second concert of the Milan Orchestral Society which was conducted by Franco Faccio.

Giulio Ricordi, of course, also did his best to lead Verdi back to opera with frequent suggestions regarding possible subjects. One of Ricordi's plans was to encourage Verdi to begin writing again by revising his *Simon Boccanegra*, which had been only moderately successful at the time of its first performances twenty-two years earlier. In pursuance of this idea, which he had mentioned in Genoa without receiving any positive reaction, Ricordi sent the score of the opera to the composer at Sant' Agata. Verdi's response to this, on 2 May 1879, was distinctly discouraging:

> . . . Yesterday I received a large package, which I assume contains the score of *Simon*! If you come to Sant' Agata in six months, a year, two, or three years etc., you will find it unopened, just as you sent it to me. I told you in Genoa that I detest useless things. It's true that everything I have ever done has been useless, but there were extenuating circumstances in the past. There would be nothing more useless to the theatre at this time than one of my operas. And then, and then, it is better to end with *Aida* and the *Requiem Mass* than with a rehash.[3]

Doubtless, Verdi would have been as good as his word. However, Ricordi was determined to succeed in persuading the composer not only to take another look at *Simon Boccanegra*, but also, eventually, to embark upon a Shakespeare opera with Boito as his librettist. Events now played into Ricordi's hands, for the Verdis went to Milan in June, Verdi having agreed to conduct a benefit performance of his *Requiem Mass* at La Scala on 30 June, for the victims of the spring floods in the Po Valley.

The River Po had flooded earlier in the month. Verdi wrote to Senator Piroli:

> Our misfortunes are not as great as in the regions of Mantua and Ferrara, but the crops are almost entirely destroyed. The mulberry trees are ruined, the hay almost entirely ruined, only one seed of wheat remains, two at the most. Maize grows poorly and rots. Grapes virtually entirely wiped out. There will be famine and deaths this winter. . . . And all the time, the government contrives to raise taxes, increase spending on armaments, and build railway lines of low priority, under the pretext of giving work to the people. It really is a mockery! For goodness' sake, if you have millions, spend them on repairing the rivers before they submerge us all![4]

At the benefit performance Teresa Stolz and Maria Waldmann both came out of retirement to sing the soprano and mezzo-soprano roles together for the last time, and the occasion was a triumphant success, raising 37,000 lire for the flood victims. Verdi received a tremendous reception, not only in the theatre but afterwards in the streets and at the nearby Grand Hotel, where he and Giuseppina were staying. The salutation 'Viva Verdi' was spelled out in flowers across the hall of the hotel, and outside in the Via Manzoni the road was blocked with hordes of people cheering and calling for the composer. When Verdi appeared on the balcony of the hotel the orchestra from La Scala arrived to serenade him, under the direction of Franco Faccio, with the overture to *Nabucco*, the prelude to Act III of *La traviata*, and other excerpts from his operas.

All of this could hardly fail to improve the temper of even the crustiest of men. When, two or three days later, Verdi and Giuseppina invited Faccio and Giulio Ricordi to supper in their suite at the Grand Hotel, Verdi was obliged at least to listen as Ricordi steered the conversation around to Shakespeare and to Boito. Probably several Shakespeare plays were mentioned, among them *King Lear*, about which, however, Verdi was known to have inhibitions. Some of the other tragedies, such as *Romeo and Juliet* and *Hamlet*, had within recent years been set by other composers. Somehow, the choice narrowed down to *Othello*. Ricordi later told his biographer that when he first mentioned *Othello* Verdi's eyes fixed on him with suspicion and with interest. Boito, who had written the libretto of Faccio's *Hamlet* opera

(*Amleto*, 1865), was suggested as a possible librettist, and Verdi, while being careful not to commit himself to anything, agreed to meet Boito, whom he had spoken to only twice, and briefly, since Paris in 1862 when he had commissioned from the young poet the text for his *Hymn of the Nations*.

The following day, Faccio brought his friend Boito to the hotel. Boito, now in his late thirties, was no longer the hot-blooded young rebel who thought that Italian opera needed to be rescued from Giuseppe Verdi, if indeed he had ever thought that. He was now a fervent admirer of the man whom he considered, as did most of his fellow countrymen, to be Italy's greatest composer, living or dead. Three days later he delivered a scenario for an opera to be based on *Othello*. (Either Boito worked very quickly or, which is more likely, urged by Ricordi he had prepared his synopsis in advance.) Verdi liked it. Still without committing himself, he encouraged Boito to write a complete verse libretto, pointing out to him that it would always be useful, whether for either of them (for Boito was, of course, also a composer) or for someone else to set.

Boito immediately and enthusiastically set to work, at first in Milan and then in Venice where he had planned to take a cure. However, the project almost foundered at the outset when Verdi, back at Sant' Agata, happened to read in Ricordi's magazine, the *Gazzetta Musicale di Milano*, an extract from the memoirs of the sculptor Giovanni Dupré, whom he had met in Florence at the time of the *Macbeth* premiere in 1847. Dupré quoted Rossini as having said that Verdi, a composer of dark and tragic calibre, would never be able to write a lighter work like Donizetti's *Linda di Chamounix*, much less an *opera buffa* like *L'elisir d'amore*. Verdi, apparently still smarting from the psychic wound inflicted upon him by the public's rejection of his comic opera *Un giorno di regno* nearly forty years previously, reacted by hitting out at Ricordi. 'I have read in your paper', he wrote,

> Dupré's words on our meeting, and the sentence pronounced by Jupiter Rossini, as Meyerbeer called him. But just a moment: for the last twenty years I've been looking for an *opera buffa* libretto; and, now that I may have found it, you print an article that will encourage the public to damn the work before it is even written, thus prejudicing my interests and yours. But have no fear! If by chance, misfortune or destiny, despite the Great Sentence, my evil genius drives me to write this *opera buffa*, I repeat you need have no fear. I'll ruin some other publisher.[5]

Ricordi was understandably perplexed by this, for he thought he had started Verdi thinking about *Othello*, which was hardly a subject for an *opera buffa*. Indeed, it is difficult to imagine what subject for a comic opera the composer can have had in mind at this time, unless it was Molière's *Tartuffe*, which he had discussed with Camille du Locle immediately before *Aida*, and of which he had retained a scenario. But, whatever the *opera buffa* subject may have been, nothing was to come of it. Ricordi, in his reply to Verdi's outburst, poured all the oil in his possession on the troubled waters of the composer's paranoia, and suggested that he 'and a friend' visit Sant' Agata in the first half of September. Verdi's response to this was characteristically cautious:

> A visit from you with a friend, who would of course be Boito, will always be a pleasure. But on this subject let me speak very clearly and frankly. A visit from him would commit me too definitely, and I wish absolutely to avoid committing myself. You know how this 'chocolate project' [*progetto di cioccolata:* the name by which Verdi and his colleagues referred to the *Othello* plan] came into being. You and a few other friends dined with me. We spoke about *Othello*, about Shakespeare and about Boito. The next day, Faccio brought Boito to visit me at the hotel, and three days later Boito brought me his *Othello* scenario which I read and liked. 'Write the libretto,' I told him. 'It will come in handy for yourself, for me, or for someone else.' If you come here now with Boito, I shall have to read the finished libretto he will bring with him. If I find it completely satisfactory, then I am somewhat committed to it. If I like it, but suggest modifications which he accepts, then I'm even more committed. If, however good it is, I don't like it, it would be difficult to say so to his face. No, no, you have gone too far, and must stop before there is any gossip or unpleasantness.[6]

Boito's libretto was not finished until the late autumn, for he was held up by bouts of facial neuralgia and toothache which culminated in a painful abscess. Ricordi kept urging him on, and Boito assured the publisher that

> the fatal influence hostile to this work shall be overcome. For the rest, whatever happens, even if Verdi won't have me any more as collaborator, I shall finish this work as best I can, so that he may have proof that I, though physically tormented, have dedicated to him, with all the affection he inspires in me, four months of my time. By that I would not wish, heaven forbid, to claim any material reward, either from him or from you, if the thing does not turn out well. It would be enough for me to have given Verdi proof that I am very much more truly devoted to him than he believes.[7]

Ricordi cleverly passed that letter, and others in similar vein, on to Verdi. When at the beginning of November a partly finished libretto was sent to Sant' Agata, the publisher invoked the aid of Giuseppina, who suggested that Boito send the remainder of the libretto, and then discuss it with Verdi when she and the composer were next in Milan. 'Between ourselves,' the wise Giuseppina wrote to Ricordi, 'what Boito has so far written of the African seems to please him, and is very well done.' She advised that they refrain from putting any pressure on Verdi:

> I want us to be able to say: 'All's well that ends well.' Don't write or speak to Verdi, then, of fears, desires or hesitations; and I add: Don't even tell Verdi that I have written to you on this subject. I believe that is the best way to avoid arousing in his mind the idea of even the slightest pressure. Let us allow the stream to find its own way down to the sea. It's in the wide open spaces that certain men are destined to meet and to understand one another.[8]

On 18 November Verdi told Ricordi, 'I have just received the chocolate,'[9] and two days later he and Giuseppina travelled to Milan where Verdi and Boito presumably discussed Boito's libretto. But the composer still refused to commit himself to the project. Writing to an old friend of her husband's in December, Giuseppina confided that Boito's *Otello* had been put 'beside Somma's *Re Lear*, which has slept profoundly and without disturbance for thirty years in its portfolio'.[10]

In August, a daughter had been born to Maria Verdi and Alberto Carrara, and had been named Giuseppina. Early in October, Verdi had been visited at Sant' Agata by two representatives of the Paris Opéra, one of whom was Auguste Vaucorbeil, the new Director. Their purpose was to persuade Verdi to allow *Aida* to be produced in French at the Opéra. Vaucorbeil's colleague was one Achille de Lauzières-Thémines (probably the son of Achille de Lauzières, co-translator of *Don Carlos* into Italian) who, on his return to Paris, published an account of their visit:

> When I recently visited [Verdi] with my excellent friend M. Vaucorbeil, to request something most difficult to obtain, the Director of the Opéra feared that he would not be able to converse at leisure with the Maestro who, he thought, would be surrounded by a host of friends or guests. We found him alone, walking in the garden, followed by an enormous dog called Leda, perhaps to mock those people who call him the Swan of Busseto. Mme Verdi, seated a little further away, was reading in the shade of an ash tree.

'Listen, my friend,' said the Maestro, when I broached the important question next morning, 'when I wish to stage an opera here, I am offered the most advantageous terms; all the great opera houses of Italy vie with one another in gaining my consent. The best artists are engaged, even at the cost of paying for broken contracts. The musicians fête me, the conductor hands me his baton, the singers compete with one another to give of their best. Why should I go abroad? To hear that I am ousting their own composers? But I don't wish to oust them. Let them leave me here in peace! Look about you – it is really quite comfortable here. If you knew what awaited me over there! . . .'

It would not have needed much for him to cry out, believing that his garden at Sant' Agata was the garden of Gethsemane: '*Transeat a me calix iste!*' [Let this cup pass from me!] It would have needed even less for me to say to M. Vaucorbeil, in view of the Maestro's magnificent property and his calm, contented life: 'Forget your mission, the Opéra, everything, and let us raise three tabernacles here.' But we had not visited Verdi to surrender ourselves to biblical recollections. The Director of the Opéra and I therefore returned to our task of obtaining the Maestro's permission to stage his latest opera. He finally agreed. The bear was tamed.[11]

Verdi's agreement to allow a production of *Aida* at the Paris Opéra in the French translation of du Locle and Nuitter did cause several French composers to feel slighted. Saint-Saëns wrote publicly that *Aida* was 'of less worth than *Les Huguenots*, *Guillaume Tell*, *Faust*, and even *Hamlet* and *Le Roi de Lahore*, and [would] gradually disappear from the repertoire, as had happened, one after the other, with *Jérusalem*, *Luisa Miller*, *Les Vêpres siciliennes*, *Il trovatore* and *Don Carlos*'.[12] Feeling that he owed an explanation to Emanuele Muzio, who had been conducting at the rival theatre, the Théâtre-Italien, which had just closed its doors after several years of unsuccessful productions, Verdi wrote to his old friend and ex-pupil. 'Dear Em,' he began,

> As matters stood, even I saw that I could not have refused to let them have *Aida*. But, between ourselves, I am not very happy about it. Either I don't go to Paris, and the opera will be performed flabbily, lifelessly, without any effect, or I go, and find my body and spirit eaten up.[13]

When Vaucorbeil wrote to him from Paris in November wanting to increase the number of trumpets in the triumphal scene, and also asking him to add several movements to the ballet music, since *Aida* as it stood was a trifle short for the Opéra, Verdi refused both requests.

He considered that the six trumpets already stipulated for the march, three in A flat, and three in B, would be sufficient ('La Scala and the San Carlo in Naples are larger than the Opéra, and the six trumpets were completely sufficient there'), and

> as for the ballet, the matter is more serious. I know well that *Aida* is a little short for your theatre, but I could not, and I would not, know where to put another ballet. What can I say? It seems to me (if you will make allowance for a composer's vanity) that *Aida* must be what it is, and that in adding something you would spoil, pardon the phrase, the architecture of the whole.[14]

To Ferdinand Hiller, the composer who, since the Cologne performance of the *Requiem*, had become a friend, Verdi wrote, 'You know that *Aida* will be done at the Opéra and that Saint-Saëns seems to be antagonistic about it. If they only knew how I feel about it! But many times in life there are circumstances that force you to do something you don't want to do, and I had no desire whatever to do *Aida* at the Opéra at this time.'[15] It is difficult to see how circumstances were in any way forcing Verdi to allow a French-language production. Nevertheless, he not only authorized it but also agreed to conduct the initial performances. Whatever he thought of the Opéra, he was cognizant of its prestige. And he loved Paris.

Before the Paris *Aida*, however, Verdi and Giuseppina had to deal with a certain unpleasantness at Sant' Agata when it was discovered that Mauro Corticelli, Giuseppina's old friend who had for some years been managing the estate, had embezzled the savings of the cook and another member of the staff, a woman named Maddalena with whom he had apparently been having an affair. Verdi dismissed Corticelli who, a few days later, attempted to drown himself in the canal at Milan. When she heard of this, Giuseppina immediately and with great generosity of spirit wrote to Teresa Stolz in Milan:

> In view of the catastrophe, which could end in the death of that unfortunate man, any comment or recrimination would be out of place. Compassion is all one can feel in such grave circumstances, and it is compassion that impels me to ask you to go to him in my name . . . and ask if I can do anything for him, and what, for I'll do it to the limit of my resources. Let him reply without reticence.[16]

Corticelli survived this disgrace and near-tragedy by several years. A stout, good-humoured man, he is said to have been the inspiration for Verdi's musical portrait of Falstaff many years later.

The year 1880 began with Verdi being made an honorary member of the Gesellschaft der Musikfreunde (Society of Music-lovers) in Vienna. On 12 February the composer left for Paris, accompanied by Giuseppina, to rehearse and conduct the French *Aida*. They were joined in Paris by Teresa Stolz: the *ménage à trois* had, it seems, been temporarily resumed. After several weeks of rehearsal, the first performance was given on 22 March, with Gabrielle Krauss (Aida), Rose Bloch (Amneris), Henri Sellier (Radames) and Victor Maurel (Amonasro). Verdi, who had agreed to conduct the first three performances, was persuaded to conduct an additional two, and was able to write to several friends that the opera had been very favourably received, that the performers, especially the soprano Krauss and the baritone Maurel, were 'stupendous', and that the production was 'beyond comparison'. Teresa Stolz wrote to a friend in Milan, after the dress rehearsal:

> I am in the company of my dearest friends, the Verdis, a great deal. . . . The dress rehearsal was on Thursday, and they closed the doors to everyone, but the Maestro permitted his wife to bring me along. . . . The orchestra and chorus were stupendous, never out of tune, altogether stupendous. In the orchestra one could detect certain subtleties of execution which I have never heard in our Italian orchestras. Among the artists who surprised me was the baritone Maurel; he is a wonderful artist of great intelligence. La Krauss did not sing her entire role in full voice, but what she sang was perfect, as far as expression goes, and well interpreted. The voice is not of such beautiful timbre, but she sang very well, and she is an artist of the greatest resources.[17]

To the same friend, Katinka Evers (a German soprano who, after her retirement from the stage, had become a theatrical agent in Milan), Stolz wrote again after the premiere:

> *Aida* and Maestro Verdi have made a triumphal entrance at the Opéra. The success for the great Maestro could not have been more complete. Here everyone is saying that this spontaneous success of the opera and the celebrations honouring the Maestro are exceptional . . . one can see that the public, the press, and the entire musical world have combined to celebrate Maestro Verdi, and, in fact, when he appeared there was such a hurricane of prolonged applause as almost to terrify one!!!! . . . The staging is simply superb. The grand march succeeds very beautifully here, first because the famous trumpets play extremely well, and then because the total effect fascinates the audience . . .
>
> Oh! What a world. With the exception of some envious composers, all

are now proclaiming Verdi a composer of great genius. As if, some years ago, he hadn't done anything!!!! . . .[18]

Before he left Paris, Verdi was nominated Grand Officer of the Foreign Legion. At the beginning of April, he and Giuseppina travelled to Genoa and, after spending some days in Turin at an International Exposition, attended the Milan Orchestral Society's concert at La Scala on 18 April, at which Verdi's 'Pater Noster' and 'Ave Maria' were being heard for the first time, conducted by Faccio, and at which a statue of Verdi was unveiled in the foyer of the theatre. Both of the new compositions were applauded so vociferously that they had to be repeated, and the composer was called upon to make a speech. After the concert, it was announced that King Umberto had conferred upon him the title of Knight of the Grand Cross of the Order of the Crown of Italy. After these excitements, Verdi returned to Sant' Agata, while Giuseppina went to Genoa. From there she wrote an extraordinary and most loving letter to the man whose life she had been sharing for the past thirty years. 'My dearest Verdi,' she addressed him,

> I am writing a few lines to accompany a note from Perosio [a Genoese friend] and a telegram from Rome that, in parenthesis, cost over five francs!
>
> The posthumous enthusiasms for *Aida* and the *Mass* must lead you to strange reflections on human nature and at the same time to exclamations of 'Enough! Enough!' Such is the world! And yet, not only are you the same man of genius as six months ago, but you are what you appeared to me at the time of *Nabucco* and the old artistic struggles. The difference lies in this: then, good glasses were needed to see the star that was rising in the sky; now, that star illuminates wherever it shines – they all want to be lit up by it in order to be seen, and everyone would like to catch more light than the others, in order to attract more attention, and so that he can say, 'I am the first!' Vanity of vanities, all is vanity!
>
> You can call me what you like, but I am a bit different from the common crowd. One must take off one's sandals before entering the tabernacle and must contemplate the Highest, prostrate on the ground! To shout out hosannas at the top of one's voice is a profanation and deprives the deepest feeling of that mystic tint that transports us to the infinite. But perhaps I am wrong, and that is a mistake to be added to my many mistakes concerning God and his creatures! So let's allow the scale of ovations to mount up to heaven, as long as you take me with you. You will see that I shall not disturb you, but only tell you, *sotto voce*, how much I love and esteem you, when the others are silent in order to get their breath back and

blow their noses! God! – *et des petits pois*, as poor Maggioni would say if he were alive!

I got up less tired than yesterday and absolutely without any desire to speak a word. I am, however, content that, apart from the donkeys which are braying at this moment, today at least no one will come to disturb the profound quiet of this Wednesday, April 21st. If the weather is fine I shall occupy myself tomorrow with the furs and winter clothes that have to be put in pepper and camphor.

Don't work too hard, my dear Pasticcio, and think that, however little is left, it will always be too much for the merits of the heirs! In your art, in the matter of glory (except for a comic opera) you can rise no higher. Try then to arrange things so that you live as long as Methuselah (966 years), if only to give pleasure to those who love you, despite the French composers, not excluding the best! If Fetid, i.e. Fétis, were still alive, he would die of jaundice, seeing the colour of things today!

Now I salute you, I kiss and embrace you. I wish you a good appetite, and hope to see you arrive soon, very soon, because I still love you with a crazy affection, and sometimes when I am in a bad mood it's a kind of loving fever, unknown to the doctors, Todeschini included!

What stupid things I have written! I'll be seeing you soon, then.[19]

It does not seem, from the tone of that letter, that Giuseppina was any longer worried about Verdi's feelings for Teresa Stolz. And Stolz's letter of thanks for the Verdis' hospitality in Paris confirms that the relationship was now an innocent one, unless she was being extremely hypocritical. 'What am I to say to you, my dear friends,' she wrote to Verdi and Giuseppina, 'about the delicious month I spent in your dear company in Paris? I ask your pardon for having perhaps too much abused your cordiality; my presence may have been sometimes inopportune; the pleasure of being with you made me exceed the limits, did it not? Well then, when you come here you can thoroughly abuse me, and I'll love you (if that's possible) even more.'[20]

Early in May, Verdi and Giuseppina paid a second visit to the Exposition in Turin, and by the middle of the month they were in residence at Sant' Agata. The 'chocolate project' was reanimated in the summer and autumn when Boito sent Verdi a revised version of the opera's Act III, which Verdi thought an improvement on the first draft, but dramatically ineffective. In criticizing it, he adumbrated a finale involving a renewed outbreak of war with the Turks, 'warriors' cries, cannon fire, drums, trumpets and all the fury of battle', but then immediately began to have doubts about ending the act in such a manner. 'Can Otello,' he wrote, 'overcome with sorrow, gnawed by jealousy, disheartened, physically and morally ill – can he suddenly pull himself together and become again the hero that he was? And if he can, if glory can still fascinate him, and he can forget love, sorrow, jealousy, why should he kill Desdemona and then himself? Are these scruples, or serious objections?'[21] In his reply, Boito revealed himself to be the librettist for whom Verdi had been, or at least should have been, searching all his life; a man who, far from being intellectually overawed by Verdi, was able to open the composer's mind to wider vistas and lead him to more complex levels of thought than he had hitherto contemplated. 'When you ask me, or rather yourself, "Are these scruples or serious objections?",' Boito wrote,

> I reply that they are serious objections. Otello is like a man moving in circles, under an incubus; and under the fatal and growing domination of that incubus, he thinks, he acts, he suffers, and commits his tremendous crime. Now, if we invent something that must necessarily excite and distract Otello from his tenacious incubus, we destroy all the sinister spell created by Shakespeare, and we cannot logically reach the climax of the action. That attack by the Turks is like a fist breaking the window of a room where two persons were on the point of dying of asphyxiation. That intimate atmosphere of death, so carefully built up by Shakespeare, is suddenly dispelled. Vital air circulates again in our tragedy, and Otello and Desdemona are saved. In order to set them again on the way to death we must enclose them again in the lethal chamber, reconstruct the incubus, patiently reconduct Iago to his prey, and there is only one act left for us to begin the tragedy over again. In other words, we shall have found the end of an act, but at the cost of the effect of the final catastrophe.[22]

Once this was pointed out to him, Verdi understood and agreed. But now *Otello* was put aside again; for, perhaps realizing that his composer needed to be coaxed back to work and into collaboration with Boito by way of some less arduous task than the creation of an entirely new opera, Giulio Ricordi had begun again to raise the question of a revised *Simon Boccanegra*, the original score of which he had sent to Sant' Agata the previous year. By November, Ricordi had persuaded Verdi to consider seriously the possibility of revising *Boccanegra* for production at La Scala in 1881. The composer opened his 1857 score again and looked through it: 'The score as it stands will not do,' he wrote to Ricordi on 26 November. 'It is too sad, too desolate. There is no need to touch anything in the first act [i.e. the Prologue] or in the last, and nothing in the third, except a few bars here and there. But the whole of the second act needs to be redone, and given relief, variety and more life. . . . Who could redo it? How can we find someone?'

The obvious answer to this was Boito, but instead of pausing for an answer Verdi continued, in the same letter to Ricordi,

> In this connection, I remember two magnificent letters by Petrarch, one to the Doge Boccanegra, and the other to the Doge of Venice, telling them that they were about to take part in a fratricidal war, and reminding them that they were sons of the same mother, Italy, etc. etc. This feeling for a united country of Italy at that time was sublime. All this is political, not dramatic, but an ingenious writer could turn it into drama very well. For example, Boccanegra, struck by this thought, wishes to follow the poet's advice. He calls together the Senate or a Privy Council, and expounds the letter and its feeling. Horror on the part of all, speeches, anger, the Doge is even accused of treason etc. etc. The argument is interrupted by the abduction of Amelia. . . . I'm talking just for the sake of it. Anyway, if you find a way to adjust and smooth over the difficulties I've listed, I am ready to rewrite the act.[23]

Boito was pressed into service, albeit at first without much enthusiasm, for he was by now fully engrossed in *Otello*. However, he warmed to the task, and even proposed writing an entire new act, to take place in the church of San Siro. Verdi did not want to compose an entire new act. He could see that the alternatives were to write either the Council Chamber scene that he had outlined, or Boito's new act in the church, or to do nothing. 'To do nothing', he told Boito,

> would be the best thing. But reasons, not very interesting, but of, so to speak, professional concern, prevent me from abandoning the idea of revising this *Boccanegra*, without at least trying to think of something. Among other things, it's in the interests of us all that La Scala should survive. Alas, this year's programme is deplorable! Ponchielli's opera [*Il figliuol prodigo*] is all very well, but the rest . . . ye Gods! There is one opera which could arouse great interest on the part of the public, and I don't understand why neither composer nor publisher wants it to be performed. I'm speaking of *Mefistofele* [by Boito: first produced, unsuccessfully, at La Scala in 1868]. The moment is propitious, and you would be rendering a service to art and to all of us.
>
> The act that you have sketched out to take place in the church of San Siro is really superb in every way. Fine for novelty, fine for historical colour, fine in the scenic and musical aspects; but it would be too much of a chore for me, and I don't think I could tackle so big a job. So, regretfully giving up the idea of this act, let's consider the scene in the Senate which, as written by you, I've no doubt will be a great success. Your criticisms are

just; but, immersed as you are in much more elevated work, and having *Otello* in mind, you are aiming at a perfection it would be impossible to achieve. Setting my sights lower, I feel more optimistic than you, and I do not despair. I agree that the table is wobbly, but with minor adjustments to a leg or two it can be made to stand. I agree, too, that there are no characters in this work (they're rare enough, anyway) to make you exclaim 'How true to life.' Nevertheless, it seems to me that we can get something out of the characters of Fiesco and Simone.[24]

Boito wrote the Council Chamber scene as envisaged by Verdi, who, when he received it, complimented his librettist on having produced something 'most beautiful, full of movement and of local colour, with your usual very elegant and forceful verses', but then complained that 'the piece is vast in the extreme, and difficult to set to music, and I don't know whether, now that I am no longer *dans le mouvement*, I shall be able to get back into practice in time to do this and patch up all the rest'.[25] Nevertheless he did so, beginning his revision of *Simon Boccanegra* early in January 1881, and, after receiving the rest of Boito's alterations to the libretto, completing the new version by late February. On 24 February he left Genoa for Milan to direct rehearsals, and the revised *Boccanegra* was given its premiere at La Scala on 24 March 1881. Boito, who, as he told Ricordi, attributed 'no artistic or literary merit' to the revision he had made to 'the work of poor Piave',[26] insisted that neither his name nor his anagram (Tobia Gorrio, which he had used as librettist of Ponchielli's *La Gioconda*) should appear on the programme. The opera was conducted by Franco Faccio, the title role was undertaken by Victor Maurel (who had sung Amonasro in the French *Aida* of the previous year), and the other principals included Francesco Tamagno (Gabriele), Anna d'Angeri (Maria) and Edouard de Reszke (Fiesco). The first night was a triumphant success, ten performances were given during the season, and Verdi admired the French baritone Maurel sufficiently to promise that he would write the role of Iago in *Otello* for him. (He is not known to have made any similar promise to the tenor, Francesco Tamagno, who did, however, become the creator of the title role in *Otello*.)

Verdi and Giuseppina returned to Genoa, and at some time, probably during the spring when Verdi had gone off on a trip to Sant' Agata, she wrote him (or, at any rate, drafted in her letter-book: there is no evidence that it was sent) a curious letter which suggests that they were not entirely happy in Genoa:

I'm glad to hear, and not surprised, that your indisposition cleared up as soon as you were past the mountains. You will perhaps remember that I have pointed out several times recently the necessity of a talk between us on certain matters which concern us both, and which it would be well to settle without delay, since time for us is getting short. The opportunity presents itself and I seize it, since quiet permits me to write a letter instead of talking.

It is certain that the climate of Genoa doesn't suit you. The coal smoke that, with the new commercial developments, now reaches us, has worsened, so to speak, the atmospheric conditions of this locality and has made a move, sooner or later, almost inevitable. It is true that you haven't made any effort to get to know it, but instinctively you don't like Genoese society. So we shall have the bother of a removal, we shall be forced to move away from the sea, light and air, without any compensation from society for these sacrifices.

Now listen carefully, my Verdi, hear me out with a little patience, and believe that what I am going to say is the result of long reflection, and set forth in all sincerity. You love Milan, and its climate is not harmful to you. You like its society, you have in that city your old friends, memories of your first successes, and, to use a modern term, there is in Milan the *milieu* suited to an artist. I suggest we go to Milan. The climate cannot harm me, since it's almost my native climate. You will be able to have, at least in the evenings, a bit of company; and, should there be none, will be able to go to the theatre or a cafe, to pass an agreeable hour or so. As you know, I have no need of society, but only of one or two good people, now and then, with whom to exchange a few words. I ask only for an apartment with light and air, and that you don't abandon me completely in these last years of life. [She was now sixty-six.] By that I mean: don't be always out of the house.

In the level streets of that city I shall be able to walk more, to pay a few calls, and shall have occasion to spend a little money, on myself even, which in Genoa I never have either the occasion or wish to do. If this project suits you, we'll come to an agreement about the apartment, etc. If it doesn't suit you, then I propose another arrangement. With the addition of the two rooms at Sant' Agata, we shall be able to put there the best of our furniture now in Genoa. We'll sell what we can of the inferior stuff, and if we can't sell it profitably we'll distribute it among relatives, who are all in need and will be glad to have a better bed, table or chair. With just the one house we shall be able to spend the winter in Milan, Rome, Naples or any other town that attracts us, without cares and responsibilities. Think it over and choose. But it's a continual vexation to me to stay in Genoa, and of no benefit to you, physically or morally.[27]

Whether Giuseppina's suggestions were discussed is not known, but the Verdis continued for the rest of their lives to reside in Genoa in the winter and Sant' Agata in the summer, with usually a brief summer visit to the spa of Montecatini to take the waters. Perhaps, a little earlier, Verdi might have been interested in considering a change in the pattern of his life; but now, in the summer of 1881, the gestation period of *Otello* was about to move, at least temporarily, into a more active phase. There can have been room for little else in his mind.

Chapter Twenty-one

1881–87

When a revised version of Boito's *Mefistofele* was produced at La Scala in May 1881, Verdi sent its composer a telegram: 'Delighted with the success. I send my most cordial, sincere congratulations. Let's have *Nerone* soon.'[1] Boito now turned his attention again to the *Otello* libretto and worked on one or two scenes with which Verdi had not been completely satisfied. Very early in July, Boito and Giulio Ricordi visited Sant' Agata for discussions with Verdi, and before the end of the month Boito had sent the composer his revised text for the Act III finale. That Verdi, although he treated Boito with more respect than he had ever shown to his earlier collaborators, was nevertheless a very active participant in the creation of the *Otello* libretto, is revealed by the correspondence of the two men on the subject. In August 1881, having gone to Milan to visit the Industrial Exposition of that year, Verdi wrote from there to acknowledge receipt of the new Act III finale:

> The finale is very well done indeed. What a difference between this one and the first! I shall add the four lines for Rodrigo. Perhaps the other four for Desdemona will not be needed.
>
> It's so true that a silent Otello is grander and more terrible, that my opinion would be not to have him speak at all during the whole ensemble. It seems to me that Iago alone can say, and more briefly, everything that must be said for the spectator's understanding, without Otello replying. Iago: 'Hurry! Time is flying! Concentrate on your task, and on that alone. I'll see to Cassio. I'll pluck out his infamous, guilty soul. I swear it. You shall have news of him at midnight.' (Altering the verses, of course.)
>
> After the ensemble, and after the words, '*Tutti fuggite Otello*' [All of you, flee from Otello], it seems to me that Otello does not speak or cry out

enough. He is silent for four lines, and it seems to me that (scenically speaking), after '*Che d'ogni senso il priva*' [That robs him of all feeling] Otello ought to bellow one or two lines: 'Away! I detest you, myself, the whole world!'

And it seems to me too that a few lines could be spared when Otello and Iago remain together:

OTELLO:	But I cannot flee from myself. Ah, the serpent.
IAGO:	Signor!
OTELLO:	To see them together, embracing, Accursed thought. Blood, blood. The handkerchief. (He cries, and faints.)
IAGO:	My poison is working.
OFFSTAGE CRIES:	Long live the hero of Cyprus!
IAGO:	Who can stop me from stamping my heel on that brow?
OFFSTAGE CRIES:	Glory to the Lion of Venice!
IAGO:	Here is the Lion!

A strangled cry on the word 'handkerchief' [*fazzoletto*] seems to me more terrible than a commonplace exclamation like '*O Satana*'. The words '*svenuto*', '*immobil*' and '*muto*' somewhat hold up the action. One stops to think, and here it's a case of hurrying on to the end. Let me have your opinion.

I haven't finished. The chorus has little or nothing to do. Could one not find a way of moving it about a bit? For example, after the words, 'In Cyprus my successor is to be – Cassio!', the chorus could have four lines, not of revolt but of protest: 'No, no, we want Otello!'

I know perfectly well that you will reply at once: 'Dear Signor Maestro, don't you know that nobody dared to breathe after a decree of the Serenissima, and that sometimes the mere presence of the Messer Grande sufficed to disperse the crowd and subdue the tumult?'

I would dare to reply that the action takes place in Cyprus, the Serenissima were far away, and perhaps for that reason the Cypriots were bolder than the Venetians.

If you come to Milan, I hope to see you. I'm not sure, but I think you have all the poetry of the third act.[2]

Though he was prepared to continue discussing the libretto, Verdi seemed reluctant actually to begin composing *Otello*. Three Christmases were to go by, at each of which Ricordi dropped a hint by sending to Sant' Agata a large cake with the figure of Otello in chocolate on the top, and it was not until March 1884 that Verdi finally began to write the opera. Meanwhile he thought deeply about the characters, especially the pivotal character of Iago. He urged his friend the painter Domenico Morelli to paint a portrait of Iago, and when Morelli pointed out the difficulty of creating a visual image of hidden wickedness, Verdi offered a few suggestions:

> If I were an actor, and had to play Iago, I would rather have a long, thin face, thin lips, small eyes close to the nose like a monkey, a high, receding forehead, the head well developed at the back. An absent-minded air, nonchalant, indifferent to everything, sceptical, a cutting manner, speaking good and evil lightly as though he were thinking of something else, so that, if anyone were to say to him, in reproof: 'What you say, what you propose, is monstrous,' he could reply: 'Really . . . I didn't think so. . . . Let's talk no more of it.' Someone like that could deceive everybody, even, up to a point, his own wife. But a malicious little fellow puts everyone on his guard, and deceives no one![3]

Boito wanted to call the opera *Iago*, and indeed many of the references to the hoped-for new work in newspapers and magazines referred to it under that title. But 'All this talking and writing about *Iago*!!!' Verdi complained to Boito much later. 'I reply in vain that "*Otello*, pas *Iago*, n'est pas fini," but they go on writing and talking about *Iago*, *Iago*!! . . . I'd rather people said "He wanted to do battle with the giant [i.e. Shakespeare's *Othello*] but was crushed" than "He wished to hide behind the title *Iago*." If you agree, let's begin to baptize the work *Otello*, and inform Giulio immediately.'[4]

During a visit to Paris in the spring of 1882 to protect his copyright interests as a consequence of the death of Léon Escudier, Verdi was approached by a representative of the Vienna Hofoper, and persuaded to undertake a revision and shortening of *Don Carlos* to render it suitable for performance in Vienna. As the composer later told his friend Piroli, 'In that city . . . operas that are too long are savagely amputated. . . . Since my legs have to be cut off, I prefer to sharpen and apply the knife myself.'[5] The revision, which resulted in the four-act version of the opera (the original Act I, set in Fontainebleau, being removed), took from September 1882 to March 1883, and involved him in indirect correspondence with the librettist Camille du Locle, through Charles Nuitter. He composed much new music for the four-act version, and made a number of important alterations to his 1867 score.

On 13 February 1883, Wagner died in Venice. 'Sad. Sad. Sad! Wagner is dead!' Verdi wrote to Giulio Ricordi. 'When I read the newspaper yesterday I was really horrified! Let us not discuss it. It is a great individual who has disappeared! A name that leaves the most powerful imprint on the history of art!'[6]

Verdi had been brooding for some time on the differences between the opportunities afforded to German composers by the long seasons and permanent companies of a multitude of theatres in the German-speaking countries, and those available to Italian composers. The season in Italy was a very short one, and the theatres comparatively few. The failure and closure of several Italian theatres was a source of distress to Verdi in whose view the only hope for the future of Italian opera lay in government subsidy for the opera houses. He said as much in February to his friend Senator Piroli, and developed his theme in conversation with a German visitor in Genoa. 'Theatres, in the sense of stable German Court theatres, do not and cannot exist in Italy,' he said. 'That is because of our climate, our national institutions and social customs. Our winter is not long, and our opera is still the short-lived child of the Carnival, in the care of the impresario.'[7]

The Verdis were now making annual visits to the baths at Montecatini – and were to continue to do so for the rest of their lives – and in 1883 they were accompanied by Teresa Stolz. On their way back to Busseto the three stopped off in Florence to visit the Laurentian Library, which housed an important collection of historical books and illuminated manuscripts. They were shown over the library by the Assistant Librarian Italo Pizzi, who was later to become a distinguished Orientalist and a friend of the composer:

> Verdi observed with great attention the precious things housed in that distinguished library, the illuminated pages displayed, the autographs of Petrarch, Cellini, Alfieri, the second-century Virgil, the Tacitus found in Westphalia, the Paulus Orosius. He asked about many things and, among others, also about the celebrated Foligno edition of *The Divine Comedy*. . . . But he did not reveal himself simply as an admirer, he was also erudite. . . . I was amazed at him when, as I showed him a very rare edition of the works of Aristotle in Greek, made in Venice and adorned with beautiful miniatures of animals, he said: 'I know no Greek but this must be the History of Animals of Aristotle.' And he was right.[8]

In October Verdi celebrated his seventieth birthday very quietly. A day or two afterwards, he had occasion to write a letter of condolence to Clarina Maffei whose lover Carlo Tenca had died. (Tenca's liaison with the Countess Maffei had been one of the principal reasons for her separation from Andrea Maffei thirty-seven years earlier.) Verdi's words cannot have given much consolation: 'I think that life is such a stupid thing, and, what is worse, a useless thing. What do we do? What shall we do? Taking it all together, there is only one answer, humiliating and extremely sad: NOTHING!'[9]

The proposed Viennese production of *Don Carlo* failed to material- ize, and Verdi's new version of the opera was first staged in Achille de Lauzières's existing Italian translation, revised by Angelo Zanardini, at La Scala on 10 January 1884. Verdi's letter of 13 December to Ricordi concerning the forthcoming production is typical of the composer's exchanges with his publisher:

'Maestro Verdi will come to Milan to preside over the rehearsals of *Don Carlo* and, naturally, to attend, we hope, the first performance' etc. etc. These words in the *Corriere* place me under an obligation to the public which can now claim that I must go, for Heaven's sake, and make the usual pirouettes and display my beautiful face!! I wrote a pencilled note yesterday on a card from Fiorenzuola to have this *réclame* denied before I came to Milan. I repeat the same thing today. It is not possible, as you ask, to produce *Don Carlo* on the 2nd or the 3rd or . . . it's impossible to fix a date. Don't tell me the singers have been studying the opera, and that they know it. I don't believe any of it. Two things they certainly don't know: clear enunciation and how to keep in time, qualities essential in *Don Carlo*, more so than in any of my other operas.

Faccio can begin, or continue, to rehearse *Don Carlo*. I recommend, indeed I demand, that he insist above all on enunciation and keeping in time. This may be mere pedantry on my part, but what do you expect? The opera is written like that, and must be performed that way if you hope to have any success with it.

As soon as I have seen a denial of the aforementioned article, I shall come to Milan and, allow me to repeat it to you, shall attend only a few rehearsals, principally of the new pieces. Nothing else, nothing else! Absolutely nothing else!!! Farewell, farewell.[10]

The four-act *Don Carlo*, conducted by Faccio, was given a successful first performance with Francesco Tamagno in the title role, Alessandro Silvestri as Philip II, Paul Lhérie as Rodrigo, Abigaille Bruschi-Chiatti as Elisabetta and Giuseppina Pasqua as Eboli. When asked by Arrivabene if he did not regret having sacrificed much of the original score, Verdi replied that he did not. He had already told his friend that he thought the new version had 'more concision, more muscle', and he now added that 'those who are dissatisfied on principle, that is to say the subscription holders, are complaining that the first act, whose music they say is so beautiful, is no longer there. It is "very beautiful" now; then, they quite probably didn't notice its existence.'[11] (However, two years later *Don Carlo* was performed in Modena with the Fontainebleau act, the original Act I, tacked onto the four-act revision, an arrangement which, it was claimed, was 'allowed and approved by the illustrious author'. The following year this 'Modena version' was published, which could hardly have happened without Verdi's consent.)

On 20 March 1884 Boito wrote to Giulio Ricordi with the good news that Verdi had at last begun work on *Otello*, and that he had already composed a large part of the opening scene. Unfortunately, in that same month Boito, in answering a question put to him by a journalist at a banquet in Naples (where he had gone for the first performances of his *Mefistofele* in that city), said that, having written the libretto of *Otello* for Verdi, he now regretted not being able to compose the opera himself. Verdi read a newspaper account of this, and as hyper-sensitive and eager to imagine a slight as ever, immediately wrote to Franco Faccio:

> The worst of it is that, by regretting he cannot set it to music himself, Boito creates the impression that he does not expect me to be able to set it in the way he would like. I admit this possibility, and so I ask you, as Boito's oldest and best friend, to tell him when he returns to Milan, not in writing but by word of mouth, that I am ready, without any resentment, to return the manuscript to him.[12]

Given this message by Faccio, Boito hastened to assure Verdi that he had been misreported, and that he wanted nothing other than to collaborate with him on *Otello*. 'This theme and my libretto are yours by right of conquest,' Boito wrote. 'You alone can set *Otello* to music. All the dramatic creations you have given us proclaim this truth.'[13] In reply, Verdi wrote to Boito:

> Since you do not accept my offer, the letter I wrote to Faccio has no longer any significance or purpose.
>
> I read hastily, and I never believe anything I see in the newspapers. If something strikes me, I stop, consider, and try to get to the bottom of it and see it clearly. The question fired point-blank at you like that at the Naples banquet was at the very least a strange one, and no doubt it contained hidden meanings that the words did not express. Perhaps you could not have answered differently, I agree. But it is also true that the overall effect of this interview could easily cause the kind of comment that I alluded to in my letter to Faccio.
>
> But it is pointless now to talk about this at length, since you absolutely

refuse to accept my offer, which, believe me, was made without the slightest trace of irony.

You say 'Either I shall finish *Nerone* or I shall not finish it.' For my part, I will repeat the same words concerning *Otello*. There has been too much talk about it! Too much time has gone by! I am too old, and I have seen too many years of service!! So there's no need for the public to tell me too plainly that they have had enough!

My conclusion is that all this has led me to cool off somewhat on *Otello*, and has stiffened the hand that had begun to sketch a few bars.[14]

Boito had to coax the composer back to work by sending him some more pieces of revised text: in April, he sent the words of 'a kind of evil Credo' for Iago, to which Verdi responded, 'Most beautiful, this Credo; most powerful and wholly Shakespearian.'[15] The composer began slowly to resume work on the opera, writing spasmodically, bouts of intense creativity alternating with periods of neurotic inactivity.

On 31 May, *Le villi*, the first opera of Giacomo Puccini, was performed at the Teatro dal Verme in Milan, on the recommendation of amongst others, Boito, and Ricordi promptly put its young composer under contract. 'I have heard the composer Puccini well spoken of,' Verdi wrote to Arrivabene:

I have seen a letter in which he is highly praised. He follows the modern tendencies, which is natural, but he adheres to melody, which is neither modern nor antique. The symphonic element, however, appears to be predominant in him. Nothing wrong with that, but one needs to tread cautiously here. Opera is opera, and the symphony is the symphony, and I do not believe it's a good thing to insert a piece of symphony into an opera, simply for the pleasure of making the orchestra perform.[16]

No work was done on *Otello* in the summer months, during which Verdi and Giuseppina went to Turin for the Exposition and to Montecatini for the baths. But at the end of September Boito visited Sant' Agata for a few days with his friend Giuseppe Giacosa (who was later to become co-librettist of Puccini's most popular operas, *La Bohème*, *Tosca* and *Madama Butterfly*), and the 'chocolate project' was stirred into life again. In the course of a lecture which he gave the following year in Trieste, entitled 'The Art of Reading', Giacosa recalled this visit:

One of my most perfectly satisfying spiritual experiences was listening to Giuseppe Verdi read from the drama that he is at present setting to music.

In the company of Arrigo Boito, I had the great honour of being his guest at the villa of Sant' Agata. This was last October. While I listened, the great Maestro discussed with Boito several parts of the libretto that the latter had written for him; together they worked their way through Shakespeare's drama, which Verdi discussed with profound dramatic perspicacity. He ended up reading entire scenes from the drama. Boito and I looked at each other, and our gazes expressed the devout feeling of admiration that filled our souls.[17]

Five years after their visit, Giacosa published an account of it in the *Gazzetta Musicale di Milano*, some paragraphs of which describe a sociable evening at Sant' Agata. (It is interesting to note that Teresa Stolz was present.)

Verdi is a gourmet, not a gourmand: the table he keeps is truly hospitable, that is magnificent and cultured. The cuisine at Sant' Agata would be worthy of a standing ovation: it is picturesque, lavish and varied, resembling a laboratory of sublime Pantagruelian alchemy. There is no danger of going without dinner merely because the cook is indisposed. At Sant' Agata, in addition to the regular cook, there are *emeritus* cooks in the shape of the gardener, the coachman and the serving woman: *uno avulso non deficit alter*. It should be noted that all this apparatus has an essentially hospitable function. Verdi is not a great eater, nor is he difficult to please. He enjoys food, like all healthy, wise and moderate men, but above all he loves to see his guests display that sincere and keen joy which accompanies and follows beautiful and exquisite meals. Verdi is a man of discipline, and as such he believes that every activity in life must at times prevail over other activities; he is also an artist, and as such he considers, quite rightly, that a dinner is a work of art.

Verdi is a concise and lively raconteur. I recall the evening he told us of the first performance of *Rigoletto* in Venice. The senior member of the chorus was a certain individual who had once been a leading singer in provincial theatres, and considered his joining the ranks of the chorus a colossal act of condescension. The poor fellow assumed the dignified air of a misunderstood and persecuted genius, so typical of those actors who had high hopes and on whom fortune did not smile. In the storm scene, the Maestro required the chorus to utter a sort of muffled roar, an indistinct sound through closed lips, accentuated merely by dynamics, to render the rise and fall of the wind. But he had to teach by example and rehearse the scene a hundred times. Our singer could not convince himself that it was this and not something else that was required of him, and when finally he could no longer doubt the composer's intentions, he advanced proudly and placed himself firmly in front of the Maestro, angrily summoning his malevolent star to witness such an outrage, saying: 'You mean I'm even expected to be the wind!' Whereupon he returned to his place with the stride of an Aristodemus.

Verdi also recounted the astonishment and dismay of certain old gentlemen at Florian's who, on hearing how the rôle of Rigoletto sometimes bordered on the comic, all but considered La Fenice dishonoured and the artistic tradition of the Serenissima offended. But such fears were expressed on the eve of the first performance; at the premiere, those old moralists were themselves forced to applaud from that sincere and unprejudiced feeling for art, which is the privilege of our country's great musical public.

In the evening there is a game of billiards or cards. One evening, immediately after dinner, we went out into the courtyard. Verdi and his wife sat down on the steps that lead up to the house, while Miss Stolz, Boito and I stayed in the open. The moon was shining, and divided the courtyard neatly in two: silvery brightness here, dense darkness there. I forget who first started it, but a tune from *Ernani* was definitely heard. One of us took up the tune from the other and, what with the help of the shadows, the warmth of the dinner, the nocturnal exaltation, and the rarefied theatrical atmosphere, the three of us ended up by singing and acting scenes from that opera. Verdi and his good lady Giuseppina laughed and applauded.[18]

'It seems impossible, but it's true!!' Verdi wrote to Boito in December 1884. 'I am busy, I am writing!!'[19] He worked on *Otello* assiduously throughout most of the winter, but abandoned the opera again in April, and appears not to have returned to it until the end of the summer.

When he read in the *Corriere della Sera* one day in February 1885 that he intended 'to restore the church of Sant' Agata, which is falling to ruins', Verdi wrote to the church's architect to make it clear that he had no such intention. His social conscience led him to be generous with his money in his own locality, but he would not allow himself to be bullied into acts of charity by cunningly placed newspaper items. He had already made several large donations to the communities of Busseto and Sant' Agata, and had recently built three new dairy farms merely in order to give employment in bad years to two hundred men who would otherwise have had to seek work in other parts of the country. He now decided to pay for the construction of a hospital at Villanova, near Sant' Agata. He himself was largely responsible for the simple design, carefully supervised the actual building, engaged the medical staff, and enlisted the aid of Giuseppina in choosing furniture and linen. The hospital had been badly needed in the district, and when it eventually opened its doors on 6 November 1887 all its beds were quickly filled. Verdi declined to have his name on the façade, which, until after his death, had the single word 'Ospedale' imprinted upon it. The hospital still serves the local community.

At the beginning of May 1885 Verdi was in Milan for a day or two to visit his dentist, and later in the year he was fitted with dentures. There were visits to the baths at Montecatini, in July, and at Tabiano, probably in August. When Boito wrote early in September to propose visiting the composer, if such a visit would not disturb his work, Verdi replied, urging him to come:

> And have no fear of interrupting the course of my work, as you put it! Alas! Since I've been here (I blush to say it) I've done nothing! The country, to some extent, the baths, the excessive heat and, let us add, my unimaginable laziness have prevented it. Until Sunday, then. If you leave Milan by the 11.40 train, you get out at two o'clock in the afternoon at Fiorenzuola, where you will find a Bucephalus* of mine to bring you here.[20]

After Boito's visit, Verdi resumed work on *Otello*. It would seem that the opera was composed in three comparatively brief but intense bouts of energy: the first in Genoa in March 1884, the second in Genoa during the winter of 1884–85, and the third at Sant' Agata from the middle of September to early October 1885. Orchestration and revision occupied Verdi, on and off, for a further year. In the middle of October 1885 Boito and Ricordi visited Sant' Agata to discuss a number of matters, among them arrangements for the opera's premiere and the casting of the principal roles. When the French baritone Victor Maurel read in a Paris newspaper that Verdi had finished composing the opera, he wrote to remind the composer of the promise he had made at the time of the *Boccanegra* rehearsals four years earlier, that he would write the role of Iago for him. Taking fright at this, Verdi replied that he did not remember making any such promise. 'I may very likely have said that the role of Iago was one which perhaps no one would interpret better than you,' he wrote. 'If I said that, I'm willing to confirm what I said. That, however, does not include any promise; it is simply a desire, which may well be realized

*Bucephalus was the favourite horse of Alexander the Great. His father, Philip of Macedonia, had determined to destroy the high-spirited horse that no one could mount, but allowed his son to try his skill first. Observing that the horse was terrified by its own shadow, Alexander turned its eyes towards the sun, and was able to mount. Verdi, it seems, was either testing Boito's classical education, or attempting to make him nervous!

as long as no unforeseen circumstances arise.'[21] To the tenor Francesco Tamagno, who attempted to stake a claim to the role of Otello, the composer was even less forthcoming: 'You know better than I do that, however fine an artist may be, he is not suited to every role, and I don't want to sacrifice anyone, least of all you!'[22]

During 1886 there were several meetings between Verdi, Boito and Ricordi, both in Genoa and at the Villa Sant' Agata, to discuss plans for the premiere of *Otello*. At the beginning of February, Teresa Stolz came to stay with the Verdis in Genoa for a few days, 'full of health and merriment' according to Giuseppina who, after Stolz's departure, wrote to a friend who was a country priest: 'She left yesterday for Milan, where she will certainly not dedicate herself to meditation on the miseries of humanity, or the world to come!'[23]

On 17 March, accompanied not only by Giuseppina but also by Emanuele Muzio, Verdi travelled to Paris where he remained until 11 April, staying, as had become his habit, at the Hôtel de Bade in the Boulevard des Italiens. The main purpose of his visit was to hear Victor Maurel, of whose current vocal condition he had received conflicting reports. At the Opéra-Comique he heard Maurel in Hérold's *Zampa* and was greatly impressed, no doubt deciding at this time that the French baritone would definitely be his Iago. He side-stepped requests that *Otello* be performed for the first time in Paris and in French by asserting that Boito's fine libretto would lose greatly in translation. (He had already, some weeks earlier in Genoa, refused this request when it was made to him personally by Pierre Gailhard, a former baritone who was now joint-Director of the Paris Opéra.) He spoke enthusiastically to interviewers about some of the new young singers he had heard this time in Paris, among them Joseph Duc, a tenor, and Rose Caron, a dramatic soprano who would, eight years later, sing the role of Desdemona at the Opéra. When asked by an Italian journalist why he had come to Paris, Verdi replied, 'One cannot afford to neglect Paris for long, and besides, I simply had to talk to my tailor.'[24]

It was during this visit that two famous portraits of Verdi were painted by the Italian artist Giovanni Boldini (1842–1931), at his studio in the Place Pigalle. The first, the portrait which today hangs in Verdi's Rest Home for Musicians (Casa di Riposo per Musicisti) in Milan, was painted early in April. The presence in the artist's studio of Giuseppina, who was apparently impatient, and Muzio, with whom Verdi continued to discuss business affairs throughout the sitting, made the artist nervous. He expressed dissatisfaction with the painting (which, however, he presented to Verdi seven years later, after the premiere of *Falstaff*), and persuaded the composer to return to his studio on 9 April when the second portrait, a pastel in which Verdi is wearing a top hat and scarf, was painted. According to Boldini's biographer, Verdi on this occasion 'went unwillingly to the studio; but after two hours the painting was so far advanced that the Maestro was impressed and agreed to stay for luncheon and another two-hour sitting – after which the portrait was finished.'[25] Boldini was pleased with this pastel portrait, and refused to sell it, even to the Prince of Wales. (In 1918, the artist presented it to the National Gallery of Modern Art in Rome.)

In the summer, Verdi's annual three weeks in Montecatini were interrupted by the news that his old friend the Countess Maffei was dying of meningitis. He hurried to Milan, but she had already lost consciousness and died on 13 July without recognizing him. 'You will have heard about poor Countess Maffei,' Verdi wrote ten days later to Ghislanzoni in acknowledging the gift of a book by his former collaborator. 'I arrived in Milan in time to see her die! Poor Clarina! So kind, so considerate and so sensible. Oh, I shall certainly never forget her. We had been friends for forty-four years!! Poor Clarina!!'[26]

On 1 November the orchestration of *Otello* was complete. 'Dear Boito,' Verdi wrote, 'It's finished! Greetings to us (and also to Him!!).'[27] (By 'Him' it is more likely that Verdi was referring to Shakespeare than to God.) But it was not quite finished. Boito sent a variant of two lines for Iago in Act II, which Verdi acknowledged on 18 December, informing the librettist that he had now finally handed all of *Otello* over to Ricordi. 'Poor Otello,' he wrote. 'He won't come back here any more.' Boito's reply was consolatory: 'The Moor will come back no more to knock at the door of Palazzo Doria, but you will go to meet the Moor at La Scala. *Otello* exists. The great drama has become reality.'[28]

It had been accepted for some months by Verdi, Boito, Ricordi and Faccio (who was to conduct the premiere) that Francesco Tamagno was the best available tenor for Otello, although Verdi especially had grave doubts concerning the tenor's musicianship and intelligence. On 4 November the composer wrote to Ricordi:

> Even after Tamagno has learned the music, there will be a good deal to do in the way of interpretation and expression. I shall have to say things to your 5,000 lire tenor that are quite unnecessary for the others, and that may

wound his *amour-propre* and his susceptibilities, especially when Maurel is present. This kind of thing makes for bad humour. Ill-natured words follow, and then one never knows how it will end. We must avoid this pitfall at all costs. But what can one do?

If the season were not so far advanced, I might ask him to come here [Sant' Agata]. But how should we pass the time? I could not make him sing the whole day long, and after working for a couple of hours he would be on my hands. I should have to entertain him, talk to him, play billiards or stroll about with him, which would tire me, and just now I cannot do it. It would be quite impossible.

Another alternative would be to ask him to Genoa, anticipating our arrival by getting there on the 15th or 20th of this month. Tamagno could learn the role with Faccio, and then come on to Genoa on the 20th. He might find rooms at the Londra or the Milano, come to me at noon for a couple of hours' work; then he could go for a walk and return at six for a meal with us. After a cup of coffee and a cigar, we could revise the morning's work. This would be an excellent plan, but I dare not suggest it to him. I have not the courage to ask him to spend a hundred lire after seeing him travel second class with his daughter on this very line between Genoa and Milan.[29]

This second plan was adopted, and Tamagno was coached by both Faccio and Verdi. The composer also offered advice to Faccio in coaching Romilda Pantaleoni, the soprano who had been entrusted with the role of Desdemona. 'Mme Pantaleoni's voice,' he told the conductor, who was Pantaleoni's lover, 'accustomed to violent parts, many times has high notes a bit too harsh. I would say there is something too metallic in them. If she could accustom herself to sing a little more with a head voice, she would produce a more attenuated sound, and her voice would also be more steady and more accurate.'[30] Even after the premiere, Verdi continued to complain that the soprano did not understand Desdemona who, in his view, was really not a character but an ideal type of goodness, resignation and sacrifice. 'The most perfect Desdemona will always be the one who sings best,' he concluded.[31]

At the beginning of January 1887 Verdi and Giuseppina travelled to Milan, and Verdi began to rehearse *Otello*, his first completely new opera since *Aida* fifteen years earlier. A special edition of the *Illustrazione Italiana*, published immediately before the premiere under the title of *Verdi e l'Otello*, contained a fascinating account of the composer in rehearsal:

. . . That first day, after Boito, Faccio, Maestro Coronaro (Faccio's assistant conductor) and Giulio Ricordi had all exchanged the usual compliments (briefly, because Verdi is not by nature loquacious), as people who have not seen each other for some time are wont to do, the Maestro approached the piano and requested the artists to sing through the great ensemble of Act 3, scene viii. The sheer excitement of finding themselves in the presence of Verdi defeated them all: the Maestro was not pleased, the ladies were frightened and the men exchanged questioning looks. The second time, however, the piece went better, and a smile of satisfaction appeared on every face.

In addition to the usual hall for the piano rehearsals, the theatre management had prepared another room, especially reserved for Verdi, with a fine Erard piano. And there the Maestro went with the principal singers. He himself sat at the piano to run through the solo numbers and duets; he gave advice and encouragement, and every now and then uttered one of those words which are worth more to an artist than any triumph. Verdi was anxious, however, to fuse singing and acting together as soon as possible, and he could teach actors as well as singers. He would insist upon the greatest degree of naturalness, and with a keen eye he studied every movement, every gesture to discover what seemed to him most natural and true. Pantaleoni sang the Willow Song sweetly, interrupting it with the words that Desdemona must address to Emilia, who helps her take off her jewellery. She sings the lines '*Scendean gli augelli a vol dai rami cupi/ Verso quel dolce canto. . .*' [The birds came flying down from the dark branches towards that sweet song], and then to Emilia: '*Riponi questo anello.*' [Put this ring away.] The Maestro pointed out that, to make the interruption seem less brusque, she should let the ring be seen on her finger, as she made the gesture with which she indicated so gracefully the birds flying down from the branches. With such a Maestro, is it possible to interpret a role with anything but great refinement?

Tamagno's turn came. At the end of the final scene, Otello must fall. Verdi required a tragic fall *à la* Salvini. Tamagno rehearsed it several times, but the Maestro was not completely satisfied. Seeing that the artist was tired, he postponed rehearsing the fall to another day; and meanwhile, adoring children as he does, he went to cuddle and play with the famous tenor's daughter, who had come to La Scala to collect her daddy.

Tamagno fell ill and had to stay at home for several days. Giulio Ricordi stood in for him, singing softly in the ensembles. But Giulio Ricordi during these days is needed by everyone at La Scala; he is called away, and Verdi himself takes his place in a scene with Desdemona, in which he considers the embrace to be too cold, too restrained. Changing roles for a moment, the Maestro demonstrates to Pantaleoni a fervent, passionate embrace.

Many will not believe it, but it is true: at five o'clock in the afternoon, when the singers, Faccio, Coronaro and even Giulio Ricordi are exhausted, Verdi, with all of his 73 years, descends as fresh as a rose into the courtyard, which opens onto Via Filodrammatici, and climbs once more into the carriage in which he arrived at midday, to return to the Hôtel de Milan [usually known as the Grand Hotel, its full name is Grand Hôtel et de Milan].

The general rehearsals of *Otello* began on 27 January, and took place at the same time as the stage rehearsals. It is easy to imagine how the excellent Scala orchestra listened with affectionate respect to Verdi's occasional observations. . . . Despite numerous requests, Verdi has remained adamant in his policy of admitting no intruders to either the rehearsals or the dress-rehearsal, as he knew they would not keep silent about what they had seen and heard. His wish is that the audience should receive an impression that has not been coloured by the gossip of the privileged few. And he is absolutely right.

For any lover of art, the sight of Verdi conducting a general rehearsal has something truly awe-inspiring about it. The eye can hardly make out the long rows of empty seats in the vast, dark and empty stalls. The silk curtains of many boxes are drawn, thus increasing the general air of respectful mystery. The orchestral players are in their places several minutes before the fixed hour; they talk in whispers; and, as you would expect, they talk of the opera and the Maestro. . . . At half past eight, the Maestro arrives. Boito, Giulio Ricordi and Faccio are already present, and have gone to meet him at the entrance on the Via Filodrammatici side. The Maestro is dressed as usual in his fur coat, with a silk scarf around his neck. On stage he unbuttons his coat and loosens his scarf a little, and sometimes removes it. . . . He sits down; Faccio is already on the rostrum and has twice rapped his desk to gain the attention of his players. It is the normal custom, but the players are already intent upon the music and ready to begin.[32]

By the day of the premiere, 2 February, the whole of Milan was raised to a fever-pitch of excitement which had been building up for weeks. The American soprano Blanche Roosevelt, who was in Milan for the premiere, produced a vivid account of the occasion:

The Piazza della Scala was a sight to see, and the cries of '*Viva Verdi! Viva Verdi!*' were so deafening that I longed for cotton in my ears. Poor Verdi! Had he been there, he would certainly have been torn to pieces, as a crowd in its enthusiasm rarely distinguishes between glory and assassination. You will ask what I was doing in the streets at such a time, and I will answer, 'I don't know.' I merely obeyed the common impulse – went where the others did. The truth is, I also wanted to watch the Scala billboard, to see that no change would be made in the announcements. We all stood staring at the old theatre, just as those idiots on the Paris boulevard on a summer night watch the magic lantern, to read the different advertisements for enterprising firms: and this, you say, in dead of winter? Oh, an Italian does not feel the cold on an occasion like this.

But to return. In case there had been any change of programme, I need not say there would not have been found a person in all Milan courageous enough to have put up the notice. There was death in the eyes of some of those men, waiting like hungry wolves since the night before, to be the first to crowd into the pit and galleries. Well, at last – after dinner – I didn't dine, I swallowed food – we started to the theatre. The carriage had to be sent off long before we reached the door, the horses could not make their way through the crowd. At best, human beings one by one between a line of police could struggle towards the entrance. I expected my dress would be in rags; however, I managed to get in whole, and once there the sight was indescribable.

La Scala has never before held such an audience, and although it was fully an hour before the time to commence, every seat was occupied. The light murmur of expectant voices issuing from three thousand throats, audible, but discreetly indistinct, reminded me of the sounds in an enchanted forest on a summer night. . . .

From pit to dome, the immense auditorium was one mass of eager faces, sparkling eyes, brilliant toilettes, and splendid jewels. The Italian Court was a rainbow of colours, and Queen Margherita's ladies of honour like a hothouse bouquet of rarest exotics. The first and second tiers of boxes were so packed with the Milanese high-bred women, so covered with dazzling jewels and filmy laces, that the house seemed spanned with a river of light, up, up, up to where the last gallery was lost in a dainty cornice of gold. The gleam of diamond tiara and corsage bouquet shot oblong rays on the black-coated background; while the new electric lights, imprisoned in their dead-white globes, shed so unearthly a radiance over the auditorium that we all looked like spectres uprising from some fantastic dead-and-gone rout. . . .

If Blanche Roosevelt is to be trusted as a critic of singers, the first-night performance left much to be desired:

Victor Maurel is the only real artist in the opera, and he is a Frenchman. In voice, acting, appearance, and dress he is the ideal of what an operatic artist should be, and the ideal of what any operatic Iago could be. He sang as even his best friends never dreamed he could sing, and his acting was the consummate work which we always have at his artistic hands. . . . Tamagno, the tenor, looked and acted Otello, but he did not sing – he bleated. . . . Madame Pantaleoni is an excellent person, but as Desdemona she ought to have been suppressed the night before at her dress rehearsal. Her voice is naturally fine and dramatic, but she has no more knowledge of the pure art of singing than I have of the real science of astronomy. She has a vile emission of tone in the medium open notes; the upper notes are clear, but rarely in tune. . . . In appearance Madame Pantaleoni is likewise unfortunate: she is short, slightly cross-eyed, and of a physical plainness. . . . Giovanni Paroli as Cassio was a really fair second tenor; he, at least, knows how to sing, but Nature evidently never intended him to sing at La Scala.[33]

Despite any shortcomings in the performance, however, it was clear that Verdi's new opera was a magnificent achievement, perhaps the greatest in the famous and much-loved composer's career. When Verdi took Boito's hand and walked out onto the stage at the end of the opera, the ovation was tremendous. Verdi was called out a further twenty times by an audience weeping with the sheer emotion of the occasion, and eventually his carriage was drawn back to his hotel by a cheering crowd which serenaded him for several hours.

Music critics and journalists had come to Milan from all over the world for the *Otello* premiere, and their reports all spoke of the new opera as a masterpiece. Verdi, who a few days before had been decorated by King Umberto I with the Great Cross of the Order of Saints Maurizio and Lazzaro, was given the Freedom of the City of Milan. The reception of *Otello* must have seemed, even to the composer, to make a wonderful and appropriate end to a half-century of glorious achievement.

Chapter Twenty-two

1887–93

To Verdi's distress, his old friend Count Opprandino Arrivabene died shortly before the premiere of *Otello*, at the age of eighty-two. On the day after the premiere, Tito Ricordi, head of the family firm, gave a luncheon at Verdi's hotel for the visiting celebrities, critics, foreign journalists, musicians and impresarios who had been present at the previous evening's performance. Verdi, claiming to be a little tired, did not attend but stayed upstairs in his suite. If not tired, he was certainly sad, not only at the loss within a short period of two of his oldest friends, Clarina Maffei and Opprandino Arrivabene, neither of whom had been able to share in the triumphant success of *Otello*, but also at the loss, in a sense, of Otello and the other characters with whom he had lived for several years. 'How painful it is to have finished it,' he told Giuseppe Giacosa a few days after the premiere:

I shall now suffer such loneliness. Till now I used to wake each morning and return to the love, anger, jealousy, deceit of my characters. And I would say to myself, 'Today I have this scene to compose', and if it did not progress according to my wishes, I would arm myself for the struggle, confident of victory. And then, when the opera was finished, there were the rehearsals, the uncertainties, the task of explaining my thoughts clearly to the actors, to make them move on stage as I wished; and then the new ideas for the staging, that I was for ever thinking up in the name of representational realism. I would arrive home, still excited by the glorious life of the theatre, happy at the goals I had reached, thinking about those I intended to reach tomorrow, and I was not conscious of fatigue, and I did not feel my age. But now? Since *Otello* now belongs to the public, it has ceased to be mine, it has become totally detached from me; and the place that it occupied within me was so great that I now feel an enormous void, which I think I shall never be able to fill.[1]

This post-creative depression fortunately did not last. Within weeks he was having second thoughts about the decor and staging of *Otello*, and passing those thoughts on to Giulio Ricordi. He had apparently never been completely satisfied with the look of Act II, and it was not until he descended the grand staircase of the Eden Hotel in Nervi, a winter resort near Genoa, in the company of Boito and Camille du Locle several weeks after the premiere, that he saw what he wanted. The lobby of the hotel, with its three large windows looking onto a garden and the sea beyond, was ideal for the scene in which, as he put it, 'two actions are taking place simultaneously: a festivity for Desdemona and a conspiracy between Iago and Otello'.[2] Zuccarelli's set at La Scala, he admitted, was beautiful, but it was wrong, for it did not reveal to the public the two distinct locales: a park or garden for Desdemona, and a grand room for Otello and Iago.

On 25 May the Opéra-Comique in Paris was destroyed by fire, with the loss of many lives. At a concert at the Opéra for the benefit of the victims and their families, Victor Maurel, Verdi's Iago, wished to sing the 'Credo' from *Otello*. Given the circumstances, Verdi found it difficult to forbid this, but he was reluctant to have the 'Credo' extracted from its place in his opera and performed out of context in Italian to a French audience. He made his feelings known, and Maurel performed a different aria. In June, in a letter to Giuseppe Piroli criticizing the conductor Edoardo Mascheroni, Verdi gave some valuable advice about the rehearsing of operas. Having been told that Mascheroni tended to neglect piano rehearsals with the singers, preferring to concentrate on orchestral rehearsals, Verdi wrote:

> This is a very serious mistake!! There can be no good performance if first the rehearsals with the singers are not conducted well. The players of the orchestra have the music in front of their eyes. In general they know music better than singers, and they have the conductor in their midst to guide them, etc. etc. The singer is left to himself, preoccupied with the action, the movements, the voice; and, in addition, those three or four thousand eyes fixed on him. Therefore the expert and practised conductor must concern himself first of all with the vocal ensemble. . . .[3]

In August, Faccio conducted *Otello* in Brescia with somewhat less famous principal singers than those of the Milan premiere. When he wrote to inform Verdi of the success of the Brescia performances, he received a reply in the composer's most heavily ironic vein:

> Well, then, *Otello* is making its way even without its creators!! I had got so

used to hearing people proclaim the glories of those two [Tamagno and Maurel] that I was almost persuaded they had written this *Otello*. Now you deprive me of my illusions by telling me that the Moor is going well without these stars! Can it be possible? I also hear, which consoles me greatly, that in Brescia, as also in Venice, the first night audience was sparse. 'Good,' I said to myself. 'This is a progressive public.' It was an act of distrust against a composer of the past, an act which revealed a passionate and praiseworthy desire for the new and the beautiful. All that was logical and just. But now, if they go to the theatre and applaud, oh dear, my arms drop to my side. It is I who lose all faith. Finally, I can only congratulate us both on having made this crazy boat sail![4]

Before leaving Milan, Verdi had been approached by the directors of La Scala to compose another opera; perhaps, this time, a comic opera. But he was adamant in his professed desire to do nothing but relax in the country and play at being a farmer. 'Don't you know how old I am?' ('*Connaissez-vous mon acte de naissance?*') he countered Blanche Roosevelt's query about his next work. For some months, he and Giuseppina led quiet lives, settling into their familiar routine in Genoa, Montecatini and Sant' Agata. In September Boito visited the composer at Sant' Agata, bring with him the French translation of *Otello* which he had completed. 'We must do another piece of work together,' he told Verdi. 'Otherwise, since neither of us likes writing useless letters, our correspondence will dwindle.'[5] Verdi, however, preferred to discuss Boito's own opera, *Nerone*, which he had been urging his colleague to finish. 'Are you having trouble with your librettist?' he would ask jokingly. But Boito, as far as musical composition was concerned, appeared to be deep in the throes of writer's block. He never completed *Nerone*, despite Verdi's urgings. (In 1891, Boito read the libretto of *Nerone* to Verdi. In 1901, after Verdi's death, he published it. In 1912 Giulio Ricordi, shortly before he died, persuaded Boito to discard the fifth act and announce a production of the remaining four acts. Boito agreed, but then withdrew his score. He died in 1918, and *Nerone* finally reached the stage in 1924, when it was performed in a version edited by Arturo Toscanini and Vincenzo Tommasini, sixty-two years after the opera's first mention in Boito's correspondence: a somewhat lengthy gestation.)

Throughout the winter of 1887–88, which he and Giuseppina spent in Genoa, Verdi displayed no signs of wanting to compose, though he dealt assiduously with matters of business connected with his operas, even down to details of the German translation of *Otello*, which he insisted on examining and upon which he commented. 'In the Willow Song,' he instructed Ricordi, 'the repetition of the word *"Salce"* neither has nor should have any meaning . . . and therefore one should not say at that moment "Green Willow" – what difference does it make whether it is green or yellow? Arrange it so that *"Weide, Weide, Weide"* is always performed.'[6]

On 6 November 1888 the hospital at Villanova which Verdi had built for his locality was opened, and the first twelve patients were admitted. Verdi kept a close watch on the institution's administration, and as early as January 1889 found occasion to write a stern letter to the president of the board:

I think it only right to let you know that I have received reports of the hospital at Villanova, which I hope are not true. This is what is said:
1 That the food is sparse.
2 That the wine is even more sparse (yet the cellar is well stocked).
3 That the milk costs more than it's worth, and that it is poor in quality.
4 That the oil is of the poorest kind, and so both food and lighting are affected.
5 That the management wanted to buy rice which was half rotten, and black, home-grown pasta.
6 That funeral expenses are being charged, even to people who haven't the means to pay.
   From far away I can't comment on this, and I can neither believe nor disbelieve it. In any case, these reports distress me very much, and make me feel I have not achieved the purpose I had in mind when I decided to dedicate part of my wealth to endowing this charitable institution.
   I believe the hospital is well provided for, and there should be no need to practise economies. But, to tell you the truth, rather than hear these complaints, I would prefer to close down the hospital and say no more about it.
   I hope, however, that none of this is true, and that you will be able to reassure me immediately with a few words.[7]

Towards the end of the year, having read in the newspapers that plans were being made to celebrate in 1889 the fiftieth anniversary of the production of his first opera, *Oberto*, Verdi did his best, by writing to Ricordi and to Boito, to scotch the proposals. However, he was unable to prevent La Scala from performing *Oberto* on 17 November 1889, the exact date of the anniversary. Tributes flowed in to Sant' Agata from all over Italy, and congratulations arrived from the King and from the Premier. Verdi was kept busy for quite some time acknowledging what he regarded as useless messages. He must have begrudged the time spent on this exercise even more because by then he had, to his own surprise, embarked upon the composition of another opera.

It was while the Verdis were in Montecatini in July 1889 for their annual visit that Boito, who knew of the composer's desire to find a suitable subject for an *opera buffa*, and knew, too, of his fascination with the character of Falstaff, made a synopsis for a libretto based on Shakespeare's *The Merry Wives of Windsor*, and sent it to Verdi. From Montecatini on 6 July Verdi replied:

Excellent! Excellent!

Before reading your sketch, I wanted to re-read *The Merry Wives*, the two parts of *Henry IV*, and *Henry V*, and I can only repeat: Excellent, for one could not do better than you have done.

A pity that the interest (it's not your fault) does not go on increasing to the end. The culminating point is the finale of the second act; and the appearance of Falstaff's face amid the linen, etc., is a true comic invention.

I'm afraid, too, that the last act, in spite of its touch of fantasy, will be trivial, with all those little pieces, songs, ariettas etc. etc. You bring back Bardolph – and why not Pistol too, both of them, to get up to some prank or other?

You reduce the weddings to two! All the better, for they are only loosely connected with the principal plot.

The two trials by water and fire suffice to punish Falstaff. Nevertheless, I should like to have seen him thoroughly well beaten also.

I am talking for the sake of talking – take no notice. We have now very different matters to discuss, so that this *Falstaff*, or *Merry Wives*, which two days ago was in the world of dreams, can now take shape and become reality! When? How? Who knows? I'll write to you tomorrow or the next day.[8]

The next day, however, when Verdi wrote again, it was to express some doubts about the project. He was conscious of his advanced age, and also anxious not to be responsible for deflecting Boito from his own opera, *Nerone*:

I said yesterday that I would write today, and I am keeping my word even at the risk of vexing you. As long as one wanders in the realm of ideas, all is serene, but when one comes down to earth, and to practical matters, doubts and discouragement arise.

In outlining *Falstaff*, have you ever thought of my enormous weight of years? I know that in replying you will exaggerate the robust state of my health. But even if it is as you say, you must agree that in taking on such a task I may over-tax my strength. What if I could not stand the strain? What if I could not finish the music? Then you would have wasted time and trouble for nothing. For all the money in the world, I would not want that to happen. The idea is insupportable to me, and all the more so if you, in writing *Falstaff*, were to, I won't say abandon, but were to move your energies away from *Nerone*, or delay its production.[9]

But he virtually invited Boito to talk him out of his doubts, and at the end of the letter failed to suppress his delight at the prospect of composing *Falstaff*: 'What a joy to be able to say to the public, "Here we are again!! Come and see us!" '[10] Boito immediately returned to the attack. 'I don't think you will find writing a comic opera fatiguing,' he assured Verdi. 'A tragedy makes its composer really suffer. His mind dwells on grief, and his nerves become unhealthily agitated. But the jests and laughter of comedy exhilarate both mind and body. . . . You have longed for a good subject for a comic opera all your life, which proves you have a natural aptitude for the noble art of comedy. Instinct is a good guide. There is only one way to end your career more splendidly than with *Otello*, and that is to end it with *Falstaff*.'[11]

Verdi needed no further persuasion. From Montecatini on 10 July he wrote to Boito: 'Amen. So be it! We'll do this *Falstaff*, then. Let's not think now of the obstacles, of age, or of illness! But I want to keep it the deepest secret: a word I underline three times to tell you that no one must know anything of it.'[12]

Verdi returned to Sant' Agata on 23 July, and a few days later began to compose *Falstaff*, almost before he had received any of the actual text. Boito visited him for a week in November, bringing the completed Acts I and II of the libretto, and in March of the following year sent the third and final act. On 17 March, Verdi was able to report that he had finished composing Act I without having made any alterations at all to Boito's verse.

Before writing a note of *Falstaff*, however, Verdi had already begun to compose again. In late February or early March 1889, he had gone to Milan to examine a piece of property which he was planning to buy. While there, he saw mentioned in an old number of the *Gazzetta Musicale* an 'enigmatic scale' (C, D flat, E, F sharp, G sharp, A sharp, B; with the F sharp replaced by F natural in its descending form). He began to work out its harmonic implications, and told Boito that he was toying with the idea of writing an 'Ave Maria' based on this scale: 'It would be the fourth I have written. In this way, I might hope to be beatified after my death.'[13] Boito replied that a large number of 'Ave Marias' would be needed to persuade the Pope to pardon Verdi for Iago's 'Credo'. Verdi pointed out, however, that, since Boito had written the words of the blasphemous 'Credo', he was the greater culprit, and had better compose a four-part 'Credo' *à la* Palestrina and put it into a certain work he thought he had better not mention by name [*Nerone*]. Verdi then proceeded to compose his 'Ave Maria', a curiously haunting piece for four-part unaccompanied chorus, which is not without echoes of Palestrina.

In October the composer completed his purchase of a large piece of land in Milan, near the Porta Garibaldi. He had decided to build a rest home for elderly and indigent singers and musicians, and to endow it with an annual income. As architect he engaged Arrigo Boito's brother Camillo, and during the next few years he himself supervised work on the construction of the Casa di Riposo, the last and most imposing of his large-scale acts of charity. At about this time, Verdi was invited to compose an opera to celebrate the four-hundredth anniversary of the discovery of America by Columbus. He declined.

In April 1890 there came an episode that could at best be labelled as unfortunate. Boito wrote to Verdi to recommend 'a certain Signor Rouillé-Destranges . . . a Frenchman, but one of the nice ones' who was in Genoa for a few days and whose most fervent wish was to meet the composer ('He has nothing to ask you, he merely wishes to pay his respects'). Verdi replied, 'Send the Frenchman whenever you like.' But Etienne Rouillé-Destranges was a twenty-seven-year-old journalist who had chosen this method of gaining an interview with a composer notoriously reluctant to be interviewed. Before the end of the month, his account of his visit to Verdi had appeared in the Paris review *Le Monde Artiste*, after which it was reprinted throughout Europe and in the United States, to the fury of the French, who considered that Verdi's comments on French composers were insulting, and of the Italians, who thought the article gave a distorted picture of their greatest composer.

A fervent Wagnerian, the journalist began his piece with a *de haut en bas* assessment of Verdi as a composer:

> I am far from being a follower of the Italian school, and many of the works of Verdi himself have a particular knack of getting on my nerves. None the less I profess, in spite of everything, a sincere and profound admiration for

the musician who, having written *Nabucco*, *Il trovatore* and *Ernani*, could compose *Aida* and *Otello*; and for the artist who, having scaled the heights of his profession, at least in his own country, did not rest on his laurels, as, sadly, Gounod has done in France. Verdi openly recognized that, while he was writing with great natural facility so many operas which have for the most part already been forgotten, art had taken great strides forward along the new path opened up by the genius of the Titan of Bayreuth. The composer of *Rigoletto* did not shrink from this fact. Without hesitating, he set to work again, mugged up with a most youthful enthusiasm the new treatises on harmony and instrumentation, studied assiduously the scores of the great German masters, partially re-educated himself, and finally to the amazement of the musical world, composed *Aida*.[14]

Rouillé-Destranges's description of Verdi's apartment in the Palazzo Doria is equally haughty in tone:

At first one enters a vast antechamber, whose walls are hung with colour prints, modestly framed, of the type that English newspapers offer as free gifts to their subscribers. I then passed into the very tall drawing-room, decorated with a beautiful ceiling and lit by large windows, which opens onto a terrace that overlooks the Palace gardens and offers a splendid view of the harbour. While I waited for the composer, I quickly examined the drawing-room: red curtains, gilt chairs, mantelpiece ornaments in gilded bronze, two or three pieces of Boule furniture, and finally, in a corner, a couch, with a cushion tapestried in garish colours and representing a pheasant. Oh, such a cushion would tempt a country priest!! Everything in this room breathes an atmosphere of profound bourgeois luxury. How different from the majestic severity of Wahnfried [Wagner's villa in Bayreuth], the great artistic order of Gounod's residence, the picturesque, oriental jumble of Reyer's bachelor abode! To the left of the fire-place, Verdi's innumerable decorations are displayed in a glass case, containing souvenirs of very different kinds: medals, laurel crowns in gold or silver, with the names of his operas engraved on the leaves, a conductor's baton in ivory, and finally the magnificent sceptre of ivory and gold adorned with precious stones, which was presented to the composer at the premiere of *Aida* in Milan.[15]

Thinking that he was talking privately with a French admirer, Verdi doubtless expressed himself with greater freedom than would have been the case had he known that his remarks were to be published. As reported by Rouillé-Destranges, he said of Gounod's *Roméo et Juliette*: 'What a tempting subject! I envisage the work, I live this work. It is there in my head. Background: hatred, bloody strife between Montagues and Capulets. Foreground: the tragic love of the two children. Then there's the entire comic side, which Gounod ignored. I would have wanted to create a more spirited work with greater contrasts, not a long duet.' Told by the journalist that Ambroise Thomas's ballet *La Tempête* (after Shakespeare's *The Tempest*) had been 'very poor, a deserved flop', Verdi exclaimed, 'What do you expect? He is old, like me [Thomas was two years older than Verdi], and finished. . . . As for his *Hamlet*, most of it is not successful. If you wish to set Shakespeare you must not hesitate, as the French say, to take the bull by the horns. What musical situations there are in *Hamlet*, and how I would have loved to tackle them.'

Verdi, who in younger days would have exploded at this, reacted mildly. He wrote later to Boito, sending him a copy of the offending piece: 'Read the enclosed article. I only send it to you to tell you to take the necessary precautions, when you next speak to that gentleman whom you introduced to me. Superfluous to tell you that everything in that article is distorted.'[16]

Work on *Falstaff* proceeded steadily, at least in the autumn and winter months, for as he grew older Verdi was increasingly reluctant to work during the summer. To his question as to how Falstaff's name should be stressed Boito answered that, like all English bisyllabic names, it was accented on the first syllable. 'Ask Signora Giuseppina if I am right or wrong,' he continued, for Verdi's wife by now wrote quite fluent English. 'Only the French, who are incorrigible garblers of foreign names, pronounce it Fal*staff*.'[17]

At some time during the year, Verdi composed another piece of sacred music, the gentle and attractive 'Laudi alla Vergine Maria', a setting for four-part female chorus of words from the last canto of Dante's 'Paradiso'. In the autumn, he returned to *Falstaff*. By now, Giulio Ricordi had been let in on the secret: unfortunately, the news appeared in the Milan *Corriere della Sera* on 26 November, and the composer began to be inundated with inquiries about the date of the opera's premiere, and requests for permission to perform it abroad. 'I began to write *Falstaff*', Verdi warned Ricordi,

> purely to pass the time, without preconceived ideas, without plans. I repeat: to pass the time! Nothing else! But now the talk that is going on, and the proposals that are made, however vague, the words they extract from you, will all turn into obligations and undertakings which I absolutely refuse to accept. I said to you, and I repeat: 'I am writing to pass the time.' I told you that the music was about half-finished, by which I meant to say, 'half-sketched out'. By far the greater part of the work is still

to be done, the assembling of the parts, revision and adjustment, as well as the instrumentation which will be extremely fatiguing. To cut a long story short, the whole of 1891 will be insufficient time to finish it. So then, why make plans and undertake obligations, however indeterminately worded? Furthermore, if I thought myself in any way bound, even in the slightest, I would no longer feel *à mon aise*, and wouldn't be able to work well. When I was young, despite ill-health I was able to stay at my desk for ten or twelve hours, working constantly. More than once, I set to work at four in the morning and continued until four in the afternoon, with only a cup of coffee to sustain me, working without a break. I can't do that now. In those days, I was in command of my health and my time. Now, alas, I am not. So, to conclude: the best thing to say now, and in the future, to everyone, is that I cannot and will not make the slightest suggestion of a promise in connection with *Falstaff*. If it is to be, it will be, and it will be as it is to be![18]

Of all the exits from the world which his old friends seemed now to be making, probably none saddened Verdi more than that of his ex-pupil, Emanuele Muzio, at the age of sixty-nine. Muzio had adored Verdi from the day of their first meeting in Milan in 1844 when the thirty-one-year-old composer began to give lessons to the twenty-three-year-old student. Throughout his life, Muzio never wavered in his unquestioning loyalty and devotion to Verdi. His own career, though hardly spectacular, was a perfectly respectable one. He conducted operas in a number of European countries, as well as in the United States of America where he gave the first performance in the New World of *Un ballo in maschera* in 1861, *Aida* in 1873 and the *Requiem* in 1874. He conducted *Rigoletto* at the opening of the Cairo Opera House in 1869, and the French premiere of *La forza del destino* in 1876. He also composed four operas, all of which were staged in the 1850s. For some years, Muzio had been chief conductor at the Théâtre-Italien in Paris, and after the destruction of the theatre by fire he stayed on in Paris as a teacher of singing. In the mid-1860s, on one of his visits to the United States, he married Lucy Simmons, a young American singer. They had a daughter, who died, after which Muzio's wife left him. In the autumn of 1890, he fell ill. Knowing that he had not long to live, he wrote, on 22 October, to his old teacher:

My dearest Maestro and friend Verdi,
    There is a little nuisance in my will; I beg you to do as I ask. Soon I shall leave for the next world, full of affection and friendship for you and for your good and dear wife. I have loved you both; remember that, since 1844, my faithful friendship has never wavered.

Remember me occasionally, and we shall meet again as late as possible in the next world. Kisses and kisses from your faithful and loving friend.[19]

Verdi confided to Ricordi that he was 'absolutely desolate' to hear of Muzio's condition. He wanted to hasten to Paris, but the winter and his seventy-seven years prevented him. Instead, he asked Giulio Ricordi to find out if there was anything he could do for his old friend and colleague. On 27 November Muzio died in a Paris nursing home. In his will, he left an annual income of six hundred lire to the Busseto Monte di Pietà to be used each year to help a student complete his studies, 'hoping that the good example will be followed by other students who will receive the same help and will succeed in their careers, accumulating great riches, or very modest ones like mine, for it is not given to all to be born with the genius of the great-hearted Verdi, whose friendship and that of his good and dear wife I carry with me'.[20] Muzio also stipulated that his letters from Verdi, which he had kept throughout the years in neat packets, should be burned, 'for I do not wish them to be made gifts of, nor do I wish that commerce in autographs be made with them for profit'.[21]

Senator Giuseppe Piroli, two years Verdi's junior and another long-standing friend, died in the same month as Muzio. 'Your letters, my dearest Maria,' Verdi wrote to Maria Waldmann, his Amneris, who was now the Countess Massari,

> are always a consolation to me, but the last one was a cure, a balm, in this moment which is so sad for me. I have lost my two oldest friends!
>
> Senator Piroli, a learned, frank, sincere man, of a rectitude not to be equalled. A constant friend, unchanging in sixty years! Dead!!
>
> Emanuele Muzio, whom you knew when he conducted the orchestra in Paris for *Aida*. A sincere friend, devoted to me for fifty years. Dead!!
>
> And neither of them as old as I!! Everything is ending! Life is a sad business!
>
> I leave you to imagine the sorrow I felt, and still feel! And that is why I am not very keen to continue writing an opera which I have begun, but not got very far with. Pay no attention to what you read in the newspapers. Will I finish it? Will I not finish it? Who knows? . . .[22]

One of Verdi's last letters to Piroli had been instigated by the poverty, social unrest and rioting in southern Italy. 'Tell me something, you who find yourself in the bustle of a riot!' he had written to Piroli:

> These sad events will unhappily have a sequel! If they repress them, arrest

people and exile the leaders, it will serve no purpose. In the crowd, certainly, there are always agitators, evil creatures, thieves, but there is also, almost always, hunger.

I do not like politics, but I admit its necessity, the theory, the form of government, patriotism, dignity, etc. etc., but above all a man must live. From my window [in Genoa] every day I see a ship, and sometimes two, each carrying at least a thousand emigrants! Poverty and hunger! I see, in the country, land-owners of a few years ago who have now become peasants, casual labourers and emigrants (poverty and hunger). The rich, whose fortunes decrease every year, can no longer spend as before, and so poverty and hunger!

And how can we progress? It is not our industry that will save us from ruin! . . . Perhaps you, as a politician, will say that there is no other road. Well then, if that is so, let's get ready for rioting and disorder, first in one city, then in another, then in the villages and the countryside, and then *le déluge!*[23]

For the first three months of 1891, Verdi neglected the new opera. When he received, on his name-day, the gentle reproach of another of Ricordi's chocolate figurines and a sketch of Falstaff by Boito, he replied: 'What a surprise! Old Fat-Gut! I haven't heard of him for four months. Meanwhile, completely drunk, he has probably gone to sleep for ever! Let him sleep on! Why awaken him? He might commit some piece of villainy that would shock the world.'[24] But by the spring he was at work again: 'Old Fat-Gut is on the way to going crazy. There are days when he won't budge, but sleeps or is in a bad humour. At other times, he shouts, jumps, and makes a terrible row. I let him indulge his whims a little, but if he goes on like this, I'll put him in a muzzle and a strait-jacket.'[25]

'Bravo! Let him have his way,' Boito replied. 'Let him cavort, let him run. He will break all the windows and all the furniture in your room, but it doesn't matter, you can buy some more. Let everything be turned upside down, so long as the great scene is finished.'[26]

Verdi worked on with renewed energy, but when he thought the tone of Ricordi's encouragement too importunate, he threatened, half jokingly, to have his opera performed not at La Scala but at Sant' Agata for his own amusement.

On the day that he and Giuseppina returned from their summer visit to Montecatini, Verdi read in the *Corriere della Sera* of the death of the conductor Franco Faccio. For the past year, Verdi, Boito and Ricordi had been worried about the decline in Faccio's health and mental condition: Boito had taken over Faccio's duties as Director of the

Parma Conservatorium to ensure the continued payment of his friend's salary. In April Faccio had been taken to Krafft-Ebing's clinic for mental diseases in Graz, but there was nothing that could be done for him: he died of general paralysis of the insane, which in those days was the inevitable final stage of syphilis.

Had he lived, Faccio, as artistic director of La Scala, would no doubt have conducted the first performance of *Falstaff*. Boito attempted to involve Verdi in the choice of a successor, and the composer replied that he was opposed to holding a competition, for in his view a conductor could be judged only in public performance. He was inclined to think Edoardo Mascheroni the best of the available candidates, 'because I'm told he is both a hard worker (and a worker is necessary for La Scala) and a conscientious man without particular sympathies and, better still, without antipathies'. He went on to give some extremely sensible advice:

> But it isn't enough just to choose a conductor. He must be independent of the management, and he must assume complete musical responsibility in the eyes of the Committee, the management and the public.
>
> Further, you need a good chorus master, who should always be subordinate to the musical director, and who not only is to look after the musical instruction, but also to concern himself with the staging, as though he were a director. At all the performances, either the chorus master or his assistant should put on a costume and sing with the chorus.
>
> Further, you need a stage manager, always subordinate to the conductor.
>
> Finally, a clear and exact programme should be drawn up, so that the operas will not be selected haphazardly (as they have been in recent years), nor the singers who perform them. Get the right singers for the operas, or the right operas for the singers.[27]

Italo Pizzi, the Orientalist whom Verdi had first met in 1883 as Assistant Librarian at the Laurentian Library in Florence, had got into the habit of visiting the composer at Sant' Agata each year, in late summer or early autumn. He made notes of their conversations which he later collected in a volume and published after the composer's death. Verdi told Pizzi that Shakespeare

> analyses the human mind so acutely and penetrates it so profoundly that the words he puts into his characters' mouths are essentially human, essentially true, as they should be. He remarked that Victor Hugo inflated his characters too much and, by exaggerating them, robs them of truth; that Schiller, too good, too naive and too idealistic, fails to penetrate as

much as Shakespeare into the human mind, and for this reason does not analyse it so profoundly.[28]

Verdi, apparently, had a strong distaste for Nordic myth, and for the entire paraphernalia of Wagner's *Ring*. 'Oh, Sigurdh and all those other heroes – how horrible!' he exclaimed to Pizzi, whose Italian translation of the *Nibelungenlied* he promised to read, although he had not cared much for the poem in an earlier translation.

When the singing teacher Salvatore Marchesi wrote to him from Paris, suggesting that his wife Mathilde's pupil Nellie Melba should visit the composer to study Desdemona with him in the hope that she might subsequently be offered the role in Paris, Verdi icily rejected the proposal. (After Verdi's death, Melba spread the story that she had met the composer and studied the roles of Desdemona and Violetta with him!)

In September, despite the fact that he had not yet completed Act III of *Falstaff*, Verdi departed from his usual custom of leaving the orchestration till the end and began to score the music he had already written, 'because,' he told Boito, 'I'm afraid of forgetting certain blends and colours of instrumentation.'[29] In the winter, he was slowed down by influenza and for much of the time felt too listless to work. When Ricordi sent him the score of *L'amico Fritz*, a new opera by the young Mascagni whose *Cavalleria rusticana* had been successful two years earlier, Verdi was not impressed:

> In my life I have read many, many, very bad librettos, but I have never read a libretto as idiotic as this. As for the music, I got some way ahead with it, but I soon became bored with so many discords, and all those false relations, and those interrupted cadences and side-slips. . . . No doubt the music is very good. I just look at it from my point of view. But then I'm an old reactionary – well, old, at any rate, but not so much of a reactionary.[30]

By the beginning of April 1892, Act I of *Falstaff* had been scored. On 8 April, as one of the participants in a concert at La Scala commemorating the hundredth anniversary of the birth of Rossini, Verdi conducted the Prayer from that composer's *Mosè*, for solo voices, chorus and orchestra. Two newspaper reviews describe his conducting style. The critic of *Il Commercio* wrote: 'Verdi conducted the entire piece standing up, waving the baton energetically and jerkily, staring at the players in the pit, and the singers on stage, marking with his left hand – a white, diaphanous, almost waxen hand – the rhythmical development of the piece.'[31] *L'Italia del Popolo* reported: 'He conducted with ample, resolute gestures, while the fingers of his right hand rested on the stand and quivered nervously: with an imperious "ssshh" he obtained a *piano* from orchestra and singers, while a movement of his entire body drew crescendos and tone from the players.'[32]

Hans von Bülow, the German conductor who had written so scathingly of Verdi's *Requiem* eighteen years earlier without having heard the work, wrote him an effusive letter in April 1892, beginning 'Illustrious Maestro, Deign to hear the confession of a contrite sinner.' Bülow had now heard the *Requiem* and had been moved to tears by it. Formerly, his mind had been 'blinded by fanaticism, by an ultra-Wagnerian prejudice', but now, 'Illustrious Maestro, I admire you, I love you! Will you absolve me and exercise the royal prerogative of clemency? . . . Long Live Verdi, the Wagner of our dear allies.'[33] 'He is definitely mad!' Verdi told Ricordi,[34] before replying politely to Bülow.

In September, Verdi sent off to Ricordi the third and final act of *Falstaff*, accompanied by a note of affectionate farewell to the character of Falstaff scribbled on the manuscript, paraphrasing a passage in Boito's libretto:

> *Tutto è finito.*
> *Va, va vecchio John.*
> *Cammina per la tua via*
> *Fin che tu puoi.*
> *Divertente tipo di briccone*
> *Eternamente vero sotto*
> *Maschera diversa in ogni*
> *Tempo, in ogni luogo.*
> *Va, va,*
> *Cammina, cammina,*
> *Addio.*

[It's all finished. Go, go, old John. Go on your way for as long as you can. Amusing rogue, forever true beneath the masks you wear in different times and places. Go, go, on your way. Farewell.]

Verdi agreed to produce *Falstaff* at La Scala at the beginning of February 1893, provided that he could have the theatre completely at his disposal from 2 January. He sent some changes to Act I, and two sketches to show the designer, Adolfo Hohenstein, how he wanted the stage to look: 'Don't say anything to anyone about these blotchy sketches of mine, not even Boito, but make sure that Hohenstein's ideas conform reasonably to mine.'[35]

The cast was chosen by Verdi and his colleagues with the utmost care. The composer pointed out that the role of Alice called for a singer of wit and vivacity: 'She must have a bit of a devil about her. It's she who stirs the porridge.'[36] After initial misgivings about her ('I felt let down when I heard the pieces from *Aida* which are her war-horses'[37]), Verdi agreed to Ricordi's recommendation of Emma Zilli and, after coaching the soprano, professed himself delighted. For the role of Ford, he rejected a baritone named Pescina ('a good artist, but he's more of a singer than an actor, and a bit too heavy for the part of Ford, who when he's mad with jealousy yells and shouts and jumps about, and so on, and unless he can do this the Act II finale will fall flat'[38]); he gave the part to Antonio Pini-Corsi, who three years later would be Puccini's first Schaunard in *La Bohème*. A highly intelligent mezzo-soprano, Giuseppina Pasqua, whom Verdi at first thought might be too fiery and dramatic for Mistress Quickly, delighted him when she visited Sant' Agata; he not only gave her the role, but built it up somewhat in Act III, taking occasional lines away from Alice and Meg in order to do so.

Verdi wanted Angelo Masini for the tenor 'juvenile lead', Fenton ('but I'm afraid of his sulks when he finds out at rehearsals that the roles of Falstaff, Alice, Quickly, Ford etc., are more important than his'[39]). However, Masini was reluctant to give up an engagement in St Petersburg which would have caused him to miss the early *Falstaff* rehearsals, so Verdi settled for Edoardo Garbin, although

> he's had no experience, and he knows nothing about music. I don't know how he'll manage in the final fugue. . . . Almost all the operas written in the past are scored so that violins, trumpets and horns double the vocal line, and in those he's all right. With his magnificent high notes, he can drag applause from an over-indulgent public. But *Falstaff* is another matter. Each note and syllable has to be given its proper due.[40]

In the event, Garbin, who was inclined to be lazy and 'only too happy to miss a rehearsal',[41] was happily paired as Fenton with the Nannetta of his fiancée, Adelina Stehle. Verdi informed Ricordi more than six months before the premiere:

> I should add that the piano and stage rehearsals will be lengthy, because it won't be easy to perform the work the way I want it done, and I shall be very demanding, and not as I was in *Otello* when, out of deference to this

or that person, and in order to pose as someone serious, grave and venerable, I put up with everything. No, no. I shall go back to being a bear, as I used to be, and we shall all profit by it.[42]

For the title role it was assumed almost from the beginning that there could be no one but the French baritone, Victor Maurel, whose intelligence, technique, vocal quality, musicianship and dramatic ability had made him an outstanding Iago. Unfortunately, Maurel initially proved troublesome, demanding an exorbitant fee, payment for rehearsals (which was then unheard of, rehearsal pay being assumed to be included in the artist's fee), and sole rights to the role in a number of European cities for a specified period. After the baritone's wife had visited Sant' Agata to negotiate, Verdi expostulated to Ricordi: 'Never has such a thing happened to me in my fifty years in the galleys. There are no words to describe such a claim, and there can be no argument about it. You mustn't hesitate, but must immediately make Maurel's claim known publicly together with my telegram [to Maurel], and add that, for this reason, *Falstaff* cannot be staged.'[43] To Teresa Stolz, Verdi wrote:

> I have spent an infernal week with Maurel. His demands were so outrageous, exorbitant, incredible, that the only course was to consign the whole affair to the devil. Four thousand lire a night! Paid rehearsals at ten thousand lire! Rights for him alone to do *Falstaff* in Milan, Florence, Rome, Madrid, America, etc. etc.!
>
> Then I bared my talons and said, 'The opera is mine and I do not allow rights to my property. I will not allow them to pay you for rehearsals, something that has never been done. I don't want any manager to be ruined by an opera of mine, not even Piontelli [impresario of La Scala]. . . .'[44]

In due course Maurel withdrew his extravagant demands, and was engaged. Piano rehearsals under the composer's direction began at Sant' Agata in November, and on 2 January 1893 Verdi and Giuseppina arrived in Milan, where Verdi supervised the orchestral rehearsals conducted by Mascheroni, at La Scala. On some days the composer rehearsed for as long as eight hours, his colleagues marvelling at his energy and quick-witted resilience. In his eightieth year, he seemed as lively as any of them, and as much a perfectionist as ever.

As the date of the premiere approached, the world's musical press began to arrive in Milan. A few days before the great event,

Giuseppina wrote to her sister: 'Admirers, bores, friends, enemies, genuine and non-genuine musicians, critics good and bad are swarming in from all over the world. The way people are clamouring for seats, the opera house would need to be as big as a public square.'[45]

Not surprisingly, the occasion itself was a triumph. Although the performance on the first night was apparently far from perfect, the work was received rapturously. Verdi, leading Boito onto the stage to share the applause, was recalled time and time again. When, eventually, they and Giuseppina left the theatre by a side exit to avoid the crowds at the stage door, and made their way to the Grand Hotel, they found another cheering mass of people awaiting the composer there. Although he managed to fight his way through them to the entrance, Verdi had to appear on his balcony three times before the crowd finally dispersed.

Critical opinion was, for the most part, highly favourable, although some reviewers were puzzled by what they thought to be a lack of melody. The French critic Alfred Bruneau discerned the influence of Rossini and his predecessors, as well as that of Mozart and Haydn. The English composer Charles Villiers Stanford, who reviewed the opera for the London *Daily Graphic*, thought that Beethoven was the dominant influence, though he also noticed a trace of Meyerbeer and even a 'twinkle' of *Die Meistersinger*. Stanford's long review, published in two parts on consecutive days, was thoughtful and perceptive. 'After first principles,' he wrote,

> the resemblance [to Wagner] ceases. Verdi's workmanship is as totally different from Wagner's as the Italian nation is from the German. The whole work is as sunny as the composer's garden at Busseto. Clear as crystal in construction, tender and explosive by turns, humorous and witty without a touch of extravagance or a note of vulgarity. Each act goes as quickly as lightning, without halt, almost without slow tempi; and the general impression is that, not of an opera written for musical effect or for the glorification of the singers, but of an admirable comedy which music has helped to illustrate, to accentuate, and to idealize.[46]

Before the premiere, the *Daily Graphic* had published an interview with Verdi on the subject of *Falstaff*, in the course of which the composer had said that certain passages were 'so droll that the music has often made me laugh while writing it'. The puritanical *Daily Graphic* journalist was shocked by this, and expressed his regret that the composer of great tragic operas had 'lived to employ his magnificent genius for the purpose of making himself and others laugh'.[47]

It is still occasionally asserted that *Falstaff*, though a work of enormous vitality and skill, lacks the melodic fecundity of Verdi's youth and middle age. In fact, however, the most striking aspect of the work is its melodic prodigality. Verdi scatters tunes throughout *Falstaff* as though he were trying to give them away. It is the very profusion of melody in the opera which has occasionally led the casual hearer to suppose that it contains no tunes at all, for in it Verdi rarely repeats his melodies, being more inclined to discard many of them after only a few bars. Also, the general tempo of *Falstaff* is extraordinarily brisk; it is not until the beginning of the final scene that there comes a moment of repose, and of lyrical relaxation. There is no time for the listener to remember the tunes as they fly past.

There is so much to admire in *Falstaff*, a masterpiece whose wit and wisdom are equalled only by Mozart's three great Italian operas: scoring of great delicacy allied to a wide, Beethovenian range of expression; the magical evocation of forest and fancy in the last scene; and the remarkable pace of the entire opera, which seems to last no longer than one sudden flash of inspiration. There is no reason to be astonished that Verdi, in extreme old age, wrote such a superb comic opera, even if one has forgotten the *Giorno di regno* of the composer's youth. It was George Bernard Shaw who drew attention to the humour in *Un ballo in maschera*, *Rigoletto* and *Otello* (and he might well have included *La forza del destino*, for the character of Melitone). In the same article, published two months after the premiere of *Falstaff* when he had examined a vocal score of the opera, Shaw wrote:

> It is not often that a man's strength is so immense that he can remain an athlete after bartering half of it to old age for experience; but the thing happens occasionally, and need not so greatly surprise us in Verdi's case, especially those of us who, long ago, when von Bülow and others were contemptuously repudiating him, were able to discern in him a man possessing more power than he knew how to use, or indeed was permitted to use by the old operatic forms imposed on him by circumstances.[48]

When Verdi and Giuseppina left Milan after the first performance of the opera to return to their winter quarters in Genoa at the end of February 1893, the composer must have felt that, having in his eightieth year given *Falstaff* to the world, he could at last confidently consider his 'account settled'. It was highly unlikely that he would compose again.

Chapter Twenty-three

1893–1901

Before leaving Milan, Verdi read in a newspaper that the title of Marquis was about to be conferred upon him by the Italian government; he immediately wrote to the appropriate minister, requesting that this be averted: 'I call on you, as an artist, to do all you can to prevent this. My gratitude will be much greater if I am not given the title.'[1] His plea was successful.

Once back at Sant'Agata, he decided to make a slight adjustment to the finale of *Falstaff*'s Act II. He sent this off to Ricordi on 8 March, and ten days later followed it with a somewhat more substantial alteration to the first scene of Act III. Both these variants were first performed when the opera was staged at the Teatro Costanzi in Rome on 15 April, and were thereafter incorporated in the definitive score. Verdi was persuaded to attend, reluctantly, the first Rome performance: when he arrived in the city on the evening of the 13th, he was greeted by a crowd of two thousand admirers, and on the following day the Mayor conferred honorary citizenship of Rome upon him. The Viennese critic Eduard Hanslick, who had come to Rome to hear *Falstaff*, described the premiere in an article in the Vienna newspaper *Die Neue Freie Presse*:

What an evening! A national celebration, an *affaire de cœur* for the whole people! The enthusiasm that greeted Verdi's appearance on stage can hardly be imagined in Germany. And the applause was even more thunderous when Verdi appeared in the Royal Box and took his seat on the right of the King. To see a very elderly, very famous artist fêted in such a way is infinitely uplifting and moving, even for a foreigner.[2]

On the day of the performance, Hanslick had met Verdi and asked him why he had not previously written a comic opera. *'Parce que l'on n'en voulait pas'* (Because no one wanted me to) was the composer's reply. Verdi denied that he had already begun to compose an opera based on *King Lear*. 'I am not twenty [*vingt*], but eighty [*quatre-vingts*], he said, smiling roguishly to excuse the pun in French. He responded somewhat evasively to Hanslick's suggestion that he had been influenced by Wagner: 'Song and melody', he asserted, 'should always remain a composer's prime concern.'[3]

Productions of *Falstaff* were now proliferating throughout Europe, and even the Americas. In July the opera was performed in Buenos Aires and Rio de Janeiro: in the latter city it was produced on the same evening at two different theatres. Edoardo Mascheroni, the conductor of the Milan premiere, also conducted *Falstaff* in Trieste and in Vienna. After the first Trieste performance, Verdi wrote light-heartedly to Mascheroni, who had become a valued and trusted friend, and whom he called the third author of *Falstaff*. He enclosed a message for Giuseppina Pasqua (Mistress Quickly in Trieste as in Milan):

> Thank her [for her letter] and say that I shall answer her later, because I am now very busy putting the finishing touches to an opera in twelve acts plus a prologue and an overture which is as long as the nine symphonies of Beethoven put together. What's more, there is a prelude to each act in which all the violins, cellos and double basses play a melody in octaves. Not like those in *Traviata*, *Rigoletto* etc. etc., but a modern melody, one of those beautiful ones with neither beginning nor end, which stays suspended in air like the tomb of Mahomet. I have no more time now to explain how the singers must perform the accompaniment, but I am hoping to find an inspiration and imitate the clashing of the cymbals with the singers' voices. I shall tell you about that another time.[4]

In September, Boito visited Sant'Agata for a few days to complete his French translation of *Falstaff* in collaboration with the composer. In December, invited by Giuseppe Gallignani, Faccio's successor as Director of the Parma Conservatorium, to write a vocal piece on the occasion of the three-hundredth anniversary of the death of Palestrina, Verdi replied: 'Do you mean it? No, no, you're joking. You must know well that I can't do anything else now, except to have myself sent off to the asylum. I'll just send you my widow's mite, and the rest is up to you.'[5]

Verdi and Giuseppina travelled to Paris in April 1894 for the French premiere of *Falstaff* which was being staged at the Opéra-Comique, again with Maurel as Falstaff, this time singing in his native language.

Arriving in Paris at seven in the morning, after a sleepless night on a train, Verdi was at the theatre by lunchtime and ready to begin rehearsing:

> Sitting beside the accompanist, he explains and analyses a nuance, indicating accents by tapping the piano. Then he sings the phrase as he wishes it to be sung; he takes the pianist's place, corrects the metronome markings which were too vaguely indicated on the score. From time to time he exclaims 'I beg you, ladies and gentlemen, I beg you, don't lapse into sentimentality! Gaiety! Gaiety! That is the essence of *Falstaff*.'⁶

Verdi tried to persuade the conductor, Jules Danbé, to move his desk closer to the audience, so that he could take in the entire orchestra at a glance; but Danbé was wedded to the traditional placing of the conductor behind the prompter's box, as close as possible to the singers, with the orchestra behind him. Verdi admitted that his suggested placing of the conductor (which is now normal practice) would 'hardly delight the singers, but they are supposed to know their roles, are they not?'⁷

He showed more of his humour in the course of a French newspaper interview, when he was asked if he could explain why Wagner's *Die Walküre* had recently failed in Milan. He replied that the performance had been far from perfect. 'And then the large audience found the opera frankly boring. After a week they had had enough.'⁸ (Whether Verdi had actually attended one of the Milan performances of *Die Walküre* is not known. Probably he had not. But Boito had been present on the first night, and had written to him: '. . . Then there is the insipid action which moves more slowly than a passenger train stopping at every station, and the interminable sequence of duets during which the stage stays miserably empty and the characters stupidly motionless.'⁹)

On 15 April, Verdi attended a concert at the Paris Conservatoire, of which the eighty-three-year-old composer Ambroise Thomas was at that time the Director. Thomas greeted Verdi and Giuseppina at the foot of the grand staircase, and escorted them and Boito to his box:

> As soon as Verdi and Thomas appeared at the balustrade of their box, the crowded audience burst into great applause, rising to their feet and joining together in this imposing, rare and perhaps unique demonstration. It was most moving to see Thomas and Verdi holding each other by the hand, standing in the centre of the box; there is a marked resemblance between the two composers, even though Thomas's expression is rather suffering

as a result of a long nervous disease, while Verdi's preserves all its manly vigour.[10]

A Hungarian journalist visited Verdi in his suite at the Grand Hotel. (The composer had reluctantly deserted his old favourite, the Hôtel de Bade, his friends having reported to him that it had seen better days.) In answer to the journalist's question about a possible visit to Budapest to stage *Falstaff* there, Verdi replied, 'No, no, this I cannot do. I'm not travelling any more. This trip to Paris is the last.' Then, turning to Giuseppina for confirmation and support, 'We're not going to travel any more, are we?' he asked. (In fact, they would both return to Paris six months later for the first French performances of *Otello*.)

The Paris dress rehearsal of *Falstaff* was held on 16 April 1894, and the first public performance in French on the 18th was favourably received. The following month Boito went to Sant' Agata to discuss the French premiere of *Otello* which was to take place in the autumn. Verdi had insisted that *Falstaff* be performed at the Opéra-Comique, as he considered the Opéra too large an auditorium for so intimate a work; the French premiere of *Otello*, however, was to be at the Opéra, and it was necessary now for Verdi to compose music for the ballet which was mandatory at that theatre. Rather than write anything new, he hoped to make use of existing sixteenth-century dance music if he could find something suitable. He began to search, and instructed Ricordi and others also to search, for suitable tunes. Various specimens of folk music from Turkey, Cyprus, Greece and Venice were sent to him but none appealed. Ricordi then sent him the national anthems of several countries. 'They're all modern,' Verdi complained. 'The oldest, and also the most beautiful, is Haydn's [the Austrian anthem].' He then remembered a Prayer to Allah from Félicien David's 1844 symphonic ode, *Le Désert*: six bars of this in due course became the 'Invocation à Allah' in the *Otello* ballet, the rest of which was newly composed at Montecatini, timed meticulously to last for five minutes and fifty-nine seconds, and sent off to Ricordi on 21 August with a detailed synopsis which Verdi had written, and an accompanying note in which he made it clear that he was not taking the ballet too seriously: '. . . I've found a Greek song dating from 5,000 years before Christ. If the world didn't exist then, so much the worse for the world. I've also found a piece from Murano that was composed 2,000 years ago for a battle that was fought between Venice and Murano, and won by the Muranese. It doesn't matter if Venice didn't then exist. . . .'[11]

Giuseppina was ill in the summer, but was well enough to travel with Verdi to Paris at the end of September for the rehearsals of *Otello*. The first performance at the Opéra on 12 October, with Maurel in his old role of Iago, Albert Saléza in the title role, and Rose Caron as Desdemona, was conducted by Paul Taffanel. It was received with the greatest enthusiasm: after the first act, Auguste Casimir-Perier, President of the Republic, invited Verdi to his box and awarded him the Grand Cross of the Legion of Honour. He presented the composer to the audience, who applauded Verdi throughout the interval.

On 18 October, the first anniversary of the death of Gounod, Verdi and Ambroise Thomas attended a memorial service, and the following day the Verdis were guests at a luncheon in Verdi's honour given by the President of the Republic at the Elysée Palace. On 22 October they left Paris to return to Genoa. At the end of November, Verdi wrote to Boito who had been in Parma attending a series of concerts in honour of the great sixteenth-century composer Palestrina. He was keen to know whether Boito had been to see the paintings of Correggio: 'Such a marvellously seductive painter! So splendid, and yet so simple that every time I see his work I feel that he could never have had a master. Sometimes he is as grandiose as Michelangelo. But whereas Correggio's prophets and apostles move me to love, those of Michelangelo inspire me with fear.'[12]

For the benefit of victims of an earthquake in Sicily and Calabria, Verdi wrote his last song, '*Pietà, Signor*', a dignified and restrained prayer whose text Boito had adapted from the 'Agnus Dei'. The song's appearance in November, in a publication called *Fata Morgana*, renewed rumours that Verdi and Boito were at work upon another opera, but they were not. Boito had suggested *Antony and Cleopatra*, the Shakespeare play which he had translated some years earlier for the great Italian actress Eleonora Duse, whose lover he had been. He had also planned his own *King Lear* libretto, and even began to write its opening scene although Giuseppina warned him that his collaborator was now too old and tired to embark upon another major work.

In November Verdi received a visit in Genoa from the fifty-two-year-old French composer Jules Massenet, who later wrote of the occasion in an article which concluded with his recollection of Verdi's demeanour on the terrace of the Palazzo Doria:

> I shall always see him bareheaded and upright beneath the scorching sun, showing me the iridescent town and the golden sea beneath us, with a gesture as proud as his genius and as simple as his beautiful artist's soul. It

was almost an evocation of one of the great Doges of the past, stretching over Genoa his powerful and beneficent hand.[13]

Verdi returned to Milan at the end of January 1895, to discuss with Camillo Boito the construction of the Casa di Riposo per Musicisti (Rest Home for Musicians). This generous and imaginative project was to occupy much of the composer's energies in his last years. He had purchased the land in 1889, but had not been able to proceed with the actual building while he was still engaged on *Falstaff*. Now that he was free to devote time and attention to it, he did so unstintingly. The Home was planned to be large enough to accommodate one hundred residents. Boito had drawn up plans but Verdi, typically, behaved as though the architect were one of his librettists: he interfered, made suggestions for improvements, and insisted that private bedrooms be provided instead of dormitories, for he wanted there to be not the slightest suggestion of institutionalism. He later stipulated that the ratio of residents was to be sixty men to forty women, that they should be Italian citizens who had reached the age of sixty-five, who had practised the art of music professionally, and who found themselves in poverty. Composers were to be given preference, followed by singers, conductors and orchestral musicians. Construction of the Casa di Riposo – Verdi had rejected Camillo Boito's suggestion that it be called an Asylum – began in 1896, and Verdi visited the site often to watch the building going up: after all, as he told more than one friend, it was his favourite of all his works, musical or otherwise. Known locally as the Casa Verdi, the Casa di Riposo per Musicisti, on the Piazzale Michelangelo Buonarotti, still functions. Some very distinguished opera singers have been content, indeed proud, to end their days in this home provided for them by their beloved Verdi. A visitor, wandering into its courtyard to visit the graves of Giuseppe and Giuseppina Verdi, can sometimes hear the elderly voice of a resident, singing a Verdi aria.

The cost of all this charity was high, and Verdi was still enough of a landlord-farmer to insist on the prompt payment by his tenants at Sant'Agata of rents due to him. 'Will you please prepare the contracts of the tenant farmers for me with a guarantee that the rents will be paid when they are due,' he instructed his land agent in March 1895. 'In one of your letters you wrote to me concerning this, "I hope they will be prompt." Hope is an alarming word in this context. Why did I make the sacrifice of reducing the land rentals so generously?'[14]

Verdi had not entirely abandoned composition, despite his frequent assertions that he was no longer capable of it. In April he began composing a 'Te Deum' which occupied him, on and off, for the next twelve months or more. Scored for double chorus and large orchestra, it is one of his finest choral works. The composer himself evidently thought so, for he asked that the score be buried with him. He had made a study of other composers' settings of this fourth- or fifth-century canticle, and had decided that the poem was more than the simple exclamation of praise it was often made to sound. 'Towards the middle it changes colour and expression,' he observed. *'Tu ad liberandum* – it is Christ born of the Virgin who opens to mankind *Regnum coelorum.* Mankind believes in the *Judex venturus,* invokes him in *Salvum fac,* and ends with a prayer, *Dignare Domine die isto,* moving, and sad to the point of terror.'[15] Verdi's 'Te Deum' captures all of these moods, doubt and uncertainty as well as praise and jubilation. Towards the end, a solo soprano voice emerges from the chorus to assert its faith, but it is with six bars of doubt and gloom in the orchestra that this subtly scored masterpiece ends.

In June 1895 Verdi declined a proposal from a German publisher that he write his autobiography. 'Never, never shall I write my memoirs!' he replied. 'It's good enough that the musical world has put up with my notes for so long a time. I shall never condemn it to read my prose.'[16] In July Arnaldo Bonaventura, an Italian musicologist, introduced himself to Verdi at his hotel in Montecatini and talked to him for half an hour on a variety of subjects. 'Art and systems of art are opposites,' Verdi had said. 'The great Wagner left much evil in his wake.' The composer also stated that one must not be reactionary, but must move with the times, without, however, disregarding the past. It was wrong to ignore the importance of tradition and do precisely the opposite of what had been done before, simply to be modern at all costs. The most serious fault of modern music was its tendency to over-elaborate. Other phrases of Verdi's that the young musicologist jotted down were: 'Simplicity in art is everything'; 'Spontaneity and inspiration are crucial'; and 'When form is intricate, contorted and difficult, communication fails, and communication is the aim of art.' From Bonaventura one also learns that the Verdis' circle of companions at Montecatini in the summer of 1895 included Teresa Stolz, Giuseppina Pasqua and the conductor Leopoldo Mugnone. The morning after their talk, Bonaventura caught sight of Verdi at two of the bathing establishments, the Regina and the Tettuccio. Noticing that the composer drank two glasses of water at the Regina, and four at the Tettuccio, Bonaventura followed his example.[17]

In Germany the young Richard Strauss had just published his first opera, *Guntram*, which had been performed in May 1894 at Weimar. The following January Strauss sent a copy of the score to Verdi, the living composer whom he most admired. 'Illustrious Maestro,' he wrote in an accompanying letter,

> From my own experience I know how annoying dedications can be. Nevertheless, I dare to send you, the true master of Italian opera, a copy of my first work in this category, *Guntram*, as a token of my sincere admiration, and with the hope that you will kindly accept it.
>
> I can find no words to describe the impression made on me by the extraordinary beauty of *Falstaff*. Consider my dedication as thanks for this reawakening of your genius. Should, one day, the occasion ever present itself, I should be most happy to converse with you about the divine art of music. . . .[18]

Verdi replied courteously and promptly:

> A few days ago I received a work which you so kindly sent me, and which enjoyed such a success. I am now on my way to Milan, where I shall spend a few days, and therefore I do not have time now to read your score. However, dipping into it here and there, I can tell that your *Guntram* is a work fashioned by a knowledgeable hand. It is a pity that I cannot understand the text, not because I wish to pass judgment (this I would not presume to do), but rather because I wish to admire and to share your pleasure.[19]

Strauss treasured Verdi's letter all his life. He might not have done so had he known that, before sending it, Verdi had written to Ricordi to enquire if a certain Richard Strauss of Munich was the same person as the composer of the waltzes. Ricordi had replied that Richard Strauss was not connected with the waltz kings of Vienna, but was 'a puffed-up braggart'.[20]

Rumours continued to circulate to the effect that Verdi was at work on this or that major project. One was *Il conte Ugolino*, because it was discovered that Verdi had asked the librarian of the Florence Musical Institute if he could borrow a copy of a cantata of that title by the sixteenth-century composer Vincenzo Galilei, father of the astronomer Galileo Galilei. One of the most persistent rumours, of course, concerned *King Lear*. However, in 1896 the eighty-three-year-old composer offered his synopsis and Antonio Somma's libretto of

King Lear to Mascagni, the most popular of the newest generation of composers. Mascagni revealed that he asked Verdi why he had never written the opera. 'Verdi closed his eyes for a moment, perhaps to remember, perhaps to forget. Then softly and slowly he replied: "The scene in which King Lear finds himself on the heath terrified me." '[21]

Giulio Ricordi had lost control of La Scala, which was now under the influence of a rival publisher, Edoardo Sanzogno. As a consequence, the operas of Ricordi's composers, even those of Verdi, were temporarily excluded from that august theatre. At the beginning of 1896 Ricordi entreated Verdi to intercede with the Prime Minister, Francesco Crispi, but Verdi refused. He disapproved of the majority of Crispi's domestic and foreign policies, especially Italy's imperialist war with Ethiopia ('We are playing the tyrant in Africa; we are in the wrong, and we shall pay for it'[22]), and had also been distressed at the Prime Minister's ruthless suppression of peasant uprisings in Sicily. Increasingly, he regarded politics as a sordid business and had strong feelings about imperial oppression, as is seen in this comment to Italo Pizzi in September 1896 in a conversation about India:

> Here you have a great and ancient people who have now fallen prey to the English. But the English will be sorry! A people might suffer tyranny, oppression, maltreatment – and the English can really be bastards. Then comes the moment when national sentiment, which no one can withstand, reawakens. That's how we dealt with the Austrians. Unfortunately, we are now behaving like tyrants in Africa, and we shall have to pay for it. It is said that we are going there to bring our own civilization to those people. A fine civilization we have, with all its unhappiness. Those people will not know what to make of it, and in many respects they are much more civilized than we are![23]

Verdi began another choral work in the winter of 1896–97, a 'Stabat Mater' for four-part chorus and orchestra. This was the last composition he was to complete, a work of deeply expressive beauty. The medieval Latin poem is set as a dramatic text, and Verdi's involvement is with the reality of the situation, the weeping mother standing by the cross on which her son is dying, rather than with mystical religious reflections upon the scene.

One morning in January 1897, Giuseppina entered Verdi's bedroom to find him lying in bed seemingly paralysed and unable to speak. He managed to make a sign indicating that he wished to write, and when pencil and paper were brought he scrawled with difficulty the one word 'coffee', a beverage which he was in the habit of drinking black, strong, and in great quantities. After being assisted to drink several cups, he began to recover, and eventually was himself again. This apparently was not the first such incident: on another occasion he was found semi-conscious on his bed. These mild strokes warned him that he must now conserve his energies, and in consequence he proceeded to complete his 'Stabat Mater' more slowly than he might otherwise have done. By October, however, it was finished, and he sent to Ricordi all four of the religious pieces he had composed in the previous few years: the 'Laudi alla Vergine Maria' and 'Ave Maria' of 1888–89, and the two longer and more recent pieces, the 'Te Deum' and 'Stabat Mater'. At the beginning of 1898 they were published together in vocal score as *Quattro pezzi sacri (Four Sacred Pieces)*.

At Montecatini in July, an acquaintance noted that Verdi looked vigorous, held himself erect, walked briskly, displayed an excellent memory for dates and names, and set forth his ideas about art clearly, but that Giuseppina 'hobbles along, all bent over, on his arm, although something about her still bears witness to her past beauty'.[24] Verdi used to complain about being stared at by passers-by at Montecatini as though he were a wild beast. He put up with it because, according to him, the spas had done him much good over the years.

Giuseppina's health had been declining for some time. On 9 September 1897 Verdi wrote to Giulio Ricordi: 'Peppina gets up for a few hours. Her cough and catarrh have improved, but she is extremely weak. She doesn't eat, and she says she cannot?! It's distressing, and we are at our wits' end.' Later in the month he had similar news to report, adding, 'Her extreme weakness robs her of almost all desire to speak or to listen.'[25] On 14 October the eighty-two-year-old Giuseppina was strong enough to pay a visit to her sister Barberina in Cremona, but on 11 November she took to her bed at Sant' Agata with severe pneumonia. Late in the afternoon of 14 November she died. One of the first visitors to the house after her death was Giuseppina's solicitor, Amilcare Martinelli, who was the executor of her will. Martinelli wrote an account of his visit:

> At Sant' Agata I found gathered, in the Villa Verdi, only the affectionate Carrara family of Busseto, the great Maestro's only relatives. They told me, in tears, the pathetic stories of the last three days. On Thursday poor Signora Giuseppina had carefully made a note of the objects that were to remain in the villa, and those that were to be gradually packed in cases, to

be sent to Genoa. On Sunday, Verdi and the Signora were to have left for Milan and thence to Genoa. But on Sunday, instead, at 4.30 p.m. Giuseppina Verdi drew her last breath! A violent pneumonia had attacked her that same Thursday. At dinner she felt a sharp chest pain and a great chill. The doctor judged the case desperate, especially since, for some time, the poor Signora had taken scant nourishment.

There was a consultation, and unfortunately the consultation confirmed the terrible sentence! But the patient did not show great suffering. . . . A few hours before serenely closing her eyes, her Verdi brought her a violet, saying, 'Smell the perfume!' And she said, 'Thank you, but I don't smell anything, because I have a slight cold.' Verdi kissed her in her death agony, and kissed the lifeless body again. . . .

As I was about to take my leave, the kindly Signora Maria Carrara [the Verdis' adopted daughter] told me that, though Verdi didn't feel up to talking, he wished to see me. I entered his room, sustained by I don't know what superhuman spirit. The Maestro was standing erect, at his armchair, between the bed against the wall, the broad desk, all covered with papers, and the closed piano. His chin was against his chest; his cheeks flushed a bright scarlet; his hair and beard very white, more silver than snowy. I ran to him, bowed, and using gentle violence made him sit. He didn't want to. He stammered these few words. . . . 'I don't feel up to speaking. . . . Tell Barberina it was better that she obeyed and left yesterday. It was better. . . .'[26]

As she had requested, Giuseppina's funeral was a simple ceremony, held at dawn, with only family and servants present. On 17 November, after a service in the chapel at Sant' Agata, her coffin was carried to Fiorenzuola, with Verdi following it, bare headed. Her body was taken by rail to Milan, where Boito and Vigoni, the Mayor, were waiting to escort it to the municipal cemetery. There, Giuseppina was buried in a plot of earth which Verdi had reserved for them both.

Apart from a number of small bequests to relatives, friends (among them Teresa Stolz, to whom she left three pieces of jewellery), servants and the local poor, Giuseppina Verdi left everything she possessed to the man whose life she had shared for fifty years. Her will, made only six months before she died, ended: 'Now farewell, my Verdi! As we were united in life, may God join our spirits together again in Heaven.'[27]

Giuseppina's death left Verdi lonely and desolate. He could not bring himself to leave Sant'Agata to spend the winter in Genoa, but remained at the villa, refusing the suggestions of friends such as

Ricordi and Boito that he move to Milan. At Christmas he was still at Sant' Agata, where Boito joined him. Hoping to please the composer, Boito had made provisional arrangements for the *Quattro pezzi sacri* to be performed at the Paris Opéra during Holy Week 1898, which he now needed to confirm. Verdi was at first reluctant to allow the four works to be performed, but was finally persuaded, insisting only that the 'Ave Maria', which he regarded as a 'charade', be withdrawn.

In January, Verdi went to Milan, accompanied by Maria Carrara and Teresa Stolz, both of whom now tried to spend as much time with him as possible. His main purpose in visiting the city was to supervise the printing of the *Quattro pezzi sacri*. Friends gathered around him in Milan, keeping him company at meal times and in the evenings, and when the weather was fine he went for long carriage rides. 'To live without being able to do anything! It's very hard,' he wrote to the conductor Mascheroni.[28] At the end of February, he finally left for Genoa and the Palazzo Doria. Life there, however, was empty without Giuseppina, for he had never cared for Genoese society and had made few friends in the city. He was now occasionally to be seen at the railway station buffet, eating a sandwich or gazing at the passers-by. But if any stranger ventured to address him by name, he took himself off.

Verdi had hoped to travel to Paris to supervise rehearsals of what were now only three sacred pieces, but his doctors advised against it. Boito agreed to go in his place, travelling via Genoa to receive last-minute instructions regarding interpretation from the composer who, after Boito's arrival in Paris, continued daily to send suggestions and instructions to him at the Grand Hotel. On 7 April, the 'Stabat Mater', 'Laudi alla Vergine Maria' and 'Te Deum' were performed by the chorus and orchestra of the Paris Opéra, conducted by Paul Taffanel. Verdi had expressed his doubts about the quality of the Paris Opéra chorus, but the performance went well, though the most enthusiastic reception was given to the 'Laudi', sung not by a four-part female chorus but by four distinguished soloists, the sopranos Ackté and Grandjean and the mezzo-sopranos Heglon and Delna. The following day, Verdi sent a dignified letter of thanks to Boito:

> In going to Paris in my place you have rendered me a service for which I shall always be grateful. But if you reject any form of recognition I remain crushed by a burden I cannot and ought not to support. Well then, my dear Boito, let's talk frankly, without reticence, like the true friends we are.
> To show you my gratitude, I could offer you some trifle or other, but

what use would it be? It would be embarrassing for me and useless to you.

Permit me, therefore, when you are back from Paris, to clasp your hand here. And for this handclasp you will not say a word, not even 'Thank you'. Further, absolute silence on the present letter. Amen. So be it.[29]

Disappointed that the premiere of those three of the *Four Sacred Pieces* whose public performance Verdi was willing to allow had not taken place in Italy, Giulio Ricordi arranged that they be performed in Turin in May, as part of the celebrations being held there in connection with the fiftieth anniversary of the Italian Constitution. The musical part of the celebrations was being arranged by Giuseppe Depanis, a prominent figure in the musical life of Turin, who had engaged the thirty-one-year-old Arturo Toscanini as conductor. In April, Depanis, Toscanini and the chorus master Aristide Venturi visited Verdi in Genoa to discuss details. The young conductor and the old composer got on extremely well, Verdi expressing his amazement at Toscanini's quickness of perception, and all three visitors being equally astonished at the energy Verdi rediscovered as he sat at the piano. Depanis described the occasion:

> His voice was veiled at first, but grew clear and imperious. His eyes sparkled, and no detail of the performance escaped him. He explained his own intentions with brief, precise, vivid phrases, which said much more than a long commentary. One phrase in particular remained in my memory and made us all smile, the Maestro included. Towards the end of the choral 'Te Deum', a single soprano voice suddenly cries out for mercy. This solo of very few bars in a piece that is essentially choral arouses a certain surprise. To enhance its effect Verdi recommended that the singer be placed as far away as possible, hidden from the audience, almost as a voice from beyond, a voice of awe and supplication. 'It is the voice of humanity in fear of hell,' he said, to explain the idea more graphically, stressing in the French manner the 'ü' of '*umanità*' [humanity] and '*paura*' [fear], as our forefathers used to in Piedmont.[30]

When the Academy of Saint Cecilia in Rome gave a performance of Verdi's *Requiem Mass*, Queen Margherita, a connoisseur of music and a devoted admirer of Verdi, was present. The following day, she despatched a telegram to the composer:

> Yesterday I heard your religious and musical masterpiece. My mind was filled with admiration for the grandeur of the musical concept, my heart was soothed by the melodic sweetness, and my soul stirred by the loftiness and strength of the prayer, which seems to rise directly to God. I felt I must

communicate these feelings to you, along with my profound admiration for the glory and honour which you bring to our art.

Verdi replied: 'I am deeply touched by the telegram which Your Majesty has so kindly sent me. Nothing could give me greater pleasure. In my sad old age, your good words are a comfort and a consolation.'[31]

In the summer of 1898, Teresa Stolz and Giuseppina Pasqua were among Verdi's companions at Montecatini, where the composer stayed at his usual hotel, the Locanda Maggiore, from 11 July to 1 August. The Tettuccio was the most abundant spring and therefore the most frequented, which is probably why Verdi tended to take the waters more frequently at two of the other springs, the Rinfresco and the Savi. On his return to Sant' Agata, he read something in the *Corriere della Sera* on 9 August which annoyed him so intensely that he immediately wrote to Ricordi:

> It is now five in the afternoon, and I read in the *Corriere*, 'The Milan Conservatorium is to be re-named after Giuseppe Verdi.'
> My God, this was all that was lacking to plague the soul of a poor devil like me who desires only to be serene and to die serenely! No, sir! Even this isn't allowed me! What wrong have I done that I should be tormented like this!??[32]

He was still furious four days later: ' "Giuseppe Verdi Conservatorium" is a discord!' he told Ricordi. 'A Conservatorium that (I do not exaggerate) tried to kill me, and whose memory I should try to escape.'[33] This was, to put it mildly, a trifle unfair, and distinctly ungracious of Verdi. His mind, however, was soon distracted from baleful thoughts of the Milan Conservatorium by the news that La Scala, which had been closed for nearly an entire year, was to be re-opened and run by a committee which had appointed Giulio Gatti-Casazza as artistic director and Arturo Toscanini as chief conductor. At the suggestion of Boito, it had been agreed to perform the three *Pezzi sacri* during the first season, although Verdi was opposed to the idea ('My name is too old and boring: it bores me even to pronounce it'[34]), and the three pieces were duly given on 16 April 1899, as part of what was said to be a badly organized concert conducted by Toscanini, whose programme included Schumann's Fourth Symphony and Liszt's orchestration of a Schubert march. In reporting on the event to Verdi, who had remained in Genoa, Boito admitted that he had been wrong to suggest inserting the *Sacred Pieces* into an operatic season, and that Verdi had been right to object. Verdi thanked his colleague for a thoughtful and friendly letter, adding: 'Kindly applause and indulgent reviews for the benefit of the "grand old man" do not touch me. No, no, I ask for neither indulgence nor pity; in fact, I prefer downright hissing.'[35]

A revival of *Falstaff* the previous month, also conducted by Toscanini, had been much more successful, but again Verdi's reaction to a report of it was that it would be better to go back to the more modest conductors of the old days. 'When I began to shock the musical world,' he told Ricordi, 'there was the calamity of the prima donnas and their rondos. Now there is the tyranny of the conductors! Bad, bad! But the former was less bad!'[36]

Verdi was at Montecatini again in July, accompanied by Teresa Stolz. This year, he seemed more tolerant of the crowds that gathered around him: it was as though he were now keen to accept any manifestation of life that offered itself. In August he returned to Sant' Agata, taking pleasure in the wedding of Maria Carrara's daughter, Giuseppina, for he regarded Maria and her family as his heirs. In September Verdi wrote to the Minister of Education asking if, after his death, his wife's grave could be moved so that he and she could be buried together in the chapel of his Rest Home for Musicians, whose construction was now almost complete.

Verdi's request was granted. In December, he went to Milan to sign the act of foundation, legally establishing the Casa di Riposo. His friends were hoping to be able to bring the official opening forward to 1 January 1900, as a New Year present to him; after the cutting of much red tape, which necessitated a hurried visit to Rome by the Rest Home's legal adviser, the Casa di Riposo per Musicisti was made the subject of a Royal Decree on 31 December, and the Acting Mayor of Milan was able to go with the entire City Council to Verdi's hotel to announce this to him on New Year's Day, to thank him for his generosity, and to offer him the good wishes of the season.

The newspapers were predicting that the Collare dell' Annunziata, the highest royal decoration Italy could offer, was about to be bestowed on Verdi by King Umberto. To Verdi, however, this seemed as irksome as being made Marquis of Busseto, an honour he had refused seven years earlier, and he succeeded in deflecting it. But curiously, he appears not to have demurred when, some months later, in April 1900, the Austrian Emperor Franz Joseph, who held Verdi in high personal regard, conferred upon him the highest Austrian honour for intellectual attainment.

In April the three sacred pieces were heard at a concert of the Academy of Saint Cecilia in Rome. (After Verdi's death, the 'Ave Maria' was allowed its rightful place with the others: performances nowadays are of the entire *Four Sacred Pieces* [*Quattro pezzi sacri*], although the most substantial piece, the 'Te Deum', is occasionally performed on its own.)

Verdi made his last will in Milan in May, and sent it to his notary, Angelo Carrara (father of Alberto Carrara who had married Verdi's adopted daughter, Maria). The will reveals that the composer was a very large landowner, the possessor of a great many farm properties in the country around Busseto. He named Maria as his residuary legatee, made a number of bequests to charitable institutions, family, friends and staff, left his numerous farms to various relatives and to the Busseto Monte di Pietà which had helped him when he was a student, and gave the use of one of the farms to Giuseppina's sister Barberina Strepponi for the rest of her life. He left eight farm properties to the hospital he had built at Villanova, adding a note: 'Because the rent of these farms comes to an amount larger than that necessary to support the hospital, I request the hospital director to contribute a thousand lire a year to the Orphanage of Cortemaggiore.' Money was set aside for the Busseto Orphanage and hospital, and for scholarships to agricultural students.

Special provision was made for the Rest Home for Musicians in Milan, which was to receive a large sum in Treasury Bonds, all Italian and foreign royalties from Verdi's operas, and his credit of 200,000 lire with the firm of Ricordi ('upon which 4 per cent interest is currently paid'). The board of the Rest Home was empowered to spend no more than 5,000 lire annually for the first ten years, in order that the remainder could be used to increase the capital. The will ends as follows:

> I ask my residuary legatee to keep up my house and garden at Sant' Agata, and the fields around the garden, all just as they are today. This obligation is to devolve upon her heirs or their representatives. I wish my funeral to be extremely simple and to take place either at daybreak or at the hour of the 'Ave Maria', without either music or song. I do not desire publication of any of the conventional death announcements.
>
> On the day after my death, one thousand lire should be distributed to the poor of the village of Sant' Agata.[37]

King Umberto was assassinated by an anarchist at Monza, an industrial town near Milan, on 29 July 1900, a crime that horrified Verdi. When the Queen wrote a prayer which was published in the newspapers, he was moved by its simplicity:

> O Lord, he sought to do good in this world. He felt rancour towards none. He always forgave those who acted evilly against him. He sacrificed his life to duty and to the good of his country. Till his last breath he struggled to fulfil his task. For his red blood which flowed from three wounds, for the good and just works he performed, merciful and just Lord, take him into your arms and grant him his eternal reward.[38]

When an acquaintance, Countess Giuseppina Negroni-Prati, wrote to Verdi suggesting that he set the Queen's prayer to music, Verdi replied that he had hoped to do so but that he was not well, and did not feel able to attempt its composition. 'In its pure simplicity,' he wrote, 'the Queen's prayer reads as though it was written by one of the early fathers of the church. Inspired by her deep religious feeling, she has found words of such truth and, as it were, primal feeling, that it would be impossible to equal them in music, which would appear affected and inflated. We should have to go back three centuries to Palestrina.'[39] A professor from Salerno also wrote to Verdi, enclosing his own rhymed verse version of the prayer, but the composer's reply was that, even if he could have undertaken the task, he would not have wanted to set a rhymed version, as he preferred the sincerity and spontaneity of the Queen's prose. He had, in fact, already begun to sketch a few bars of a setting of the prayer on a plain sheet of paper on which he had ruled musical stave-lines, but had not found the strength to continue.

Verdi was slowly becoming weaker. When Italo Pizzi called on him at Sant' Agata on 12 September, the composer greeted him affably but said, 'I'm sorry, Pizzi, that I can't welcome you as I used to, but I don't feel well today, not at all well.' Their conversation was brief, and as Pizzi took his leave Verdi continued to complain about the state of his health:

> 'My legs no longer carry me!' he said, and indeed, as he accompanied me to the door, he leaned heavily on my hand, and moved with difficulty, taking very short steps. I said to him, 'Don't lose heart, Maestro! Your doctor, Battistini, told me a few hours ago in Busseto that you have a very strong constitution.' Verdi replied, slightly peevishly, 'I know, I know. If I hadn't, I wouldn't have reached the age of eighty-seven. But those eighty-seven years are weighing me down!'[40]

The staff at Sant' Agata would occasionally hear their master singing softly and mournfully to himself. Maria Carrara revealed that, after Giuseppina's death, Verdi sometimes sat at the piano and sang the aria of King Philip from *Don Carlos* in its Italian translation, '*Dormirò sol nel manto mio regal*' (I shall sleep alone in my regal mantle). He grieved still for his long-dead first wife and his children, as well as for his life-long companion and second wife, Giuseppina. Perhaps, now more than ever, he regretted that neither of his two children had lived to reach adult age and to provide him with a long line of direct descendants. He had kept the wedding rings he had exchanged with Margherita Barezzi, together with a lock of her hair, in a box on which he had written 'Souvenirs of my poor family'. After his death, it was given at his wish to the niece of Antonio Barezzi, the father of Verdi's first wife.

On 4 December, after arranging to collect and destroy any surviving musical manuscripts of his student days that he could discover, Verdi left Sant' Agata to spend Christmas in Milan at his usual suite in the Grand Hôtel et de Milan, in the company of his closest friends and associates, among them Maria Carrara, Teresa Stolz, Arrigo Boito and the Ricordi family. 'Our beloved Maestro is well, despite his eighty-seven years,' Teresa Stolz, the original Aida, wrote to her friend Maria Waldmann, the original Amneris. 'He enjoys a good appetite, sleeps well, often goes out for drives, sometimes walks a little, but complains of his legs, saying he would take longer walks but his legs are too weak. For the rest, he is in good humour, likes company, and every evening has a gathering of his most intimate friends at his hotel. Later, in March, he will leave for Genoa.'[41]

But Verdi was to see neither Genoa nor Sant' Agata again. A few days into January 1901 he wrote to a friend, Giuseppe de Amicis, 'Even though the doctors tell me I am not ill, I feel that everything tires me. I can no longer read or write. I can't see very well, my feeling grows less, and even my legs don't want to carry me any more. I'm not living, I'm vegetating. What am I doing still in this world?'[42] He received a visit from the composer Umberto Giordano, whose opera *Andrea Chenier* had been a resounding success four years earlier at La Scala, and asked Giordano why he did not attempt to make an opera from Sardou's play *Madame Sans-Gêne*:

'But what about the character of Napoleon, Maestro?' Giordano asked. And Verdi, with the intuition of a genius, replied, 'I could not imagine

Napoleon coming to the footlights to sing a romance with his hand across his heart. Certainly not. But a Napoleon who uttered dramatic recitative would be perfectly fitting, even in an opera.'[43]

The last letters Verdi wrote were probably those of 17 January, in French, to Victor Sauchon, an officer of the Société des Auteurs et Compositeurs Dramatiques in Paris, acknowledging receipt of his French royalties up to the end of the previous year, and of 18 January to his sister-in-law, Barberina Strepponi, which consists entirely of small talk: '. . . I write little because writing tires me; but you have a steady hand, write to me. I know that Maria tells you my news – she is well and sends her love. I shake you warmly by the hand.'[44]

On New Year's Day, Giuseppe Gallignani (who, as well as being Director of the Parma Conservatorium, was choir-master of the Duomo, the Milan Cathedral) had called on Verdi to convey the best wishes of the Archbishop of Milan. The composer considered this an ill omen. It was on 21 January, at about ten-thirty in the morning, that the catastrophe occurred. Verdi's Milan physician, Dr Caporali, had made his usual visit and, finding his patient in good health, had agreed to allow him to go for a drive in his carriage. As Verdi was dressing, seated on the edge of his bed, his housekeeper noticed that he was fastening the buttons of his waistcoat into the wrong buttonholes, and drew his attention to the fact. 'What's a button here or there?' Verdi replied. They were the last words he was ever to utter, for he suddenly lost consciousness and fell backwards onto the bed. Maria Carrara was called from her adjacent room and arrived with the hotel doctor who, together with Dr Caporali who had been urgently recalled, administered first aid. The composer showed clear signs of having suffered a cerebral haemorrhage which had paralysed his entire right side. Professor Grocco, who for several years had tended Verdi at Montecatini, was summoned from Florence by telegram, but there was nothing that could be done except wait for the end. When this seemed imminent three days later, on 24 January, the Catholic rite of extreme unction was administered to the still-comatose composer. However, his condition improved slightly, and he lingered on for another three days. He recovered consciousness only briefly when Dr Grocco put his gold watch, which struck the hours with a musical phrase, close to his ear. Verdi opened his eyes, smiled and relapsed into unconsciousness.

The news that the great Verdi lay dying spread quickly. Messages arrived from the new King, Vittorio Emanuele III, son of the assassinated Umberto, and from leading politicians, friends and admirers from all parts of the world. A sad and silent crowd gathered in the street outside the hotel to await news, traffic was halted and straw laid down in the street in order to deaden the noise of traffic in case it disturbed Verdi. The hotel draped itself in black. Adolfo Hohenstein, the stage designer of *Falstaff*, visited the composer on his deathbed on 25 and 26 January, and made a series of drawings of his head, meticulously noting the date and the hour on each drawing.

Verdi died on 27 January, at about a quarter to three in the morning. On the evening of that same day, the following account of the composer's last hours, written by the playwright and librettist Giuseppe Giacosa, appeared in the *Corriere della Sera*:

All yesterday the Maestro remained in a state of peaceful sleep, not dissimilar, it seemed, to his condition on the preceding days. There was nothing to suggest to those present that he was close to death. And yet the pupils of his eyes no longer reacted in the slightest to the light, nor did the back of his throat contract when tickled with a feather moistened with glycerine. His hand, which on previous days had often been raised to his face, or engaged in weak attempts to button his shirt or throw back the blankets, had lain inert since morning.

On previous days the Maestro tended to lie with one arm across his chest. Since then, the doctors had tried several times to move the arm away to prevent it from pressing on those poor muscles which, though already extremely weak, were helping him to breathe. But whether by an act of will or a reflex action, he would immediately move his arm back into its former position. Yesterday, Grocco tried once more, and placed the arm by the composer's side. This time, the dying Maestro no longer had the strength to move it. But it was only the doctors who were able to note his physical decline from such external signs. His face remained flushed throughout the day, the rhythm of his breathing did not appear to alter, and he uttered no sound that resembled a death rattle.

His pulse fluctuated between 150 and 180, and his temperature remained feverish, above 39 degrees.

Towards midnight his face grew pale and suddenly began to appear emaciated, and a hissing noise indicated that his breathing was obstructed. It gradually grew shorter and more laboured, and was very soon reduced to a mere gurgle. Dr Grocco, Dr Caporali, Dr Odescalchi and Dr Bertarelli were present, and the glances they exchanged seemed to announce that the struggle was about to begin. Who had alerted all the relatives and friends who had been snatching a few hours of sleep in various rooms of the hotel? Suddenly they were all assembled around the bed.

Every ten or twelve breaths were followed by a pause, and the pauses gradually became longer and more frequent. And then the rhythm would resume. Towards one o'clock, it all seemed over. For several interminable seconds he neither moved nor made a sound. But then life returned. Soon there was another long pause. Grocco was already rising to his feet to certify him dead, when Verdi's chest rose once more, and he resumed his laboured breathing. Everyone exchanged glances of awe. It seemed that death had been conquered.

In fact, an hour of relatively peaceful sleep followed, and the people surrounding his bed dispersed once again to go to their nearby rooms. At half past two, hurried footsteps in the corridor and frantic calls suddenly brought everyone together again in the hallowed room. Short breaths were followed by long pauses. At 2.45, after an interminable and painful wait for the breath of life to resume, the weeping Grocco bent over Verdi's motionless face and kissed his forehead. Thus was his death announced.[45]

There is no evidence to suggest that Verdi had ever expressed any desire to be taken under the wing of the church before he died; it seems, rather, that he maintained his independent anti-clerical stance to the end. It was his heir, Maria Carrara, who had arranged for the Catholic rite of extreme unction to be administered on 24 January as he lay in a coma. The priest who administered the rite, one Don Adalberto Catena of the church of San Fedele, returned on the evening of 26 January to offer prayers for the composer's soul. Around Verdi when he died were Maria Carrara, Teresa Stolz, Giulio Ricordi and his wife, Arrigo Boito, Giuseppe Giacosa, Umberto Campanari (Verdi's solicitor), Giuseppe Spatz (proprietor of the hotel) and the four doctors. The only person who claimed that Verdi regained consciousness some hours before he died was the priest, Don Adalberto Catena, whose proselytizing zeal led him later to recall something which appears to have been missed by everyone else present, some of whom presumably (and Maria Carrara certainly) were devout Catholics: 'A long clasp of the hand, a meaningful look, and a deeply conscious expression', said the priest, 'assured me that he understood the religious significance of what I was saying. There was only a moment, but for both of us it was precious. He could not speak, but his eyes and his handclasp spoke for him. This was the last look, the message of the great Italian musician. After I had caught it, he gave no further signs of consciousness, and died serenely.'[46] More reliable, surely, is the testimony of Boito, expressed in a letter to his friend Camille Bellaigue, a French music critic who wanted Boito to collaborate on a biography of the composer:

He gave the example of Christian faith by the moving beauty of his religious works, by the observance of rites (you must recall his handsome head bowed in the chapel of Sant' Agata), by his homage to Manzoni, by the ordering of his funeral, found in his will: one priest, one candle, one cross. He knew that faith is the sustenance of the heart. To the workers in the fields, to the unhappy, to the afflicted around him, he offered himself as example, without ostentation, humbly, severely, to be useful to their consciences.

And here one must arrest the inquiry: to proceed further would take me far in the meanderings of psychological research, where his great personality would have nothing to lose, but where I myself would fear to miss my way. In the ideal, moral and social sense he was a great Christian, but one must be very careful not to present him as a Catholic in the political and strictly theological sense of the word: *nothing could be further from the truth.*[47]

In accordance with his wishes, Verdi's funeral was extremely simple. At six-thirty on the morning of 30 January, a cold and foggy day, a hearse left the Grand Hotel and made its way to the municipal cemetery. His grave had already been dug beside that of Giuseppina, and the composer's coffin was lowered into it without any funeral oration, while a crowd watched from a respectful distance. On 1 February at La Scala a solemn commemoration was held, at which a eulogy was delivered by Giacosa, and excerpts from seven Verdi operas were conducted by Toscanini, the ten soloists including Francesco Tamagno (the first Otello), Enrico Caruso, Giuseppe Borgatti, Antonio Magini-Coletti (a distinguished Amonasro), Amelia Pinto and Emma Carelli (who had sung Desdemona at La Scala in an 1899 revival of *Otello*).

On 28 February, one month after the funeral, the bodies of Giuseppe and Giuseppina Verdi were removed at eight o'clock in the morning to the completed Casa di Riposo, as Verdi had requested. The occasion was made a state ceremony. Two hundred thousand people lined the black-draped streets of Milan to say farewell to the greatest and most popular Italian of the nineteenth century. Toscanini conducted a choir of eight hundred in the moving chorus '*Va, pensiero, sull' ali dorate*' from *Nabucco*, as a hearse designed for the occasion by two architects carried the bodies through the city, followed by a prince of the reigning house and a vast crowd of people from all social levels. Wreaths which had arrived from around the world were conveyed in the procession to the Rest Home for Musicians, where the bodies of Italy's greatest composer and his wife still rest. Verdi's music lives on in his operas, whose humanity, strength, vibrant melody and dramatic truth are more appreciated than ever in an age in which these qualities are so sadly lacking.

Notes

COV refers to *The Complete Operas of Verdi* by Charles Osborne (London, 1969). LGV refers to *Letters of Giuseppe Verdi*, selected, translated and edited from the *Copialettere* by Charles Osborne (London, 1971).

CHAPTER 1: 1813–32

1. To Caterina Pigorini-Beri; quoted in *The New Grove*, Vol. 19, p. 635
2. In Adolfo Rossi, *Roncole Verdi* (Fidenza, 1969)
3. Quoted in Franco Abbiati, *Giuseppe Verdi* (Milan, 1959), I, pp. 6–7
4. Manuscript in the library of the Monte di Pietà, Busseto
5. Quoted in Abbiati, *op. cit.*, I, p. 10

CHAPTER 2: 1832–34

1. Letter to Jacopo Caponi, 13 October 1880; quoted in Arthur Pougin, *Verdi* (English translation, London, 1887), pp. 27–28
2. Quoted in Ludovico Corio, *Ricerche storiche sul R. Conservatorio di Musica di Milano* (Milan, 1908); reprinted in Frank Walker, *The Man Verdi* (London, 1962), p. 9
3. Letter to Francesco Florimo, 9 January 1871; quoted in Walker, *op. cit.*, p. 13
4. Dictated by Verdi to Giulio Ricordi on 19 October 1879; published in Pougin, *op. cit.,* pp. 48–67 (the 1887 English translation has been revised by the present author)

CHAPTER 3: 1834–42

1. Letter of 28 July 1835; quoted in Walker, *op. cit.*, p. 25
2. On 24 January 1836: Walker, *op. cit.*, p. 25
3. On 16 September 1836: Walker, *op. cit.*, p. 25
4. Walker, *op. cit.*, p. 26
5. On 3 November 1837: Walker, *op. cit.*, p. 26
6. On 14 May 1871: Abbiati, *op. cit.*, p. 326
7. The *Rocester–Oberto* question is discussed in more detail in COV, pp. 19–21
8. Abbiati, *op. cit.*, I, p. 352
9. *La Moda*, Milan, 17 September 1840
10. Quoted in *Atti del I congresso internazionale di studi verdiani* (Venice, 1966), p. 92

11. Letter to Antonio Vasselli; quoted in Guido Zavadini, *Donizetti* (Bergamo, 1948), p. 580
12. *Gazzetta di Milano*, 13 March 1842
13. *Otto Nicolais Tagebücher* (Leipzig, 1892), p. 130
14. Michele Lessona, *Volere e potere* (Milan, 1869), p. 299

CHAPTER 4: 1842–44

1. Arrivabene to Verdi, 17 March 1870; quoted in Weaver and Chusid (eds), *A Verdi Companion* (London, 1980), p. 175
2. On 31 March 1854; quoted in Werfel and Stefan (eds), *Verdi: The Man in his Letters* (New York, 1942), p. 185 (1973 reprint)
3. Abbiati, *op. cit.*, I, p. 472
4. On 19 August 1843: Abbiati, *op. cit.*, I, p. 472
5. On 5 September 1843: Abbiati, *op. cit.*, I, pp. 473–74
6. On 26 September 1843; quoted in David R.B. Kimbell, *Verdi in the Age of Italian Romanticism* (Cambridge, 1981), p. 124
7. On 30 November 1843: Abbiati, *op. cit.*, I, p. 478
8. LGV, pp. 18–19
9. Kimbell, *op. cit.*, p. 130
10. *Ibid.*
11. Letter of 12 January 1844 to Francesco Pasetti; original in Harvard University Library, Theatre Collection
12. LGV, p. 19
13. *Gazzetta Privilegiata di Venezia*, 11 March 1843
14. The other operas of the season in Venice: *Lucrezia Borgia* (Donizetti), *Gemma di Vergy* (Donizetti), *Fidanzata Corsa* (Pacini) and *Giuditta* (Levi)
15. *Il Gondoliere*, 10 March 1844
16. LGV, pp. 21–22
17. Luigi Garibaldi, *Giuseppe Verdi nelle lettere di Emanuele Muzio ad Antonio Barezzi* (Milan, 1931), pp. 157–58; quoted in Weaver (ed.), *Verdi: A Documentary Study* (London, n.d.)
18. Original in Civico Istituto Musicale Gaetano Donizetti, Bergamo
19. LGV, pp. 22–23
20. Garibaldi, *op. cit.*, p. 162
21. LGV, p. 25
22. Postscript by Piave to a letter from Verdi to Luigi Toccagni, 4 November 1844; quoted in Walker, *op. cit.*, p. 124
23. COV, p. 96

CHAPTER 5: 1844–46

1. Letter to Barezzi, 22 December 1844: Garibaldi, *op. cit.*, p. 177
2. Letter to Barezzi, 29 December 1844: *ibid.*, p. 179

3. Letter to Barezzi, 9 December 1844: *ibid.*, p. 175
4. Letter to Barezzi, *ibid.*, p. 179
5. Letter to Barezzi, 12 January 1845: *ibid.*, p. 181
6. Letter to Barezzi, 17 March 1845: *ibid.*, p. 191
7. In September 1844: Abbiati, *op. cit.*, I, p. 534
8. Garibaldi, *op. cit:*, p. 199
9. Signed only with the initial 'E', this appeared in *La France Musicale*, Paris, on 25 May 1845
10. Cesari and Luzio (eds), *I Copialettere di Giuseppe Verdi* (Milan, 1913), p. 429
11. In a letter to Tommaso Persico, written from Vienna on 14 June 1843: Zavadini, *op. cit.*, p. 670
12. Kimbell, *op. cit.*, p. 155
13. Letter of 14 May 1845: LGV, p. 26
14. LGV, pp. 26–27
15. *Ibid.*, p. 28
16. *Ibid.*, pp. 28–29
17. Quoted in Walker, *op. cit.*, p. 135
18. On 12 July 1845: *Copialettere*, p. 431
19. LGV, p. 30
20. Abbiati, *op. cit.*, I, p. 567
21. 5 November 1845: LGV, p. 31
22. *Copialettere*, p. 432
23. 12 September 1845: *ibid.*, p. 439
24. On 21 April 1845; quoted in Walker, *op. cit.*, p. 180
25. 5 November 1845: *Copialettere*, p. 432
26. 5 November 1845; quoted in Walker, *op. cit.*, pp. 180–81
27. Abbiati, *op. cit.*, I, p. 596
28. On 1 November 1845: *Copialettere*, p. 439
29. Abbiati, *op. cit.*, I, p. 591
30. On 27 August 1846; quoted in Conati (ed.), *Interviews and Encounters with Verdi* (London, 1984), p. 33
31. Weaver (ed.), *Verdi: A Documentary Study* (London, n.d.), p. 165
32. *Copialettere*, p. 441
33. Letter to Gina Somaglia: Abbiati, *op. cit.*, I, pp. 606–7
34. On 18 March 1846

CHAPTER 6: 1846–48

1. On 14 April 1846: LGV, p. 33
2. *Ibid.*, pp. 34–35
3. *Ibid.*, pp. 35–36
4. *Ibid.*, pp. 36–37

5. 4 September 1846: Abbiati, *op. cit.*, I, p. 643
6. *Copialettere*, p. 451
7. Walker, *op. cit.*, pp. 451–52
8. In the *Gazzetta Musicale di Milano* in 1887; quoted in Conati, *op. cit.*, p. 27
9. On 21 January 1847: LGV, p. 42
10. *Copialettere*, p. 448
11. Garibaldi, *op. cit.*, pp. 300–301
12. On 2 January 1847: Rosen and Porter (eds), *Verdi's Macbeth: A Sourcebook* (Cambridge, 1984), pp. 29–30
13. Abbiati, *op. cit.*, I, pp. 676–77
14. Garibaldi, *op. cit.*, pp. 262–63
15. Quoted in Gino Monaldi, *Verdi, 1839–1898* (Turin, 1899), 1926 reprint, p. 75
16. On 14 February 1847: Abbiati, *op. cit.*, I, p. 680
17. Ricordi Archives, Milan (draft in *Copialettere*, pp. 34–35)
18. Postmarked 9 June 1847: *Copialettere*, p. 457
19. Letter to Barezzi, 4 June 1847: Garibaldi, *op. cit.*, pp. 325–26
20. LGV, p. 44
21. Garibaldi, *op. cit.*, p. 328
22. Letter to Barezzi, 29 June 1847: *ibid.*, p. 334
23. LGV, p. 46
24. 29 June 1847: Garibaldi, *op. cit.*, pp. 334–35
25. Letter to Barezzi; quoted in Walker, *op. cit.*, p. 162
26. From Paris, on 30 July 1847: LGV, pp. 47–48
27. On 23 July 1847: *Copialettere*, p. 459
28. COV, p. 167
29. Queen Victoria's Journal, kept at Buckingham Palace
30. LGV, pp. 49–50
31. 27 November 1847; quoted in *Quaderno no. 2 dell' Istituto di studi verdiani* (Venice, 1963), p. 103
32. Letter to Giuseppina Appiani, 22 September 1847: *Copialettere*, p. 461
33. Quoted in Conati, *op. cit.*, p. 318
34. On 6 October 1848: *ibid.*, p. 319

CHAPTER 7: 1848–50

1. On 9 March 1848: LGV, pp. 51–52
2. Abbiati, *op. cit.*, I, p. 745
3. *Copialettere*, p. 466
4. *Ibid.*, pp. 449–50
5. Abbiati, *op. cit.*, I, pp. 691–92
6. Letter to Giuseppina Appiani, 25 February 1854: LGV, p. 91
7. 18 October 1848: *ibid.*, p. 56

8. 22 July 1848: Abbiati, *op. cit.*, I, p. 751
9. 24 September 1848: *Copialettere*, p. 56
10. 23 November 1848: *ibid.*, p. 60
11. LGV, pp. 52–53
12. On 5 February 1849; quoted in Weaver (ed.), *Verdi: A Documentary Study*, p. 176
13. Letter to Cammarano, 24 September 1848: LGV, p. 55
14. 18 January 1849: Abbiati, *op. cit.*, I, p. 781
15. LGV, pp. 63–65
16. 11 June 1849: *Copialettere*, p. 473
17. Walker, *op. cit.*, pp. 195–96
18. Letter of 15 May 1849: Abbiati, *op. cit.*, II, p. 9
19. Quoted in Dyneley Hussey, *Verdi* (London, 1940), 1973 edition revised by Charles Osborne, pp. 65–66
20. LGV, pp. 69–73
21. Abbiati, *op. cit.*, II, pp. 56–57
22. 17 June 1850: *Copialettere*, pp. 482–83

CHAPTER 8: 1850–51

1. 28 April 1850: Abbiati, *op. cit.*, II, pp. 59–60
2. *Ibid.*, pp. 62–63
3. 13 October 1850: *ibid.*, pp. 69–70
4. On 17 November 1850: *Quaderno no. 3 dell' Istituto di studi verdiani* (Parma, 1968), pp. 101–2
5. *Ibid.*, p. 114
6. On 4 December 1850: *ibid.*, p. 121
7. *Ibid.*, p. 113
8. On 5 January 1851: *Copialettere*, pp. 112–13
9. On 5 December 1850: LGV, p. 75
10. *Ibid.*, pp. 76–77
11. 14 December 1850: *Copialettere*, p. 111
12. *Ibid.*, pp. 489–90
13. *Ibid.*, pp. 491–92
14. Giulia Cora Varesi, 'L'interpretazione di Macbeth' in *Nuova Antologia*, CCCLXIV (1932), p. 440
15. 12 March 1851: M. Nordio, *Verdi e la Fenice* (Venice, 1951), p. 44
16. Abbiati, *op. cit.*, II, p. 111
17. On 8 September 1852: LGV, pp. 87–88

CHAPTER 9: 1851–53

1. On 19 December 1850: *Bollettino no. 8 dell' Istituto di studi verdiani* (Parma, 1973), p. 860

2. Monaldi, *op. cit.*, pp. 118–119
3. 29 March 1851: Abbiati, *op. cit.*, II, p. 121
4. 4 April 1851: *ibid.*, pp. 122–23
5. 9 April 1851: LGV, p. 80
6. *Ibid.*, pp. 82–84
7. Alessandro Luzio, *Carteggi Verdiani* (Rome, 1935–47), I, p. 9; quoted in LGV, p. 86
8. Léon Escudier, *Mes Souvenirs* (Paris, 1863), pp. 84–86
9. Abbiati, *op. cit.*, II, p. 203
10. On 20 January 1853
11. On 29 January 1853: LGV, p. 89
12. On 4 February 1853: Nordio, *op. cit.*, pp. 48–49
13. Abbiati, *op. cit.*, II, p. 217
14. *Ibid.*, pp. 220–21
15. *Copialettere*, p. 333
16. 10 March 1853: Abbiati, *op. cit.*, II, p. 229
17. Pougin, *op. cit.*, p. 152, footnote
18. F. Schlitzer, *Mondo teatrale dell' ottocento* (Naples, 1954), p. 156
19. Luzio, *op. cit.*, I, pp. 23–24
20. 26 May 1854: *ibid.*, pp. 24–25

CHAPTER 10: 1853–55

1. Letter of 12 March 1853: *Verdi: The Man in his Letters*, p. 173
2. Letter of 22 April 1853: *ibid.*, p. 175
3. 30 April 1853: Luzio, *op. cit.*, II, p. 65
4. 22 May 1853: Alessandro Pascolato, *Re Lear e Ballo in maschera: lettere di Giuseppe Verdi* (Città di Castello, 1902), p. 48
5. 29 June 1853: *ibid.*, p. 51
6. 30 August 1853: *ibid.*, p. 54
7. 19 November 1853: *ibid.*, p. 61
8. 31 March 1854: *ibid.*, p. 65
9. 5 May 1854: Abbiati, *op. cit.*, II, p. 271
10. 17 May 1854: Pascolato, *op. cit.*, p. 67
11. Quoted in Julian Budden, *The Operas of Verdi* (London, 1978), II, p. 174
12. LGV, pp. 91–92
13. *Ibid.*, pp. 92–93
14. *Ibid.*, pp. 94–95
15. Abbiati, *op. cit.*, II, p. 279
16. 29 November 1854; quoted in Weaver (ed.), *Verdi: A Documentary Study*, p. 194
17. 3 January 1855: LGV, pp. 96–98
18. Hector Berlioz, *Correspondance inédite* (Paris, 1888), p. 229

19. Charles Santley, *Student and Singer* (London, 1892), p. 53
20. 28 June 1855: LGV, p. 98
21. On 7 October 1855
22. 21 October 1855, to Dr Ercolano Balestra: LGV, p. 100

CHAPTER 11: 1855–57

1. Reprinted in Conati, *op. cit.*, p. 32
2. Luzio, *op. cit.*, I, p. 32
3. *Ibid.*, p. 25; quoted in LGV, p. 106
4. 25 November 1855: LGV, p. 106
5. *Ibid.*, p. 108
6. 3 September 1856: Abbiati, *op. cit.*, II, p. 371
7. COV, p. 80
8. Letter to Vincenzo Torelli, 22 April 1856: LGV, pp. 108–9
9. 7 December 1856: *ibid.*, p. 113
10. *Bollettino no. 3 dell' Istituto di studi verdiani* (Parma, 1960), p. 1387
11. Abbiati, *op. cit.*, II, p. 375
12. 23 March 1857: *ibid.*, pp. 395–96
13. 13 March 1857: *ibid.*, p. 393
14. 11 April 1857: LGV, pp. 114–15
15. 4 February 1859: *ibid.*, pp. 118–19
16. 4 July 1857: Abbiati, *op. cit.*, II, p. 420
17. Girolami Bottoni, *Giuseppe Verdi a Rimini* (Rimini, 1913), p. 69
18. Abbiati, *op. cit.*, II, p. 426
19. *Ibid.*, p. 425
20. Bottoni, *op. cit.*, p. 74
21. Abbiati, *op. cit.*, II, pp. 444–45

CHAPTER 12: 1857–59

1. 19 September 1857: LGV, pp. 115–16
2. 14 October 1857: *Copialettere*, p. 563
3. Abbiati, *op. cit.*, II, p. 458
4. *Ibid.*, pp. 458–59
5. *Omnibus*, Naples, January 1858; quoted in Abbiati, *op. cit.*, p. 467
6. *Ibid.*, p. 469
7. 13 February 1858: *ibid.*, p. 470
8. *Ibid.*, p. 471
9. Luzio, *op. cit.*, I, p. 269
10. *Copialettere*, p. 572
11. *Bollettino no. 2 dell' Istituto di Studi Verdiani* (Parma, 1960), p. 634
12. *Ibid.*, pp. 636–37
13. 8 July 1858: Pascolato, *op. cit.*, p. 92

14. Abbiati, *op. cit.*, p. 506; quoted in COV, p. 316
15. 20 October 1858: Abbiati, *op. cit.*, II, pp. 512–13
16. *Ibid.*, p. 515

CHAPTER 13: 1859–61

1. In *Omnibus*, Naples, March 1859
2. 5 September 1859: LGV, p. 122
3. 21 September 1859: *Copialettere*, pp. 582–83
4. 10 February 1860: Abbiati, *op. cit.*, II, p. 568
5. LGV, pp. 124–25
6. Quoted in Walker, *op. cit.*, p. 312
7. Gustavo Marchesi, *Verdi* (Turin, 1970), p. 265
8. 4 May 1860: Abbiati, *op. cit.*, II, p. 578
9. November 1860: *ibid.*, p. 591
10. 23 January 1861: LGV, pp. 127–28
11. Quoted in Hussey, *op. cit.*, p. 124
12. 14 June 1861: Annibale Alberti, *Verdi intimo* (Milan, 1931), pp. 9–10
13. 8 February 1865: LGV, pp. 138–39

CHAPTER 14: 1861–63

1. 5 June 1859: LGV, pp. 119–20
2. *Copialettere*, p. 599
3. 11 December 1860: Abbiati, *op. cit.*, II, p. 625
4. 17 January 1861; quoted in Budden, *op. cit.*, II, p. 427
5. 17 April 1861; quoted in Walker, *op. cit.*, p. 239
6. *Bollettino no. 4 dell' Istituto di studi verdiani* (Parma, 1961), p. 13
7. *Ibid.*, p. 16
8. 12 October 1861: Luzio, *op. cit.*, III, p. 18
9. Abbiati, *op. cit.*, II, p. 665
10. 20 January 1862: *ibid.*, p. 14; quoted in COV, p. 333
11. 21 February 1862: *Bollettino no. 5 dell' Istituto di studi verdiani*, pp. 1096–97
12 *The Times*, London, 24 April 1862
13. 2 May 1862: *Bollettino no. 5 dell' Istituto di studi verdiani*, p. 724; quoted in COV, p. 459
14. 3 May 1862: *ibid.*, p. 725; quoted in COV, p. 459
15. *Morning Post*, London, 25 May 1862; quoted in COV, p. 459
16. COV, p. 460
17. Postmarked 4 May 1862: Walker, *op. cit.*, p. 245
18. 1 August 1862: Luzio, *op. cit.*, II, p. 205
19. *Ibid.*, p. 62
20. *Journal de St Pétersbourg*, issue no. 245, 11 November 1862 (30 October, Russian calendar); quoted in COV, p. 334

21. Letter to Cesare de Sanctis, 26 November 1862: Luzio, *op. cit.*, I, p. 86
22. Censor's Report, Rome, 14 November 1862; in State Archives, Rome
23. LGV, p. 131
24. LGV, p. 132
25. Letter to Arrivabene, 22 February 1863: Alberti, *op. cit.*, p. 23
26. Letter to Arrivabene, 22 March 1863: *ibid.*, p. 24

CHAPTER 15: 1863–67

1. 'L'Orchestre de l'Opéra' in 23 July 1863 issue of *L'Art Musical*, pp. 271–72
2. 31 July 1863: Abbiati, *op. cit.*, II, p. 755
3. 13 December 1863: LGV, p. 133
4. 12 March 1876; quoted in Hans Busch, *Verdi's Aida* (Minneapolis, 1978), p. 390
5. 14 May 1863: Abbiati, *op. cit.*, II, p. 733
6. 1 January 1865: *ibid.*, p. 804
7. 24 October 1864: LGV, pp. 134–35
8. In January 1865: *ibid.*, p. 137
9. 3 February 1865: *ibid.*, pp. 137–38
10. 11 March 1865: autograph in Folger Library, Washington; quoted in Conati, *op. cit.*, p. 28
11. Alberti, *op. cit.*, p. 51
12. *Ibid.*
13. 28 April 1865: *ibid.*, III, p. 8
14. In July 1865; quoted in Walker, *op. cit.*, p. 257
15. Alberti, *op. cit.*, p. 58
16. *Ibid.*, p. 61
17. 16 February 1866: *ibid.*, p. 68
18. 6 May 1866: *ibid.*, p. 79
19. 9 June 1866: Luzio, *op. cit.*, III, p. 39
20. Alberti, *op. cit.*, p. 73
21. 7 December 1866: *ibid.*, p. 113
22. *La France Musicale*, issue of 23 December 1866, p. 402
23. Jules Claretie, 'Une répétition de Don Carlos – Verdi', *Le Figaro*, 17 February 1867
24. Alberti, *op. cit.*, p. 75
25. 1 April 1867: *ibid.*, p. 131

CHAPTER 16: 1867–69

1. 11 June 1867; quoted in Budden, *The Operas of Verdi*, III (London, 1981), p. 27
2. 4 June 1867: *Copialettere*, p. 499
3. 24 May 1867: Abbiati, *op. cit.*, III, p. 141

4. *Ibid.*, p. 157
5. 14 January 1868: autograph in Bibliothèque de l'Opéra, Paris; quoted in Conati, *op. cit.*, p. 217
6. 12 March 1868: autograph in Bibliothèque de l'Opéra, Paris; quoted in *ibid.*, pp. 217–18
7. 19 February 1868: Busch, *op. cit.*, p. 3
8. Luzio, *op. cit.*, II, p. 359
9. May 1868; quoted in Werfel and Stefan (eds), *Verdi: The Man in his Letters*, p. 256
10. Antonio Ghislanzoni, ' La casa di Verdi a Sant' Agata', *Gazzetta Musicale di Milano*, 26 July 1868, pp. 1–3
11. Quoted in Walker, *op. cit.*, p. 274
12. Abbiati, *op. cit.*, III, p. 215
13. 20 November 1868: *ibid.*, p. 224
14. *Ibid.*, p. 231
15. *Ibid.*, p. 233
16. *Ibid.*
17. *Ibid.*, p. 235
18. 1 March 1869: *ibid.*, pp. 99–100
19. 1 March 1869: LGV, p. 146
20. Quoted in Conati, *op. cit.*, p. 81
21. 13 October 1869: LGV, p. 150

CHAPTER 17: 1869–71

1. 9 August 1869: Busch, *op. cit.*, p. 3
2. 7 December 1869: LGV, pp. 151–53
3. Abbiati, *op. cit.*, III, p. 328
4. January 1870: *ibid.*, p. 329
5. Letter to Giulio Ricordi, 13 April 1870: *ibid.*, p. 335
6. 26 May 1870: *ibid.*, p. 371
7. 28 April 1870: Busch, *op. cit.*, p. 12
8. Abbiati, *op. cit.*, III, p. 372
9. Busch, *op. cit.*, p. 24
10. *Ibid.*, p. 25
11. LGV, p. 156
12. 9 July 1870: Busch, *op. cit.*, p. 30
13. 17 August 1870: LGV, pp. 159–60
14. 22 August 1870: *ibid.*, pp. 160–61
15. 30 September 1870: *ibid.*, pp. 161–62
16. Probably 12 November 1870: *ibid.*, p. 165
17. *Ibid.*, p. 167
18. 4 January 1871: *ibid.*, pp. 168–69

19. 30 January 1871: Abbiati, *op. cit.*, III, p. 359
20. 13 October 1871: LGV, pp. 182–83
21. Letter to Carlino del Signore, 20 November 1871: Abbiati, *op. cit.*, III, p. 506
22. *Ibid.*, p. 508
23. 8 December 1871: *ibid.*, p. 517
24. 8 December 1871: LGV, p. 184
25. *La Perseveranza*, Milan, 27 December 1871

CHAPTER 18: 1871–75

1. 9 July 1871: Busch, *op. cit.*, p. 182
2. 10 July 1871: LGV, pp. 178–79
3. Busch, *op. cit.*, pp. 268–69
4. *Ibid.*, p. 276
5. Giuseppe Adami, *Giulio Ricordi e i suoi musicisti* (Milan, 1933), pp. 51–52
6. Alberti, *op. cit.*, pp. 138–42; quoted in COV, p. 377
7. LGV, p. 186
8. 7 May 1872: Pougin, *op. cit.*, p. 219
9. *Ibid.*, p. 221
10. *Ibid.*, p. 237
11. 16 April 1873: Busch, *op. cit.*, p. 340
12. 25 February 1878: *Copialettere*, pp. 301–2; quoted in COV, p. 461
13. 23 May 1873: LGV, pp. 189–90
14. Abbiati, *op. cit.*, III, p. 643
15. 29 May 1873: LGV, p. 190
16. 9 May 1872; quoted in Walker, *op. cit.*, p. 280
17. 13 September 1873: Busch, *op. cit.*, p. 347
18. 6 September 1873: *ibid.*, p. 346
19. Pougin, *op. cit.*, pp. 232–34
20. Abbiati, *op. cit.*, III, p. 700
21. 21 November 1874: *ibid.*, p. 721
22. 3 January 1875: Busch, *op. cit.*, p. 374
23. 27 February 1875: *ibid.*, p. 378
24. 5 March 1875: Abbiati, *op. cit.*, III, p. 740
25. Letter to Giulio Ricordi: Busch, *op. cit.*, p. 379
26. 25 March 1875: *ibid.*, p. 380
27. *Ibid.*, p. 381
28. *Ibid.*, p. 382
29. Abbiati, *op. cit.*, III, p. 750
30. Blanche Roosevelt, *Verdi: Milan and Othello* (London, 1887), pp. 77–78
31. Quoted in COV, p. 339
32. 21 July 1872: Luzio, *op. cit.*, II, p. 37

33. 7 June 1875; quoted in Conati, *op. cit.*, p. 107
34. 12 June 1875: Werfel and Stefan, *op. cit.*, p. 330
35. Reprinted in Eduard Hanslick, *Music Criticisms 1846–1899* (New York, 1950); revised UK paperback edition, 1963, pp. 160–62
36. *Neue Freie Presse*, 9 June 1875
37. Walker, *op. cit.*, p. 425
38. *Ibid.*, pp. 425–26
39. 29 December 1875: Luzio, *op. cit.*, III, p. 115
40. Letter from Giuseppina Verdi to Dr Angiolo Carrara, 7 August 1875; quoted in Walker, *op. cit.*, p. 424

CHAPTER 19: 1875–78

1. *Rivista Indipendente*, Florence, 22 August and 4 September 1875; quoted in Walker, *op. cit.*, pp. 427–29
2. *Ibid.*, pp. 429–30
3. 25 May 1875: Busch, *op. cit.*, p. 383
4. 5 March 1874: Walker, *op. cit.*, p. 419
5. *Ibid.*, pp. 431–32
6. Busch, *op. cit.*, p. 393
7. 22 April 1876: *ibid.*, p. 395
8. 21 June 1876: Abbiati, *op. cit.*, IV, p. 8
9. 1 July 1876: Busch, *op. cit.*, pp. 402–3
10. 16 December 1876: Walker, *op. cit.*, pp. 436–37
11. LGV, pp. 200–201
12. 22 May 1877: Alberti, *op. cit*, pp. 203–4
13. *Kölnische Zeitung*, 22 May 1877
14. 22 October 1877: Alberti, *op. cit.*, p. 204
15. 6 October 1877: LGV, pp. 201–2
16. 12 February 1878: LGV, p. 203
17. 12 March 1878: Busch, *op. cit.*, p. 409
18. 18 March 1878: *ibid.*, p. 410
19. 19 March 1878: autograph in Library of the Martini Conservatorium, Bologna; quoted in Conati, *op. cit.*, p. 298
20. 18 June 1878: Walker, *op. cit.*, p. 439
21. *Ibid.*, p. 439
22. 11 August 1878: *ibid.*, p. 439
23. *Ibid.*
24. Letter to Daniele Morchio, 18 October 1878: *ibid.*, p. 440
25. 14 October 1878: Alberti, *op. cit.*, pp. 221–22
26. Raffaelle De Rensis, *Franco Faccio e Verdi* (Milan, 1934), pp. 185–89

CHAPTER 20: 1879–81

1. 30 March 1879: Alberti, *op. cit.*, p. 226

2. 4 April 1879: LGV, pp. 207–8
3. Abbiati, *op. cit.*, IV, p. 82
4. 11 June 1879; quoted in Conati, *op. cit.*, p. 154
5. 26 August 1879: *Copialettere*, pp. 308–9; quoted in COV, p. 408
6. End of August 1879: *Copialettere*, p. 311; quoted in *ibid.*, p. 409
7. Walker, *op. cit.*, p. 475
8. 7 November 1879: *ibid.*, p. 476
9. *Ibid.*
10. 18 December 1879: *ibid.*
11. In *Le Figaro*, Paris, 11 October 1879
12. In *Voltaire*, 19 October 1879
13. 7 October 1879: LGV, pp. 209–10
14. 24 November 1879: Busch, *op. cit.*, pp. 417–18
15. 11 November 1879: *ibid.*, p. 417
16. Walker, *op. cit.*, p. 445
17. 13 March 1880: Busch, *op. cit.*, p. 420
18. 25 March 1880: *ibid.*, p. 422
19. 21 April 1880: Walker, *op. cit.*, pp. 441–42
20. *Ibid.*, p. 441
21. Letter to Boito, 15 August 1880: *ibid.*, p. 477–78
22. 18 October 1880: Abbiati, *op. cit.*, IV, p. 173
23. LGV, pp. 212–13.
24. 11 December 1880: *ibid.*
25. 28 December 1880; quoted in COV, p. 297
26. 21 January 1881: Abbiati, *op. cit.*, IV, p. 175
27. Walker, *op. cit.*, pp. 442–43

CHAPTER 21: 1881–87

1. Walker, *op. cit.*, p. 485
2. *Ibid.*, pp. 486–87; quoted in COV, pp. 409–10
3. 24 September 1881: LGV, pp. 216–17
4. 21 January 1886: Medici and Conati (eds), *Carteggio Verdi-Boito* (Parma, 1978), pp. 99–100
5. 3 December 1882: Luzio, *op. cit.*, III, p. 158–59
6. 14 February 1883: *ibid.*, p. 219
7. A. von Winterfeld, 'Unterhaltungen in Verdis Tuskulum', *Deutsche Revue*, XII (Stuttgart, 1887); quoted in Conati, *op. cit.*, p. 147
8. Italo Pizzi, *Ricordi verdiani inediti* (Turin, 1901), pp. 9–12
9. 11 October 1883: LGV, pp. 220–21
10. *Ibid.*, p. 221
11. 15 March 1883 and 29 January 1884: Alberti, *op. cit.*, pp. 300 and 306
12. 27 March 1884: *Copialettere*, p. 324; quoted in COV, p. 411
13. Piero Nardi, *Vita di Arrigo Boito* (Milan, 1942), p. 494; quoted in COV, p. 411

14. 26 April 1884: LGV, pp. 223–24
15. 3 May 1884: autograph in Istituto di Studi Verdiani, Parma
16. 10 June 1884: LGV, p. 225
17. Reported in *Gazzetta Musicale di Milano*, 17 May 1885, pp. 176–77
18. *Gazzetta Musicale di Milano*, special supplement for Verdi jubilee, 27 November 1889, pp. 774–75
19. 9 December 1884: autograph in Istituto di Studi Verdiani, Parma
20. 10 September 1885; quoted in Walker, *op. cit.*, p. 492
21. 30 December 1885: LGV, p. 229
22. 31 January 1886: *ibid.*, pp. 229–30
23. Letter to Canon Avanzi, 5 February 1886: Walker, *op. cit.*, p. 446
24. Jacopo Caponi, 'Verdi à Paris', *Le Figaro*, Paris, 17 April 1886
25. Ettore Camesasca, 'L'opera completa di Boldini' in the series *Classici dell' arte* (Milan, 1970), p. 103, note 141
26. 22 July 1886: LGV, p. 230
27. *Ibid.*, p. 231
28. December 1886: Walker, *op. cit.*, pp. 493–94
29. 4 November 1886: Ferruccio Bonavia, *Verdi* (Oxford, 1930); 1947 reprint, p. 99
30. 2 September 1886; quoted in *A Verdi Companion*, pp. 159–60
31. Letter to Giulio Ricordi, 11 May 1887: Abbiati, *op. cit.*, IV, p. 337
32. Ugo Pesci, 'Le prove dell' Otello' in *Verdi e l'Otello*, special number of the *Illustrazione Italiana*, February 1887, pp. 39–40
33. Roosevelt, *op. cit.*, pp. 185–86 and 197–99

CHAPTER 22: 1887–93

1. Giuseppe Giacosa, 'Verdi e il Falstaff', special number of *Vita Moderna*, Milan, 12 February 1893, pp. 50–52
2. Letter to Giulio Ricordi, 14 March 1887: Abbiati, *op. cit.*, IV, p. 328
3. 28 June 1887: *ibid.*, p. 342
4. 19 August 1887: LGV, p. 232
5. Quoted in Carlo Gatti, *Verdi* (English translation, London, 1955), p. 300
6. 22 January 1888: Abbiati, *op. cit.*, p. 356
7. 16 January 1889: LGV, pp. 235–36
8. Autograph in Istituto di studi verdiani, Parma; quoted in Weaver, *op. cit.*, p. 245
9. 7 July 1889: *Copialettere*, p. 711
10. *Ibid.*
11. 7 July 1889: Luzio, *op. cit.*, II, p. 146; quoted in COV, pp. 434–35
12. Abbiati, *op. cit.*, p. 387
13. *Ibid.*, p. 375

14. Etienne Rouillé-Destranges, 'Une visite à Verdi', *Le Monde Artiste*, Paris, April 1890; reprinted in *Carteggio Verdi–Boito*, pp. 395–98
15. *Ibid.*
16. *Carteggio Verdi–Boito*, p. 281
17. 20 March 1890: Abbiati, *op. cit.*, IV, p. 397
18. 1 January 1891: LGV, pp. 242–43
19. *Copialettere*, p. 359
20. Abbiati, *op. cit.*, IV, p. 409
21. *Ibid.*
22. 6 December 1890: LGV, pp. 241–42
23. Quoted in George Martin, *Verdi* (London, 1965), p. 450
24. Letter to Giulio Ricordi, 19 March 1891: Abbiati, *op. cit.*, IV, p. 418
25. Letter to Boito, 12 June 1891: *Carteggio Verdi–Boito*, p. 190
26. 14 June 1891: *ibid.*, p. 191
27. 26 April 1891: LGV, pp. 244–45
28. Pizzi, *op. cit.*; quoted in Conati, *op. cit.*, pp. 341 and 343
29. 10 September 1891: *Carteggio Verdi–Boito*, p. 196
30. 6 November 1891: Abbiati, *op. cit.*, IV, pp. 426–27
31. On 9 April 1892
32. Issue of 9–10 April 1892
33. 7 April 1892: Weaver, *op. cit.*, p. 247
34. 11 April 1892: Abbiati, *op. cit.*, IV, p. 439
35. Letter to Giulio Ricordi, 18 September 1892: LGV, pp. 250–53
36. Letter to Giulio Ricordi, 17 June 1892: Abbiati, *op. cit.*, IV, pp. 442–44
37. Letter to Giulio Ricordi, 14 July 1892: *ibid.*, p. 447
38. Letter to Giulio Ricordi, 17 June 1892: *ibid.*, pp. 442–44
39. *Ibid.*
40. Letter to Giulio Ricordi, 16 November 1892: *ibid.*, p. 466
41. Letter to Giulio Ricordi, 21 December 1892: *ibid.*, pp. 468–69
42. Letter to Giulio Ricordi, 17 June 1892: *ibid.*, pp. 442–44
43. 30 August 1892: *ibid.*, p. 454
44. 9 September 1892: *ibid.*, p. 457
45. Letter to Barberina Strepponi: *ibid.*, p. 472; quoted in COV, p. 436
46. *Daily Graphic*, London, issues of 15 and 16 February 1893
47. *Ibid.*, issue of 14 January 1893
48. George Bernard Shaw, article in *The World*, London, 12 April 1893; reprinted in Shaw, *Music in London* (Standard Edition, 1932), II, pp. 281–82; quoted in part in COV, p. 449

CHAPTER 23: 1893–1901

1. Letter to Minister Ferdinando Martini, 11 February 1893: LGV, pp. 253–54

2. In *Die Neue Freie Presse*, Vienna, April 1893; reprinted in Eduard Hanslick, *Aus meinem Leben* (Berlin, 1894), II, pp. 281–83

3. *Ibid.*

4. 15 May 1893: LGV, pp. 255–56

5. 27 December 1893: *ibid.*, p. 259

6. Jules Huret, 'Deux interviews – Giuseppe Verdi', *Le Figaro*, Paris, 5 April 1894

7. H.F.G., 'Une entrevue avec M. Verdi', *Journal des Débats*, Paris, 5 April 1894

8. *Ibid.*

9. 31 December 1893: *Carteggio Verdi–Boito*, p. 221

10. *Gazzetta Musicale di Milano*, 22 April 1894, pp. 251–52

11. Abbiati, *op. cit.*, IV, pp. 551–52

12. Gatti, *op. cit.*, p. 328

13. Jules Massenet, 'Visite à Verdi', *Le Gaulois du Dimanche*, Paris, 9–10 October 1897

14. Letter to Dr Angelo Carrara, 23 March 1895: *Copialettere*, pp. 396–97

15. *Copialettere*, p. 412; quoted in COV, p. 465

16. Letter to the Director of the Deutsche Verlags-Anstalt, Stuttgart, 21 June 1895: LGV, pp. 262–63

17. Arnaldo Bonaventura, 'Un ricordo personale'; reproduced in Conati, *op. cit.*, pp. 280–85

18. 18 January 1895: Luzio, *op. cit.*, IV, p. 35; quoted in part in COV, p. 447

19. Quoted in Conati, *op. cit.*, p. 293

20. Autograph in Villa Verdi, Sant' Agata; quoted in Conati, *op. cit.*, p. 293

21. Luzio, *op. cit.*, II, p. 64

22. Quoted in Julian Budden, *Verdi* (London, 1985), pp. 141–42

23. Pizzi, *op. cit.*; quoted in Conati, *op. cit.*, p. 351

24. Gatti, *op. cit.*, p. 335

25. Letters of 9 and 22 September 1897: autographs in Ricordi Archives, Milan; quoted in Conati, *op. cit.*, p. 372

26. Amilcare Martinelli, *Verdi, raggi e penombre* (Genoa, 1926); quoted in Weaver, *op. cit.*, p. 250

27. Abbiati, *op. cit.*, IV, p. 618; quoted in COV, p. 467

28. January 1898: Abbiati, *ibid.*, p. 621

29. 8 April 1898; quoted in Walker, *op. cit.*, p. 507

30. Giuseppe Depanis, 'Verdi a Torino – Una visita di Toscanini a Verdi'; quoted in Conati, *op. cit.*, pp. 304–8

31. Gatti, *op. cit.*, pp. 339–40

32. 9 August 1898: Abbiati, *op. cit.*, IV, p. 632

33. 13 August 1898: *ibid.*

34. Letter to Boito, 15 December 1898: *Copialettere*, p. 414

35. April 1899: Gatti, *op. cit.*, p. 344

36. 18 March 1899: Abbiati, *op. cit.*, IV, p. 638
37. Dated 14 May 1900, the will is reproduced in Gatti, *op. cit.*, pp. 355–58
38. Reproduced in LGV, pp. 264–65
39. 16 August 1900: *ibid.*
40. Pizzi, *op. cit.*, pp. 18–19
41. Quoted in Hussey, *op. cit.*, p. 311
42. Gatti, *op. cit.*, p. 351
43. Quoted in Conati, *op. cit.*, p. 374
44. Facsimile of autograph in Martinelli, *op. cit.*; quoted in Conati, *ibid.*, p. 376
45. *Corriere della Sera*, Milan, 27–28 January 1901
46. Quoted in Gatti, *op. cit.*, p. 352
47. Walker, *op. cit.*, p. 506

Select Bibliography

BIOGRAPHY, LIFE AND WORKS

G. Demaldè, *Cenni biografici* (pub. in *Newsletter of the American Institute for Verdi Studies*, nos. 1–3, 1976–77)

A. Pougin, *Giuseppe Verdi: vita aneddotica* (Ital. trans. Milan, 1881; Fr. orig., 1886; Eng. trans. from French, 1887)

G. Monaldi, *Verdi* (Turin, 1899)

C. Gatti, *Verdi* (Milan, 1931; Eng. trans., 1955)

F. Toye, *Giuseppe Verdi: His Life and Works* (London, 1931)

F. Abbiati, *Giuseppe Verdi* (Milan, 1959)

F. Walker, *The Man Verdi* (London, 1962)

M. Conati, *Interviste e incontri con Verdi* (Milan, 1980; Eng. trans., 1984)

J. Budden, *Verdi* (London, 1985)

MUSICAL STUDIES

S. Hughes, *Famous Verdi Operas* (London, 1968)

C. Osborne, *The Complete Operas of Verdi* (London, 1969)

G. Baldini, *Abitare la battaglia: la storia di Giuseppe Verdi* (Milan, 1970; Eng. trans., 1980)

J. Budden, *The Operas of Verdi*, 3 vols (London, 1973, 1978, 1981)

W. Weaver and M. Chusid (eds), *The Verdi Companion* (New York, 1979)

D. Kimbell, *Verdi in the Age of Italian Romanticism* (Cambridge, 1981)

LETTERS AND DOCUMENTS

G. Cesare and A. Luzio, *I Copialettere di Giuseppe Verdi* (Milan, 1913)

A. Luzio, *Carteggi verdiani* (Rome, 1935; 1947)

C. Osborne (trans. and ed.), *Letters of Giuseppe Verdi* (London, 1971)

W. Weaver (ed.), *Verdi: A Documentary Study* (London, 1977)

M. Medici and M. Conati, *Carteggio Verdi–Boito*, 2 vols (Parma, 1978)

List of Works

OPERAS (year in brackets is that of first performance)

Oberto (1839)
Un giorno di regno (1840)
Nabucco (1842)
I lombardi (1843)
Ernani (1844)
I due Foscari (1844)
Giovanna d'Arco (1845)
Alzira (1845)
Attila (1846)
Macbeth (1847; revised version, 1865)
I masnadieri (1847)
Jérusalem (adapted from *I lombardi*, 1847)
Il corsaro (1848)
La battaglia di Legnano (1849)
Luisa Miller (1849)
Stiffelio (1850)
Rigoletto (1851)
Il trovatore (1853)
La traviata (1853)
Les Vêpres siciliennes (1855)
Simon Boccanegra (1857; revised version, 1881)
Aroldo (adapted from *Stiffelio*, 1857)
Un ballo in maschera (1859)
La forza del destino (1862; revised version, 1869)
Don Carlos (1867; revised version, 1884)
Aida (1871)
Otello (1887)
Falstaff (1893)

OTHER WORKS (excluding juvenilia; unless otherwise noted, year in brackets is that of publication, which is usually also that of composition)

Sei romanze, songs for voice and piano (1838)
    i. 'Non t'accostare all' urna'
    ii. 'More, Elisa, lo stanca poeta'
    iii. 'In solitaria stanza'

iv. *'Nell' orror di notte oscura'*

v. *'Perduta ho la pace'*

vi. *'Deh, pietoso, oh Addolorata'*

'L'esule', song for voice and piano (1839)

'La seduzione', song for voice and piano (1839)

'Guarda che bianca luna', nocturne for soprano, tenor, bass, flute and piano (1839)

'Chi i bei dì m'adduce ancora', song for voice and piano (composed 1842; published 1948)

Sei romanze, songs for voice and piano (1845)

i. *'Il tramonto'*

ii. *'La zingara'*

iii. *'Ad una stella'*

iv. *'Lo spazzacamino'*

v. *'Il mistero'*

vi. *'Brindisi'*

'Il poveretto', song for voice and piano (1847)

'Suona la tromba', for three-part male chorus and orchestra (composed 1848)

'L'abandonée', song for voice and piano (1849)

'Fiorellin che sorge appena', song for voice and piano (composed 1850; published 1951)

'La preghiera del poeta', song for voice and piano (composed 1858, published 1941)

Inno delle nazioni, for tenor (or soprano), chorus and orchestra (1862)

'Il brigidino', song for voice and piano (composed 1863; published 1941)

'Stornello: Tu dici che non m'ami', song for voice and piano (1869)

String Quartet in E minor (composed 1873; published 1876)

Messa da Requiem, for soprano, mezzo-soprano, tenor, bass, chorus and orchestra (1874)

'Pater Noster', for unaccompanied five-part chorus (1880)

'Ave Maria', for soprano and string orchestra (1880)

Pietà, Signor' (1894)

Quattro pezzi sacri, for chorus and orchestra (composed between 1888 and 1897; published 1898)

Index

Verdi's works are indexed under the entry for Verdi himself

Index

Index

Index

Index

Roosevelt (Rosavela), Blanche, 236–7, 285–7, 290

Roqueplan, Nestor, 77

Rossi, Giovanni, 227

Rossini, Gioacchino, 5, 20, 130, 137, 176, 210, 239; Verdi visits, 31, 192; on Verdi's genius, 108, 197; death, 204; proposed Requiem Mass for, 204–5, 206, 208; on Verdi's incapacity for *opera buffa*, 258; centenary, 301

Rouillé-Destranges, Etienne, 294–6

Royer, Alphonse, 76, 77

Ruy Blas (Hugo), 171–2

St Petersburg, 171–5, 179–80

Saint-Saëns, Camille, 261, 262

Saléza, Albert, 311

Salvi, Lorenzo, 13

Salvi, Matteo, 129

Salvini-Donatelli, Fanny, 119, 120, 121, 122

Sanctis, Cesare de, 127, 156; letters to, 94, 112, 116, 123, 125, 133, 137, 138

Sant' Agata, 1, 92, 279; *see also* Villa Sant' Agata

Santley, Sir Charles, 135

Sanzogno, Edoardo, 315

Sardou, Victorien, 209, 212, 324

Sass, Marie-Constance, 196

Sauchon, Victor, 325

Sbriscia, Zelinda, 157

Schiller, Johann C. F. von, 47, 62, 71, 75, 76, 89–90, 94, 192, 300

Scott, Sir Walter, 35

Scribe, Eugène, 128–9, 133–4, 148, 149, 154

Seletti, Emilio, 22

Seletti, Giuseppe, 6, 10

Seletti, Don Pietro, 4, 6

Sella, Quintino, 170

Sellier, Henri, 263

Semiramide (Rossini), 131

Severi, Giovanni, 113

Shaw, George Bernard, 306

Shaw, Maria, 23

Silvestri, Alessandro, 275

Simmons, Lucy, 297

Simon Boccanegra (Gutiérrez), 139

Sole, Il, 233

Solera, Temistocle, 12, 13, 20, 22, 34; and *Nabucco*, 15–17, 27; and *I lombardi*, 31–2, 33, 78; and *Giovanna d'Arco*, 47–8; and *Attila*, 55, 56, 57, 59; death, 252

Solferino, battle of (1859), 161

Somma, Antonio, 33; and *King Lear*, 125–8, 140, 260, 314; and *La vendetta in domino*, 149–50, 151–2, 155–6, 158

Sonnambula, La (Bellini), 30, 72, 131, 250

Souvestre, Emile, 101

Spezia, Maria, 123, 128

Stabat Mater (Rossini), 239

Staël, Madame de, 40, 41

Stehle, Adelina, 303

Steller, Francesco, 219

Stiffelius (orig. *Le Pasteur*), 101

Stolz, Teresa, 206, 225, 229, 255, 257, 262, 279, 304; close friendship with Verdi and Giuseppina, 221, 244, 247, 248, 252–3, 263, 265, 274, 278, 281, 313; as Aida, 224, 226, 227, 238, 246; in *Requiem*, 232, 233, 234, 252; alleged liaison with Verdi, 242–7; retirement from stage, 247, 248; devotion to widowed Verdi, 318, 320, 321, 324; and Verdi's death, 327

Strauss, Richard, 314

Strepponi, Adelina, 92

Strepponi, Barberina, 316, 317, 322, 325

Strepponi, Camillo, 92

Strepponi, Giuseppa, 92

Strepponi, Giuseppina, 111, 138, 144, 157, 167, 182, 184, 281, 283, 304, 308, 310, 315; and Verdi's first opera, 12, 13; and *Nabucco*, 16, 17, 27, 28, 33, 38; support for Verdi, 27, 31, 33–4; and *Ernani*, 43; liaison with Verdi, 71, 76, 78, 82, 84, 91, 92–3, 113–15, 117, 127–8, 130, 136, 145, 148, 150, 156; her children, 92; at Sant' Agata, 83, 92, 113 and *passim*; letters to Verdi, 92, 117, 120, 245–6, 264–5, 268–9; ill-health and depression, 120, 139, 244–5, 255, 268–9, 311; offended by Countess Appiani, 131; pet dogs, 138, 150, 156, 178–9, 191; marriage to Verdi, 161–2; winters in Genoa, 163–4, 187, 189, 193, 194, 199, 201, 234, 248, 251, 255, 270, 290, 306, 311; Russian visits, 171, 172, 174–5, 179; her English style, 178, 196; and Verdi's family affairs, 195, 196, 248, 252, 253; escape from drowning, 207–8; and Verdi's religious views, 231; on proposed German tour, 238; and Ricordi dispute, 240–1; purchase of Palazzo Dordoni from Verdi, 241; attitude to Stolz, 243, 244–7, 248, 253, 262, 265, 281; increasing infirmity, 255, 316; and *Otello*, 260; and dishonest Sant' Agata agent, 262;

356

Index

Index

Index

About the Author

Charles Osborne has written numerous books on music and musical figures, including *The Complete Operas of Verdi*, *The Complete Operas of Mozart*, *The Complete Operas of Puccini*, *The World Theatre of Wagner*, *The Dictionary of Opera*, and *Schubert and His Vienna*. He is also the author of a biography of Agatha Christie, and he has been the Literature Director of the Arts Council of Great Britain since 1971. A native of Australia, Mr. Osborne lives in England.

A Note on the Type

The text of this book was set in a digitized version of Bembo, a well-known Monotype face. Named for Pietro Bembo, the celebrated Renaissance writer and humanist scholar who was made a cardinal and served as secretary to Pope Leo X, the original cutting of Bembo was made by Francesco Griffo of Bologna only a few years after Columbus discovered America.

Sturdy, well-balanced, and finely proportioned, Bembo is a face of rare beauty, extremely legible in all of its sizes.

Composed in Great Britain

Printed and bound by Fairfield Graphics,
Fairfield, Pennsylvania

Display typography and binding design by
Claire M. Naylon

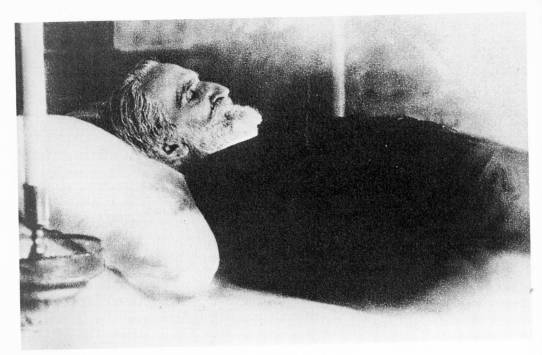

Verdi on his death-bed, 27 January 1901

The funeral procession: the coffins of Giuseppe and Giuseppina Verdi are taken to their final
resting-place in the Casa di Riposo, Milan, on 26 February 1901

Victor Maurel, the first
Falstaff

Casa di Riposo, Milan,
built and endowed by
Verdi as a home for
impoverished elderly
musicians

Verdi, aged seventy-nine, with Arrigo Boito, in the Perego garden, Milan, in the summer of 1892

Verdi with friends at the spa of Montecatini, 1898; Teresa Stolz is seated at his right

Verdi with the conductor and cast
of *Otello*

Verdi's study at Sant' Agata

Verdi in the garden of his villa, Sant' Agata, *c.* 1899

Below left: Giuseppina Strepponi in middle age

Below: First page of the *Requiem* manuscript, 1874, inscribed to Teresa Stolz

The conductor Angelo Mariani

Teresa Stolz

Caricature of the first performance of the
Requiem. From left to right: Giuseppe
Capponi (tenor), Verdi, Armando Maini
(bass), Teresa Stolz (soprano), Maria
Waldmann (mezzo–soprano)

Caricature of the conductor Franco Faccio

Teresa Stolz as Aida

Emanuele Muzio: painting by Giovanni
Boldini

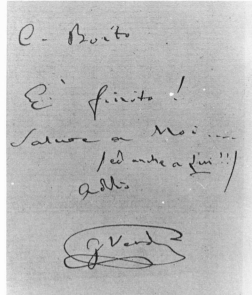

Above: Verdi acknowledging applause for *Falstaff* in Paris, April 1894

Above right: Verdi's note to Boito, on 1 November 1886, the day he completed work on *Otello*: 'Dear Boito, It's finished! Greetings to us ... (and also to Him!!) Farewell.'

An 1866 cartoon: Vittorio Emanuele (Manrico) clasps Italy (Leonora), and sings 'Ah! sì, ben mio' from Act III of *Il trovatore*